Emerging Technologies for Innovation Management in the Software Industry

Varun Gupta
Universidad de Alcalá, Madrid, Spain

Chetna Gupta
Jaypee Institute of Information Technology, Noida, India

A volume in the Advances in Systems Analysis,
Software Engineering, and High Performance
Computing (ASASEHPC) Book Series

Published in the United States of America by
IGI Global
Engineering Science Reference (an imprint of IGI Global)
701 E. Chocolate Avenue
Hershey PA, USA 17033
Tel: 717-533-8845
Fax: 717-533-8661
E-mail: cust@igi-global.com
Web site: http://www.igi-global.com

Library of Congress Cataloging-in-Publication Data

Names: Gupta, Varun, 1987- editor. | Gupta, Chetna, editor.
Title: Emerging technologies for innovation management in the software
  industry / Varun Gupta, and Chetna Gupta, editors.
Description: Hershey, PA : Business Science Reference, [2022] | Includes
  bibliographical references and index. | Summary: "This book will
  highlight the role of technology to assist software companies,
  especially small start-ups, to innovate their products, processes or
  business models"-- Provided by publisher.
Identifiers: LCCN 2021042348 (print) | LCCN 2021042349 (ebook) | ISBN
  9781799890591 (hardcover) | ISBN 9781799890607 (paperback) | ISBN
  9781799890614 (ebook)
Subjects: LCSH: Computer software industry--Management. | Technological
  innovations. | Computer software--Development.
Classification: LCC HD9696.63.A2 E55 2022 (print) | LCC HD9696.63.A2
  (ebook) | DDC 005.068/4--dc23/eng/20211014
LC record available at https://lccn.loc.gov/2021042348
LC ebook record available at https://lccn.loc.gov/2021042349

This book is published in the IGI Global book series Advances in Systems Analysis, Software Engineering, and High Performance Computing (ASASEHPC) (ISSN: 2327-3453; eISSN: 2327-3461)

British Cataloguing in Publication Data
A Cataloguing in Publication record for this book is available from the British Library.

All work contributed to this book is new, previously-unpublished material. The views expressed in this book are those of the authors, but not necessarily of the publisher.

For electronic access to this publication, please contact: eresources@igi-global.com.

Advances in Systems Analysis, Software Engineering, and High Performance Computing (ASASEHPC) Book Series

Vijayan Sugumaran
Oakland University, USA

ISSN:2327-3453
EISSN:2327-3461

MISSION

The theory and practice of computing applications and distributed systems has emerged as one of the key areas of research driving innovations in business, engineering, and science. The fields of software engineering, systems analysis, and high performance computing offer a wide range of applications and solutions in solving computational problems for any modern organization.

The **Advances in Systems Analysis, Software Engineering, and High Performance Computing (ASASEHPC) Book Series** brings together research in the areas of distributed computing, systems and software engineering, high performance computing, and service science. This collection of publications is useful for academics, researchers, and practitioners seeking the latest practices and knowledge in this field.

COVERAGE

- Computer Graphics
- Performance Modelling
- Metadata and Semantic Web
- Human-Computer Interaction
- Computer System Analysis
- Computer Networking
- Engineering Environments
- Storage Systems
- Network Management
- Enterprise Information Systems

IGI Global is currently accepting manuscripts for publication within this series. To submit a proposal for a volume in this series, please contact our Acquisition Editors at Acquisitions@igi-global.com or visit: http://www.igi-global.com/publish/.

Titles in this Series

For a list of additional titles in this series, please visit: http://www.igi-global.com/book-series/advances-systems-analysis-software-engineering/73689

Technology Road Mapping for Quantum Computing and Engineering
Brojo Kishore Mishra (GIET University, India)
Engineering Science Reference • © 2022 • 243pp • H/C (ISBN: 9781799891833) • US $225.00

Designing User Interfaces With a Data Science Approach
Abhijit Narayanrao Banubakode (MET Institute of Computer Science, India) Ganesh Dattatray Bhutkar (Vishwakarma Institute of Technology, India) Yohannes Kurniawan (Bina Nusantara University, Indonesia) and Chhaya Santosh Gosavi (MKSSS's Cummins College of Engineering, India)
Engineering Science Reference • © 2022 • 325pp • H/C (ISBN: 9781799891215) • US $245.00

Implementation of Machine Learning Algorithms Using Control-Flow and Dataflow Paradigms
Veljko Milutinović (Indiana University, Bloomington, USA) Nenad Mitić (University of Belgrade, Serbia) Aleksandar Kartelj (University of Belgrade, Serbia) and Miloš Kotlar (University of Belgrade, Serbia)
Engineering Science Reference • © 2022 • 296pp • H/C (ISBN: 9781799883500) • US $245.00

Advancing Smarter and More Secure Industrial Applications Using AI, IoT, and Blockchain Technology
Kavita Saini (Galgotias University, India) and Pethuru Raj (Reliance Jio Platforms Ltd., Bangalore, India)
Engineering Science Reference • © 2022 • 309pp • H/C (ISBN: 9781799883678) • US $245.00

Deep Learning Applications for Cyber-Physical Systems
Monica R. Mundada (M.S. Ramaiah Institute of Technology, India) S. Seema (M.S. Ramaiah Institute of Technology, India) Srinivasa K.G. (National Institute of Technical Teachers Training and Research, Chandigarh, India) and M. Shilpa (M.S. Ramaiah Institute of Technology, India)
Engineering Science Reference • © 2022 • 293pp • H/C (ISBN: 9781799881612) • US $245.00

Design, Applications, and Maintenance of Cyber-Physical Systems
Pierluigi Rea (University of Cagliari, Italy) Erika Ottaviano (University of Cassino and Southern Lazio, Italy) José Machado (University of Minho, Portugal) and Katarzyna Antosz (Rzeszow University of Technology, Poland)
Engineering Science Reference • © 2021 • 314pp • H/C (ISBN: 9781799867210) • US $225.00

Methodologies and Applications of Computational Statistics for Machine Intelligence
Debabrata Samanta (Christ University (Deemed), India) Raghavendra Rao Althar (QMS, First American India, Bangalore, India) Sabyasachi Pramanik (Haldia Institute of Technology, India) and Soumi Dutta (Institute of Engineering and Management, Kolkata, India)
Engineering Science Reference • © 2021 • 277pp • H/C (ISBN: 9781799877011) • US $245.00

IGI Global
PUBLISHER of TIMELY KNOWLEDGE

701 East Chocolate Avenue, Hershey, PA 17033, USA
Tel: 717-533-8845 x100 • Fax: 717-533-8661
E-Mail: cust@igi-global.com • www.igi-global.com

Table of Contents

Detailed Table of Contents

The chapter reported the results of investigation of existing product and business model development frameworks and identified any gaps or scopes for improvement that can benefit aspiring software startups by improving their chances of success in their entrepreneurial ventures. Accordingly, current literature in the space of both product and business model development including overlapping areas are reviewed, and their values along with potential for improvement are highlighted.

This chapter investigated the way digital technologies impact the innovation process and ultimately reshape the way business processes are designed and managed. It also sheds light on the link between digital innovation and BPM and the means by which they complement and reshape one another. The following sections explain the characteristics of digital technology, the impact of digitalization on innovation processes, and the link between digital innovation and BPM.

Chapter 3

This chapter introduces an area of research related to the implementation of emerging unified communications and collaboration (UC&C) technologies for productivity and innovation management within the context of large-scale automotive design, manufacturing, and business operations at General

Motors (GM), a leader in the global automotive industry. It further discusses how the chapter bridges the gaps presented through the design of the research developed with the purpose of evaluating the impact of said emerging technologies. In terms of mentioning what problems existed, prior to the research undertaking reported on in this chapter, General Motors had not implemented unified communications within its manufacturing, design, or business operation functions and had not engaged in the development of an internet of things (IoT)-related digitization strategy.

Chapter 4
Khalid Khan, Karachi Institute of Economics and Technology, Pakistan
Faiza Khan, Karachi Institute of Economics and Technology, Pakistan
Trung Nguyen Quang, Thuongmai University, Vietnam
Anh Nguyen Duc, University of South-Eastern Norway, Norway

This chapter reported the results of an empirical investigation on five hardware startup companies about hardware startup product development. This chapter reported some common good practices among hardware startups (i.e., process definition, evolutionary development process, and document management). We reveal several factors that are different from software startups, such as low priority of product quality, product pipeline, and unrecognized product platform. This chapter also proposes an integrative process model of hardware product development that shows the connections between human factors in the startups, their speed-prioritized development processes, and the consequence of hindered productivity in the later phases. The model has some implications for hardware startup founders to plan for the trade-off between team, speed, quality, and later productivity.

Chapter 5
Varun Gupta, University of Alcala, Spain
Chetna Gupta, Jaypee Institute of Information Technology, India
Luis García Piedrabuena, University of Alcala, Spain

In highly dynamic situations, entrepreneurs build value propositions in resource-constrained conditions. The activity is set up as a series of experiments, with each one aimed at validating value proposition-related assumptions with customers. Validation entails interactions between potential customers and the startup team utilizing prototypes, which leads to the confirmation of current assumptions as well as the discovery of new insights that lead to more experiments. The main features of the value proposition identification model are highlighted in this chapter, and a novel value prioritizing approach is proposed.

Chapter 6
Şükran Sirkintioğlu Yildirim, Kastamonu University, Turkey
Özlem Atay, Ankara University, Turkey

This chapter searches how knowledge management and innovation activities, which enable an advantageous position for firms over their opponents, influence ambidexterity and business performance. These enable firms to gain an advantage over their competitors, concerning ambidexterity and organizational performance. The population for this study comprises firms, operating in technology development zones in Ankara,

Turkey. According to the sectoral distribution of the enterprises in the technology development zones, the majority operate in the software sector. No sampling methods were used because the sensus method was adopted. Three hundred sixty high-tech enterprise top managers form the basis of this empirical research. In this study, structural equation modeling was used for testing research model. As a result of the structural equation modeling, it was understood that firms' knowledge management and innovation usage preferences have a positive impact on ambidexterity and organizational performance. This outcome is important for firms to gain a competitive advantage.

Chapter 7

This chapter provided the discussion about innovation management with reference to the software industry. Much attention is drawn to the importance of knowledge management in this chapter. Knowledge management covers four phases: create, structure, share, and apply. Successful management of these phases leads to successful knowledge management outcomes. From the moment it emerged, the internet of things has made a positive difference in providing high-volume and instant data communication, especially between computer systems, which are one of the basic components of knowledge management systems. Artificial intelligence (AI) uses modern technologies to simplify the discovery of knowledge. Thus, knowledge management could be aided by the use of AI.

Chapter 8

Software startups bring innovative products to the market. However, such innovation is at the cost of highly educated guesswork about customer expectations and quick decision making by persons responsible for strategic planning and implementation. It is therefore of interest to understand the challenges and practices faced by startups that aim to release something innovative in selected market segments. Hence, this chapter investigates the challenges faced by entrepreneurs of startups and the practices they follow to become successful. The specific challenges explored include (1) how startups handle software evolution, (2) challenges faced in releasing products to the market, and (3) the state of affairs of software engineering in startups. Results indicate that despite guidance and support in terms of well-known and documented development methods, practitioners find it difficult to implement and apply these in practice. They must quickly evolve their products to sustain in the market, and the market is highly uncertain, which makes the complete process highly probabilistic.

Chapter 9

This chapter identifies the factors considered when prioritising requirements for five popular prioritisation approaches. This research also compares these factors to the agile requirement re-prioritisation process to see how well these popular approaches support the agile process. The five popular requirement prioritisation approaches are analytic hierarchy process (AHP), quality functional deployment (QFD), planning game, binary search tree, and $100 allocation. Framework synthesis was used to identify a best-fit framework developed by a robust methodology and relevant for the agile requirement re-prioritisation process. The chosen best-fit framework considers six factors when prioritising requirements, business value, risk, effort estimation, learning experience, external change, and project constraints. First, the factors considered by the five popular approaches were identified. The results show that five factors were reported in literature for the planning game, three were reported for AHP, one was reported for QFD, and no factors were identified for binary search tree and $100 allocation. Although the factor business value was not identified in the literature for $100 allocation or binary search tree, it is likely that stakeholders consider business value for $100 allocation as they allocate more dollars to the requirements, which are more important. It is also likely that business value is considered for binary search tree, while determining the placement of each candidate requirement on the tree. Second, the factors from the agile requirement re-prioritisation process were compared with the factors considered by the five popular approaches. The results confirm five of the factors identified in the agile requirement re-prioritisation process. The sixth factor, external change, was not reported in the literature for the five popular approaches. The planning game covers five of the factors whereas AHP covers three of the factors. QFD only covered one factor, and both the binary search tree and £100 allocation approaches did not report any of the factors although the binary search tree and $100 allocation approaches have numerous benefits, including being fast and easy to use. This may influence the choice of approach used for agile requirement re-prioritisation. This study contributes insights that are important for requirement prioritisation literature and practice.

Chapter 10

    Quang-Trung Nguyen, ThuongMai University, Vietnam
    Thananya Phromwongsa, University of Southern Denmark, Denmark
    Sharanka Shanmugalingam, University of Southern Denmark, Denmark
    Victor Steenfeldt Laursen, University of Southern Denmark, Denmark
    Indira Nurdiani Jabangwe, University of Southern Denmark, Denmark
    Anh Nguyen-Duc, University of South-Eastern Norway, Norway

The success and survival of software startup companies depend on the decision-making of entrepreneurs. Risk management is an important part of making both business and product-related decisions. In contrast to the popularity of research on risk management in the context of established organizations, there is relatively limited research on risk management in early-stage startup companies. In this work, we aim at understanding the perception and practices of managing risks in software startups. We interviewed CEOs and CTOs of nine early-stage software startups in Denmark and Norway. The results revealed an awareness of common types of risks among software startups. However, risks are not measured or managed by any established approaches. We found that startups founders do not believe in risk management methods and prioritize other tasks on their to-do list. The findings have direct implications for startup founders in their early stages in Nordic countries.

Chapter 11

Varun Gupta, University of Alcala, Spain
Chetna Gupta, Jaypee Institute of Information Technology, India
Lawrence Peters, Software Consultants International Limited, USA & Universidad
*   Politecnica de Madrid, Madrid, Spain*
Leandro Pereira, ISCTE, University Institute of Lisbon, Lisboa, Portugal

The importance of scholarly literature on startup capacities to stimulate innovation in pandemic times is highlighted in this chapter. The scholarly literature can help startups looking for opportunities or solutions in the face of a pandemic, but knowledge acquisition from secondary materials may be limited due to the growing number of publications, retractions, and preprints. The growing number of publications and venues makes it more difficult for entrepreneurs to get the information they need, analyse it, and then use collective intelligence to turn it into useful business knowledge. Retractions may steer startups in the incorrect direction, resulting in a waste of financial resources. Preprints are non-peer reviewed research articles that may provide some direction to startups but should not be relied upon entirely. The solutions to these issues are finally provided. Addressing these concerns could make scholarly literature beneficial to startups, allowing the global community to respond to the pandemic as a whole.

Chapter 12

Anastasia Sergeevna Samoylova, Federal State Autonomous Educational Institution of
*   Higher Education, Moscow Polytechnic University, Russia*
Ekaterina Olegovna Bobrova, Federal State Budgetary Educational Institution of Higher
*   Education Lomonosov, Moscow State University, Russia*
Valentina Valentinovna Britvina, Federal State Autonomous Educational Institution of
*   Higher Education, Moscow Polytechnic University, Russia*
Galina Pavlovna Konyukhova, Moscow State University of Technology, Russia

This chapter reported the innovative IT-technologies in the field of mechanical engineering, allowing to increase the efficiency of production. This chapter reflects a particular task of automation of a particular branch of mechanical engineering – the technology of mechanical engineering. New methods of calculation of typical multivariable tasks are considered as well as the effectiveness of the introduction of automation at the level of the design office.

Chapter 13

Zoe Hoy, University of Portsmouth, UK

This chapter pertains to process innovation in requirement prioritisation. The research identifies the limitations associated with five requirements prioritisation approaches, namely analytic hierarchy process (AHP), quality functional deployment (QFD), the planning game, binary search tree, and $100 allocation. A search of academic literature was conducted to identify sentences and paragraphs describing the limitations. With little research on prioritisation approach limitations, grounded theory was chosen. Verbatim text about the limitations was inductively analysed to identify which were reported for each of the five popular prioritisation approaches. The findings contributed 16 limitations associated with the five popular prioritisation approaches: nine limitations for AHP and QFD, seven for the planning game, six for $100 allocation, and four for binary search tree. While analysing these, limitations dependencies were reported among them. For example, the quality of the requirement limitation could impact the validity issues limitation. Therefore, this study also contributes a framework showing these dependencies and how the limitations can impact or influence other limitations. The results could help software developers to understand the limitations of each approach and inform the approach they choose for requirements prioritisation. With the fewest limitations, this study shows that the binary search tree could be the best approach. However, an approach with a high number of limitations may be preferred if the benefits outweigh the limitations. Therefore, further research is needed to provide a balanced view and also consider the benefits of these five popular approaches. Future research could also be used to verify the framework.

This chapter pertains to technology-enhanced business model innovation. The innovative business model must be capable of producing new business ideas by combining the technology along with the business values so as to come up with solution to new customer requirements. This chapter highlights the trends across the technology innovation, how technology can be a tool for fostering innovation, associated challenges with technology-driven innovation, how to enable IT-enabled innovation in enterprises, and how technology-driven innovation could lead to business growth. Finally, various approaches for innovation are presented.

Preface

AN OVERVIEW

Innovation is the key to maintain competitive advantage. Innovation in products, processes, and business models help companies to provide economic value to their customers. Identifying the innovative ideas, implementing those ideas, and absorbing them in the market requires investing many resources that could incur large costs. Technology encourages companies to foster innovation to remain competitive in the marketplace.

Emerging Technologies for Innovation Management in the Software Industry serves as a resource for technology absorption in companies supporting innovation. It highlights the role of technology to assist software companies—especially small start-ups—to innovate their products, processes, and business models. This book provides the necessary guidelines of which tools to use and under what situations. Covering topics such as risk management, prioritization approaches, and digitally-enabled innovation processes, this premier reference source is an ideal resource for entrepreneurs, software developers, software managers, business leaders, engineers, students and faculty of higher education, researchers, and academicians.

TARGET AUDIENCE

Entrepreneurs, Software Engineers, Scientists working as Researchers with research organizations, Universities, and Research & Development Units, Academicians, Business consultants, and others will benefit from the research findings presented in this book. This book gives readers a single point of entry to research on startup innovation in terms of empirical investigations and research solutions. The book's information provides significant direction to the startup community and other stakeholders for incorporating it into their actual business processes. The research papers presented in this book will assist the audience in the following ways:

Entrepreneurs

- Improving their current innovation strategies.
- Using the knowledge imparted in this book to solve their current business difficulties.
- Developing dynamic capacities to maintain a market competitive advantage.

Academicians

- Lecturing students on current innovation management strategies used by startups.
- Developing new research lines and innovating existing research lines using the book.
- Creating strong research proposals that can be submitted to funding agencies.

Scientists/Researchers

- Using the book as a source of information to start new research projects or improve on existing ones.
- Developing strong research project proposals for possible funding agency submissions.
- Strengthening their ties with industry and addressing real-world issues.
- Using a book as a main research study to find knowledge gaps and acquire ideas for future research in their professional and academic fields.

Software Engineers

- Improving startup business operations, for example, by making them better and more suited to startup working environments, based on knowledge imparted in the book.
- Incorporating the findings presented in the book into their daily work routines.

CONTRIBUTOR DEMOGRAPHICS

This book includes contributions from 39 authors from prestigious universities throughout the world. These authors contributed to 14 of the book's chapters. Contributors came from all over the world, including North America (United States of America (USA)), Europe (Denmark, Norway Portugal, Russia, Spain, Turkey, United Kingdom (UK)), Australia (Australia), Asia (India, Pakistan, Vietnam, Malaysia) and Africa (South Africa) as graphically represented in Figure 1).

Figure 1. Contributor demographics (based on their affiliations)

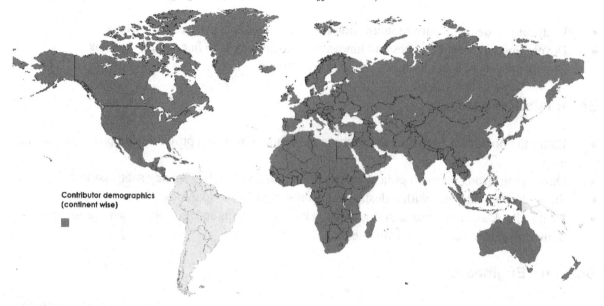

Contributor demographics
(continent wise)

ORGANISATION OF BOOK

This book is divided into 14 chapters, each of which focuses on innovation management in the context of a startup. These investigations are organized into 14 chapters, each of which is detailed in detail in the following lines.

Chapter 1 highlighted that Software startups have been widely known for their potential for disruptive innovation and their ability to generate wealth through unique value propositions and business models. The benefits that such organizations provide to the local and global economy are well documented. There is however that a concern when it comes to software startups is that most such startups fail in less than 2 years of inception. Given the invaluable contributions that these emerging organizations bring to the lives of their founding teams and the overall economic system alike, the causes, the current constructs contributing to the failure and possible success of software startups should merit further study.

From the perspective of business model development, much of the software startup space is presently dominated by the agile paradigm of business model creation using methodologies such as the Business Model Canvas, the Lean Startup and the Lean Canvas. The traditional business model development methodology has largely been abandoned given that it takes too much time to work through and the ever-changing fast paced nature of the software market would need business modelling methods which can easily pivot and is quick to develop, form hypothesis and test. The situation is not very different in the product development space, as the agile manifesto was originally conceived with the needs of the software space in mind. User stories are one of the most popular methodologies used when capturing requirements and prioritization is done using techniques like QFD, pair-wise analysis and MoSCoW analysis. Prototyping is used as a tool to help with testing out product concepts and getting user feedback. Some of the shortcomings observed during the creation of the startup is the lack of a holistic approach to the startup's development. The product and business model development efforts are rather created in silos with little interconnections. For instance, there is no commercial validation efforts done during the product development process. All efforts during that point is made to ensure that the product being developed is useful to the user and has good usability. There are similar issues when it comes to business model development. A better paradigm could be to explore an integrated approach for development of the startup, where both product and business model development are explored as a part of the same process with a common goal in mind. Ideally, a framework developed using such a perspective will incorporate additional aspects such as making use of product evangelists to promote the value proposition, keeping a close watch on the evolutions within the user's problem space, creating potential product ecosystems around the core value proposition and leveraging metrics for better decision making.

Chapter 2 highlighted that the widespread use of digital technology in innovation processes and outcomes, has prompted scholars to develop new theories on innovation management. These theories challenge long-held beliefs about the relationship between company performance and innovation processes, as well as the boundaries between innovation and organizations. Researchers must study and investigate digital technology implementation in order to foster innovative activity, which necessitates new digital technology theorization. Scholars have developed various research directions to theoretically understand digital technology in relation to developing digital business strategies, reassembling current capabilities with digital resources to establish digital capabilities, and capturing or creating value using digital technologies.

A thorough understanding of how digital technology affects the management of the innovation process might lead to the creation of an innovation process framework. Based on these premises and the research streams mentioned, researchers argue that incorporating and using digital technologies in innovation processes forces organizations to reorganize their business models and manage the innovation process in a different way than previously stated in the literature. The mechanisms that digital innovation supports are sometimes forgotten in the story of digital innovation. The potential of digital innovation to reconfigure, revitalize, challenge, and rethink the way things are viewed and comprehended is its primary impact. To put it another way, digital innovation is all about what it changes and how it affects how things are done as a result of the use of digital technologies. To comprehend change, one must first comprehend the mechanism through which change occurs, and vice versa. As a result, in the context of digital innovation, business process management is becoming increasingly important.

Digital innovation is expected to alter the process by balancing new innovation features with immediate feedback, balancing adaptation freedom with predefined structure, balancing positive deviation with process compliance, and balancing inter-organizational emergence with intra-organizational optimisation, according to researchers' attempts to link digital innovation to BPM. A new stream of research has recently emerged at the interface of digital innovation and business process management. This stream presents new ideas to describe how digital innovation affects the design, analysis, and management of business processes by enabling, hindering, shifting, or constraining them. It also looks at how BPM theory, technology, and practices can help us understand the processes and outcomes of digital innovation. The goal of this stream is to bring together those two disparate and isolated fields so that their insights, ideas, and theories can collide and transcend the bounds of their own literature streams.

Despite the fact that the literature on BPM and digital innovation is fragmented, it is apparent that the two sectors are complementary and mutually beneficial. Scholars in both fields must examine their techniques, questions, and assumptions in order to assess this complementarity. Scholars must start listening in on each other's talks in order to contribute to this complementarity. Context comprehension is a significant source of research prospects in both digital innovation and business process management. Contextual factors have a significant impact on both digital innovation and business process management.

The BPM field has produced context-aware methodologies, tools, and conceptualizations. To address context, the digital innovation area has used computational and empirical methodologies. The possibility arises from using digital innovation research methodology to the development and improvement of BPM technology, such as process analysis and process mining, and vice versa.

Chapter 3 introduced an area of research related to the implementation of emerging Unified Communications and Collaboration (UC&C) technologies for productivity and innovation management within the context of large-scale automotive design, manufacture and business operations at General Motors (GM), a leader in the global automotive industry. It further discusses how the chapter bridges the gaps presented through the design of the research developed with the purpose of evaluating the impact of said emerging technologies. In terms of mentioning what problems existed, prior to the research undertaking reported on in this chapter, General Motors had not implemented unified communications within its manufacturing, design or business operation functions and had not engaged in the development of an Internet of Things (IoT)-related digitization strategy.

Chapter 4 highlighted that the hardware startups are increasingly popular due to recent advancements in hardware technologies. Nowadays, hardware product development involves the process innovation not only at the hardware level but also at software components. The scarce of knowledge on hardware startup product development motivates us to carry an empirical investigation on five hardware startup companies. This chapter reported some common good practices among hardware startups, i.e., process definition, evolutionary development process and document management. Several factors that are different from software startups, such as low priority of product quality, product pipeline and unrecognized product platform, are revealed. An integrative process model of hardware product development that shows the connections between human factors in the startups, their speed-prioritized development processes, and the consequence of hindered productivity in the later phases, is finally proposed. The model has some implications for hardware startup founders to plan for the trade-off between team, speed, quality, and later productivity.

Chapter 5 highlighted that in highly dynamic situations, entrepreneurs build value propositions in resource-constrained conditions. The activity is set up as a series of experiments, with each one aimed at validating value proposition-related assumptions with customers. Validation entails interactions between potential customers and the startup team utilizing prototypes, which leads to the confirmation of current assumptions as well as the discovery of new insights that lead to more experiments. The main features of the value proposition identification model are highlighted, and a novel value prioritizing approach is proposed in this chapter.

Chapter 6 highlighted that in today's world of strong competition, firms aim to minimize costs as much as possible while enhancing efficiency and quality. As a result, in order to keep the company afloat, managers must manage multiple crises at the same time. Organizations are putting a larger focus on concepts like novelty, creativity, and speed as a result of the rapid rise of technology and globalization, which allows knowledge to become a strategic value. To manage turbulence while maintaining long-term survival, businesses must participate in innovative operations. The notions that are currently separating companies are knowledge and the human factor that creates knowledge. The development, sharing, application, and management of knowledge are all elements of the organizational culture. The relevance of knowledge management is demonstrated by the fact that knowledge may be exploited as a competitive weapon by businesses in a global society, and that capital-intensive enterprises are being replaced by knowledge-intensive businesses. Organizations, on the other hand, may encounter a knowledge gap between their existing level of knowledge and the amount of knowledge required to create new items, processes, or services. Businesses will need to conduct new research to close this gap. The most important factors for a corporation at this time are the quality and quantity of knowledge, as well as how it will be employed to carry out innovative operations. Integration of knowledge management and knowledge processes boosts a company's innovation and performance.

Knowledge management strategies and initiative actions used by businesses include knowledge development, transmission, application, and storage. A company's ability to innovate is boosted by effective knowledge management. Knowledge development in enterprises serves as a foundation for innovation and competition. As a result, companies can use knowledge management to help them launch new goods and services. In knowledge-based economies, knowledge is a critical resource for businesses to develop effective management policies and practices. Thanks to knowledge management, businesses improve their ability to innovate, increase productivity, and, as a result, gain a competitive advantage in the medium to long term. Firms aim to extend their innovation activities and produce value with their growing expertise. In terms of businesses, knowledge management is at the heart of the innovation process and organizational harmony.

Businesses should focus on a variety of activities that allow them to both follow and develop innovations while also taking advantage of available capabilities since exploratory and exploratory activities compete for precious resources. The purpose of this chapter was to investigate the impact of ambidexterity on company success via knowledge management and innovation. As a result of the analysis within the context of a designated model, we concluded that there is a positive and significant effect of knowledge management over innovation, a positive and significant effect of innovation over ambidexterity, and a positive and significant effect of ambidexterity over business performance. After using the structural equation modeling linearity hypothesis to run the model, it became clear that seeking ambidexterity through inventive activities had a greater impact than other approaches.

In today's environment of fierce competition, businesses must make numerous modifications. These changes emphasize the provision of higher-quality products and services, as well as the development of new strategies and innovation. Firms that place a stronger emphasis on innovation are more likely to use knowledge management successfully and seek out new skills while sharpening old ones. The complexity and dynamism of the firms' environment can hinder their shift from short-term to long-term success. Businesses can both carry their existing successes into the future and respond to probable future environmental changes due to their ambidexterity.

Chapter 7 highlighted that Software development is one of the most knowledge-intensive jobs possible. Moreover, it requires you to have different kinds of constantly updated information about the software processes themselves, in addition to the products and services you are working on. Software developers repeatedly create various processes for development, which causes software development to be inherently experimental; software engineers thus continually gain knowledge with every development project. Therefore, knowledge management is vital for the software industry.

Knowledge Management covers 4 phases which are: Create, Structure, Share and Apply. Successfully management of these phases leads to successful knowledge management outcomes. Knowledge management has become more efficient by using emerging technologies. These emerging technologies allow the above-mentioned phases of knowledge management to be implemented more effectively.

The Internet of Things (IoT) applications have radically changed our lives by adding great value to the lives of both individuals and organizations. Today, billions of everyday objects are equipped with advanced sensors, wireless networks and innovative computing capabilities. This means that very large data can be transmitted quickly. One of the biggest operational challenges for knowledge management systems is to access the real-time data necessary for optimal and effective decision making. From the moment it emerged, the Internet of Things has made a positive difference in providing high-volume and instant data communication, especially between computer systems, which are one of the basic components of knowledge management systems.

Today, the opportunity to have big data has also led to the need to use advanced technologies in transforming this data into information and knowledge. As the amount of information created and shared increases, the difficulty of discovering information increases in coordination. Artificial intelligence uses modern technologies to simplify the discovery of knowledge. Artificial intelligence powered knowledge bases use new technologies such as semantic search, natural language processing, and machine learning to make it easy for employees to find the information they are looking for quickly and easily. Artificial intelligence powered tools help us consolidate information across multiple systems, making information accessible to all employees, wherever they are.

Artificial intelligence connects data from different sources. Artificial intelligence helps us keep our knowledge base content up to date. Artificial intelligence tools provide key knowledge management metrics. Artificial Intelligence contribute to knowledge management in software industry in some major activities:

- Knowledge distribution: Online databases can provide AIs with knowledge spanning different fields and application areas according to software.
- A well-built machine can extract from the actual data store, which increases with the number of interactions with users feeding new information into the algorithm. This means new information retrieval and therefore a larger data repository for customers or system users.
- The act of delivering (or transferring) knowledge is often performed by chatbots: artificial technologies based on NLP that analyze and interact with human language through a speech-like simulation environment during software development.
- The information caught from the software running on production can automatically be analyzed and fix or improvement areas can be automatically determined.

Chapter 8 highlighted that Software Startups bring innovative products to the market. However, such innovation is at the cost of highly educated guess work about customer expectations and quick decision making by persons responsible for strategic planning and implementation. It is therefore of interest to understand the challenges and practices faced by startups that aim to release something innovative in selected market segments. Hence this paper investigates the challenges faced by entrepreneurs of startups and the practices they follow to become successful. The specific challenges explored include: (i) How startups handle software evolution (ii) Challenges faced in releasing products to the market, and (iii) the state of affairs of Software Engineering in startups. Results indicate that despite guidance and support in terms of well-known and documented development methods, practitioners find it difficult to implement and apply these in practice. They must quickly evolve their products to sustain in the market and the market is highly uncertain which makes the complete process highly probabilistic.

Chapter 9 pertains to the innovations in requirement prioritisation process. Software requirements prioritisation is an important task that ultimately determines whether the software is successful and achieves customer satisfaction. Most software projects have a large number of requirements, so there is a need to prioritise which requirements to include. Startups use agile methodologies to deliver innovative software solutions, as agile adapts to requirement changes well and delivers software quickly in short increments, called sprints. Benefits may be more notable for smaller companies and startups as they tend to have a greater focus on the customer and on process improvement, whereas large companies may suffer from a rigid organisation and functional silos. The product owner is responsible for managing and prioritising a dynamic product backlog, to reflect the continuous re-prioritisation of the requirements. Developers are often delegated this decision-making role, particularly for small organisations or startups who may not have IT domain knowledge and cannot afford an IT consultant to act on their behalf. However, there is little research about the practices of agile requirements re-prioritisation, the activity to reprioritise requirements at the start of each sprint. This research contributes to this gap by identifying the factors considered when prioritising requirements for five popular prioritisation approaches. This research also compares these factors to the agile requirements re-prioritisation process to see how well these popular approaches support the agile process. The five popular requirements prioritisation approaches are Analytic Hierarchy Process (AHP), Quality Functional Deployment (QFD), planning game, binary search tree, and $100 allocation. Framework synthesis was used to identify a best-fit framework developed by a robust methodology, and relevant for the agile requirements re-prioritisation process. The chosen best-fit framework considers six factors when prioritising requirements, business value, risk, effort estimation, learning experience, external change, and project constraints. First. the factors considered by the five popular approaches were identified. The results show that five factors were reported in literature for the planning game, three were reported for AHP, one was reported for QFD and no factors were identified for binary search tree and $100 allocation. Although, the factor business value was not identified in the literature for $100 allocation or binary search tree, it is likely that stakeholders consider business value for $100 allocation as they allocate more dollars to the requirements, which are more important. It is also likely that business value is considered for binary search tree, while determining the placement of each candidate requirement on the tree. Second, the factors from the agile requirements re-prioritisation process were compared with the factors considered by the five popular approaches. The results confirm five of the factors identified in the agile requirements re-prioritisation process, the sixth factor external change, was not reported in the literature for the five popular approaches. The planning game covers five of the factors whereas AHP covers three of the factors. QFD only covered one factor and both the binary search tree and £100 allocation approaches did not report any of the factors. Although, the Binary search tree and $100 allocation approaches have numerous benefits, including being fast and easy to use. This may influence the choice of approach used for agile requirements re-prioritisation. This study contributes insights that are important for requirements prioritisation literature and practice.

Chapter 10 pertains to innovation in risk management. Risk is an inherent part of a startup journey, and software startups need to deal with different type of risks, including technical and product risks. In established companies, risk management is well-established research and practice area, and proof to be helpful for successfully managing software development projects. However, it is less known in a software startup context whether risk management also work as they are in established contexts. This paper reports a result from qualitative studies in nine software startups in Denmark and Finland. The outcomes indicates that startups founders do not believe in risk management methods and prioritize other tasks on their to-do list. These findings might not be generalized for a larger population; however, they could be useful for startups companies in Nordic countries, which share similar environmental contexts with our cases. We believe that the insights from this study would be helpful for people who are doing or want to start their software business. However, there is a need to further explore if there is any impact on startup performance when risk management is used versus when it is not.

Chapter 11 highlights the importance of scholarly literature on startup capacities to stimulate innovation in pandemic times is highlighted in this chapter. The scholarly literature can help startups looking for opportunities or solutions in the face of a pandemic, but knowledge acquisition from secondary materials may be limited due to the growing number of publications, retractions, and Preprints. The growing number of publications and venues makes it more difficult for entrepreneurs to get the information they need, analyse it, and then use collective intelligence to turn it into useful business knowledge. Retractions may steer startups in the incorrect direction, resulting in a waste of financial resources. Preprints are non-peer reviewed research articles that may provide some direction to startups but should not be relied upon entirely. The solutions to these issues are finally provided. Addressing these concerns could make scholarly literature beneficial to startups, allowing the global community to respond to the pandemic as a whole.

Chapter 12 reported the innovative IT-technologies in the field of mechanical engineering, allowing to increase the efficiency of production. This chapter reflects a particular task of automation of a particular branch of mechanical engineering - the technology of mechanical engineering. New methods of calculation of typical multivariable tasks are considered, as well as the effectiveness of the introduction of automation at the level of the design office.

Chapter 13 pertains to process innovation in requirement prioritisation. Agile software development is popular among startup companies, who quickly develop software with a focus on innovation. Software can be developed for a variety of applications, including mobile phones and the controls of an aeroplane. Prioritisation is an essential process of any software development project, as there are usually more requirements than there is time and budget. There are various approaches available, to help decide which requirements to prioritise for inclusion in the software. The wrong approach could waste resources and cause customer dissatisfaction. There are also constraints for startups, such as small teams and multiple influencers which must be considered when choosing a suitable approach. An awareness of limitations with prioritisation approaches could help inform software developers with this decision. However, there is limited research linked to the limitations of requirements prioritisation approaches. This research helps to address this gap by identifying limitations for five popular approaches. The five requirements prioritisation approaches studied were Analytic hierarchy process (AHP), quality functional deployment (QFD), the planning game, binary search tree, and $100 allocation. A search of academic literature was conducted to identify sentences and paragraphs describing the limitations. With little research on prioritisation approach limitations, Grounded Theory was chosen. Verbatim text about the limitations was inductively analysed to identify which were reported for each of the five popular prioritisation approaches. The findings contributed sixteen limitations associated with the five popular prioritisation approaches. Nine limitations for AHP and QFD, seven for the planning game, six for $100 allocation, and four for binary search tree. While analysing these limitations dependencies were reported among them. For example, the quality of the requirements limitation could impact the validity issues limitation. Therefore, this study also contributes a framework showing these dependencies, how the limitations can impact or influence other limitations. The results could help software developers to understand the limitations of each approach and inform the approach they choose for requirements prioritisation. With the fewest limitations, this study shows that the binary search tree could be the best approach. However, an approach with a high number of limitations may be preferred if the benefits outweigh the limitations. Therefore, further research is needed to provide a balanced view, and also consider the benefits of these five popular approaches. Future research could also be used to verify the framework.

Chapter 14 pertains to technology enhanced business model innovation. Innovation is critical for any forward-thinking organization. This is where technology plays a major role. Choosing technologies that will empower an organization is challenging. Even a good development strategy needs to be implemented properly. To innovate enough, start thinking about what kind of technology is actually required in order to be benefited with outcomes. Information technology (IT) innovation in an enterprise involves using technology in new ways to create a more efficient organization and improve alignment between technology initiatives and business goals. IT innovation can take many forms like turning business processes into automated IT functions, developing applications that open new markets, or implementing desktop virtualization to increase manageability and cut hardware costs. Information and Communication Technologies (ICT) are emerging as a promising paradigm for creating a profound change in digitizing technologies. Technology innovation can take many forms, for instance, novel software implementing new algorithms and data processing models; or new hardware components (sensors, processors, components); or improved user interfaces offering seamless experiences; it can also happen at a higher level, in the form of new processes, business models, monetization engines, and so on.

To bring in technology into business model entrepreneurs must involve themselves into research and development (R&D), generating new ideas, conducting experiments, designing and implementing new changes into the system. To achieve better performance appropriate strategy has to be followed. To bring in technology into business the first step of the entrepreneur must be recognizing the unanswered or unresolved customer needs. There are three characteristics to be considered for technology with respect to the business model development. Technology supports business model through various supporting functions for a specific business model. Technology acts as the enabler for a business model and business model enables an innovative technology.

Both innovation and technology are tightly interlaced. Two very notable ways technology propels innovation forward is that it boosts tinkering and experimentation, and that in itself accelerates innovation processes. Earlier experimentation with new technologies was only possible by multinational corporations or government-funded research labs. Today, affordable technology digital and others make it possible for most enterprises big and small to experiment with ideas and concepts in whole new ways, and also in reality instead of only in test labs. Innovation must be socially desirable, economically profitable, and technologically feasible.

Technology, Innovation and Ventures capabilities should be brought together to support the clients' needs for sustainable growth. Approaches to anticipate the new trends, assess their potential, validate their enterprise-readiness, and exploit them responsibly should be enabled. Applied innovation in industries has enabled scaling, with certainty and trust, and with the power of data and intelligence built in.

This book includes research articles on several forms of startup innovations, such as process innovations, business model innovations, and product innovations. The expertise imparted by the book will assist its readers in adapting the knowledge to their startup context in order to overcome difficulties that are specific to their situation. Furthermore, the book makes a significant contribution to the body of knowledge by expanding on innovation-specific knowledge in the context of startups. This book will be especially valuable to startups with a high failure rate and minimal resources. By embracing an interdisciplinary approach integrating computer engineering and business management, this book provides a good range of research studies to stimulate further research in innovation management relevant to startups. Interdisciplinary solutions are needed by the startup community to be inventive and gain a lasting competitive edge in extremely dynamic markets. This book will be an amazing source of instant knowledge for startups, boosting their innovative capabilities and success rates, with a perfect blend of empirical research and evaluation study kinds.

The editors hope that the intended audience will benefit from this book, and we wish them a Happy Reading, Learning, and Adoption.

Varun Gupta
Universidad de Alcalá, Madrid, Spain

Chetna Gupta
Jaypee Institute of Information Technology, Noida, India

Acknowledgment

The editors would like to express their gratitude to everyone who contributed to this project, especially the authors and reviewers who participated in the review process. This book would not have been possible without their help.

First and foremost, the editors would like to express their gratitude to all of the contributors for their contributions. The authors of the chapters who offered their time and expertise to this book have our heartfelt gratitude.

Second, the editors like to thank the reviewers for their substantial contributions to improving the quality, coherence, and content presentation of the chapters. The majority of the authors also worked as referees, which we greatly appreciate.

Chapter 1

Development Frameworks for Software Startups:
A Literature Review

Narendranath Shanbhag
La Trobe University, Australia

Eric Pardede
La Trobe University, Australia

ABSTRACT

Although software startups are seen as engines of rapid growth and sources of disruptive innovation, these entities are known to have a high failure rate. In addition to this, owing to the rapidly evolving technology sector and the ever-changing needs of the modern business and consumer markets, it might be worth reviewing the development methodologies presently in use for relevance. Considering newer technological constructs such as cloud computing and corresponding impact that could have on the development process such as the ability to quickly scale will need to be studied as part of such a review. This research works reviews current literature for product, business model, and integrated frameworks involving the two spaces to present the various aspects covered as part of the different paradigms of startup development within the software space. The resultant review presents the areas covered by the different paradigms and presents a view of the various areas from the viewpoint of software startup success factors.

INTRODUCTION

Software startups have been acknowledged for their potential for disruptive innovation, rapid growth and massive revenue generation. Indeed, Software products dominate work and personal spaces for most peoples. It must be noted that most early stage startups fail in less than two years on their inception (Tripathi et al., 2019). One of the reasons for this include not taking into account the problem solution fit of the product (Paternoster et al., 2014).

DOI: 10.4018/978-1-7998-9059-1.ch001

Software startups are startup entities for whom the development of software forms a core portion of their product or service offering (Gutbrod et al., 2017; Melegati et al., 2019). As pointed out by Paternoster et al. (2014) and later by Tripati et al. (2019), the term software startup surfaced in early literature in a research article by Carmel (1994). Paternoster et al. (2014) define software startups as "newly created companies with no operating history and fast in producing cutting-edge technologies". Another commonly accepted meaning of the term software startups is startup entities which conceive and produce software intensive products (Tripathi et al., 2019). In this work, the scope is limited to software products and not software services. It must be noted that software offered as a service (SaaS) are included in the scope of software products. Xu and Brinkkemper (2005) define a software product as "... *a packaged configuration of software components or a software-based service, with auxiliary materials, which is released for and traded in a specific market*".

As stated by Sutton (2000) and later pointed out by Paternoster et al. (2014), some key challenges faced by software startups include

- Resource constraints – software startups have limited resources in terms of time, finance and human capital, their primary focus is on getting the products in the hands of consumers, promotion of the product and developing strategic alliances.
- Turbulent and ever-changing market conditions – with disruptive technologies and adoption of globalization, the constantly changing market needs and software startups need to ensure their products keep up with these changes.
- Continually evolving technologies – software startups need to work with evolving and disruptive technologies.
- A wide and diverse range of influences – Software startups are influenced by wide ranging, interconnected sets of factors including customers, industry partners, investors, the competitive forces, the industry, and the overall market.
- Little to no accumulated experience – Since software startups have little to no operating history, they do not have an established development process or other management processes for their organization.

In the initial stages of most startups, the focus is on product development, as without a product offering there is not much else to create a business around (Trimi & Berbegal-Mirabent, 2012), and this holds true in the area of software. Software products are typically defined as standardized systems which are produced for mass market consumption aimed at either consumer or enterprise user bases (Aramand, 2008). Software startups however find it difficult to adopt development process for software products owing to various factors and influences. These varied range of factors and influences can make every development context different and unique in its own regard.

Most software development techniques involve requirements gather and specification, design of the product, implementation of the product and testing, most often in this given sequence. Prominent software development methodologies include traditional and agile methodologies. Traditional software development involved the creation of formal project plans, detailed documentation of requirements, more documentation and detailed testing (Rico et al., 2008). This development paradigm was well suited to create products where the requirements did not change often and did not have rigid time constraints (Aitken & Ilango, 2013). However, the very nature of software products and the modern technology driven market in general, was characterized by frequent change and uncertainty. A different approach was required to successfully develop products for the software space. This is where agile methodologies came in. Agile development methodologies are a collection of development methods which use incremental and iterative development cycles to produce software products in a collaborative manner with the aid of cross-functional teams (R. G. Cooper, 2019).

A few key benefits of agile include the ability to quickly respond to change, improved time to market, evolutionary method of development and delivery of products, focus on productivity and quality, adaptive approach to development planning, reduced costs and its time-bound iterative approach to product development (R. G. Cooper, 2019; Reifer, 2002). These benefits would be greatly useful to software startups, given their limited resources and necessity to get products out early to market. Agile methodologies might therefore be better suited to the needs of software startups when compared to traditional software development methodologies. However, agile methodologies are not without its challenges. A major challenge for the adoption of agile is its dependence on effective collaboration and the needed experience and expertise for the practical adoption of the methodology (Smoczyńska et al., 2018). Cho (2008) asserts that overly simplified documentation produced when working with agile can be both a boon and bane, as simplified documentation will lack the needed level of detail required for proper development of features of system. Lastly and importantly, agile focuses on the short term perspective of development and does not consider the longer term perspective of strategy, particularly from a business model standpoint (R. G. Cooper & Sommer, 2018). Hence, although it can serve as a good base for software product development, it cannot be used as an end-to-end methodology for software startups for product and business (model) development.

The main aim of this research work is to study existing product and business model development frameworks and identify any gaps or scopes for improvement, that can benefit aspiring software startups by improving their chances of success in their entrepreneurial ventures. Accordingly, current literature in the space of both product and business model development, including overlapping areas are reviewed and their values, along with potential for improvement are highlighted.

The sections of this review of research are structured as follows: in section two, the concepts involved in business model creation are reviewed, along with the multitude of frameworks available for business model development. Section three covers product development frameworks such as agile, along with relevant processes such as requirement capture, prioritization, and development of prototypes, among others. Section four discusses integrated approaches to product and business model development, including the shortcomings of said methods. Section five covers the newer considerations in product and business model development domains and section six discusses the observed gap in the reviewed literature. A summarized analysis is presented as part of this section. Finally, section seven outlines the conclusion and scope for future work.

BUSINESS MODELS AND BUSINESS MODEL DEVELOPMENT

Business Models

Startups run a race against time to find a business model that works. To begin this race, products along with associated services serve as value propositions which the business can offer to the customers. However, businesses can stay afloat only if these offerings can be monetized enough to eventually turn a profit. Therefore innovating and consequently creating great products would need to be followed by efficient business model planning for the survival of any startup (Teece, 2010). Although there is no universally accepted definition for the term "business model" (Rajala et al., 2003), it generally refers to how any business intends to create value (Morris et al., 2005), be it for the customers, investors or other stakeholders. Chesbrough and Rosenbloom (2002) describe business models as an general outline of how an organization or person does business. Ostwalder and Pigneur (2010) define business models as how organizations or entities create, deliver and capture value. Teece and Linden (2017) specify that the ideal business model should strike a balance between providing value to customers and a proportional capture of value by its provider. Fernandes and Afonso (2018) point out the three important questions mentioned by Markides (1997) which should be deliberated upon by entrepreneurs working on business models: *Who*, *What* and *How*. To elaborate, *Who* the customers will be, *What* the nature of the product or service being offered should be and *How* these offerings should be made to the customers, keeping in mind efficiency. Fernandes and Afonso (2018) also note the addition of a fourth question by Osterwalder and Pigneur (2010) which seeks the answer to *How much*, implying how much value a company can derive from its offerings (ideally in terms of profit). Business models should also be adaptable based on changing circumstances, owing to the fact that the modern market is increasingly networked, knowledge based and technology driven (Fjeldstad & Snow, 2018).

Blank (2018), on the other hand mentions that established organizations are focused on execution of tried and tested business models whereas startups are in search of a business model, which can work. This implies that business model development is an experimentation driven journey of discovery, as reiterated by McGrath (2010). However, Teece and Linden (2017) stress the importance of determining the path to profitability being a core component of business modeling which should be planned beforehand. Osterwalder and Pigneur (2010) highlight that sustained value creation can only be achieved through constant and iterative adaption and renewal of an underlying successful business model. The role that strategy and experimentation play in this process has been acknowledged in literature (McGrath, 2010; Teece & Linden, 2017).

In terms of other benefits provided by business models, Ritter and Lettl (2018) point out that business models provide contextual explanation on how actors within the system are positioned inside value networks and how businesses produce output using inputs, while accomplishing their business goals. Business models also help describe the working of the business and can be used by management personnel to determine future directions and next steps for the organization to explore (Teng & Lu, 2016).

Frameworks and Paradigms for Business Model Development

Business model frameworks help define the various components or elements of the business model and can serve as a foundation to the planning process for business models. Frameworks also help articulate the value provided by the business to the customer and the value captured by the business, on behalf of its stakeholders. The two most common paradigms in business model development is the traditional business planning paradigm and the more modern business planning paradigm based on "Lean" and "Agile" techniques, which perfectly describes techniques such as the Business Model Canvas (BMC) by Osterwalder and Pigneur (2004).

The traditional business planning paradigm plays an important role in the entrepreneurship process. Kraus and Kauranen (2009) highlight this importance in the context of its linking of entrepreneurship with the domain of strategic management. Honig and Karlson (2004) point out and Ghezzi et al. (2015) reiterate the importance of the traditional business plan in outlining the enterprise strategy and its subsequent role in presenting the vision, along with the process it intends to follow to attain this vision. Ghezzi et al. (2015) further note that the business plan document serves as a foundation for the business strategy and represents its formalization.

However, the usefulness and applicability of the traditional business plan in the modern business landscape have been a subject of debate (Burke et al., 2009; Ghezzi et al., 2015; Kraus & Kauranen, 2009). Conventional business model development methodologies create products with the assumption and without any evidence that the final product will be both useful and usable by the mainstream customer (Ries, 2011). Furthermore, both Blank (2013b) and Ries (2011) highlight that traditional methodologies focus on testing either the developed product or the value proposition. They go on to highlight that all elements of the business model need to be tested and not just the value proposition, which is characteristic of conventional business model planning methods. In the same context, traditional software product development techniques such as *waterfall* consumes more time and resources when compared to newer techniques such as the Lean startup, thereby helping startups and other resource constrained organizations quickly discard poor ideas or ideas which have no market (Yoo et al., 2017).

On the business side, many successful entrepreneurs have avoided the process of writing business planning documents (Honig & Karlsson, 2013), which are emblematic to the traditional business planning paradigm. One of the reasons for this is that the process of documenting a formal business plan takes a long time and the startup's development process remains mostly stagnant during that phase (Blank, 2013a). Also, many entrepreneurs do not update the business plans after they are formalized/documented and rarely even refer to them, making the adoption of the business plan development as a purely symbolic process (T. Karlsson & Honig, 2009). Blank (2013b) suggests using methodologies based on Lean for business undertakings, over traditional planning and business model techniques to reduce the chances of failure with such undertakings. Bosch et al. (2013) also mention the benefits of using lean along with agile practices, particularly in the case of early stage startups. Blank (2013a) also suggests the use of customer development methodology over traditional business plans as a means to quickly validate and subsequently outline the product and business model elements of a startup.

The most popular methodology that embodies the "Lean/Agile" vision of business model development is the Business Model Canvas (BMC) by Osterwalder and Pigneur (2004). The BMC is seen as a 'user-friendly' business model development approach (2013b). The idea behind the BMC is that instead of investing a huge amount of time creating business plans, entrepreneurs can use the BMC structure to quickly create summaries of their best business model hypothesis, which they believe can succeed (Ojasalo & Ojasalo, 2015). The value proposition is typically seen as the 'centerpiece' of this business modeling structure (Lima & Baudier, 2017). When using the BMC, the business model is divided into nine blocks or 'segments' relating to their underlying value provided to the business model creation process (Osterwalder & Pigneur, 2010): Value proposition, Distribution channel, Customer Segments, Revenue streams, Cost structure, Key resources, Key partners, Customer relationships, Key activities.

Borseman et al. (2016) suggest that the BMC can simply serve as a good foundation over which other derived frameworks and models can be based. The authors point to two such variations of the BMC: the *Lean Canvas* by Maurya (Maurya, 2012) and the *Business Model Snapshot* by Furr and Dyer (2014), where the focus is placed on providing tools for risk mitigation in new product and business development. Besides variations, there have also been many extensions and integrations to the BMC. A BMC integration with the technological roadmap was proposed by Toro-Jarrín et al. (2016), in which the authors explored a technique which allowed for the creation of a better proposal for a business strategy.

Another example of a model derived from the BMC to suit a particular paradigm is the *Triple layered business model canvas*, which places emphasis on sustainability-focused business model innovation. This variation of the model has found relevance in many sectors such as manufacturing (García-Muiña et al., 2020) and agriculture (Furqon et al., 2019). Another example can be seen in the tailoring of the BMC for the services sector, aptly named the *Service Business Model Canvas* (Zolnowski et al., 2014), designed to capture details specific to business models in the service space such as co-creation. The BMC has also been applied in combination with data analysis techniques such as multidimensional cluster analysis in an attempt to discover newer markets in an existing sector (Urban et al., 2018). Such an application could help businesses better understand their business models and help with creating new value propositions and cater to a wider range of customer segments. Hence, the BMC can serve as a good foundational base for proposing product and/or business model development frameworks.

There are other business model frameworks which do not fit into any single paradigm but have been crafted with a specific niche or purpose in mind. These include Components Business model and the objectives, goals, strategies and measures (*OGSM*) model. The Components Business model, which was introduced by IBM, was designed to analyze and model the business elements or "components" of an organization. This simulation based technique provided organizations with a way to play around with different business modeling techniques before allocating any resources to any component or the realization of the business model as a whole (Chesbrough, 2010). However, this approach assumes that there is an existing business model structure, which can then be re-envisioned from a new perspective.

The *OGSM* model places strategy as its foundation pillar and then guides the user to derive actionable plans based on the set OGSM. The primary advantage of the OGSM model is that it packs the critical information of a 50 page business plan into a single page document (Fisler, 2012). However, although the average OGSM model is a single page concise document, it runs the risk of turning into a list of desirable initiatives rather than an action oriented plan which directs the users on where they should focus on and how they can achieve success, as evidenced by the application of the technique by Procter & Gamble (Lafley & Martin, 2013).

In the interest of not reinventing the wheel, we dig deeper into the facets of traditional business planning and a deeper analysis of the BMC framework, as these can provide a strong foundation and a good starting point for the conception of any startup development framework.

Facets of Traditional Business Plans

Schneider (1998) outlines the critical elements which need to be included in the typical traditional business plan:

- A holistic description of the product/service offering and the business.
- Clearly established SMART goals.
- A plan for business growth.
- An anticipated timeframe with reference to the goals.

Schneider (1998) likens a well-drawn business plan to a "road map", which empowers the person creating and using the plan to define objectives, determining milestones, measure progress based on goals and provides the option to change course, when needed. The strategic foundation of any organization can start with the purpose of its existence. Helpful artefacts which provide insight on this matter include the mission and vision of the organization. Pearce and David (1987) point out that defining the mission is the first step in the strategic planning process. Alt and Zimmerman (2001) define mission as *"a high-level understanding of the overall vision, strategic goals and the value proposition including the basic product or service features"*. Ideally the mission should provide details on key market (who the customer or target group is), the key contribution (what the business can do for the customer) and the distinction (why the customer should choose this organization's offering) (Dahle et al., 2020). A good business plan should help a startup define its mission, among other aspects of the business model (Kiznyte et al., 2016). The mission plays a vital role in the strategic planning process of an organization, given its strong relationship to the business model (Dahle et al., 2020). A well-crafted mission and vision are among the eight factors sought out by investors when considering startups to invest in (Cremades, 2019).

Another interlinked artefact of the strategic planning process is the vision of the organization. Maurya (2012) recommends taking steps to capture the vision of the business, owing to its importance from the overall business standpoint. The lean startup approach also advocates for this, through the defining of the vision as a hypothesis to test as a consequence of developing a prototype in conjunction with the business model (Reis et al., 2019; Ries, 2011). The startup's established vision can serve many purposes. One such purpose is when the startup is looking to recruit talent, since a clear vision can fill the gap of appeal which established organizations possess due their brand presence in the market (Kiznyte et al., 2016; Razdan & Kambalimath, 2019). Another purpose is pointed out by Gralha et al. (2018), when providing an instance of how the alignment of the organization's vision to the planning process, coupled with an in-depth understanding of the client, product and market can result in a higher quality product.

High-level business goals tend to define the strategies and goals of other initiatives within an organization (Basili et al., 2009), such as product development. It must be noted that as the startup evolves, these goals have been observed to evolve as well (Brun, 2016). However, startups conventionally have business goals which involve generating revenue and achieving high growth (Nguyen-Duc et al., 2017), among others. A clearly articulated goal (or set of goals) with a defined time frame can help business pave the way for easily achieving their vision (Collins & Porras, 1996).

Owing to the substantial skill, knowledge and efforts needed by the core startup team, understanding the core competence of the startup can be critical to its success (Seppänen et al., 2015). Seppanen et al. (2015) define competence as *"a complete set of skills and knowledge required for successful progress of a startup along its evolutionary path"*. Identification of core competencies along with identification of strategic opportunities, creating strategic alliances and management of intellectual capital can serve as a foundation for the creation of sustainable competitive advantage for organizations (Nowak & Grantham, 2000). Although every organization will evolve over time, certain competencies might be more relevant during its initial phase (startup) than others, which is why it is beneficial to identify and maintain a portfolio of competencies (Ahmed & Koubaa, 2013). There is a case to be made for considering even the outsourcing process itself as a core competence (Fine & Whitney, 2002).

Giardino et al. (2014) highlight the absence of organizational culture as a general characteristic of initial phases of startups, owing to its lack of operating history. Due to this fact, methodologies which will be adopted by startups during this time point should be flexible, adaptable and support a quicker learning process (Paternoster et al., 2014). The organization culture which is created and developed during these initial phases (of startups) have a strong impact on the nature of outcome produced, how the startup operates and the general evolution of the startup (Gralha et al., 2018). This fact is supported by cases from literature. For instance, Giardino et al. (2015) cite a case where a 'hacker' culture along with a 'just-do-it' approach helped a team to rapidly go from idea to implementation for a product. Yang and Choi (2009) highlight that fostering a culture of creativity, wherein attempts are encouraged and rewarded instead of punishments doled out for negative outcomes, can greatly improve performance. Hence, cultural aspects can be considered an important area of focus, alongside identification and management of core competencies.

Even in the space of product development, clearly defined goals can improve the chances of success, and are even seen as one of the best practices in product development (Barczak & Kahn, 2012; Foroutan & Baski-Reeves, 2017). Product goals also provide benchmarks, which can be used to evaluate the design (A. Joshi, 2009). In the context of the strategic foundation, product goals can be used to verify if there is an alignment of product goals with the goals of the organization (Barczak & Kahn, 2012), since business goals tend to guide development efforts in organizations (Lindgren & Münch, 2016). For the desired outcome within startups, having optimal alignment between (product) development goals and business goals of the organization is considered vital (Klotins et al., 2019).

Facets and Shortcomings of the Business Model Canvas (BMC)

The 'lean' nature of the BMC can benefit technology-based startups by ensuring that the product in development is tailored to requirements of the customer from the start. The built in system of validation can result in a good amount of cost savings for startups, since early validations can root out poor product concepts before investments are poured in and the startup scales its product development initiatives (Dal Lago et al., 2016). Blank (2018) mentions that the BMC is a great tool to capture the nine key details which entrepreneurs need to be concerned with on "day one". However, it must be noted that the BMC serves more as a guideline for business model development rather than a confirmed contract of product or business success as a consequence of filling up the BMC segments (Borseman et al., 2016). Some of the derived models or variations of the BMC were discussed in the previous sections (Section number 2.2.) such as the Lean Canvas, the Value Proposition Canvas. A comparative analysis of these models along with others such as the Lean Startup and the Customer Development method is presented in table 1.

Shortcomings of the BMC

While the BMC serves as a great foundation for business model planning and innovation, there are some notable shortcomings of the framework which deserves attention. To start with, Spanz (2012) highlights that the core BMC structure does not include the tracking of goals for startups. This is compounded by the fact that the structure of the BMC does not mandate the determination of strategic foundation elements (such as mission, vision or goals) for the startup (Kraaijenbrink, 2012), nor does it has provisions to verify if the startup has the necessary competencies to implement and fulfil the desired vision of the founding team (Spanz, 2012). Kraaijenbrink (2012) also points out that a study of competing entities are not taken into account as part of the traditional BMC structure, even though its exclusion was most likely to simplify the business modeling process during the early stages of the startup.

Another notable missing element is the consideration of metrics for tracking various aspects of the startup such as performance and revenue (Maurya, 2010; Spanz, 2012). A shortcoming of the BMC, as noted by Vanhala and Saarikallio (Vanhala & Saarikallio, 2015) is that the lines between segments at many time can be blurred and it is hard to categorize them specifically to one segment. The authors provide an example wherein a venture capitalist can be seen as a part of the revenue stream segment, since in this case, venture capitalists add to the capital pool for a startup. However, they can also be seen as a key resource since the provided capital can be used in the development process. The BMC also does not provide a platform for the conduction of visualization and analysis of the business model (Ide et al., 2015). Finally, Maurya (2010) points out the missing 'differentiation' factor in the form of determination of a Unique selling proposition (USP), which is not part of the BMC structure.

Competitor analysis is another area which has not received the attention that it deserves, which can be immensely useful during the strategic formulation process (Hatzijordanou, 2019) and/or the product development process (Rafiq et al., 2017; Tripathi et al., 2017). Product differentiation can be useful to startups as means of setting their offering apart from the competition and providing better product visibility in a competitive market. In today's highly competitive global market, the competition can have a significant impact on the development of product or business, resulting in possible pivots depending on the strength of the competition (Bajwa et al., 2017). Although variations of mainstream business model development methodologies such as the Lean Canvas by Maurya (2012) take the study of the competition into account, the mainstream methodologies themselves do not provide structures to study this area (García-Gutiérrez & Martínez-Borreguero, 2016). Aside from this factor, Maurya (Maurya, 2012) suggests that it is ideal to hone in on the early adopter to get insights on what matters to the customer base. Rasmussen and Tanev (2016) also note that seeking the assistance of early adopters for an early validation of the customer problem with the solution can be highly beneficial to the startup.

Based on the reviewed shortcomings, the following criteria can be used when comparing the different startup development approaches: the consideration of strategic foundation elements as part of the planning process (Kraaijenbrink, 2012), the checking for the availability of core competence within the startup to achieve its vision and goals (Spanz, 2012), the ability to visualize and analyse of the business model (Ide et al., 2015), the employment of an iterative method for the validation of the primary value proposition (Ries, 2011), the usage of a metric driven framework as part of the startup development process (Klein, 2013; Maurya, 2012), the study of competing products or services (Kraaijenbrink, 2012; Maurya, 2012) and the planning for vertical/horizontal integration as part of the startup development framework (Hanssen, 2012; Van Den Berk et al., 2010). These factors were selected as ideal for the comparative analysis since they span the entire process timeline of the startup development process.

Table 1. Comparative analysis of business model development techniques

	Strategic Foundation Established Using Mission and Goals	Checking for the Availability of Core Competence Within the Startup	Ability to Visualize and Analyze of the Business Model	Can be Used as an Iterative Value Proposition Development and Validation Method	Guided by Metrics (Using a Metrics Framework)	Incorporates Competitor Analysis for Value Proposition Differentiation	Future Planning for Vertical/Horizontal Integration (Ecosystems)
Traditional Business Planning	✓	-	-	-	-	-	-
Business Model Canvas	-	-	-	✓	-	-	-
Lean Startup	-	-	-	✓	-	-	-
Customer Development	-	-	-	✓	-	-	-
Lean Canvas	-	-	-	✓ Promotes employment of early adopters to test concepts	Metrics defined but not guided by any specific framework	✓	-
Value Proposition Canvas	-	-	-	✓ (Product Focused)	-	-	-

AGILE - PRODUCT DEVELOPMENT PARADIGMS

The primary reason that the philosophy of agile methodologies resonates with software and business communities alike, is that it takes into account the ever-changing nature of the domains to which they are applied. Both business and software share a common trait, in that its state is constantly evolving and methodologies which can adapt to change could significantly improve the chances of success of such undertakings. As evidence of this, software development initiatives which utilized agile methodologies were found to be three times as successful as traditional software development methodologies (Sutherland & Schwaber, 2012). From the perspective of businesses, the customer requirement is always changing and from the perspective of the software community, the technology is rapidly evolving. Hence agile methods have become popular in product development initiatives among IT product and service providers. Agile techniques focus on rapidly creating value for its customers (Dzamashvili Fogelström et al., 2010), which provides obvious benefits to software startups. Agile methodologies, however, do have some shortcomings. Agile methodologies can have a tendency to be overly dependent on the customer interaction (J. Cho, 2008). Haunts (2014) mentions that the development team might incur time and costs overheads owing to the requirements of resources for testing. Besides this, it is usually hard to accurately estimate cost and effort required, during the initial phases of the development undertaking (Haunts, 2014).

Agile methodologies have even been used in combination with other techniques to better adapt to ever evolving customer requirements. The *agile-stage-gate* model is a classic example of one such approach (R. G. Cooper & Sommer, 2018). The conventional agile methodology is embedded as part of an existing stage-gate implementation. This hybrid model features a deeper integration of the voice of the customer as part of the process, better collaboration and overall shorter time to market. Such integrations, however, serve as evidence that agile methodologies have some inherent shortcomings and has room for structural and process related improvements, in the broader content of the overall business. The remainder of this section will involve the review of relevant aspects of agile product development such as gathering requirements using user stories, prioritization of requirements and prototyping of the product concept, among others.

User Stories and Capturing User Requirements

User stories are often the most common technique for capturing requirements in agile projects (Wang et al., 2014). A technique popularized by Cohn (2004), user stories help the business craft requirements in collaboration with customers using simple business-like English syntax. As described by Cohn (2004), user stories capture only the essential elements of the requirement which includes *who* the requirement is for, *what* feature is expected from the system and *why* the (user) considers this requirement is important. For example, In the context of a Learning management system (LMS), a user story could be: "*As a student, I want to see the feedback on my submission, so that I make needed changes as a part of future submissions*".

In the context of agile methodologies, user stories are not meant as a complete replacement for the traditional requirements engineering process, which is characterized by detailed documentation (Wagner, 2001). This is because they do not contain the same level of detail as traditional requirements. User stories are used due to their flexible nature and ease of use for non-technical users (Silva et al., 2016). Beck (2000) goes as far as to describe user stories as "*units of customer-visible functionality*". User stories are also one of the most preferred requirements engineering practice for customers, owing to their ability to quickly capture rapidly changing requirements (Wang et al., 2014), which could translate to rapid product development and in-turn to quicker time to market. Every user stories even captures a product feature, as part of its structure (Lucassen et al., 2016). These features can be collected, prioritized, and later used in product development efforts.

However, it must be noted that user stories are not relevant for every software development context, for instance in safety critical systems, where high-quality, detailed documentation is critical in order to create robust systems (Heeager & Nielsen, 2018). Some of the challenges of using agile requirements engineering techniques such as user stories include lack of detailed documentation and adequate presence/quality of customer participation in the requirements engineering efforts (Bjarnason et al., 2011; Cao & Ramesh, 2008; Paetsch et al., 2003). Stakeholder motivation for requirements engineering efforts (Bjarnason et al., 2011) and neglecting quality issues in requirements (Cao & Ramesh, 2008) are some of the other challenges faced. The challenge of quality issues in requirements can to a certain degree be mitigated by using qualitative techniques of capturing feedback such as user quotes (after interaction with a prototype). The rationale is that a qualitative approach can allow for an in-depth analysis of any phenomenon in context (Hummel & Epp, 2015; Myers, 2019). There is literature to support the fact that capturing qualitative feedback during early stages development can improve the quality of the product in development (Olsson & Bosch, 2015). Other challenges such as lack of documentation can be overcome by the use of prototypes and subsequently gathering customer feedback based on user interaction with the prototypes, along with adoption of complementary good practices (Käpyaho & Kauppinen, 2015). In particular, the authors point to the main benefits of using prototypes (in the context of usage with agile requirements engineering) being the improved quality of communication between the various stakeholders involved, greater motivation to discuss requirements/changes to requirement and the benefit that the tangential nature of prototypes provide when discussing evolving requirements.

However, user stories are not the only source of information on user needs. The requirements of users can also be studied during their experiences when they come into contact with the product, related service(s) or a prototype of the product (Kawano et al., 2019). These are called as *touchpoints* and can provide details on how users interact with the product, that can be then used to inform further design and development decisions (Sauvola et al., 2016). Noting and tracking touchpoints can let the team shape the user experience of the product in a certain direction (Howard, 2007), which can lead to creation of compelling user experiences. The touchpoints concept can be applied alongside agile based requirement elicitation techniques such as user stories since both approaches treat customers as partners in the design and development process of applications (Sauvola et al., 2016; Schön et al., 2017). In addition, many recent product and business development approaches often uses *personas* to represent the user archetype. A persona is a fictional narrative, along with clear and detailed description of a fictional customer who can be seen to represent the whole customer base (Haas & Kunz, 2010). A persona typically includes a set of information which is created based on the insight derived out of interviews, interactions and observations of potential real world users of the product being built (Wölbling et al., 2012). These details can include a person's demographic, psychographic and behavioral details, also with describing the user's needs (Perdana et al., 2017). Personas help in understanding the problem space from a user's viewpoint (Müller & Thoring, 2012).

Another newer and less utilized technique for studying user needs is the study of competing products, which are not covered as part of most commonly used requirement elicitation techniques (Rafiq et al., 2017). A study of the competition can be considered vital to the startup owing to the fact that the actions and strategies of the competition can have a major impact on the product and business decisions of the startup. For instance, the product decisions of a competing established larger organization may cause the startup to perform a pivot since it may not be able to compete with the larger organization directly on a certain value proposition (Bajwa et al., 2017). Another reason for the study of potential competition is to check for the prospects of potential partnership opportunities (Tripathi et al., 2017).

Prioritization of Requirements

The list of user stories and correspondingly derived list of features for any project can get large, particularly in the case of projects with wide scope. To these, newer stories can be added at any time during the course of the product development process (Georgsson, 2011). In any case, the requirements (based on user stories) with the highest priority need to be implemented in a shorter timeframe, so as to maximize the business value provided to the client (Bakalova et al., 2011). In this regard, a challenge faced by teams is determining the features that need to be included in the current iteration of the development process (Racheva et al., 2008). Typically, this responsibility of requirement prioritization is taken over either by the customer, the product owner or the customer team (Ambler, 2002; Harris & Cohn, 2006). Some commonly used prioritization techniques in agile projects include *Pair-wise analysis, Ping pong balls, Quality function deployment* (QFD), *Analytic hierarchy process* (AHP) and *MoSCoW analysis* to name a few (Achimugu et al., 2014; Racheva et al., 2008). Each of these methods have a suitable application context and are relevant based on the circumstances of the project. For instance, techniques like pairwise analysis and ping pong balls do not scale well and are better suited to projects with fewer requirements

(Fehlmann, 2008; J. Karlsson et al., 1998). Similarly, the QFD technique is quite a comprehensive and robust technique for requirement prioritization (Wiegers, 1999). However, some of its shortcomings are that it requires the users of the technique to have some prior knowledge in the corresponding area, it needs a particular level of abstraction for the expression of requirements which can be hard to achieve and handling temporal relations between requirements can be quite challenging (J. Karlsson et al., 1998). AHP is another technique which uses a pairwise comparison matrix with the aim of calculating relative importance among requirements, however it is found to be not scalable and can be time consuming when the number of requirements increase (Achimugu et al., 2014).

The most common among requirement prioritization techniques is MoSCoW analysis and works by assigning requirements to *priority groups* based on their perceived importance (Racheva et al., 2008). The MoSCoW analysis technique is noted for its simplicity in the ability to prioritize requirements (Zagajsek et al., 2007). The groups include *must-haves*, *should-haves*, *could-haves* and *won't-haves*, wherein *must-haves* indicate non-negotiable requirements which need to be including in the current iteration and *should-haves* point to requirements that are good to include if possible, *could-haves* indicate nice to have requirements which are of lower priority that *should-haves* and the *won't-haves* point to lowest priority requirements which will be explored in future iterations (Achimugu et al., 2014). The MoSCow technique, similar to the other mentioned techniques, has its list of shortcomings (Popli et al., 2014). However, the key benefits of applying this technique are its speed and simplicity (Waters, 2009), which make it very attractive in the agile context and is possibly the main reason for its popularity.

Prototyping

A prototype is a model or representation of the final end product which the development team intends to build and can be presented as either a low-fidelity or a high-fidelity prototype or any range in between the two mentioned types (Nelson et al., 2016). On the other hand, a *wireframe* describes the basic app structure and flow of the application. Low-fidelity prototypes are easy, quick to develop and cost effective, making them ideal for fast continuous product development (Börsting & Gruhn, 2018). High-fidelity prototypes, on the other hand, are seen are similar in visual appearance and look & feel to the intended final product (Christoforakos & Diefenbach, 2018). The main use of low-fidelity prototypes is to study the needs of the user and validate ideas quickly, during the early stages of product design and development process (Abidin et al., 2019). Another advantage of using low-fidelity during the early stages of product development is that the user's attention can be brought to focus on singular aspects of the product whereas using high-fidelity prototypes early on might result in user attention being needless drawn towards irrelevant details of the high-fidelity prototype (Christoforakos & Diefenbach, 2018).

The ideal sequence of usage of the two prototyping techniques is to begin with a low-fidelity prototype for the purpose of quickly validating product concepts and then to evolve iteratively into a high-fidelity prototype (Abdel-Hamid, 1989). Hildenbrand et al. (2012) suggests a three-level approach to prototyping (based on captured user stories) with the intention of gathering user feedback. The bottom level (called Low-fidelity prototypes) uses paper prototypes to communicate the general application flow along with basic details used in the application. The middle level (called High-fidelity prototypes) provides digital representations of the applications visual design, typically created in an easy to design application such as Microsoft PowerPoint. The final level is the development of a working application prototype, so that the users can have a 'Hands-on' feel of the application and provide relevant feedback. It must be noted that low-fidelity prototypes can also be created using application software such as NinjaMock, rather than just pen and paper, as seen in the work done by Monteiro-Guerra et al. (2017). Using an application to develop a prototype with low-fidelity wireframes has the benefit that, in addition to being quick, it is more interactive than paper prototypes. Prototypes being quick and interactive can help in achieving the goal of quick validated learning, especially in initial stages of product and customer development.

Other Aspects in Product Development and a Comparative Analysis With Other Paradigms

In addition to the aspects discussed in section 3, most product development paradigms do not perform commercial validation of products to check if the value proposition offered by the product is lucrative enough make the product attractive to the customers. Without this, the product may be technically proficient but may not be commercially successful, from a business viewpoint. However, some development frameworks do perform technical validation of the product. Besides this, most product development paradigms do not plan for business model development as part of the framework. The implication is that, in such constructs, the products are not validated for commercial viability but rather for their technical proficiency.

Besides the matter of commercial validation, in order to improve their chances of achieving commercial success and realize its strategic goals, a startup will need to scale its product offerings and achieve sustainable growth over time. Although much of product development literature does not provide much in the way of guidance on startup growth and scale related matters, the Lean startup methodology by Ries (2011) and the customer development model proposed by Blank (2013a) provide suggestions on this topic. Blank (2013a) highlights that startups should continually remain in the process of search for a repeatable, profitable and scalable business model. Only once they find and validate this model, should they execute and scale the operation. This is done as part of the "execute" phase, which follows the "search" phase (Blank & Dorf, 2012). The Lean startup philosophy, on the other hand, does not recommend scaling the startup until the product-market fit is found (Nobel, 2011), essentially indicating that the startup has created a product which the alleviates a customer problem and at the same time is commercially monetizable. The issue of scalability is vital for startups and deserves attention as early as possible during the startup's initial phases (Yoffie & Cusumano, 1999). To enable a quicker development process improve a product's ability to scale, prominent application frameworks can be used along with pre-existing components, third party libraries and frameworks (Paternoster et al., 2014).

Another consideration for startups is the adoption of 'As a service' solutions to quickly create high quality products. With the advent of newer technologies such as cloud computing, the way software applications are created, consumed and distributed have also evolved (Giessmann & Stanoevska-Slabeva, 2012). These newer formats typically feature an 'as a service' suffix and mostly feature a different mode of delivery and business model. Some of the prominent ones include Software as a Service (SaaS), Platform as a Service (PaaS) and Infrastructure as a Service (SaaS). These service models have shared and interrelated components (Walther et al., 2012). SaaS is model of (software) product delivery in which the product is hosted online and is made available to the user though the medium of the internet, wherein tasks are performed online and data is also generally stored online (Lawton, 2008). PaaS serves as a middle layer between IaaS and SaaS (Giessmann & Legner, 2013). PaaS is defined as *"generally hosted, Web-based application-development platforms, providing end-to-end or, in some cases, partial environments for developing full programs online"* (Lawton, 2008). IaaS refers to the offering of hardware along with associated software components as a service, which features provision of resources on demand and the lack of a need for long term commitment (Bhardwaj et al., 2010).

As stated in the previous paragraph, there is evidence to back that PaaS and related offerings have changed the way software is developed, marketed, utilized and priced (Giessmann et al., 2014). PaaS solutions can benefit the development process by providing a fully managed platform for development and deployment of software products (S. Joshi, 2019). PaaS also offers 'value co-creation' though the provision of complementary application components developed by third-party entities (Tiwana et al., 2010), which can speed up the development time and therefore the time to market. The case is the same with SaaS solutions, wherein the end user is saved the additional tasks of development, regular updating and maintenance of solutions, hosting or management of application data (Lawton, 2008). Similarly, the adoption of IaaS solutions can provide startups with many benefits including cost savings, competitive advantages such as speed of development, flexibility, faster deployment times, better availability of resources and fine grained scalability (Serrano et al., 2015). A consequence of quicker development and deployment of products is that the startup can quickly perform validation and learning (Melegati & Goldman, 2015). Therefore, consideration of these cloud-based solutions by software startups can be beneficial for the realization of their strategic objectives. A comparative analysis of product development paradigms is presented in table B.

INTEGRATED APPROACHES FOR PRODUCT AND BUSINESS MODEL DEVELOPMENT

While agile methodologies serve as nimble process structures for working through product development, on its own, it does not inform the practitioners on what products needs to be built (Bosch et al., 2013). Product development initiatives in the startup context will need to take into account both the product and business aspects, rather than only focusing on the technological solution (Bosch et al., 2013; Giardino, Bajwa, et al., 2015). A lack of focus on business aspects as part of product development such as establishment of the product-market fit can result in key challenges down the road for the business, such as struggles acquiring the initial set of paying customers (Giardino, Bajwa, et al., 2015). One of the most important reasons which technology projects fail is that they do not consider the business model as part of the product development process (Meertens et al., 2011).

In cases where startups are unable to find paying customers for the product they build, they '*pivot*' to a different value proposition. A 'pivot' can be defined as a strategic change in direction with the aim of testing a new hypothesis regarding a product or business model, with the assumption that this change in direction can impact the growth and/or consolidation of the business (Fernandes & Afonso, 2018). It is worth noting that making a pivot can lead to significant changes to the business model of any organization. Therefore, product development, business strategy and business model development can be seen as deeply linked to one another. 'Pivot'ing is not uncommon among startups. As a matter of fact, Blank (2018) mentions an estimate that over 90 percent of startups eventually end up pursuing a different path and plan, when compared to the path they originally intended to pursue.

A key issue with software development methodologies from an holistic perspective, is that innovation and business-related activities are not an inherent integral part of the conventional software development framework, even though both innovation and business activities form a good portion of work done during the initial phases of software startups (Nguyen-Duc et al., 2015). Lamratanakul (2018) suggests formal business development should manage product development initiatives for a more successful undertaking. Hence, it can be noted that product and business development does not happen in a silo but are rather interlinked. Integrated approaches perceive development undertakings as a process which begins with the conception of a product all the way to business model realization.

Hence, working on an integrated product-business model development approach can be more beneficial for startups in their quest to find a commercially viable value proposition and the right user base to target. Such an integrated development approach of sorts called the lean startup was proposed by Ries (2011) for the purpose of product and business development. According to this approach, product development was done in iterative cycles alongside hypothesis-based experimentation. This approach could lead to lower market risks and quicker, more efficient validation of customer needs (Lenarduzzi & Taibi, 2016). Ries (2011) recommended the development and usage of a *minimum viable product* (MVP) to learn as much as possible about customer needs as possible.

The Lean Startup

The Lean startup is a experimentation driven approach to innovation proposed by Eric Ries (2011), which is primarily aimed at startups, with the main goal of finding the product-market fit. Ries (2011) describes the Lean startup approach as "*a set of practices for helping entrepreneurs increase their odds of building a successful startup.*" It must be noted that while the term 'lean' traditionally refers to reduced waste and a focus on providing customer value, the lean startup concept does not depend on lean production (Nguyen-Duc et al., 2015). Ries (2011) proposed the Lean startup concept to iron out the wasteful efforts within product and business development initiatives in startups, while at the same time placing an emphasis on providing value (Frederiksen & Brem, 2017), hence the term 'lean' still remains applicable to this context. Also, Innovation is considered one of the key driver of success within startups, and Ries (2011) perceives the Lean startup approach as a new way of innovating for startups (Edison, 2015).

For startups, the product development process, the business modeling efforts such as marketing and customer relationship management are all interlinked and any product development initiative will need to not only work on development but also work on the business aspects in parallel (Bosch et al., 2013). The lean startup recommends investing resources into developing MVPs and iteratively refining the product concept using the *build-measure-learn* loop with goal of satisfying the needs of early adopters (Ries, 2011). As per this approach, the early adopters will need to be targeted before the mainstream market (Rasmussen & Tanev, 2016), in order to learn about what aspects of the MVP the customers might care about. The idea is to get early feedback and learn quickly based on this feedback (Edison, 2015). Doing so can significantly reduce market risks and other related expensive investments such as product launches (Johansson, 2017). Rasmussen and Tanev (2016) point out that most startups do not have resources to build products which have all the features desired by the mainstream in a single iteration, but rather the startups which are successful typically focus on critical pain points of the early adopters. The authors go on to point out that early-adopters have one or more acute pain-points and are able to afford paying for a solution, which they are actively searching for. Therefore, their rationale is that identifying, targeting and possibly partnering with such early adopters to iteratively develop solutions before targeting the mainstream can lead to greater chances of a successful product undertaking. The Lean startup approach also sees the customer as a partner within its innovation process, as evidenced by the way in which it is utilized at a former software startup called Dropbox (Richter et al., 2018).

One of the key tenets of the Lean startup approach is the search for a product-market fit. A product-market fit refers to a state three condition are achieved: there is willingness on the part of the customer to pay for the product, what the customers are willing to pay exceeds the acquisition cost of the customer and the market is large enough to be sustainable, so as to support the business (B. Cooper & Vlaskovits, 2010). Finding the product-market fit as quickly as possible is a key priority for startups, that are looking to be successful (Giardino, Paternoster, et al., 2015). This is because startups often do not know the customer and therefore, the team must craft strategies to ensure that only they build features and products which cater to customer pain points (Chanin et al., 2017). Sometimes startups can initially look for a problem-solution fit, before exploring a product-market fit. A problem-solution fit ensures that the product being built indeed serves customer needs and therefore could have business potential at some point (Hokkanen, Kuusinen, et al., 2016). Startups can be on the lookout for this fit by quickly creating prototypes, testing to see if it serves customer needs and iterating until they find a solution that serves the customer's needs (Njima & Demeyer, 2017). After discovering a product-market fit, the innovation or solution which results from this process is considered validated (Müller & Thoring, 2012). Only after achieving the product-market fit, is it considered wise for the venture to scale its operations (B. Cooper & Vlaskovits, 2010). Hokkanen and Leppänen (2015) suggest the ideal sequence is to find the problem-solution fit, then the product-market fit and after that looking to scale the operation. This perspective is mirrored by Maurya (Aßmann, 2015). The remainder of this section will review of relevant aspects of the Lean startup methodology such as the Minimum Viable Product concept, Validating the value proposition, the shortcomings of the methodology and conclude with a comparative analysis of product and integrated development approaches discussed so far.

Minimum Viable Product (MVP)

First coined by Robinson (2001) in the early 2000s, the MVP is a technique to acquire knowledge about the pain points of the customer. As defined by Ries (2011), the MVP is *"a version of a new product, which allows a team to collect the maximum amount of validated learning about customers with the least effort"*. This definition clearly establishes the purpose of the MVP. This artefact can be used to continually test given hypotheses about the product and change directions depending on the learning outcome of the test. Ries (2011) describes this strategic change in direction as a pivot (discussed in the previous section of this work). When using the lean startup technique, this is how startups ensure that they are indeed developing a product which is relevant in the context of the customer problem, using which they can grow and eventually obtain a sustainable business model (Bajwa et al., 2016).

The MVP was also mentioned by Blank as an excellent tool to validate assumptions (Blank & Euchner, 2018). Blank proposes a similar approach called *customer development* (Blank, 2013a), which helps the business learn about customer needs and validating assumptions early on during product conception. Similar to the lean startup approach, there is the provision for the development team to pivot based on the outcome of the customer validation process, if the product is not found to cater to the user requirement as per the initial hypothesis (Blank & Euchner, 2018). A similar approach is also suggested by Maurya (Maurya, 2010), when applying the lean canvas method to developing the value proposition and the business model around it. The commonality that can be spotted between the approaches by Blank (2013a), Ries (2011) and Maurya (2012) (who propose the customer development, Build-measure-learn, and Product/Market fit approaches respectively) is that they suggest using an iterative process of finding a commercially viable product using a tangible proof of concept (Ripsas et al., 2018).

Validating the Value Proposition

With regard to the validation and collection of feedback on the usage of the MVP, Blank and Dorf (2012) along with Furr and Ahlstrom (2011) recommend qualitative means of validation of the feedback first, before attempting to use quantitative means (Rasmussen & Tanev, 2016). The authors argue that qualitative feedback provides more details about the customer's perception of the solution and is therefore superior to quantitative methods, particularly when not much is known on this subject. Ries (2011) proposes the use of quantitative methods, alongside the qualitative measures, possibly by the use of metrics. Rasmussen and Tanev (2016) suggest that the analysis of both quantitative and qualitative feedback can provide optimal insight to the development team on the best course of direction to take, i.e. procced on course or pivot.

As part of the lean canvas, Maurya (2016) mentions the role early adopters can play and their importance in validation of the value proposition. In a parallel context, Rasmussen and Tanev (2016) recommend the proposal of a *problem hypothesis* to determine if a problem exists which is worth solving, along with identifying the early adopters and how they currently resolve the problem.

Shortcomings

One of the shortcomings of the Lean startup process was that it lacked a clear guideline on when entrepreneurs should stop validating the hypothesis behind their product and start scaling (Ladd, 2016). Although the Lean startup follows a hypothesis driven approach to product and business development, developing a testable hypothesis in an ad-hoc environment, as in the case of most startups, is not an easy task (Nguyen-Duc et al., 2015). As both the hypothesis and the expected results feature a lack of clarity, the intended learning process can be negatively impacted (Markerink, 2014). Lean startup methods also do not take into account quantitative research techniques while relying solely on qualitative data by the target customer segment (Batova et al., 2016). It also overlooks the importance of the either user experience design of the end product (Batova et al., 2016). Another major challenge is to identify useful and relevant metrics which can ensure development of a successful product though creation of value for the customer (Rissanen & Münch, 2015).

A comparative analysis of development paradigms is presented in table 2. Based on the reviewed shortcomings for product development and integrated development approaches, the following criteria can be used when comparing these different development approaches: Capture of User Requirements (Wang et al., 2014), Commercial (Iterative) validation of Value proposition (Blank & Dorf, 2012; Furr & Ahlstrom, 2011), Prioritization of Requirements (Racheva et al., 2008), Prototyping or creation of an MVP to help with validation (Börsting & Gruhn, 2018; Ries, 2011), Consideration of 'As a service' solutions in product/business development (Giessmann & Stanoevska-Slabeva, 2012), when to scale (Yoffie & Cusumano, 1999).

Table 2. Comparative analysis of development paradigms

	Capture of User Requirements	Commercial (Iterative) Validation of Value Proposition	Prioritization of Requirements	Prototyping or Creation of an MVP to Help With Validation	Consideration of 'As a service' Solutions in Product/Business Development	When to Scale
Traditional (Waterfall) development paradigms	✓	-	✓	-		-
Agile development paradigms	✓	- (Technical validation is done although commercial validation is not)	✓	✓	-	-
Integrated (Hybrid) paradigms for business and product development (such as Lean Startup)	✓	- (Technical validation is done although commercial validation is not)	- (Not inherently a part of it but prioritization can be integrated)	✓	-	-

NEWER CONSIDERATIONS FOR PRODUCT AND BUSINESS MODEL DOMAINS

As technologies, economies and businesses evolve over time, the various considerations for product and business model development evolves with these changes. Newer avenues of product development are introduced to the market which potentially bring greater efficiency, innovation in the form of the potential for diverse range of business models and the opportunity to rethink the way products and business models are developed. In this section, we explore some prominent considerations of the like.

Unfair Advantage

Maurya (2012) also asserts the need for an explicit *Unfair advantage*, which is a key feature or asset which cannot be easily replicated by the competition. He reasons that with some degree of initial success, competitors will quickly try to replicate the business model and the product offering. The presence of this Unfair advantage (also sometimes known as a Unique differentiator or Unique selling proposition) can serve as a defense against newer entrants (Borseman et al., 2016). Therefore, the idea behind this is to have a differentiation aspect, which potential competitors will not be easily able to imitate. Under the right circumstances, Innovation can be a source of such unique differentiation (Bowonder et al., 2010), when offered in a manner which is hard to replicate. This unfair advantage can serve as a clear overview of the benefits of the value proposition when working on business modeling or marketing efforts for the startup (Waldenström, 2018, p. 33).

As a means of sustainable competitive advantage, organizations could focus on their core strengths and outsource the rest (Quinn et al., 1990). In the world of software, this can also translate to usage of usage of third-party rapid development frameworks or Infrastructure as a service solution. Common examples of organizations who engage in this practice include Netflix, Adobe, Airbnb, Spotify and SAP, among other prominent players in the Software market (Gewirtz, 2014). All the mentioned products focus on the application features and product experiences, leaving the backend infrastructure to Amazon Web Services. There are cases where *Multi-homing* is used as a source of competitive advantage (Hyrynsalmi et al., 2012). Netflix for instance uses this strategy to maintain its presence on multiple platforms and 'meet the customers where they are', so as to be easily accessible as a service at any time and any place (Voigt et al., 2017), which is a part of the appeal of its product experience. It must be noted that for organizations which center their offerings around software products, it does not span the entirety of the offering provided to the customer, as the offering can also include services (Vähäniitty et al., 2002).

Evangelism

Thanks to the modern technologically connected world dominated by the influence of social media, we exist in a "Referral powered community", where the actions and attitude of customers can be shaped by the expressed opinions of people who are respected and trusted in that space (Shaari & Ahmad, 2016). Evangelists are essentially powerful influencers among the target customer base, who can promote the solution to a wide range of this base, therefore increasing the visibility of the value proposition. Many organizations in the information technology sector have used the medium of evangelism to boost the adoption of their products and platforms and this trend has been observed since the early 1990s (Folz, 2019; Fontão et al., 2018; Maher, 2015).

Intellectual Property Protections

Intellectual property (IP) protections provide a way for startups to extract value from their innovations (Fisher III & Oberholzer-Gee, 2013). Technology-oriented companies can find that the strategic utilization of intellectual property assets can be a source of competitive advantage (Y. Cho et al., 2018), and its effective management can be crucial in maintaining sustainable competitive advantage (Cesaroni & Piccaluga, 2013). The importance of IP assets should therefore not be overlooked by startups and rather should take an active interest in contemplating its planning and management (Baran & Zhumabaeva, 2018), since legal issues can impact the general vision of organizations (Alt & Zimmermann, 2001). When discussing IP protections, the most common type of IP protection discussed is often patents (Fisher III & Oberholzer-Gee, 2013). This is understandable since there is evidence to support the claim that having patents improves the chances for startups to acquire VC funding (Cockburn & MacGarvie, 2009; Häussler et al., 2012). However, various other forms of IP can be used in a manner complementary to one another (Graham & Sichelman, 2016), rather than just considering just one type of protection.

Scholarly literature backs this view that IP protections which are not patents (such as copyright, trade secrets and trademark) are also found to be useful when competing in the modern market conditions (Somaya & Graham, 2006). Given that business strategy, R&D and Intellectual property management are rarely well integrated in present practice (Fisher III & Oberholzer-Gee, 2013) along with the importance of IP protections from a startup context, the presence of an effective IP management policy can greatly impact the competitiveness of any startup and should be included in the core planning aspects for startups (Baran & Zhumabaeva, 2018).

Problem Evolution

It is well documented that the nature of the customer's need is ever evolving, particularly in the domain of software (Matharu et al., 2015; Paetsch et al., 2003; Sener & Karsak, 2012). There is a case to be made for considering the evolution of customer problems during product or business model development. A good example of this can be seen when studying the rise and fall of Nokia as a smartphone superpower (Hacklin et al., 2018). Nokia was once the world's largest manufacturer of what is today referred to as *feature phones*, around the time of the dot com revolution. A decade from that point, the market looked very different, despite Nokia retaining its position as the world's largest feature phone manufacturer. Companies like RIM and LG became Nokia's primary competitors (Gartner, 2011), even though they were relatively new to that market. The main issue was that as the preference of the average technology consumer tended towards solutions which provided support for greater mobility. When RIM entered the game and offered solutions such as easy access to emails and Blackberry messenger, they were better in tune with the evolution of the customer problem. Therefore, although Nokia was still the king of the feature phone market, the size of that market itself was rapidly shrinking. Nokia's dominance quickly became irrelevant since the newly created smartphone market was growing larger, at the cost of the feature phone market.

In the case of startups, a prominent case of failure due to problem evolution is that of Quibi. Quibi was designed as a mobile-first content streaming solution, similar to the likes of Netflix and Hulu (Cheung, 2019). Catering to the needs to the modern younger audience, it served up content in smaller packages of streaming content (Williams, 2020). If the requirements remained the same, as it were during the conception and development stages of this value proposition, this might have taken off very well. However, the Covid-19 pandemic took place during the first quarter of 2020 and the Quibi service was released in April of the same year (Ellingsen et al., 2020). The core value proposition of the "On-the-go content consumption" was no longer relevant, as most nations were in lockdowns and travel from and to work was at a minimum. By not having the value proposition evolve with the evolving problem space, the solution lost relevance and resulted in a failure for the startup.

Product Ecosystems

The product ecosystem concept is a relatively new phenomena within the software product space (Bosch, 2009). Most startups begin their journeys with a single product offering based on a single idea and if this offering is found to be successful, the startup can choose to develop a new set of products based on the original offering (Knauber et al., 2000). It must be noted that very few startups start with an ecosystem of offerings, but the objective of this section is to highlight that, new enterprises should aim for the creation of their own ecosystem of offerings as a form of competitive advantage, along other benefits such as the ability to provide the user with a better user experience.

A good definition for a product ecosystem was provided by Jansen et al. (2009) as follows:

A set of actors functioning as a unit and interacting with a shared market for software and services, together with the relationships among them. These relationships are frequently underpinned by a common technological platform or market and operate through the exchange of information, resources and artifacts.

Two prominent examples of ecosystems include Android by Google and the Apple ecosystem by Apple (Sadi & Yu, 2015). Android is an example of a purely software ecosystem where the aim is to provide a platform along with associated services, whereas the Apple ecosystem provides the software ecosystem, aside from deep vertical integration of software, hardware and associated services on the platform side by Apple. Hanssen (2012) noted that the concept of ecosystems, particularly in the software product context, relates to other areas such as business strategy and technology/innovation management. The author goes on to mention that this concept can lead to new business models. Van Den Berk et al. (2010) highlight that organizations are finding that there can be significant advantages in either joining or themselves creating such ecosystems. Although the technical details of building ecosystems receive a good amount of attention, more attention needs to be paid to its business modeling aspect, which is required for the commercialization of ecosystems (Weiblen et al., 2012). Sadi and Yu (2015) point to a lack of methodology on how to model software ecosystems and align with organizational viewpoints, which potentially suggests that more work can be done in integrating the software ecosystem concept into the business modeling dimension. This is compounded by the fact that the platform economy has seen significant uptake and is poised to overtake conventional models of software business models (Still et al., 2018), which is why this space deserves more attention.

In the context of ecosystems, Multi-homing is the phenomenon of developing software products for more than one platform (Idu et al., 2011). In this context, a platform comprises an ecosystem upon which third-parties (such as developers) can create innovative solutions (Tiwana et al., 2010). Such a strategy can be useful for both product publishers, consumers and the platform developers alike. For product publishers, they increase access to a pool of current and potential customers. For consumers, they provide a variety of options in platforms to choose from, in order to access the intended functionality. Platform developers on the other hand are keen to pursue this strategy since it creates a two sided market, wherein the product publisher and consumers are attracted to the platform (Holzer & Ondrus, 2011). The consumers are attracted to the system as more products are made available on the platform and more product publishers will make their products available on the platform as more consumers adopt the platform, forming a positive feedback loop (Hyrynsalmi et al., 2012). The platform developers benefit immensely from this loop, as the positive loop will make the platform more attractive over time for both sides of the two-sided market. Studying the phenomenon of multi-homing can contribute to learning about how competitors can potentially behave (Idu et al., 2011). This can help organizations develop appropriate strategies to remain competitive themselves.

Organizations can also leverage the trait of Vertical integration to better control the user experience and keep the users coming back as returning users to their ecosystem of products/platforms. Vertical integration can be defined as a single vendor (i.e., Organization) controls much of the various parts of the supply chain (Turk, 2015). This can be either refer to the software components (as in the case of Google) or both the software and the hardware (as in the case of Apple) (Turk, 2015). The ability to control the experience from end to end provides the organization with the greater control of the end user experience.

Metrics

Klien (2013) highlights that identifying and tracking good metrics can be vital to the success of a startup. Croll and Yoskovitz (2013) echo this sentiment when they point out that utilizing metrics to design and create useful products is a tested and reliable practice which has been consistently shown to provide desired outcomes. Indeed, Data driven decision making was in part responsible for the driving organizational development at the former software startup, Dropbox (Richter et al., 2018). It must however be noted that organizations might need to strive for a balance when establishing the metrics of interest, since collecting too many metrics can prove to be counter intuitive. Maurya (2012) mentions that the issue with startups can be that they collect too much data and sometimes can even drown in it. Hence, he suggests that startups need to be watchful of what and how many metrics they track.

A variety of metric frameworks have been proposed to cater to certain phases of a startup's journey. However, many of them such as the Three engines framework by Ries (2011) and the pirate metrics framework by McClure (2019) are focused primarily on startup growth. Others such as the Lean Analytics framework by Croll and Yoskovitz (2013) take into account the subject of scale, after the product-market fit has been achieved. In keeping with this line of thinking, Maurya (2012) recommends delivering value before growth. Certain other metrics are either more user centric such as Google's HEART framework or product centric such as the Goals-Signals-Metrics (GSM) framework (Rodden et al., 2010). Maurya (2012) suggests that having a standardized set of metrics can help startups with measuring.

However, most metric frameworks do not consider aspects such as the eventual evolution of the problem space and its impact on the solution space, or phenomenon where evolutions in the problem space resulting in the need for additional newer (possibly complementary) solutions. This is important since customer problems tend to evolve with time, particularly in the software space (Matharu et al., 2015; Paetsch et al., 2003; Sener & Karsak, 2012). Therefore, there's a need for a metric framework which takes a more holistic view of the startups journey from conception to operational realization. Such a framework can help identify relevant metrics and help the startup make data driven decisions in its path to achieve its business objectives. A summary of the various startup development areas covered as a part of this literature review is presented in table 3.

Table 3. The topics and areas reviewed within startup development

Topics\Area	Area 1	Area 2	Area 3	Area 4
	User stories	Touchpoints	Personas	Competing products
Requirements elicitation	(Cohn, 2004), (Wagner, 2001), (Silva et al., 2016), (Beck, 2000), (Wang et al., 2014), (Lucassen et al., 2016), (Heeager & Nielsen, 2018), (Bjarnason et al., 2011; Cao & Ramesh, 2008; Paetsch et al., 2003), (Hummel & Epp, 2015; Myers, 2019), (Olsson & Bosch, 2015), (Käpyaho & Kauppinen, 2015).	(Kawano et al., 2019), (Howard, 2007), (Sauvola et al., 2016; Schön et al., 2017).	(Haas & Kunz, 2010), (Wölbling et al., 2012), (Perdana et al., 2017), (Müller & Thoring, 2012).	(Rafiq et al., 2017), (Tripathi et al., 2017), (Bajwa et al., 2017), (Somaya & Graham, 2006), (Kraaijenbrink, 2012), (Maurya, 2012), (Hokkanen, Xu, et al., 2016),

Continued on following page

Table 3. Continued

Topics\Area	Area 1	Area 2	Area 3	Area 4
Requirements Prioritization and Prototyping	Prioritization process and techniques	MoSCoW analysis	Prototyping	MVP
	(Georgsson, 2011), (Bakalova et al., 2011), (Racheva et al., 2008), (Ambler, 2002; Harris & Cohn, 2006), (Fehlmann, 2008; J. Karlsson et al., 1998), (Wiegers, 1999), (Achimugu et al., 2014).	(Achimugu et al., 2014; Racheva et al., 2008), (Zagajsek et al., 2007), (Popli et al., 2014), (Waters, 2009).	(Rasmussen & Tanev, 2016), (Nelson et al., 2016), (Börsting & Gruhn, 2018), (Christoforakos & Diefenbach, 2018), (Abidin et al., 2019), (Abdel-Hamid, 1989), (Hildenbrand & Meyer, 2012), (Monteiro-Guerra et al., 2017).	(Ries, 2011), (Lenarduzzi & Taibi, 2016), (Nguyen-Duc et al., 2015), (Frederiksen & Brem, 2017), (2001), (Bajwa et al., 2016), (Blank & Euchner, 2018), (Maurya, 2010), (Maurya, 2012), (Ripsas et al., 2018).
Iteration and validation	Problem-solution fit & Product-market fit	Early adopters	Pivot	User and Commercial validation
	(Nobel, 2011), (Ries, 2011), (Frederiksen & Brem, 2017), (Edison, 2015), (B. Cooper & Vlaskovits, 2010), (Giardino, Paternoster, et al., 2015), (Chanin et al., 2017), (Hokkanen, Kuusinen, et al., 2016), (Njima & Demeyer, 2017), (Müller & Thoring, 2012), (Hokkanen & Leppänen, 2015), (Aßmann, 2015),	(Ries, 2011), (Rasmussen & Tanev, 2016), (Edison, 2015), (Johansson, 2017).	(Fernandes & Afonso, 2018), (Blank & Euchner, 2018), (Nguyen-Duc et al., 2015), (Iamratanakul, 2018), (Blank, 2013a),	(Ries, 2011), (Blank, 2013a), (Lenarduzzi & Taibi, 2016), (Bosch et al., 2013), (Müller & Thoring, 2012), (Blank & Euchner, 2018), (Ripsas et al., 2018), (2012), (2011), (Rasmussen & Tanev, 2016), (Maurya, 2016), (Batova et al., 2016).
Product development and management	Metrics	Unfair advantage & Comparative analysis	Intellectual property	Scale
	(Rissanen & Münch, 2015), (Klein, 2013), (Croll & Yoskovitz, 2013), (Richter et al., 2018), (Maurya, 2012), (Ries, 2011), (McClure, 2019), (Rodden et al., 2010), (Matharu et al., 2015; Paetsch et al., 2003; Sener & Karsak, 2012).	(Bowonder et al., 2010), (Waldenström, 2018, p. 33), (Borseman et al., 2016), (Maurya, 2012), (Quinn et al., 1990), (Gewirtz, 2014), (Hyrynsalmi et al., 2012), (Voigt et al., 2017), (Vähäniitty et al., 2002).	(Fisher III & Oberholzer-Gee, 2013), (Y. Cho et al., 2018), (Cesaroni & Piccaluga, 2013), (Baran & Zhumabaeva, 2018), (Alt & Zimmermann, 2001), (Cockburn & MacGarvie, 2009; Häussler et al., 2012), (Graham & Sichelman, 2016), (Somaya & Graham, 2006),	(Yoffie & Cusumano, 1999), (B. Cooper & Vlaskovits, 2010), (2015), (Aßmann, 2015), (Ladd, 2016).

Continued on following page

Table 3. Continued

Topics\Area	Area 1	Area 2	Area 3	Area 4
	'As a service' and development frameworks	Evangelism	Problem evolution	Product ecosystems
Newer considerations for product/business development	(Paternoster et al., 2014), (Giessmann & Stanoevska-Slabeva, 2012), (Walther et al., 2012), (Lawton, 2008), (Giessmann & Legner, 2013), (Bhardwaj et al., 2010), (Giessmann et al., 2014), (S. Joshi, 2019), (Tiwana et al., 2010), (Serrano et al., 2015), (Melegati & Goldman, 2015).	(Shaari & Ahmad, 2016), (Folz, 2019; Fontão et al., 2018; Maher, 2015).	(Matharu et al., 2015; Paetsch et al., 2003; Sener & Karsak, 2012), (Hacklin et al., 2018), (Gartner, 2011), (Cheung, 2019), (Williams, 2020), (Ellingsen et al., 2020).	(Bosch, 2009), (Knauber et al., 2000), (2009), (Sadi & Yu, 2015), (2012), (Weiblen et al., 2012), (Still et al., 2018), (Idu et al., 2011), (Tiwana et al., 2010), (Holzer & Ondrus, 2011), (Hyrynsalmi et al., 2012), (Turk, 2015),

DISCUSSION (GAP)

In most cases, frameworks and practices designed for established larger organizations are reused to fit to the operation of startups (Yau & Murphy, 2013). Most of these practices either ignore or do not place enough emphasis on the critical elements which impact the success of startups such as faster time to market (Giardino, Paternoster, et al., 2015). Klotins et al. (2019) point to the previous two points and highlight the fact that very few process driven models or frameworks presently exist to cater to the product development context within software startups. Klotins (2019) goes on to state that within an optimistic failure rate of startups being 75% and an approximate amount of 429 billion dollars invested in startups (figure as of the first three quarters of 2015), more work needs to be done to improve the development practices which are employed in startups.

The importance of startup capital and time to market for the success of a software startup is paramount and are considered as two key success factors for startups (Devadiga, 2017; Giardino, Paternoster, et al., 2015; Heirman & Clarysse, 2007). To this end, many techniques such as the Agile, the Lean startup attempt to reduce the time to market and save the accumulated capital through techniques such as creation of MVPs and subsequent rapid validation of product concepts before entering production (Paternoster et al., 2014). Jansen et al. (Jansen et al., 2008) even recommend using utilization of third party components to produce finished products quickly, in order to get the products in the hands of the customer as quickly as possible, which highlights the importance of both improving the time to market and reducing the cost (and thereby conserving the capital for potential investment in other key areas such as marketing). Another critical success factor pointed out by Maurya (2012) is that of unfair advantage, which is essentially a product differentiation factor which the competition does not have and cannot easily acquire. That differentiation factor could be something as simple as focus on user experience (Hokkanen, Xu, et al., 2016), as seen in the case of product by companies like Apple. Having such a factor can enable to successfully manage competition and survive, possibly even thrive in a highly competitive global market. However, having noted these success factors and seeing their importance to the success of software startups, there is no model which places emphasis and incorporates these factors as first-class citizens of their framework, although some of them provide indirect avenues to cater to individual factors such as time to market one at a time.

The current software development models which is employed by startups to develop their first offering is found to not integrate well within the dynamic context of startups (Unterkalmsteiner et al., 2016). There is a need for more research in the area of software development with regards to the startup context (Curcio et al., 2018; Paternoster et al., 2014). Particularly, studies with regard to early stages of startup development is found to be scarce. Unlike well-established larger organizations, product and business development within startups is highly interconnected (Blank, 2013a; Ries, 2011). The business activities such as looking into customer pain points will inform the product that needs to be built and the validation of the prototype/MVP will inform the business what can be monetized. Besides the customer development framework by Blank (2013a) and the Lean startup by Ries (2011), most methodologies do not take this interconnected nature into account. However, these methodologies are not without shortcomings, as discussed in the earlier sections of this literature. Other software development methodologies such as Agile do not take the business model aspects into account. There is evidence in literature to show that startups struggle to adopt both new and traditional methodologies, despite the knowledge that finding product-market fit can dramatically improve the chances of success (Göthensten & Hellström, 2017). There is a need for the development of an end-to-end framework for software startups which provides a clear (step by step) pathway from product conception through iterative stages, all the way till business model realization. The low levels of experience among most startup founders can also be seen as an issue (Tripathi et al., 2017), which supports the case for a step by step process driven framework for software startups.

Competitor analysis is another area which has not received the attention that it deserves, which can be immensely useful during the strategic formulation process (Hatzijordanou, 2019) and/or the product development process (Rafiq et al., 2017; Tripathi et al., 2017). In today's highly competitive global market, the competition can have a significant impact on the development of product or business, resulting in possible pivots depending on the strength of the competition (Bajwa et al., 2017). Although variations of mainstream business model development methodologies such as the Lean Canvas by Maurya (2012) take the study of the competition into account, the mainstream methodologies themselves do not provide structures to study this area (García-Gutiérrez & Martínez-Borreguero, 2016). Aside from this factor, Maurya (2012) suggests that it is ideal to hone in on the early adopter to get insights on what matters to the customer base. Rasmussen and Tanev (2016) also note that seeking the assistance of early adopters for an early validation of the customer problem with the solution can be highly beneficial to the startup.

Other aspects which can be incorporated into such an end-to-end framework include the aspects of evolution and product ecosystems. As discussed in sections 5.4., the customer problem undergoes constant evolution over time. Although some frameworks such as agile keep checking in with the customer regarding the features of the system which has already been built, sometimes the market, technological, economic or political changes can cause the problem to lose relevance and hence the solution. Other times, they could give rise to opportunities to develop additional newer parallel offerings to create product ecosystems. Aspects such as these could potentially be incorporated into the framework. Additionally, there is still a need for a structured approach for validating business models (Blank & Dorf, 2012). Besides this, the limited literature surrounding the phenomenon of pivots in startups has been acknowledged (Bajwa et al., 2016). Startups find it hard to know when to pivot and when to discard a solution. At present, there is a need for a model that combines the key advantages of agile, business models, and product development into a single process driven framework which can be used for product and business development for startups in the software space. The various startup development factors discussed throughout this work is summarized in table 4 and categorized based on the critical success factors outlined in the triple cornerstones framework by the works of Shanbhag and Pardede (2021).

Table 4. Summarizing startup development factors

Startup Development Factors	Description	Category (Success Factor)	Relevant Literature
The use of 'As a service' products (such as Software-As-A-Service, Platform-As-A-Service etc) or Third-party components	Promoting the use of third-party components to speed up the product/prototype development process and can help reduce the time to market, while keeping costs low.	Time to market, Startup Capital, Differentiation	(Giessmann et al., 2014), (S. Joshi, 2019), (Tiwana et al., 2010), (Lawton, 2008), (Serrano et al., 2015), (Melegati & Goldman, 2015), (Giessmann & Stanoevska-Slabeva, 2012), (Walther et al., 2012), (Giessmann & Legner, 2013), (Bhardwaj et al., 2010), (Jansen et al., 2008)
The presence of one or more Unfair Advantage or Competitive Advantage	Gaining competitive advantage over existing market players by the acquisition or development of a differentiating factor as a part of the product or some part of the business model.	Differentiation	(2012), (Bajwa et al., 2017), (Rafiq et al., 2017; Tripathi et al., 2017), (Hatzijordanou, 2019), (García-Gutiérrez & Martínez-Borreguero, 2016)
Process driven models for business/product development	Defining the product/business model development mechanism as a process rather than an open-ended mechanism such as a canvas, with the aim of creating inclusiveness for first time or inexperienced entrepreneurs.	Time to market	(Tripathi et al., 2017), (Klotins et al., 2019), (Giardino, Bajwa, et al., 2015), (Meertens et al., 2011)
Integrated Development frameworks for early-stage startups	Defining the product/business model development mechanism as a single process rather than two processes which operate in their own silos. The aim is to acquire a holistic perspective of enterprise development with the value proposition at the core of the business.	Time to market, Startup Capital	(Blank, 2013a), (Ries, 2011), (Unterkalmsteiner et al., 2016), (Curcio et al., 2018; Paternoster et al., 2014), (Bosch et al., 2013), (Giardino, Bajwa, et al., 2015), (Meertens et al., 2011)
Collaboration with Early adopters	Using feedback from early adopters before targeting the mainstream market, in order to learn quickly and reduce risk of failure.	Time to market	(Ries, 2011), (Rasmussen & Tanev, 2016), (Rasmussen & Tanev, 2016), (Edison, 2015), (Johansson, 2017)
The consideration of Problem evolution	Keeping track of the evolving needs of customers over time to ensure that the startups value proposition remains relevant.	Differentiation	(Matharu et al., 2015; Paetsch et al., 2003; Sener & Karsak, 2012), (Hacklin et al., 2018), (Gartner, 2011), (Matharu et al., 2015; Paetsch et al., 2003; Sener & Karsak, 2012)

Continued on following page

Table 4. Continued

Startup Development Factors	Description	Category (Success Factor)	Relevant Literature
Planning for Product ecosystems	Planning for parallel value propositions with regarding the core offering to create an 'ecosystem' of offerings, with the aim of creating better customer experiences and increasing market share.	Startup Capital, Differentiation	(Hyrynsalmi et al., 2012), (Bosch, 2009), (Knauber et al., 2000), (2009), (Sadi & Yu, 2015), (2012), (2010), (Weiblen et al., 2012), (Still et al., 2018), (Idu et al., 2011), (Tiwana et al., 2010), (Holzer & Ondrus, 2011), (Turk, 2015)
Collaboration with Evangelists	Working with evangelists to improve the visibility of the value proposition among the target user base.	Differentiation	(Shaari & Ahmad, 2016), (Folz, 2019; Fontão et al., 2018; Maher, 2015)
Planning for Intellectual property protections	Finding the optimal means to leverage value out of the intellectual property assets, which the startup has created or will create.	Startup Capital, Differentiation	(Alt & Zimmermann, 2001), (Fisher III & Oberholzer-Gee, 2013), (Y. Cho et al., 2018), (Cesaroni & Piccaluga, 2013), (Baran & Zhumabaeva, 2018), (Cockburn & MacGarvie, 2009; Häussler et al., 2012), (Graham & Sichelman, 2016), (Somaya & Graham, 2006)
When to scale	Optimal determination on the subject of when to scale, so as to effectively and positively increase the profitability of the startup's value proposition(s) by serving more customers.	Startup Capital	(Ries, 2011), (Blank, 2013a), (Blank & Dorf, 2012), (Nobel, 2011), (Yoffie & Cusumano, 1999), (Paternoster et al., 2014)
The use of metric frameworks	Using metric frameworks to determine, track and leverage metrics for product and business-related decision making.	Time to market, Startup Capital, Differentiation	(Klein, 2013), (Croll & Yoskovitz, 2013), (Maurya, 2012), (2011), (McClure, 2019), (Rodden et al., 2010),

CONCLUSION AND FUTURE WORK

The intent of this research was to review the current literature for the startup development space and to research factors which impact product and business model development for software startups. In addition to this, from the view of success factors, this work aimed to determine what elements, when constituted as part of the startup development process will create a more holistic product and business model development experience for the startup.

Accordingly, this research work reviews the current literature in the areas of product development, business model developments and integrated approaches for product and business model development for software startup space. As part of the review, conventional aspects of development are discussed which includes *capture of user requirements and its prioritization, prototyping* and *validation*. Emerging trends are also covered which include *commercial validation of the value proposition, consideration of cloud and third-party components or libraries in product and business development* and *the question of when to scale.* A deeper look into some of integrated development frameworks uncovered additional areas which could provide a holistic development approach, for startups to work with. These areas include the *presence of one or more unfair advantages, collaboration with early adopters and evangelists, planning for intellectual property protections, the leveraging of metric frameworks, the consideration of problem evolution* and *planning for product ecosystems.* These factors are grouped and presented based on startup success factors, with the aim of creating an integrated approach to startup development for software startups. Another aspect of the reviewed literature highlights the benefit crafting the said approach to be process driven, rather open canvas based, as in the case of the Business Model Canvas.

As discussed, the next step would include the proposal of a holistic framework for startup development for the software space. However, it might be interesting to explore the possibility of creating component based sub-frameworks, which can integrate into an end-to-end holistic framework for startups. This could be useful in cases where the startup has a fully developed value proposition but is only interested in working on the business model development portion. Such a '*plug and play*' approach can make for a versatile framework which could be useful in a diverse range of startup scenarios.

REFERENCES

Abdel-Hamid, T. K. (1989). The dynamics of software project staffing: A system dynamics based simulation approach. *IEEE Transactions on Software Engineering, 15*(2), 109–119. doi:10.1109/32.21738

Abidin, S. R. Z., Noor, S. F. M., & Ashaari, N. S. (2019). Low-fidelity Prototype Design for Serious Game for Slow-reading Students. *Learning, 10*(3).

Achimugu, P., Selamat, A., Ibrahim, R., & Mahrin, M. N. (2014). A systematic literature review of software requirements prioritization research. *Information and Software Technology, 56*(6), 568–585. doi:10.1016/j.infsof.2014.02.001

Ahmed, S. Z. F., & Koubaa, M. B. (2013). Core competencies and phases of the organizational life cycle. *International Journal of Business and Management Studies, 5*(1), 461–473.

Aitken, A., & Ilango, V. (2013). A comparative analysis of traditional software engineering and agile software development. *2013 46th Hawaii International Conference on System Sciences*, 4751–4760.

Alt, R., & Zimmermann, H.-D. (2001). Introduction to special section-business models. *Electronic Markets-The International Journal, 11*(1), 1019–6781.

Ambler, S. (2002). *Agile modeling: Effective practices for extreme programming and the unified process.* John Wiley & Sons.

Aramand, M. (2008). Software products and services are high tech? New product development strategy for software products and services. *Technovation, 28*(3), 154–160. doi:10.1016/j.technovation.2007.10.004

Aßmann, U. (2015). *Part IV. 03.* The Lean Startup Process.

Bajwa, S. S., Wang, X., Duc, A. N., & Abrahamsson, P. (2016). How do software startups pivot? Empirical results from a multiple case study. *International Conference of Software Business*, 169–176. 10.1007/978-3-319-40515-5_14

Bajwa, S. S., Wang, X., Duc, A. N., & Abrahamsson, P. (2017). "Failures" to be celebrated: An analysis of major pivots of software startups. *Empirical Software Engineering*, *22*(5), 2373–2408. doi:10.100710664-016-9458-0

Bakalova, Z., Daneva, M., Herrmann, A., & Wieringa, R. (2011). Agile requirements prioritization: What happens in practice and what is described in literature. *International Working Conference on Requirements Engineering: Foundation for Software Quality*, 181–195. 10.1007/978-3-642-19858-8_18

Baran, A., & Zhumabaeva, A. (2018). Intellectual property management in startups—Problematic issues. *Engineering Management in Production and Services*, *10*(2), 66–74. doi:10.2478/emj-2018-0012

Barczak, G., & Kahn, K. B. (2012). Identifying new product development best practice. *Business Horizons*, *55*(3), 293–305. doi:10.1016/j.bushor.2012.01.006

Basili, V. R., Heidrich, J., Lindvall, M., Münch, J., Seanian, C., Regardie, M., & Trendowicz, A. (2009). Determining the Impact of Business Strategies Using Principles from Goal-oriented Measurement. *Wirtschaftsinformatik*, (1), 545–554.

Batova, T., Clark, D., & Card, D. (2016). Challenges of lean customer discovery as invention. *2016 IEEE International Professional Communication Conference (IPCC)*, 1–5. 10.1109/IPCC.2016.7740514

Beck, K. (2000). *Extreme programming explained: Embrace change*. Addison-Wesley Professional.

Bhardwaj, S., Jain, L., & Jain, S. (2010). Cloud computing: A study of infrastructure as a service (IAAS). *International Journal of Engineering and Information Technology*, *2*(1), 60–63.

Bjarnason, E., Wnuk, K., & Regnell, B. (2011). A case study on benefits and side-effects of agile practices in large-scale requirements engineering. *Proceedings of the 1st Workshop on Agile Requirements Engineering*, 1–5. 10.1145/2068783.2068786

Blank, S. (2013a). *The four steps to the epiphany: Successful strategies for products that win*. BookBaby.

Blank, S. (2013b). Why the lean start-up changes everything. *Harvard Business Review*, *91*(5), 63–72.

Blank, S., & Dorf, B. (2012). *The startup owner's manual: The step-by-step guide for building a great company*. BookBaby.

Blank, S., & Euchner, J. (2018). The genesis and future of Lean Startup: An interview with Steve Blank. *Research Technology Management*, *61*(5), 15–21. doi:10.1080/08956308.2018.1495963

Borseman, M., Tanev, S., Weiss, M., & Rasmussen, E. S. (2016). Lost in the canvases: Managing uncertainty in lean global startups. *ISPIM Innovation Symposium*, 1.

Börsting, I., & Gruhn, V. (2018). Toward Rapid Digital Prototyping for Augmented Reality Applications. *2018 IEEE/ACM 4th International Workshop on Rapid Continuous Software Engineering (RCoSE)*, 12–15.

Bosch, J. (2009). From software product lines to software ecosystems. *SPLC*, *9*, 111–119.

Bosch, J., Olsson, H. H., Björk, J., & Ljungblad, J. (2013). The early stage software startup development model: A framework for operationalizing lean principles in software startups. In *Lean Enterprise Software and Systems* (pp. 1–15). Springer. doi:10.1007/978-3-642-44930-7_1

Bowonder, B., Dambal, A., Kumar, S., & Shirodkar, A. (2010). Innovation strategies for creating competitive advantage. *Research Technology Management, 53*(3), 19–32. doi:10.1080/08956308.2010.11657628

Brun, E. C. (2016). Start-up development processes in business incubators. *ISPIM Innovation Symposium*, 1.

Burke, A. E., Fraser, S., & Greene, F. J. (2009). Multiple effects of business plans on new ventures. *Journal of Management Studies*.

Cao, L., & Ramesh, B. (2008). Agile requirements engineering practices: An empirical study. *IEEE Software, 25*(1), 60–67. doi:10.1109/MS.2008.1

Carmel, E. (1994). Time-to-completion in software package startups. *Proceedings of the Twenty-Seventh Hawaii International Conference on System Sciences, 4*, 498–507. 10.1109/HICSS.1994.323468

Cesaroni, F., & Piccaluga, A. (2013). Operational challenges and ST's proposed solutions to improve collaboration between IP and R&D in innovation processes. *California Management Review, 55*(4), 143–156. doi:10.1525/cmr.2013.55.4.143

Chanin, R., Pompermaier, L., Fraga, K., Sales, A., & Prikladnicki, R. (2017). Applying customer development for software requirements in a startup development program. *2017 IEEE/ACM 1st International Workshop on Software Engineering for Startups (SoftStart)*, 2–5.

Chesbrough, H. (2010). Business Model Innovation: Opportunities and Barriers. *Long Range Planning, 43*(2), 354–363. doi:10.1016/j.lrp.2009.07.010

Chesbrough, H., & Rosenbloom, R. S. (2002). The role of the business model in capturing value from innovation: Evidence from Xerox Corporation's technology spin-off companies. *Industrial and Corporate Change, 11*(3), 529–555. doi:10.1093/icc/11.3.529

Cheung, M. (2019). *Live streamed vs freely streamed content's effect on the engagement of viewers.* Academic Press.

Cho, J. (2008). Issues and Challenges of agile software development with SCRUM. *Issues in Information Systems, 9*(2), 188–195.

Cho, Y., Kirkewoog, S., & Daim, T. U. (2018). Managing strategic intellectual property assets in the fuzzy front end of new product development process. *R & D Management, 48*(3), 354–374. doi:10.1111/radm.12312

Christoforakos, L., & Diefenbach, S. (2018). Idealization Effects in UX Evaluation at Early Concept Stages: Challenges of Low-Fidelity Prototyping. *International Conference on Applied Human Factors and Ergonomics*, 3–14.

Cockburn, I. M., & MacGarvie, M. J. (2009). Patents, Thickets and the Financing of Early-Stage Firms: Evidence from the Software Industry. *Journal of Economics & Management Strategy, 18*(3), 729–773. doi:10.1111/j.1530-9134.2009.00228.x

Cohn, M. (2004). *User stories applied: For agile software development.* Addison-Wesley Professional.

Collins, J. C., & Porras, J. I. (1996). Building your company's vision. *Harvard Business Review, 74*(5), 65.

Cooper, B., & Vlaskovits, P. (2010). *Entrepreneur's Guideto Customer Development*. Academic Press.

Cooper, R. G. (2019). The drivers of success in new-product development. *Industrial Marketing Management*, *76*, 36–47. doi:10.1016/j.indmarman.2018.07.005

Cooper, R. G., & Sommer, A. F. (2018). Agile–Stage-Gate for Manufacturers: Changing the Way New Products Are Developed Integrating Agile project management methods into a Stage-Gate system offers both opportunities and challenges. *Research Technology Management*, *61*(2), 17–26. doi:10.1080/089 56308.2018.1421380

Cremades, A. (2019, January 9). How Investors Decide To Invest In Startups. *Forbes*. https://www.forbes.com/sites/alejandrocremades/2019/01/09/how-investors-decide-to-invest-in-startups/

Croll, A., & Yoskovitz, B. (2013). *Lean analytics: Use data to build a better startup faster*. O'Reilly Media, Inc.

Curcio, K., Navarro, T., Malucelli, A., & Reinehr, S. (2018). Requirements engineering: A systematic mapping study in agile software development. *Journal of Systems and Software*, *139*, 32–50. doi:10.1016/j.jss.2018.01.036

Dahle, Y., Nguyen-Duc, A., Steinert, M., & Reuther, K. (2020). Six pillars of modern entrepreneurial theory and how to use them. In *Fundamentals of Software Startups* (pp. 3–25). Springer. doi:10.1007/978-3-030-35983-6_1

Dal Lago, M., Corti, D., & Pedrazzoli, P. (2016). Turning a lean business model into a successful Startup in the wearable technology sector: The case of Clara Swiss Tech. *Workshop on Business Models and ICT Technologies for the Fashion Supply Chain*, 111–122.

Devadiga, N. M. (2017). Software engineering education: Converging with the startup industry. *2017 IEEE 30th Conference on Software Engineering Education and Training (CSEE&T)*, 192–196.

Dzamashvili Fogelström, N., Gorschek, T., Svahnberg, M., & Olsson, P. (2010). The impact of agile principles on market-driven software product development. *Journal of Software Maintenance and Evolution: Research and Practice*, *22*(1), 53–80. doi:10.1002pip.420

Edison, H. (2015). A Conceptual Framework of Lean Startup Enabled Internal Corporate Venture. In P. Abrahamsson, L. Corral, M. Oivo, & B. Russo (Eds.), *Product-Focused Software Process Improvement* (pp. 607–613). Springer International Publishing. doi:10.1007/978-3-319-26844-6_46

Ellingsen, S., Turnbull, S. E., Bassaget, J., Ryan, M., Evans, N., Burkholder, M., King, E., Cunningham, S., McCutcheon, M., & Healy, G. (2020). *Quibi disaster: How to lose $1.75 b on something you don't understand*. Screen Hub.

Fehlmann, T. M. (2008). New Lanchester theory for requirements prioritization. *2008 Second International Workshop on Software Product Management*, 35–40. 10.1109/IWSPM.2008.6

Fernandes, J. M., & Afonso, P. (2018). Changing and pivoting the business model in software startups. *International Conference of Software Business*, 157–171. 10.1007/978-3-030-04840-2_11

Fine, C. H., & Whitney, D. E. (2002). *Is the make-buy decision process a core competence?* Fisher III, W. W., & Oberholzer-Gee, F. (2013). Strategic management of intellectual property: An integrated approach. *California Management Review, 55*(4), 157–183.

Fisler, L. (2012, October 9). Do You Need an OGSM? Use Strategic Planning to Boost Your Creative Career, by Linda Fisler. *Artists Network*. https://www.artistsnetwork.com/art-business/do-you-need-an-ogsm-use-strategic-planning-to-boost-your-creative-career-by-linda-fisler/

Fjeldstad, Ø. D., & Snow, C. C. (2018). Business models and organization design. *Long Range Planning, 51*(1), 32–39. doi:10.1016/j.lrp.2017.07.008

Folz, J. (2019). *Free and Open Source Software in India: Mobilising Technology for the National Good.* University of Manchester.

Fontão, A., Estácio, B., Fernandes, J., dos Santos, R. P., & Dias-Neto, A. C. (2018). Which factors affect the evangelist's support during training sessions in mobile software ecosystems? *Proceedings of the 12th European Conference on Software Architecture: Companion Proceedings,* 1–7. 10.1145/3241403.3241427

Foroutan, M., & Baski-Reeves, K. (2017). *Need for development and validation of a new product development (NPD) assessment and improvement tool: A review of literature.* Academic Press.

Frederiksen, D. L., & Brem, A. (2017). How do entrepreneurs think they create value? A scientific reflection of Eric Ries' Lean Startup approach. *The International Entrepreneurship and Management Journal, 13*(1), 169–189. doi:10.100711365-016-0411-x

Furqon, C., Sultan, M., & Wijaya, F. (2019). Business Development of Coffee Farmers Group Using Triple Layered Business Model Canvas. *Journal of Business & Economics Research, 4*(4), 163–170.

Furr, N., & Ahlstrom, P. (2011). Nail it then scale it: The entrepreneur's guide to creating and managing breakthrough innovation (Issue 658.421 FUR. CIMMYT.). Academic Press.

Furr, N., & Dyer, J. (2014). *The Innovator's Method: Bringing the Lean Start-Up Into Your Organization.* Harvard Business Review Press.

García-Gutiérrez, I., & Martínez-Borreguero, F. J. (2016). The Innovation Pivot Framework: Fostering Business Model Innovation in Startups: A new tool helps entrepreneurs design business models by identifying the sources of competitive advantage embedded in an innovation. *Research Technology Management, 59*(5), 48–56. doi:10.1080/08956308.2016.1208043

García-Muiña, F. E., Medina-Salgado, M. S., Ferrari, A. M., & Cucchi, M. (2020). Sustainability Transition in Industry 4.0 and Smart Manufacturing with the Triple-Layered Business Model Canvas. *Sustainability, 12*(6), 2364. doi:10.3390u12062364

Gartner, I. (2011). *Gartner says worldwide mobile device sales to end users reached 1.6 billion units in 2010; smartphone sales grew 72 percent in 2010.* Academic Press.

Georgsson, A. (2011). *Introducing story points and user stories to perform estimations in a software development organisation. A case study at Swedbank IT.* Academic Press.

Gewirtz, D. (2014). *15 sites you know, that you may not know are based on Amazon Web Services.* ZD-Net. https://www.zdnet.com/article/15-sites-you-know-that-you-may-not-know-are-based-on-amazon-web-services/

Ghezzi, A., Cavallaro, A., Rangone, A., & Balocco, R. (2015). A Comparative Study on the Impact of Business Model Design & Lean Startup Approach versus Traditional Business Plan on Mobile Startups Performance. *ICEIS*, (3), 196–203. doi:10.5220/0005337501960203

Giardino, C., Bajwa, S. S., Wang, X., & Abrahamsson, P. (2015). Key Challenges in Early-Stage Software Startups. In C. Lassenius, T. Dingsøyr, & M. Paasivaara (Eds.), *Agile Processes in Software Engineering and Extreme Programming* (pp. 52–63). Springer International Publishing. doi:10.1007/978-3-319-18612-2_5

Giardino, C., Paternoster, N., Unterkalmsteiner, M., Gorschek, T., & Abrahamsson, P. (2015). Software development in startup companies: The greenfield startup model. *IEEE Transactions on Software Engineering*, *42*(6), 585–604. doi:10.1109/TSE.2015.2509970

Giardino, C., Unterkalmsteiner, M., Paternoster, N., Gorschek, T., & Abrahamsson, P. (2014). What Do We Know about Software Development in Startups? *IEEE Software*, *31*(5), 28–32. doi:10.1109/MS.2014.129

Giessmann, A., Kyas, P., Tyrväinen, P., & Stanoevska, K. (2014). Towards a better Understanding of the Dynamics of Platform as a Service Business Models. *2014 47th Hawaii International Conference on System Sciences*, 965–974.

Giessmann, A., & Legner, C. (2013). *Designing business models for platform as a service: Towards a design theory.* Academic Press.

Giessmann, A., & Stanoevska-Slabeva, K. (2012). Business models of platform as a service (PaaS) providers: Current state and future directions. *Journal of Information Technology Theory and Application*, *13*(4), 31.

Göthensten, V., & Hellström, A. (2017). *Finding product-market fit, How do software start-ups approach product-market fit?* Academic Press.

Graham, S. J., & Sichelman, T. S. (2016). *Intellectual Property and Technology Startups: What Entrepreneurs Tell Us', Technological Innovation: Generating Economic Results.* Emerald Group Publishing Limited.

Gralha, C., Damian, D., Wasserman, A., Goulão, M., & Araújo, J. (2018). The evolution of requirements practices in software startups. *2018 IEEE/ACM 40th International Conference on Software Engineering (ICSE)*, 823–833.

Gutbrod, M., Münch, J., & Tichy, M. (2017). How do software startups approach experimentation? Empirical results from a qualitative interview study. *International Conference on Product-Focused Software Process Improvement*, 297–304. 10.1007/978-3-319-69926-4_21

Haas, M., & Kunz, W. H. (2010). How to master the challenges of service mass customization–A persona-based approach. In *Handbook of Research in Mass Customization and Personalization: (In 2 Volumes)* (pp. 603–621). World Scientific.

Hacklin, F., Björkdahl, J., & Wallin, M. W. (2018). Strategies for business model innovation: How firms reel in migrating value. *Long Range Planning*, *51*(1), 82–110. doi:10.1016/j.lrp.2017.06.009

Hanssen, G. K. (2012). A longitudinal case study of an emerging software ecosystem: Implications for practice and theory. *Journal of Systems and Software*, *85*(7), 1455–1466. doi:10.1016/j.jss.2011.04.020

Harris, R. S., & Cohn, M. (2006). Incorporating learning and expected cost of change in prioritizing features on agile projects. *International Conference on Extreme Programming and Agile Processes in Software Engineering*, 175–180. 10.1007/11774129_19

Hatzijordanou, N. (2019). *Towards Conducting Viable Competitor Analysis in Early-Stage Startups: A Design Science Approach*. Academic Press.

Haunts, S. (2014, December 19). *Advantages and Disadvantages of Agile Software Development*. https://stephenhaunts.com/2014/12/19/advantages-and-disadvantages-of-agile-software-development/

Häussler, C., Harhoff, D., & Müller, E. (2012). *To be financed or not...-The role of patents for venture capital-financing*. ZEW-Centre for European Economic Research Discussion Paper, 09–003.

Heeager, L. T., & Nielsen, P. A. (2018). A conceptual model of agile software development in a safety-critical context: A systematic literature review. *Information and Software Technology*, *103*, 22–39. doi:10.1016/j.infsof.2018.06.004

Heirman, A., & Clarysse, B. (2007). Which tangible and intangible assets matter for innovation speed in start-ups? *Journal of Product Innovation Management*, *24*(4), 303–315. doi:10.1111/j.1540-5885.2007.00253.x

Hildenbrand, T., & Meyer, J. (2012). Intertwining lean and design thinking: Software product development from empathy to shipment. In *Software for people* (pp. 217–237). Springer. doi:10.1007/978-3-642-31371-4_13

Hokkanen, L., Kuusinen, K., & Väänänen, K. (2016). Minimum Viable User EXperience: A Framework for Supporting Product Design in Startups. *Agile Processes, in Software Engineering, and Extreme Programming*, 66–78. doi:10.1007/978-3-319-33515-5_6

Hokkanen, L., & Leppänen, M. (2015). Three patterns for user involvement in startups. *Proceedings of the 20th European Conference on Pattern Languages of Programs*, 1–8. 10.1145/2855321.2855373

Hokkanen, L., Xu, Y., & Väänänen, K. (2016). Focusing on user experience and business models in startups: Investigation of two-dimensional value creation. *Proceedings of the 20th International Academic Mindtrek Conference*, 59–67. 10.1145/2994310.2994371

Holzer, A., & Ondrus, J. (2011). Mobile application market: A developer's perspective. *Telematics and Informatics*, *28*(1), 22–31. doi:10.1016/j.tele.2010.05.006

Honig, B., & Karlsson, T. (2004). Institutional forces and the written business plan. *Journal of Management, 30*(1), 29–48. doi:10.1016/j.jm.2002.11.002

Honig, B., & Karlsson, T. (2013). An institutional perspective on business planning activities for nascent entrepreneurs in Sweden and the US. *Administrative Sciences, 3*(4), 266–289. doi:10.3390/admsci3040266

Howard, J. (2007, November 7). On the Origin of Touchpoints. *Design for Service*. https://designforservice.wordpress.com/2007/11/07/on-the-origin-of-touchpoints/

Hummel, M., & Epp, A. (2015). Success factors of agile information systems development: A qualitative study. *2015 48th Hawaii International Conference on System Sciences*, 5045–5054.

Hyrynsalmi, S., Mäkilä, T., Järvi, A., Suominen, A., Seppänen, M., & Knuutila, T. (2012). App store, marketplace, play! An analysis of multi-homing in mobile software ecosystems. *Jansen*, 59–72.

Iamratanakul, S. (2018). A conceptual framework of implementing business strategy for the NPD process. *Review of Integrative Business and Economics Research, 7*(1), 116.

Ide, M., Amagai, Y., Aoyama, M., & Kikushima, Y. (2015). A lean design methodology for business models and its application to IoT business model development. *2015 Agile Conference*, 107–111. 10.1109/Agile.2015.8

Idu, A., van de Zande, T., & Jansen, S. (2011). Multi-homing in the apple ecosystem: Why and how developers target multiple apple app stores. *Proceedings of the International Conference on Management of Emergent Digital EcoSystems*, 122–128. 10.1145/2077489.2077511

Jansen, S., Brinkkemper, S., Hunink, I., & Demir, C. (2008). Pragmatic and opportunistic reuse in innovative start-up companies. *IEEE Software, 25*(6), 42–49. doi:10.1109/MS.2008.155

Jansen, S., Finkelstein, A., & Brinkkemper, S. (2009). A sense of community: A research agenda for software ecosystems. *2009 31st International Conference on Software Engineering-Companion Volume*, 187–190.

Johansson, H. (2017). *Finding the Product/Market fit: Lean Canvas framework as a tool for establishing customer-validated market orientation in early-stage startup businesses.* Academic Press.

Joshi, A. (2009). Usability goals setting tool. *4th Workshop on Software and Usability Engineering Cross-Pollination: Usability Evaluation of Advanced Interfaces.*

Joshi, S. (2019, October). *PaaS (Platform-as-a-Service).* https://www.ibm.com/cloud/learn/paas

Käpyaho, M., & Kauppinen, M. (2015). Agile requirements engineering with prototyping: A case study. *2015 IEEE 23rd International Requirements Engineering Conference (RE)*, 334–343.

Karlsson, J., Wohlin, C., & Regnell, B. (1998). An evaluation of methods for prioritizing software requirements. *Information and Software Technology, 39*(14–15), 939–947. doi:10.1016/S0950-5849(97)00053-0

Karlsson, T., & Honig, B. (2009). Judging a business by its cover: An institutional perspective on new ventures and the business plan. *Journal of Business Venturing, 24*(1), 27–45. doi:10.1016/j.jbusvent.2007.10.003

Kawano, A., Motoyama, Y., & Aoyama, M. (2019). A LX (Learner eXperience)-Based Evaluation Method of the Education and Training Programs for Professional Software Engineers. *Proceedings of the 2019 7th International Conference on Information and Education Technology*, 151–159. 10.1145/3323771.3323789

Kiznyte, J., Welker, M., & Dechange, A. (2016). Applying project management methods to the creation of a start-up business plan: The case of Blendlee. *PM World Journal*, *5*(5), 1–24.

Klein, L. (2013). *UX for Lean Startups: Faster, Smarter User Experience Research and Design*. O'Reilly Media, Inc.

Klotins, E., Unterkalmsteiner, M., & Gorschek, T. (2019). Software engineering in start-up companies: An analysis of 88 experience reports. *Empirical Software Engineering*, *24*(1), 68–102. doi:10.100710664-018-9620-y

Knauber, P., Muthig, D., Schmid, K., & Widen, T. (2000). Applying product line concepts in small and medium-sized companies. *IEEE Software*, *17*(5), 88–95. doi:10.1109/52.877873

Kraaijenbrink, J. (2012). *Three shortcomings of the business model canvas*. Kraaijenbrink Training Advies Atom.

Kraus, S., & Kauranen, I. (2009). Strategic management and entrepreneurship: Friends or foes? *International Journal of Business Science and Applied Management*, *4*(1), 37–50.

Ladd, T. (2016). The limits of the lean startup method. *Harvard Business Review*, *94*(3).

Lafley, A. G., & Martin, R. (2013). Instituting a company-wide strategic conversation at Procter & Gamble. *Strategy and Leadership*, *41*(4), 4–9. doi:10.1108/SL-04-2013-0023

Lawton, G. (2008). Developing software online with platform-as-a-service technology. *Computer*, *41*(6), 13–15. doi:10.1109/MC.2008.185

Lenarduzzi, V., & Taibi, D. (2016). MVP explained: A systematic mapping study on the definitions of minimal viable product. *2016 42th Euromicro Conference on Software Engineering and Advanced Applications (SEAA)*, 112–119.

Lima, M., & Baudier, P. (2017). Business model canvas acceptance among French entrepreneurship students: Principles for enhancing innovation artefacts in business education. *Journal of Innovation Economics Management*, *2*(23), 159–183. doi:10.3917/jie.pr1.0008

Lindgren, E., & Münch, J. (2016). Raising the odds of success: The current state of experimentation in product development. *Information and Software Technology*, *77*, 80–91. doi:10.1016/j.infsof.2016.04.008

Lucassen, G., Dalpiaz, F., van der Werf, J. M. E. M., & Brinkkemper, S. (2016). Improving agile requirements: The Quality User Story framework and tool. *Requirements Engineering*, *21*(3), 383–403. doi:10.100700766-016-0250-x

Maher, J. H. (2015). *Software evangelism and the rhetoric of morality: Coding justice in a digital democracy*. Routledge. doi:10.4324/9780203762172

Markerink, E. J. P. (2014). *Enhancing Organizational Creation, Product Development and Success Through the use of Lean Startup in Relation to the Information Technology Sector*. University of Twente.

Markides, C. (1997). Strategic innovation. *Sloan Management Review, 38,* 9–24.

Matharu, G. S., Mishra, A., Singh, H., & Upadhyay, P. (2015). Empirical study of agile software development methodologies: A comparative analysis. *Software Engineering Notes, 40*(1), 1–6. doi:10.1145/2693208.2693233

Maurya, A. (2010). *Lean Canvas–How I Document my Business Model.* Http://Www. Ashmaurya. Com/2010/08/Businessmodelcanvas

Maurya, A. (2012). *Running lean: Iterate from plan A to a plan that works.* O'Reilly Media, Inc.

Maurya, A. (2016). *Scaling lean: Mastering the key metrics for startup growth.* Penguin.

McClure, D. (2019, February 19). *Startup Metrics for Pirates.* https://www.slideshare.net/dmc500hats/startup-metrics-for-pirates-long-version

McGrath, R. G. (2010). Business models: A discovery driven approach. *Long Range Planning, 43*(2–3), 247–261. doi:10.1016/j.lrp.2009.07.005

Meertens, L. O., Iacob, M.-E., & Nieuwenhuis, L. B. J. (2011). A method for business model development. *International Symposium on Business Modeling and Software Design,* 113–129.

Melegati, J., & Goldman, A. (2015). Seven patterns for software startups. *Proceedings of the 22nd Conference on Pattern Languages of Programs (PLoP'15), 20*(11).

Melegati, J., Goldman, A., Kon, F., & Wang, X. (2019). A model of requirements engineering in software startups. *Information and Software Technology, 109,* 92–107. doi:10.1016/j.infsof.2019.02.001

Monteiro-Guerra, F., Rivera-Romero, O., Mylonopoulou, V., Signorelli, G. R., Zambrana, F., & Fernandez-Luque, L. (2017). The design of a mobile app for promotion of physical activity and self-management in prostate cancer survivors: Personas, feature ideation and low-fidelity prototyping. *2017 IEEE 30th International Symposium on Computer-Based Medical Systems (CBMS),* 761–766.

Morris, M., Schindehutte, M., & Allen, J. (2005). The entrepreneur's business model: Toward a unified perspective. *Journal of Business Research, 58*(6), 726–735. doi:10.1016/j.jbusres.2003.11.001

Müller, R. M., & Thoring, K. (2012). Design thinking vs. Lean startup: A comparison of two user-driven innovation strategies. *Leading through Design, 151,* 91–106.

Myers, M. D. (2019). *Qualitative research in business and management.* Sage Publications Limited.

Nelson, S. D., Del Fiol, G., Hanseler, H., Crouch, B. I., & Cummins, M. R. (2016). Software prototyping. *Applied Clinical Informatics, 7*(01), 22–32. doi:10.4338/ACI-2015-07-CR-0091 PMID:27081404

Nguyen-Duc, A., Dahle, Y., Steinert, M., & Abrahamsson, P. (2017). Towards understanding startup product development as effectual entrepreneurial behaviors. *International Conference on Product-Focused Software Process Improvement,* 265–279. 10.1007/978-3-319-69926-4_19

Nguyen-Duc, A., Seppänen, P., & Abrahamsson, P. (2015). Hunter-gatherer Cycle: A Conceptual Model of the Evolution of Software Startups. *Proceedings of the 2015 International Conference on Software and System Process,* 199–203. 10.1145/2785592.2795368

Njima, M., & Demeyer, S. (2017). Evolution of software product development in startup companies. *CEUR Workshop Proceedings*.

Nobel, C. (2011). Teaching a 'Lean Startup' Strategy. *HBS Working Knowledge*, 1–2.

Nowak, M. J., & Grantham, C. E. (2000). The virtual incubator: Managing human capital in the software industry. *Research Policy, 29*(2), 125–134. doi:10.1016/S0048-7333(99)00054-2

Ojasalo, J., & Ojasalo, K. (2015). Using service logic business model canvas in lean service development. *Proceedings of the 2015 Naples Forum on Service*, 9–12.

Olsson, H. H., & Bosch, J. (2015). Towards continuous customer validation: A conceptual model for combining qualitative customer feedback with quantitative customer observation. *International Conference of Software Business*, 154–166. 10.1007/978-3-319-19593-3_13

Osterwalder, A. (2004). *The business model ontology: A proposition in a design science approach.* Academic Press.

Osterwalder, A., & Pigneur, Y. (2010). *Business model generation: A handbook for visionaries, game changers, and challengers.* John Wiley & Sons.

Paetsch, F., Eberlein, A., & Maurer, F. (2003). Requirements engineering and agile software development. *Enabling Technologies: Infrastructure for Collaborative Enterprises, 2003. WET ICE 2003. Proceedings. Twelfth IEEE International Workshops On*, 308–313.

Paternoster, N., Giardino, C., Unterkalmsteiner, M., Gorschek, T., & Abrahamsson, P. (2014). Software development in startup companies: A systematic mapping study. *Information and Software Technology, 56*(10), 1200–1218. doi:10.1016/j.infsof.2014.04.014

Pearce, J. A. II, & David, F. (1987). Corporate mission statements: The bottom line. *The Academy of Management Perspectives, 1*(2), 109–115. doi:10.5465/ame.1987.4275821

Perdana, R. A., Suzianti, A., & Ardi, R. (2017). Crowdfunding website design with lean product process framework. *Proceedings of the 3rd International Conference on Communication and Information Processing*, 369–374. 10.1145/3162957.3162994

Popli, R., Chauhan, N., & Sharma, H. (2014). Prioritising user stories in agile environment. *2014 International Conference on Issues and Challenges in Intelligent Computing Techniques (ICICT)*, 515–519.

Quinn, J. B., Doorley, T. L., & Paquette, P. C. (1990). Beyond products: Services-based strategy. *Harvard Business Review, 68*(2), 58–60, 64–66, 68. PMID:10106517

Racheva, Z., Daneva, M., & Buglione, L. (2008). Supporting the dynamic reprioritization of requirements in agile development of software products. *2008 Second International Workshop on Software Product Management*, 49–58. 10.1109/IWSPM.2008.7

Rafiq, U., Bajwa, S. S., Wang, X., & Lunesu, I. (2017). Requirements elicitation techniques applied in software startups. *2017 43rd Euromicro Conference on Software Engineering and Advanced Applications (SEAA)*, 141–144.

Rajala, R., Rossi, M., & Tuunainen, V. K. (2003). A framework for analyzing software business models. *ECIS*, 1614–1627.

Rasmussen, E. S., & Tanev, S. (2016). Lean start-up: Making the start-up more successful. In *Start-up creation* (pp. 39–56). Elsevier. doi:10.1016/B978-0-08-100546-0.00003-0

Razdan, R., & Kambalimath, S. (2019). Super Lean Software Startup Engineering Management. *2019 IEEE Technology & Engineering Management Conference (TEMSCON)*, 1–6.

Reifer, D. J. (2002). How good are agile methods? *IEEE Software, 19*(4), 16–18. doi:10.1109/MS.2002.1020280

Reis, D. A., Fleury, A. L., & de Carvalho, M. M. (2019). Toward a Recursive Stage-Based Framework for Supporting Startup Business Initiation: An Exploratory Study With Entrepreneurs. *IEEE Transactions on Engineering Management*.

Richter, N., Schildhauer, T., & Jackson, P. (2018). Meeting the innovation challenge: Agile processes for established organisations. In *Entrepreneurial Innovation and Leadership* (pp. 109–121). Springer. doi:10.1007/978-3-319-71737-1_10

Rico, D. F., Sayani, H. H., & Field, R. F. (2008). History of Computers, Electronic Commerce and Agile Methods. In M. V. Zelkowitz (Ed.), *Advances in Computers* (Vol. 73, pp. 1–55). Elsevier. doi:10.1016/S0065-2458(08)00401-4

Ries, E. (2011). *The Lean Startup: How Today's Entrepreneurs Use Continuous Innovation to Create Radically Successful Businesses*. Crown Publishing Group. https://books.google.com.au/books?id=tvfyz-4JILwC

Ripsas, S., Schaper, B., & Tröger, S. (2018). A startup cockpit for the proof-of-concept. In *Handbuch entrepreneurship* (pp. 263–279). Springer. doi:10.1007/978-3-658-04994-2_21

Rissanen, O., & Münch, J. (2015). Continuous experimentation in the B2B domain: A case study. *2015 IEEE/ACM 2nd International Workshop on Rapid Continuous Software Engineering*, 12–18.

Ritter, T., & Lettl, C. (2018). The wider implications of business-model research. *Long Range Planning, 51*(1), 1–8. doi:10.1016/j.lrp.2017.07.005

Robinson, F. (2001). *A proven methodology to maximize return on risk*. Academic Press.

Rodden, K., Hutchinson, H., & Fu, X. (2010). Measuring the User Experience on a Large Scale: User-centered Metrics for Web Applications. *Proceedings of the SIGCHI Conference on Human Factors in Computing Systems*, 2395–2398. 10.1145/1753326.1753687

Sadi, M. H., & Yu, E. (2015). Designing software ecosystems: How can modeling techniques help? In Enterprise, Business-Process and Information Systems Modeling (pp. 360–375). Springer.

Sauvola, T., Rontti, S., Laivamaa, L., Oivo, M., & Kuvaja, P. (2016). Integrating Service Design Prototyping into Software Development. *ICSEA, 2016*, 338.

Schneider, T. W. (1998). Building a business plan. *Journal of Property Management, 63*(6).

Schön, E.-M., Thomaschewski, J., & Escalona, M. J. (2017). Agile Requirements Engineering: A systematic literature review. *Computer Standards & Interfaces*, *49*, 79–91. doi:10.1016/j.csi.2016.08.011

Sener, Z., & Karsak, E. E. (2012). A decision model for setting target levels in software quality function deployment to respond to rapidly changing customer needs. *Concurrent Engineering*, *20*(1), 19–29. doi:10.1177/1063293X11435344

Seppänen, P., Liukkunen, K., & Oivo, M. (2015). On the feasibility of startup models as a framework for research on competence needs in software startups. *International Conference on Product-Focused Software Process Improvement*, 569–576. 10.1007/978-3-319-26844-6_42

Serrano, N., Gallardo, G., & Hernantes, J. (2015). Infrastructure as a service and cloud technologies. *IEEE Software*, *32*(2), 30–36. doi:10.1109/MS.2015.43

Shaari, H., & Ahmad, I. S. (2016). Brand evangelism among online brand community members. *International Review of Management and Business Research*, *5*(1), 80.

Shanbhag, N., & Pardede, E. (2021). A Triple Cornerstone Framework for Software Startups: A Systems Thinking-Based Analysis. In Handbook of Research on Modeling, Analysis, and Control of Complex Systems (pp. 60–90). IGI Global. doi:10.4018/978-1-7998-5788-4.ch003

Silva, T. R., Hak, J.-L., & Winckler, M. (2016). Testing prototypes and final user interfaces through an ontological perspective for behavior-driven development. In *Human-Centered and Error-Resilient Systems Development* (pp. 86–107). Springer. doi:10.1007/978-3-319-44902-9_7

Smoczyńska, A., Pawlak, M., & Poniszewska-Marańda, A. (2018). Hybrid agile method for management of software creation. *KKIO Software Engineering Conference*, 101–115.

Somaya, D., & Graham, S. J. (2006). *Vermeers and Rembrandts in the same attic: Complementarity between copyright and trademark leveraging strategies in software*. Georgia Institute of Technology TIGER Working Paper.

Spanz, G. (2012). *Startup best practice: Business Model Canvas*. Academic Press.

Still, K., Seppänen, M., Valkokari, K., Suominen, A., & Kumpulainen, M. (2018). Platform Competences of Digi-driven Startups. *ISPIM Conference Proceedings*, 1–10.

Sutherland, J. S. K., & Schwaber, K. (2012). *The Crisis in Software: The Wrong Process Produces the Wrong Results*. J. Wiley & Sons.

Sutton, S. M. (2000). The role of process in software start-up. *IEEE Software*, *17*(4), 33–39. doi:10.1109/52.854066

Teece, D. J. (2010). Business models, business strategy and innovation. *Long Range Planning*, *43*(2–3), 172–194. doi:10.1016/j.lrp.2009.07.003

Teece, D. J., & Linden, G. (2017). Business models, value capture, and the digital enterprise. *Journal of Organization Design*, *6*(1), 1–14. doi:10.118641469-017-0018-x

Teng, D., & Lu, P. (2016). Value proposition discovery in big data enabled business model innovation. *2016 International Conference on Management Science and Engineering (ICMSE)*, 1754–1759. 10.1109/ICMSE.2016.8365646

Tiwana, A., Konsynski, B., & Bush, A. A. (2010). Platform evolution: Coevolution of platform architecture, governance, and environmental dynamics (research commentary). *Information Systems Research*, *21*(4), 675–687. doi:10.1287/isre.1100.0323

Toro-Jarrín, M. A., Ponce-Jaramillo, I. E., & Güemes-Castorena, D. (2016). Methodology for the of building process integration of Business Model Canvas and Technological Roadmap. *Technological Forecasting and Social Change*, *110*, 213–225. doi:10.1016/j.techfore.2016.01.009

Trimi, S., & Berbegal-Mirabent, J. (2012). Business model innovation in entrepreneurship. *The International Entrepreneurship and Management Journal*, *8*(4), 449–465. doi:10.100711365-012-0234-3

Tripathi, N., Oivo, M., Liukkunen, K., & Markkula, J. (2019). Startup ecosystem effect on minimum viable product development in software startups. *Information and Software Technology*, *114*, 77–91. doi:10.1016/j.infsof.2019.06.008

Tripathi, N., Seppänen, P., Oivo, M., Similä, J., & Liukkunen, K. (2017). The effect of competitor interaction on startup's product development. *2017 43rd Euromicro Conference on Software Engineering and Advanced Applications (SEAA)*, 125–132.

Turk, M. (2015). Vertical integration. *Computing in Science & Engineering*, *17*(1), 64–66. doi:10.1109/MCSE.2015.27

Unterkalmsteiner, M., Abrahamsson, P., Wang, X., Nguyen-Duc, A., Shah, S., Bajwa, S. S., Baltes, G. H., Conboy, K., Cullina, E., & Dennehy, D. (2016). Software startups–a research agenda. *E-Informatica Software Engineering Journal*, *10*(1).

Urban, M., Klemm, M., Ploetner, K. O., & Hornung, M. (2018). Airline categorisation by applying the business model canvas and clustering algorithms. *Journal of Air Transport Management*, *71*, 175–192. doi:10.1016/j.jairtraman.2018.04.005

Vähäniitty, J., Lassenius, C., & Rautiainen, K. (2002). An approach to product roadmapping in small software product businesses. *ECSQ2002, Conference Notes*, 12–13.

Van Den Berk, I., Jansen, S., & Luinenburg, L. (2010). Software ecosystems: A software ecosystem strategy assessment model. *Proceedings of the Fourth European Conference on Software Architecture: Companion*, 127–134. 10.1145/1842752.1842781

Vanhala, E., & Saarikallio, M. (2015). Business model elements in different types of organization in software business. *International Journal of Computer Information Systems and Industrial Management Applications*, *7*, 139–150.

Voigt, K.-I., Buliga, O., & Michl, K. (2017). Entertainment on Demand: The Case of Netflix. In K.-I. Voigt, O. Buliga, & K. Michl (Eds.), *Business Model Pioneers: How Innovators Successfully Implement New Business Models* (pp. 127–141). Springer International Publishing. doi:10.1007/978-3-319-38845-8_11

Wagner, L. (2001). Extreme requirements engineering. *Cutter IT Journal*, *14*(12), 34–38.

Waldenström, S. (2018). *Lean Startup Approach to Develop Ideas for Internal Systems and Processes: Creating Guidelines for Working with Ideas within Software and Service Companies.* Academic Press.

Walther, S., Plank, A., Eymann, T., Singh, N., & Phadke, G. (2012). *Success factors and value propositions of software as a service providers–a literature review and classification.* Academic Press.

Wang, X., Zhao, L., Wang, Y., & Sun, J. (2014). The role of requirements engineering practices in agile development: An empirical study. In *Requirements Engineering* (pp. 195–209). Springer. doi:10.1007/978-3-662-43610-3_15

Waters, K. (2009). Prioritization using moscow. *Agile Planning, 12,* 31.

Weiblen, T., Giessmann, A., Bonakdar, A., & Eisert, U. (2012). *Leveraging the software ecosystem: Towards a business model framework for marketplaces.* Academic Press.

Wiegers, K. (1999). First things first: Prioritizing requirements. *Software Development, 7*(9), 48–53.

Williams, A. (2020). The Dawn of a New Era in Entertainment History. *Global Tides, 14*(1), 7.

Wölbling, A., Krämer, K., Buss, C. N., Dribbisch, K., LoBue, P., & Taherivand, A. (2012). Design thinking: An innovative concept for developing user-centered software. In *Software for people* (pp. 121–136). Springer. doi:10.1007/978-3-642-31371-4_7

Xu, L., & Brinkkemper, S. (2005). Concepts of product software: Paving the road for urgently needed research. *The First International Workshop on Philosophical Foundations of Information Systems Engineering (PHISE'05),* 523–528.

Yang, S.-B., & Choi, S. O. (2009). Employee empowerment and team performance. *Team Performance Management, 15*(5/6), 289–301. doi:10.1108/13527590910983549

Yau, A., & Murphy, C. (2013). *Is a Rigorous Agile Methodology the Best Development Strategy for Small Scale Tech Startups?* Technical Reports (CIS). https://repository.upenn.edu/cis_reports/980

Yoffie, D. B., & Cusumano, M. A. (1999). Building a company on Internet time: Lessons from netscape. *California Management Review, 41*(3), 8–28. doi:10.2307/41165995

YooO. S.HuangT.ArifogluK. (2017). A theoretical analysis of the lean startup's product development process. doi:10.2139/ssrn.3070613

Zagajsek, B., Separovic, K., & Car, Z. (2007). Requirements management process model for software development based on legacy system functionalities. *Telecommunications, 2007. ConTel 2007. 9th International Conference On,* 115–122.

Zolnowski, A., Weiß, C., & Böhmann, T. (2014). Representing Service Business Models with the Service Business Model Canvas—The Case of a Mobile Payment Service in the Retail Industry. *2014 47th Hawaii International Conference on System Sciences,* 718–727.

Chapter 2
Digitally-Enabled Innovation Processes:
The Emergence of a New Management Logic

Haneen Abdallah Allataifeh
https://orcid.org/0000-0001-5737-9507
Univeristy of Malaya, Malaysia

Sedigheh Moghavvemi
University of Malaya, Malaysia

ABSTRACT

Malleability, homogeneity, and transferability are three distinct characteristics of digital technology that allow the continuous evolvement of innovation and the generation of new forms of agency, both within and across processes. Scholars have developed various research directions to theoretically understand digital technology correlative to business process management. Yet, literature in this area lacks a structured view of how digital technologies modify the innovation processes, and research aimed at examining the effect of digital technology on business process management is still relatively scant and in a very early stage. This chapter sheds light on scholarly works to explain digital technology's impact on the innovation process and how it is linked to business process management.

INTRODUCTION

The emergence of digital technologies and their constantly expanding digital infrastructures, including social media, wearables, mobile computing, augmented and virtual reality, blockchain, data analytics, cloud computing, robotics, machine learning, 3D printing, and the Internet of Things (IoT) are radically modifying the processes, outcomes, and nature of innovation (Nambisan, Lyytinen, & Yoo, 2020). Digital innovation can generally be described as "the creation of (and consequent change in) market offerings, business processes, or models that result from the use of digital technology" (Nambisan, Lyytinen, Maj-

DOI: 10.4018/978-1-7998-9059-1.ch002

chrzak, & Song, 2017, p. 224). Digital innovation consists of a "new combination of digital and physical components" (Yoo, Henfridsson, & Lyytinen, 2010, p. 725) that are carried by an amorphous agency to achieve uncertain outcomes resulting from a constant flow of integrating, expanding, and augmenting digital tools and components into business infrastructure (Nambisan et al., 2020).

The widespread use of digital technologies in innovation processes and outcomes has urged scholars to formulate new theories on innovation management. These theories shake core assumptions about the boundaries between innovation and organizations and the link between firm performance and innovation processes (Nambisan et al., 2017). Digital technology has drastically impacted the business environment (Davis, Field, & Stavrulaki, 2015) and modified the way organizations and customers interact and create value (Yadav & Pavlou, 2014). Digital technologies have indeed reshaped organizations and industries and challenged themes and assumptions that underly innovation process management. Thus, scholars are urged to build and incorporate new concepts and theories that can reflect the ways digitalization of innovation processes modifies the practical outcomes and transforms process management (Ferreira, Fernandes, & Ferreira, 2019).

Business processes are considered a top priority in the context of digital innovation. Business process management (BPM) has become the field of focus for many scholars and practitioners by providing techniques, management principles, and methods to strategically position processes to achieve better results, compliance, and sustainability (Van Looy, 2021). However, BPM is challenged by the rapid emergence of digital technologies that impose fast-paced transformations in the business environment (Fichman, Dos Santos, & Zheng, 2014; Schmiedel & vom Brocke, 2015). The incorporation of new technologies in organizational strategies and business processes has become a matter of survival and growth, especially when such technologies are competitive and user-friendly (Fichman et al., 2014). For example, Uber still takes customers from A to B, and it rather modifies the process of the way it is done. Blockchain systems do not change the fact of money transfer, but it fundamentally modifies how its conducted. These types of modifications go beyond the mere substitution of one tool for another to improve speed and quality and reduce cost; as a result, it opens up new areas of activities (Mendling, Pentland, & Recker, 2020).

While BPM has essentially focused on standardization, automation, and continuous improvement, digital innovation requires flexibility and agility (Van den Bergh, Thijs, & Viaene, 2014). The core transformation characteristic of digital technologies is the openness they bring to the process they are incorporated in, which disrupts the inward-looking nature of traditional BPM and requires openness to the surrounding environment (Van Looy, 2021). Given the new challenges of digital innovation in the traditional BPM discipline, scholars have started to tap into new streams of research to understand how to manage business processes under the influence of digital technology and how BPM benefits from digital innovation. One of the main questions for further investigation is how can the transformative process of digital innovation be managed? It is widely acknowledged that digital innovation provides opportunities for change and deviation, but can this deviation be optimized? In other words, can BPM benefit from digital innovation to enhance operational efficiency (Grisold, Wurm, Mendling, & Vom Brocke, 2020; Mendling et al., 2020)?

Hence, the objective of this chapter is to elucidate the way digital technologies impact the innovation process and ultimately reshape the way business processes are designed and managed. It also sheds light on the link between digital innovation and BPM and the means by which they complement and reshape one another. The following sections explain the characteristics of digital technology, the impact of digitalization on innovation processes, and the link between digital innovation and BPM.

DIGITAL TECHNOLOGY CHARACTERISTICS

To understand the nature of the innovation, the difference between digital technology and former technologies must be considered. The term 'digital' signifies the conversion from mainly analog information into a binary language understood by computers. Digital technologies are "products or services that are either embodied in information and communication technologies or enabled by them" (Lyytinen, Yoo, & Boland Jr, 2016, p. 49). Digital technologies can come in the form of the IoT, big data, virtual reality, cloud computing, cyber-physical systems, augmented reality, and artificial intelligence, or in the form of mobiles, social media, or embedded devices (Urbinati, Bogers, Chiesa, & Frattini, 2019). Hence, there are three unique characteristics of digital technology: malleability, homogeneity, and transferability (Yoo et al., 2010).

Malleability refers to the re-programmability of digital tools and components, allowing such tools to conduct various functions, such as word processing, calculating distances, web browsing, and video editing. Homogeneity indicates how the digital representation transforms an analog signal into a combination of binary numbers, leading to data homogenization. As such, digital contents can be stored, processed, transmitted, combined, and represented to deliver various services that can loosen the boundaries of products and industries. Transferability refers to the ability of digital innovation to diffuse and establish a network of externalities that can accelerate the availability and creation of digital tools, networks, content, and services. This can further boost innovation through a cycle of low entry barriers, low learning costs, and a high diffusion rate. The radical improvements in computer price and performance and the emergence of the internet have enforced the necessity and affordability of employing digital tools in innovation processes. Digital technology, subsequently, has democratized innovation and diffused the boundaries between innovation agencies and the surrounding environment (Yoo et al., 2010).

The malleability, homogeneity, and transferability are at the core of digital technology because they enable, constrain, and intermix with human actions. These three distinct characteristics of digital technology allow innovation to evolve even after implementation and continuous use. It also allows for the creation of new forms of agency, both within and across processes (Altman, Nagle, & Tushman, 2015; Flyverbom, Huysman, & Matten, 2016; Yoo et al., 2010).

Digital technologies are distinguished into digital tools and infrastructure, digital platforms or artifacts with digitized applications, media content, or components. All categories decouple digital information from the physical form of the material device and separate semiotic functional logic from the physical embodiment that executes it. Subsequently, digital technology mediates the control of inputs, outputs, and their transformations. Digital technology can determine the type of resources that are provided as input and the way resources are converted and provided as an output (Nambisan, Wright, & Feldman, 2019).

The Impact of Digital Technology on Innovation

Nowadays, organizations use digital technologies to drive innovation, usually surpassing the traditional capabilities of their IT departments. For instance, organizations digitize their products, embed software-based technologies in physical products, and analyze big data for customer profiling (Nambisan et al., 2017). Numerous examples in the media industry, financial services, and the automotive sectors show how digital technology has changed products and services, including strategic dimensions, such as the scale, scope, source, and speed of value creation (Nambisan, 2017). Digital technology impacts the innovation process by influencing the dynamic capabilities of the company in two ways; it improves an organization's ability to sense and respond to opportunities, and it increases an organization's explorative and exploitative capabilities. Exploitation relates to the efficient use of existing capabilities and resources to improve existing products or processes, while exploration refers to discovering new ways to combine capabilities and resources to bring in more opportunities (Leonhardt, Haffke, Kranz, & Benlian, 2017).

Aside from Leonhardt et al.'s (2017) study, scholars have a relatively limited understanding of how much digital technology contributes to innovation (Ravichandran, Han, & Mithas, 2017). Innovation literature shows a progressive increase in scholarly works that considered some features of digital technology. Additionally, the scope and nature of these papers have changed. The studies from the 1990s broadly focused on examining the issues of organizations and management that are placed at the crossroad between product development and information systems. Whereas recent studies concentrate on detailed issues, are naturally empirical, and have begun to integrate IS and management concepts (Nambisan et al., 2017). Previous studies on digital technology and innovation have paid special attention to the digital technology role as an operand resource (i.e., as an enabler of innovation), while less attention is given to its role as an operant resource (i.e., as a trigger or an initiator of innovation). Both roles played by digital technology exert a different impact on the innovation process as well as the innovation outcome (Nambisan, 2013; see Table 1).

Table 1. Digital technology roles in the innovation process and outcome

The role of Digital Technology	Impact on Innovation Process	Impact on Innovation Outcome
Digital technology as operant Resource	Digital tool as a trigger	Digital component as a trigger
Digital technology as operand resource	Digital tool as an enabler	Digital component as an enabler

Digital Tool as an Innovation Enabler

Studies have examined the operand resource role of digital technology and how it influences the innovation process. Some scholars have focused on empirically investigating evidence related to the impact of digital technology on development processes and product design as well as the business's competitive advantage and value derived from digital technology inclusion in product development (e.g., Durmuşoğlu & Barczak, 2011; Kleis, Chwelos, Ramirez, & Cockburn, 2012). Other scholars have focused on applying certain IS constructs and concepts to better comprehend the work process and the collaborative structures of product development (e.g., Bardhan, 2007; Li & Qiu, 2006). A third group of researchers has studied the deployment of specific digital applications and tools (e.g., PLM, decision support systems, data mining, virtual simulation, and social media) to enable and support different activities of product development (e.g., Malins & Liapis, 2010; Nambisan & Baron, 2010). Studies in this area have empirically shown that the proper use of digital applications and tools can improve the effectiveness and efficiency of product development activities. Recent studies examined the impact of the interaction between companies' resources and mechanisms and digital tools in the context of product development. For instance, Nambisan et al. (2017) relied on the complementarities logic to propose that digital tools can be improved if they are systematically inserted into the context of product development, such as process, strategies, and structures. Future studies adopting this perspective can provide insight into the reasons why some companies have better success in acquiring value from digital applications and tools in innovation activities.

Digital Component as an Innovation Enabler

Scholars have studied the digital components as an operand resource and their impact on innovation outcomes. This role deals with the supportive functionality of digital components in product and service innovations. In this area, some studies have explored the extent and nature of the value that digital components generate as part of diverse service innovations and the capabilities and assets that companies need to improve such value (e.g., Ordanini & Rubera, 2010). Most of these studies focus on digital technology applications; hence they are considered part of traditional IS literature, yet their larger context is that of a service innovation where the IT application enables or supports the service innovation (Nambisan, 2013). The main insight from these studies is the significance of combining digital and non-digital components of service innovation in an integrated fashion to secure success and gain the maximum value out of the innovation investment. Other studies in such areas (e.g., Woodard et al., Ramasubbu, Tschang, & Sambamurthy, 2013) examined the contexts in which digital components are embedded inside diverse products. These contexts have an emerging nature; thus, there are few studies in this area. Moreover, it is progressively evident that the focus for these studies needs to move to analyze how the digital components fit in the broader product architecture and the associated strategic and managerial issues (e.g., the nature of digital components enabling role, interface specifications, trade-offs of product design, and the management of intellectual property). Accordingly, it is necessary for future studies to adopt a wider theoretical framework to combine key constructs and concepts from other business fields to investigate the value and impact of digital components (Nambisan et al., 2017).

The role of digital technology as an operant resource for product and service innovation is related to the ability of such technologies to autonomously trigger or initiate innovation. This role has been recently revealed, with digital resources claiming a central significance in diverse products and services. Thus, there is an inadequate focus on this area in existing IT and innovation literature (Nambisan et al., 2019).

Digital Tool as an Innovation Trigger

Literature has considered the impact of digital technology on the innovation process as an operant resource. This refers to the mechanism by which digital tools can trigger or initiate new processes of innovation or related organizational mechanisms and routines. Several studies have investigated the correlation between product innovation, information technology, and organizational design, focusing on how new digital tools drive innovative arrangements and processes (e.g., Dunne & Dougherty, 2012; Faraj, Jarvenpaa, & Majchrzak, 2011). Dougherty and Dunne (2012) conceded the utilization of digital tools within drug discovery projects, which has altered the knowledge that separates traditional wet therapy scientists from digital scientists and resulted in a radical transformation in the innovation activities that are performed by both groups. Other scholars (e.g., Bailey, Leonardi, & Barley, 2012; Leonardi, 2011) indicated that the impact of digital tools on innovation processes and routines is usually unpredictable, dynamic, and not positive. Essentially, such studies show the promise of this research area to provide critical insights into the way digital tools can reconfigure or transform innovation activities and processes and shed light on wider organizational implications.

Digital Components as an Innovation Trigger

Studies have investigated the triggering role of digital technology and its effect on innovation outcomes. It reflects the potential of new digital resources to release creativity and impact digital components and product design. Research on the role of digital technology role as an operant resource is limited. The display of implicit constructs (e.g., service ecosystems, layered modularity, resource liquefication, digital platforms, and resource density) in recent literature might improve this topic discourse. For instance, Lusch and Nambisan (2015) see innovation from the perspective of service-dominant logic and outline that digital components within service platforms can search for and carry on unique opportunities for resource integration and can act or engage with others in the ecosystem, leading to value co-creation or innovation (Lusch & Nambisan, 2015). As such, they considered the generative triggering nature of digital components' affordances and the implications on the innovation platforms' design, and how actors contribute to the ecosystem. However, more research is needed to clarify the underlying concepts and issues. This area is essential and abundant for future research, especially in understanding the operant role of digital technology in innovation and explaining its implications on the development and design of digital resources (Nambisan et al., 2019).

This concise assessment of digital technology and innovation literature suggests the cumulative knowledge related to the role of the operand resource in digital technology provides numerous opportunities to broaden this knowledge in an emerging field. It also indicates that the literature in product and service development has begun to build on some IS-related concepts and theories. For instance, media richness and capacity theories are applied in communication evaluation within virtual development teams as well as to evaluate its impact on performance. Another example is the functioning duality of digital technologies in decision-support and communication and their comparative influence on improving the integration between R&D and marketing. Moreover, incorporating network externalities into the technology acceptance model can help examine consumer intentions to purchase new digital products. Finally, digital embeddedness in the processes of product development can indicate the impact of digital technology on product development and performance (Nambisan, 2013; Nambisan et al., 2019).

DIGITALIZATION OF INNOVATION

Digitalization refers to the process of incorporating digital technology in institutional and social contexts, which makes digital technologies infrastructural. It "refers to the practice of taking processes, content or objects that used to be primarily (or entirely) physical or analog and transforming them to be primarily (or entirely) digital" (Fichman et al., 2014, p. 333). Digitalization supports three main affordances that shape the position of organizations' opportunities within the economy and the adequate practices to carry out such opportunities. Digitalization decouples function and form and subsequently shifts the determinants to minimize the essentiality of fixed assets in regulating power and dependency in relationships within manufacturing value chains. Digitalization boosts disintermediation, minimizes the power of the middleman in the value chain, and grants more freedom to providers to shape and develop products and services. Digitalization promotes generativity, provides the ability to coordinate geographically dispersed actors, and establishes new means to build and employ platform momentum (Nambisan et al., 2017). These key affordances allow companies to reinvent how they create, capture, and deliver value, thus enabling them to obstruct incumbents with radical new business models (Nambisan et al., 2020). This has impacted innovation and businesses in various ways. The following section explains some of these impacts, which have been documented in the literature.

Digital Technology and Innovation Management

Scholars have investigated the impact of digitalization on many key organizational processes and developed a connection between digital technology and improvements in customer satisfaction, organizational productivity, and profit (Ho, Tian, Wu, & Xu, 2017; Mithas, Krishnan, & Fornell, 2016). According to the literature, digital technology has six mechanisms of enablement: conservation (i.e., reduces resources required to take action), compression (i.e., reduces the time required to take action), substitution (i.e., replaces one resource with another), expansion (i.e., increases resource's availability), generation (i.e., builds new artifacts by modifying existing ones), and combination (i.e., combine different resources to build new artifacts; von Briel, Davidsson, & Recker, 2018). Based on Nambisan et al. (2017), digital technology has changed the innovation process nature in several ways.

The first way is that innovative ideas can be rapidly shaped, instituted, adjusted, and re-enacted through a cyclic process of implementation and experimentation, enabling it to be less obvious as to where and when a specific innovation stage begins or ends. This makes innovation an entity that lacks clear boundaries. The second way is the ability to quickly scale items up or down during the design process. This establishes fluidity in the innovation processes, enabling the process to evolve in a nonlinear way through time and space. The final way is that the digital product is always emerging and incomplete. Consequently, traditional models of innovation that generate a complete state of the product to be launched are in conflict with the logic of digitalized innovation since they are incomplete and emerge over time and space.

The digitalization of innovation challenges the core assumptions of business process management. Nowadays, such issues are more relevant since the process of innovation is becoming more open, and its different phases demand greater resources to capture, integrate, and transfer knowledge inside and outside organizational boundaries. This indicates more challenges in terms of managing the growing amount of knowledge and information (Urbinati et al., 2019). The massive employment of digital technologies in the processes of innovation has urged scholars to establish a theory for the management of digital technology (Fichman et al., 2014; Nambisan et al., 2017). The need for new digital technology theorization calls researchers to intensely analyze and investigate the implementation of digital technology to nurture innovation activity. This deep theoretical effort on how digital technology supports the innovation processes led to multiple endeavors to provide innovation and strategic conceptual frameworks (Nambisan et al., 2021). Furthermore, scholars have developed various research directions to theoretically understand digital technology and the development of digital business strategies (Nambisan et al., 2021), the reassembly of current capabilities with digital resources to establish digital capabilities, and capture or create value via digital technologies (Lobo & Whyte, 2017). However, literature in this area lacks a structured view of how and why digital technologies are utilized in the innovation processes, and research aimed at examining the effect of digital technology on innovation process management is still relatively scant and in a very early stage (Urbinati et al., 2019).

In spite of richness in practical and managerial implications, the emerging literature lacks a specific focus on methods, applications, and advantages of digital technologies in the processes of innovation. Therefore, further empirical and theoretical research is required to gain a structured perspective of the role of digital technology in the process of innovation (Urbinati et al., 2019). Extensive understanding of how digital technology impacts innovation process management can lead to the development of an innovation process framework. Drawing on these premises and building on the mentioned research streams, research debates that the incorporation and usage of digital technologies in the process of innovation urges organizations to reorganize their business models and manage the innovation process in a different way than formerly stated in the literature. The following section demonstrates researchers' attempts to explain how digitally enabled innovation processes are modifying the whole business management structure.

DIGITAL INNOVATION AND BUSINESS PROCESS MANAGEMENT

Digital innovation describes how new products, processes, or business models are embodied in or enabled by digital technology (Fichman et al., 2014). This view emphasizes two points. First, digital innovation is inherently socio-technical, addressing both changes in technological systems (such as hardware and software) and social systems (such as processes, structures, and norms) brought forward through digitalization. Second, digital innovation blurs the boundaries between process and outcome. Products as outcomes of innovation processes may spawn or be involved in further innovation processes (Kyriakou, Garagounis, Vasileiou, Vourros, & Stoukides, 2017). Conversely, innovation processes can continuously render products fluid, malleable and emergent, making them fit for change and innovation aftermarket launch (Mendling et al., 2020).

In the story of digital innovation, the processes it facilitates are often overlooked. The key impact of digital innovation is its ability to reconfigure, rejuvenate, challenge, and reframe the way things are viewed and comprehended (Mendling et al., 2020). In other words, the incorporation of digital innovation is all about what changes and how things are carried differently. To understand change, the process by which change occurs needs to be understood. Therefore, business process management (BPM) is increasingly prioritized in the digital innovation context. BPM is an essential field that provides techniques, methods, and management approaches to strategically align business processes and achieve compliance, better business results, and obtain strategic competitiveness (Ahmad & Van Looy, 2020). BPM refers to the set of techniques and methods to discover and identify a business process, establish a design for that process, and monitor, automate, and optimize the process with financial, technological, and human resources (Abrell, Pihlajamaa, Kanto, Vom Brocke, & Uebernickel, 2016). Research has traditionally viewed the BPM lifecycle as a set of iterative stages of process discovery and identification followed by process analysis and process redesign and ending with execution and monitoring (Van Looy, 2021). This BPM lifecycle is needed in every innovation stage to facilitate workflows (Fichman et al., 2014).

BPM and digital innovation might seem different at their core. For instance, BPM focuses on how processes are designed as sequential episodes of activities, while digital innovation focuses on how processes unfold with emergent technology (Mendling et al., 2018). BPM is mainly about separating the problem from the solution, while digital innovation views the problem and the solution as emergent and co-evolving (Von Hippel & Von Krogh, 2016). BPM largely emerges in a top-down approach from strategic requirements and architectural design to process implementation, while digital innovation unfolds in a bottom-up approach to release generativity emerging from the small. BPM has a stage-driven design, whereas digital innovation usually unfolds in an anarchistic and ad-hoc style driven by contextual opportunities. BPM offers tangible business values, while digital innovation is looser and often offers intangible business values. Lastly, BPM research is largely prescriptive and focuses on computational and analytical approaches to establish technology, methods, or frameworks that support the management and execution of processes. In contrast, digital innovation research is mainly explanatory and deals with understanding how processes unfold and how they can be modified (Mendling et al., 2020).

Although BPM and digital innovation may appear to be opposites in the performance spectrum ranging from operational efficiency to generative capacity, they have synergy. For instance, digital innovation has facilitated current BPM practices as much as it changed the way processes are managed. Nevertheless, for various reasons, literature in each field has been attracted to varying assumptions, phenomena, methods, and settings. Neither field is comprehensive enough to capture the emergence and coalescence of digital innovation as arising through, enacted in, and transformative of the business processes (Mendling et al., 2020).

Recent research has been increasingly focused on the intersection of digital innovation and BPM. This research proposes new theories to explain how digital innovation enables, unbends, shifts, or constrains the design, analysis, and management of business processes. Likewise, it examines how theory, technology, and techniques from BPM can help understand the processes and outcomes of digital innovation. These research objectives combine the two different and isolated fields and join their insights, ideas, and theories to meet and surpass the boundaries of their individual lines of research (Van Looy, 2021).

Bygstad and Øvrelid (2020) have begun researching this intersection by examining the link between digital infrastructure and BPM in the case of a Norwegian hospital. They identified contradictory assumptions about BPM and infrastructure and then proposed mechanisms to align architecture and governance that increase the potential of successful innovation processes. They focused on the role of digital technology in the innovation process and revealed how such technology could lead to rapid changes without extensive engineering . Baiyere, Salmela, and Tapanainen (2020) explored the link between service offerings and the introduction of new digital products and how these changes influence BPM. They argued that there was a mismatch in assumptions between digital transformation and BPM. Through their analysis, they proposed new logic that comprised mindful agencies, infrastructural flexibility, and fast-paced processes that together provided more encompassing, updated, and flexible assumptions on how an organization can manage business processes. Mikalef and Krogstie (2020) investigated the interactions between BPM and big data analytics, using data from more than two hundred top managers working in different industries. They distinguished arrangements that support different types of innovation processes. They emphasized that a combination of factors and managerial skills are required for the digital innovation process. Van Looy (2021) reported that the nature and strength of the link between digital innovation and BPM based on an international survey and an expert panel. The link was examined from the perspectives of more than four hundred companies operating in four continents, which allowed for the consideration of the contextual factors impacting this link. Van Looy combined the findings to extend the technology–organization–environment (TOE) framework and proposed a typology to classify organizations based on their digital process innovation in a readiness matrix.

Based on researchers' attempts to link digital innovation to BPM, digital innovation is expected to alter the management process in four ways.

Balancing New Innovation Features With Immediate Feedback

Due to digital innovation, BPM views process design as finding a solution to a process-related problem becoming obsolete. BPM has to be modified to be more agile, and process design must become more continuous and more fine-grained. Short learning cycles and quick feedback are needed to examine and choose the best process design for a given business environment (Satyal, Weber, Paik, Di Ciccio,

& Mendling, 2019). Short time-frame implementation approaches like process automation become progressively essential. Such small-scale and fine-grained approaches can automate tedious manual computer activities like data entry and impose a structure of emergence (Baiyere et al., 2020; Bygstad & Øvrelid, 2020).

Balancing Adaptation Freedom With Predefined Structure

To combine BPM and digital innovation, the process design must have a balance between structurally sequenced activities and adaptation freedom, where it is impossible to fully define processes prior to execution. Some insights into balancing the extreme assumptions of BPM include top-down, design-driven, while digital innovation is bottom-up, generativity-driven, and is brought by organizational routines. Research into organizational routines proposes that business processes have a clearly demonstrative aspect that embraces a variety of fixed process performances; hence the socio-technical activities in business processes cannot be fully automated or planned (Mendling et al., 2020). Since actions depend on contextual factors, there will always be room for errors, exceptions, improvisation, and innovation (Feldman, Pentland, D'Adderio, & Lazaric, 2016). However, traditional BPM assumptions contradict this proposition, as the process is expected to be supported by the technological workflow in a way that is fully identified. A variety of approaches have been suggested to introduce flexibility to business process execution (Van der Aalst, Weske, & Grünbauer, 2005). Most of the developed propositions integrate BPM with adaptive management standards and systems. The key idea of such systems is to deliberately underspecify some elements of the processes and to provide mechanisms to extend and adapt processes upon execution. Moving forward, with the exponential interest in integrating digital innovation with BPM, a stronger focus on adaptive, flexible, or partial process design is expected due to digital innovation malleability and generative capacity offerings (Mendling et al., 2020).

Balancing Positive Deviation With Process Compliance

With the modifying influence of digital innovation, BPM enforces process compliance while identifying positive deviation. While BPM anticipates a stage-gates line of thinking for identifying and executing a process, digital innovation embraces a robust process theory without a clear structure (Hernes, 2017). A weak process theoretical perspective identifies that structure and evolution are mutually defined by each other. This means that a business process design can be initially specified, yet deviation is anticipated leading to uncertainty on how it will roll out upon execution. Therefore, management is confronted by a continuous knowledge gap about how the process will practically unfold over time (Pentland, Recker, Wolf, & Wyner, 2020). To reduce this uncertainty, different digital tools are offered to monitor and analyze the process over time. For instance, process mining gathers transactional data to generate precise process diagrams that offer detailed and fast evidence regarding the real performance of a business process (Van Der Aalst, 2012). Process mining resembles a BPM tool that facilitates the management and understanding of the impact of digital innovation. However, the application of such tools must change. Digital tools should neither emphasize the stable process model discovery nor compliance checking. Instead, applications should focus on unveiling patterns and stable paths in ongoing business processes to identify the process sequences that influence, rather than determine, future process performance and recognize opportunities for positive deviation (Grisold et al., 2020).

Balancing Inter-Organizational Emergence With Intra-Organizational Optimization

BPM assumes an intra-organizational process that is supported or enabled by enclosed systems of information. Based on this mindset, business processes were designed based on a context of long-term stability; however, this is often not the case in a digital context. Digital innovation blurred the boundaries of business processes and opened them to the surrounding environment (Winter, Berente, Howison, & Butler, 2014). Digitalized processes have become unstable, emergent, and less integrated than traditionally assumed. For instance, distributed ledger technology is viewed as the first information system that fully supports open inter-organizational business processes (Mendling et al., 2018). The key characteristic of this technology is its ability to utilize smart contracts to integrate "emerging value chains of transactions" in an unpredicted and non-predefined way. Likewise, digital platforms facilitate and support reconfiguration and openness within organizations and across a wide network of complementors, customers, and partners (Nambisan et al., 2021). An example of such platforms are Netflix and Uber since they hold an implicit design of a microservice infrastructure with abundance of smaller software services that are orchestrated and loosely integrated by business processes. In sum, the restrictive interpretation of BPM as intra-business and as an inward-looking process must be abundant and replaced by managing digitally enabled, intertwined networks of open processes (Mendling et al., 2020).

FUTURE RESEARCH DIRECTIONS

Research in BPM and digital innovation fields has relied on different methodologies that further the gap in the pool of knowledge in both fields. To further deepen the link between both fields, researchers need to apply an approach that is predominant in one field to achieve the objectives of the other. Process mining, for instance, can be a bridge between data traces of digital innovation in empirical research and a pattern of recognition in PBM research. Thus, process mining and such BPM technologies can be used in hypothesis testing and theory building about process changes (Pentland et al., 2020).

Another area of research opportunities arises from context understanding in both digital innovation and BPM. The impactful influence of contextual factors is well acknowledged in both digital innovation and BPM fields. BPM has developed methods, technologies, and conceptualizations embracing this context. Digital innovation has employed computational and empirical methods to address this context. The opportunity stems from using the methodological tools of digital innovation research to develop and improve BPM technology, such as process analysis and process mining. One example mentioned in this chapter is Mikalf and Krogstie's (2020) configurational analysis.

CONCLUSION

This chapter contributes to a deeper understanding of how digital transformation can reshape business process management. This research achieves this objective by addressing the characteristics of digital technology, the way it impacts innovation processes, and how it influences and is influenced by BPM. Digital innovation is re-inventing, re-engineering, and transforming business management practices. Despite the current isolation of both digital innovation and BPM fields, their complementarity and synergistic rhythm are well noticed. Product, process, and technologies are associated and intertwined. Digital innovation and BPM can be seen as two sides of the same coin. Digital innovation is re-inventing and re-engineering the entire domain of business process, and process design increasingly displays digital methodologies' characteristics of problem-solution-driven understanding (Dittrich & Seidl, 2018; Von Hippel & Von Krogh, 2016), where both endogenous evolution and interventional design constantly trigger each other. Hence, despite the fragmentation between both fields in the literature, it is clear that digital innovation and BPM are complementary areas of inquiry. To assess this complementarity, scholars in both fields need to examine their methods and question their assumptions. To contribute to this complementarity, scholars need to start tapping into each other's conversations.

REFERENCES

Abrell, T., Pihlajamaa, M., Kanto, L., Vom Brocke, J., & Uebernickel, F. (2016). The role of users and customers in digital innovation: Insights from B2B manufacturing firms. *Information & Management*, *53*(3), 324–335. doi:10.1016/j.im.2015.12.005

Ahmad, T., & Van Looy, A. (2020). Business process management and digital innovations: A systematic literature review. *Sustainability*, *12*(17), 6827. doi:10.3390u12176827

Altman, E. J., Nagle, F., & Tushman, M. (2015). *Innovating without information constraints: Organizations, communities, and innovation when information costs approach zero. In The Oxford Handbook of Creativity, Innovation, and Entrepreneurship*. Oxford University Press.

Bailey, D. E., Leonardi, P. M., & Barley, S. R. (2012). The lure of the virtual. *Organization Science*, *23*(5), 1485–1504. doi:10.1287/orsc.1110.0703

Baiyere, A., Salmela, H., & Tapanainen, T. (2020). Digital transformation and the new logics of business process management. *European Journal of Information Systems*, *29*(3), 238–259. doi:10.1080/09 60085X.2020.1718007

Bardhan, I. R. (2007). Toward a theory to study the use of collaborative product commerce for product development. *Information Technology and Management*, *8*(2), 167–184. doi:10.100710799-007-0013-y

Bygstad, B., & Øvrelid, E. (2020). Architectural alignment of process innovation and digital infrastructure in a high-tech hospital. *European Journal of Information Systems*, *29*(3), 220–237. doi:10.1080/0 960085X.2020.1728201

Davis, M. M., Field, J., & Stavrulaki, E. (2015). Using digital service inventories to create customer value. *Service Science*, *7*(2), 83–99. doi:10.1287erv.2015.0098

Dittrich, K., & Seidl, D. (2018). Emerging intentionality in routine dynamics: A pragmatist view. *Academy of Management Journal*, *61*(1), 111–138. doi:10.5465/amj.2015.0010

Dunne, D. D., & Dougherty, D. (2012). Organizing for change, innovation, and creativity. In *Handbook of organizational creativity* (pp. 569–583). Elsevier. doi:10.1016/B978-0-12-374714-3.00022-7

Durmuşoğlu, S. S., & Barczak, G. (2011). The use of information technology tools in new product development phases: Analysis of effects on new product innovativeness, quality, and market performance. *Industrial Marketing Management, 40*(2), 321–330. doi:10.1016/j.indmarman.2010.08.009

Faraj, S., Jarvenpaa, S. L., & Majchrzak, A. (2011). Knowledge collaboration in online communities. *Organization Science, 22*(5), 1224–1239. doi:10.1287/orsc.1100.0614

Feldman, M. S., Pentland, B. T., D'Adderio, L., & Lazaric, N. (2016). *Beyond routines as things: Introduction to the special issue on routine dynamics.* INFORMS.

Ferreira, J. J., Fernandes, C. I., & Ferreira, F. A. (2019). To be or not to be digital, that is the question: Firm innovation and performance. *Journal of Business Research, 101*, 583–590. doi:10.1016/j.jbusres.2018.11.013

Fichman, R. G., Dos Santos, B. L., & Zheng, Z. (2014). Digital innovation as a fundamental and powerful concept in the information systems curriculum. *Management Information Systems Quarterly, 38*(2), 329–A315. doi:10.25300/MISQ/2014/38.2.01

Flyverbom, M., Huysman, M., & Matten, D. (2016). *Sub-theme 63: digital transformations: technology, organization and governance in the algorithmic age.* Academic Press.

Grisold, T., Wurm, B., Mendling, J., & Vom Brocke, J. (2020). *Using process mining to support theorizing about change in organizations.* Academic Press.

Hernes, T. (2017). Process as the becoming of temporal trajectory. In *The Sage handbook of process organization studies* (pp. 601–607). SAGE Publications.

Ho, J., Tian, F., Wu, A., & Xu, S. X. (2017). Seeking value through deviation? Economic impacts of IT overinvestment and underinvestment. *Information Systems Research, 28*(4), 850–862. doi:10.1287/isre.2017.0710

Kleis, L., Chwelos, P., Ramirez, R. V., & Cockburn, I. (2012). Information technology and intangible output: The impact of IT investment on innovation productivity. *Information Systems Research, 23*(1), 42–59. doi:10.1287/isre.1100.0338

Kyriakou, V., Garagounis, I., Vasileiou, E., Vourros, A., & Stoukides, M. (2017). Progress in the electrochemical synthesis of ammonia. *Catalysis Today, 286*, 2–13. doi:10.1016/j.cattod.2016.06.014

Leonardi, P. M. (2011). When flexible routines meet flexible technologies: Affordance, constraint, and the imbrication of human and material agencies. *Management Information Systems Quarterly, 35*(1), 147–167. doi:10.2307/23043493

Leonhardt, D., Haffke, I., Kranz, J., & Benlian, A. (2017). *Reinventing the IT function: the Role of IT Agility and IT Ambidexterity in Supporting Digital Business Transformation.* Paper presented at the ECIS.

Li, W., & Qiu, Z. (2006). State-of-the-art technologies and methodologies for collaborative product development systems. *International Journal of Production Research, 44*(13), 2525–2559. doi:10.1080/00207540500422080

Lobo, S., & Whyte, J. (2017). Aligning and Reconciling: Building project capabilities for digital delivery. *Research Policy*, *46*(1), 93–107. doi:10.1016/j.respol.2016.10.005

Lusch, R. F., & Nambisan, S. (2015). Service innovation. *Management Information Systems Quarterly*, *39*(1), 155–176. doi:10.25300/MISQ/2015/39.1.07

Lyytinen, K., Yoo, Y., & Boland, R. J. Jr. (2016). Digital product innovation within four classes of innovation networks. *Information Systems Journal*, *26*(1), 47–75. doi:10.1111/isj.12093

Malins, J., & Liapis, A. (2010). IT-based tools to support new product design: A case study of a design consultancy firm. In *Information Technology and Product Development* (pp. 65–79). Springer. doi:10.1007/978-1-4419-1081-3_4

Mendling, J., Pentland, B. T., & Recker, J. (2020). *Building a complementary agenda for business process management and digital innovation.* Taylor & Francis. doi:10.1080/0960085X.2020.1755207

Mendling, J., Weber, I., Aalst, W. V. D., Brocke, J. V., Cabanillas, C., Daniel, F., ... Dustdar, S. (2018). Blockchains for business process management-challenges and opportunities. *ACM Transactions on Management Information Systems*, *9*(1), 1–16. doi:10.1145/3183367

Mikalef, P., & Krogstie, J. (2020). Examining the interplay between big data analytics and contextual factors in driving process innovation capabilities. *European Journal of Information Systems*, *29*(3), 260–287. doi:10.1080/0960085X.2020.1740618

Mithas, S., Krishnan, M. S., & Fornell, C. (2016). Research note—Information technology, customer satisfaction, and profit: Theory and evidence. *Information Systems Research*, *27*(1), 166–181. doi:10.1287/isre.2015.0609

Nambisan, S. (2013). Information technology and product/service innovation: A brief assessment and some suggestions for future research. *Journal of the Association for Information Systems*, *14*(4), 1. doi:10.17705/1jais.00327

Nambisan, S. (2017). Digital entrepreneurship: Toward a digital technology perspective of entrepreneurship. *Entrepreneurship Theory and Practice*, *41*(6), 1029–1055. doi:10.1111/etap.12254

Nambisan, S., & Baron, R. A. (2010). Different roles, different strokes: Organizing virtual customer environments to promote two types of customer contributions. *Organization Science*, *21*(2), 554–572. doi:10.1287/orsc.1090.0460

Nambisan, S., Lyytinen, K., Majchrzak, A., & Song, M. (2017). Digital Innovation Management: Reinventing innovation management research in a digital world. *Management Information Systems Quarterly*, *41*(1), 223–238. doi:10.25300/MISQ/2017/41:1.03

Nambisan, S., Lyytinen, K., & Yoo, Y. (2020). Digital innovation: towards a transdisciplinary perspective. In *Handbook of Digital Innovation*. Edward Elgar Publishing. doi:10.4337/9781788119986.00008

Nambisan, S., Wright, M., & Feldman, M. (2019). The digital transformation of innovation and entrepreneurship: Progress, challenges and key themes. *Research Policy*, *48*(8), 103773. doi:10.1016/j.respol.2019.03.018

Ordanini, A., & Rubera, G. (2010). How does the application of an IT service innovation affect firm performance? A theoretical framework and empirical analysis on e-commerce. *Information & Management*, *47*(1), 60–67. doi:10.1016/j.im.2009.10.003

Pentland, B. T., Recker, J., Wolf, J. R., & Wyner, G. (2020). Bringing context inside process research with digital trace data. *Journal of the Association for Information Systems*, *21*(5), 5. doi:10.17705/1jais.00635

Ravichandran, T., Han, S., & Mithas, S. (2017). Mitigating diminishing returns to R&D: The role of information technology in innovation. *Information Systems Research*, *28*(4), 812–827. doi:10.1287/isre.2017.0717

Satyal, S., Weber, I., Paik, H.-y., Di Ciccio, C., & Mendling, J. (2019). Business process improvement with the AB-BPM methodology. *Information Systems*, *84*, 283–298. doi:10.1016/j.is.2018.06.007

Schmiedel, T., & vom Brocke, J. (2015). Business process management: Potentials and challenges of driving innovation. In *Bpm-driving innovation in a digital world* (pp. 3–15). Springer. doi:10.1007/978-3-319-14430-6_1

Urbinati, A., Bogers, M., Chiesa, V., & Frattini, F. (2019). Creating and capturing value from Big Data: A multiple-case study analysis of provider companies. *Technovation*, *84*, 21–36. doi:10.1016/j.technovation.2018.07.004

Van den Bergh, J., Thijs, S., & Viaene, S. (2014). *Transforming Through Processes: Leading Voices on BPM, People and Technology*. Springer. doi:10.1007/978-3-319-03937-4

Van Der Aalst, W. (2012). Process mining: Overview and opportunities. *ACM Transactions on Management Information Systems*, *3*(2), 1–17. doi:10.1145/2229156.2229157

Van der Aalst, W. M., Weske, M., & Grünbauer, D. (2005). Case handling: A new paradigm for business process support. *Data & Knowledge Engineering*, *53*(2), 129–162. doi:10.1016/j.datak.2004.07.003

Van Looy, A. (2021). A quantitative and qualitative study of the link between business process management and digital innovation. *Information & Management*, *58*(2), 103413. doi:10.1016/j.im.2020.103413

von Briel, F., Davidsson, P., & Recker, J. (2018). Digital technologies as external enablers of new venture creation in the IT hardware sector. *Entrepreneurship Theory and Practice*, *42*(1), 47–69. doi:10.1177/1042258717732779

Von Hippel, E., & Von Krogh, G. (2016). Crossroads—Identifying viable "need–solution pairs": Problem solving without problem formulation. *Organization Science*, *27*(1), 207–221.

Winter, S., Berente, N., Howison, J., & Butler, B. (2014). Beyond the organizational 'container': Conceptualizing 21st century sociotechnical work. *Information and Organization*, *24*(4), 250–269. doi:10.1016/j.infoandorg.2014.10.003

Woodard, C. J., Ramasubbu, N., Tschang, F. T., & Sambamurthy, V. (2013). Design capital and design moves: The logic of digital business strategy. *Management Information Systems Quarterly*, *37*(2), 537–564. doi:10.25300/MISQ/2013/37.2.10

Yadav, M. S., & Pavlou, P. A. (2014). Marketing in computer-mediated environments: Research synthesis and new directions. *Journal of Marketing*, *78*(1), 20–40. doi:10.1509/jm.12.0020

Yoo, Y., Henfridsson, O., & Lyytinen, K. (2010). Research commentary—the new organizing logic of digital innovation: An agenda for information systems research. *Information Systems Research, 21*(4), 724–735. doi:10.1287/isre.1100.0322

ADDITIONAL READING

Curley, M., & Salmelin, B. (2017). *Open innovation 2.0: The new mode of digital innovation for prosperity and sustainability*. Springer.

Grisold, T., vom Brocke, J., Gross, S., Mendling, J., Röglinger, M., & Stelzl, K. (2021). Digital Innovation and Business Process Management: Opportunities and Challenges as Perceived by Practitioners. *Communications of the Association for Information Systems, 49*(1), 556–571. doi:10.17705/1CAIS.04927

Hjalmarsson, A., Juell-Skielse, G., & Johannesson, P. (2017). Open Digital Innovation Contest. In *Open Digital Innovation* (pp. 11–21). Springer. doi:10.1007/978-3-319-56339-8_3

Lederer, M., Knapp, J., & Schott, P. (2017, March). The digital future has many names—How business process management drives the digital transformation. In *2017 6th International Conference on Industrial Technology and Management (ICITM)* (pp. 22-26). IEEE.

Ramrattan, L., & Szenberg, M. (2015). *Revolutions in book publishing: the effects of digital innovation on the industry*. Springer.

Silkina, G. Y., Shevchenko, S., & Sharapaev, P. (2021). Digital innovation in process management. *Academy of Strategic Management Journal, 20*, 1–25.

Vom Brocke, J., & Schmiedel, T. (Eds.). (2015). *BPM-driving innovation in a digital world*. Springer. doi:10.1007/978-3-319-14430-6

KEY TERMS AND DEFINITIONS

Business Process Management: Is the process of discovering, designing, automating, and monitoring business activities to detect deviations, and achieve compliance and sustainability.

Digital Innovation: Is the process of incorporating digital technologies to capture and create value.

Digital Technology: Is a tool or platform that is enabled by or embodied in information and communication technologies, such as social media, mobile devices, big data, process mining, Internet of Things, etc.

Digitalization: Is the process of transforming information into digital format.

Innovation Process: Is the set of activities from problem identification to solution recognition, formulation, and market launch.

Operand Resource: Is the set of tangible resources that shapes the competitive advantage of an organization.

Operant Resource: Is the set of intangible knowledge and skills that acts upon operand resources.

Chapter 3
Emerging Technologies for Innovation and Productivity Management in the Automotive Industry:
Impact of Digital Transformation on Communication

Anthony D. Bolton
https://orcid.org/0000-0002-1259-7479
University of South Africa, South Africa

Leila Goosen
https://orcid.org/0000-0003-4948-2699
University of South Africa, South Africa

Elmarie Kritzinger
https://orcid.org/0000-0002-5141-4348
University of South Africa, South Africa

ABSTRACT

The purpose of this chapter is to answer the primary research question associated with the empirical study, around the extent to which the introduction of emerging unified communications and collaboration (UC&C) technologies for innovation and productivity management within the context of large-scale automotive design, manufacturing, and business operations at General Motors (GM), a leader in the global automotive industry, influenced the impact of digital transformation on communication and collaboration.

DOI: 10.4018/978-1-7998-9059-1.ch003

INTRODUCTION

This section will introduce the area described in general in the chapter and end by specifically stating how the **objective** of the chapter bridges these gaps.

Boisit (1998) pointed to knowledge assets and innovation as key to securing competitive advantage in the information economy. *Innovation* in terms of "the act of creating a new product or process" (Kahn, 2012, p. 454), as well as business models, help industry to provide economic value to their customers. Discovering innovative opportunities and exploring, generating, championing and then implementing these ideas (Ngugi & Goosen, 2021), including "the work required to bring an idea or concept to" the market (Kahn, 2012, p. 454), require investing a lot of resources that could incur large costs. Enterprise management of **emerging technologies** could support industry to foster *innovation* towards remaining competitive in the marketplace (Glazer, Kenkins & Schaper, 2005). This chapter intends to serve as a platform for resources related to technology absorption in industry to impact *innovation* and productivity management. Practices, successful reporting, empirical findings and results (well-supported by validations) will be considered. **Lessons learned from** *innovation* efforts made to tackle the coronavirus are also included.

This chapter introduces an area of research related to the implementation of **emerging** Unified Communications and Collaboration (UC&C) **technologies** for productivity and *innovation* management within the context of large-scale automotive design, manufacture and business operations at General Motors (GM), a leader in the global automotive industry. It further discusses how the chapter bridges the gaps presented through the design of the research developed with the purpose of evaluating the impact of said **emerging technologies**. In terms of mentioning what **problems** existed, prior to the research undertaking reported on in this chapter, General Motors had not implemented unified communications within its manufacturing, design or business operation functions and had not engaged in the development of an Internet of Things (IoT)-related digitization strategy.

Research Approach and Justification

According to Miles, Huberman and Saldana (2014, p. 7), "research is actually more of a craft … than a slavish adherence to methodological rules. No study confirms exactly to a standard methodology; each one calls for the research to bend the methodology to the uniqueness of the setting or case."

The approach for this research comprised of literature and empirical studies on the deployment and impact of unified communications and collaboration technologies over a four-year period at General Motors, one of the world's largest automotive manufacturers. The underlying research design centered on a qualitative research approach, leveraging case study research that included documentation review and qualitative methods, including interviews and surveys. As described by Taylor, Bodgan and DeVault (2016), a qualitative methodology refers in a broad sense to a process of research that produces descriptive data. The descriptive data produced represents people's own written or spoken words and observable behavior.

The research approach, design and associated methods leveraged within the scope of this study were specially selected to facilitate evaluation of user perceptions of productivity and *innovation* post-implementation of General Motors' unified communications and collaboration architecture and service deployment. The phenomenological perspective is central to a qualitative research approach and methodology.

Open coding was leveraged to examine and analyze the perceptions of participants. Open coding techniques are frequently leveraged in qualitative research to develop a theory that is grounded in data organizationally and systematically (Yin, 2011). Open coding also facilitated the process of investigating, comparing, conceptualizing and assigning categories to specific phenomena (Urquhart, 2013).

Objective

Similar to the theme of the book, the **objective** of this chapter will be to highlight the role of emerging communication and collaboration technologies in assisting the global automotive industry to innovate their products, processes and business models. The accurate selection of such technologies can help them to innovate at lower costs. The chapter will also show how these provided them with the necessary criteria and guidelines for the selection and implementation of **emerging technologies** and in what situations to use these (Goosen, 2004).

BACKGROUND

This section of the chapter and the next will provide broad *definitions* and discussions of the topic and incorporate views of others (in the form of a literature review) into the discussion to support, refute, or demonstrate the authors' position on the topic of the chapter on emerging technologies for innovation and productivity management in the automotive industry in terms of the impact of digital transformation on communication and collaboration.

Technology-Based Innovation Amid, and Lessons Learned From Covid

In a context, which quickly became part of the daily work scenario, Skowron, Rank, Garcia and Holyst (2017) were Zooming in on studying collective cyber-emotions in cyberspace, while computer lecturers were using their institutional Learning Management System (LMS) for Information and Communication Technology (ICT) education in the cyber world (Goosen & Naidoo, 2014). Similarly, against the **background** of computer science and its applications, Martinik (2015) looked at ubiquitous rich-media information technologies and the use of these in crisis management communication. Finally, Demerouti, Derks, Lieke and Bakker (2014) investigated new ways of working in terms of the impact of ICTs on the quality of working life and conditions, as well as work-family balance and well-being.

In line with two of the **recommended topics** for the book, towards the post-**Covid**-19 era, Bolton, Goosen and Kritzinger (2021b) reported on an empirical study into the impact on innovation and productivity with regard to digital transformation of an automotive enterprise, while Ngugi and Goosen (2021) published a chapter in the same context on innovation, entrepreneurship and sustainability for ICT students. Van Heerden and Goosen (2021) answered questions in terms of students' perceptions of e-assessment in the context of **Covid**-19 regarding a case study of the University of South Africa (UNISA), whereas Goosen (Goosen, 2021) shared organizational knowledge and administration **lessons learned from** an ICT for Development (ICT4D) Massive Open Online Course (MOOC) – the latter included the use of educational technologies for an ICT4D MOOC in the 21st century (Goosen, 2015).

Corresponding to another one of the **recommended topics** for the book, a chapter by Goosen (Goosen, 2019) described research on *technology-supported* teaching and learning.

In the context of management science, Ebadi and Utterback (1984) investigated the effects of communication on *technological* **innovation**.

A chapter by Bolton, Goosen and Kritzinger (2021a) on unified communication technologies at a global automotive organization provided details on the theoretical model and design thereof, while an earlier conference paper by Bolton, Goosen and Kritzinger (2016) on enterprise digitization enablement through Unified Communication and Collaboration (UC&C) technologies, for example, supplied a definition of theory.

Primary Research Question

The primary research question associated with this study was: *To what extent do emerging technologies for innovation and productivity management in the global automotive industry influence the impact of digital transformation on communication and collaboration?*

Research Variables

Independence of observations is the assumption that the selection of any given "study participant is not related to the selection of any other participant" (Dattalo, 2013, p. 8).

Theory Development

The theory developed proposed that a subsequent increase in communication accessibility helps to foster relationships and collaboration among teams, leading to a perceived increase in productivity and capacity to drive innovation. Figure 1 presents a model showing the theoretical alignment of emerging UC&C technologies and digital transformation with the research questions and developed hypotheses. This model also highlights the proposed end user outcomes that were evaluated in the empirical study.

Figure 1. Development of hypotheses aligned to primary and secondary research questions

The structure for this model was derived from data reviewed within the research literature, identifying suggested enhancements to the communication and collaboration of end users through emerging UC&C technologies. These enhancements are aligned with the primary and secondary research questions, leading to the proposed hypotheses that were established for the empirical evaluation. End user outcomes in the form of productivity and innovation were highlighted, along with alignment to individual and organization impact. These outcomes were focused on for the purpose of the evaluation of the primary research question and explored in the empirical investigation and analysis of findings.

The consolidated model facilitated the compression of the research questions and the establishment of four related research hypotheses:

Digital Transformation Through Emerging Technologies

H1: Digital transformation of communication and collaboration achieved through **emerging technologies** results in increased inclusion and engagement of individuals and teams across the global automotive industry.

Raine and Wellman (2012) highlighted emerging technologies in the context of the new social operating system.

In their study associated with the question of social connectedness and inclusion via digital augmentation in public spaces, Brenny and Hu (2013) proposed that digital interaction through shared mediums supported a higher level of connectedness among individuals within the populations of large cities. The concept of enhanced connectedness via the leverage of unified communications and collaboration technologies is possible due to its flexible integration framework and consolidated delivery of digitally enabled and enhanced communication and collaboration functions.

Figure 2 highlights the pathways enabled for communication and collaboration, as well as the establishment of virtual inclusion via features and digital capabilities commonly found in UC&C **solutions**. The model depicted was developed within the scope of the research study and applied and evaluated via the empirical research and case study carried out through the deployment of an Enhanced UC&C (E-UC&C) framework at General Motors. This model provided a guide for the development of cyber-physical integrations, extending the communication and collaboration of people and human-social networks through the digital transformation of systems and processes.

Figure 2. Model for digital transformation

Digitally Transformed Social Presence

H2: Digitally transformed social presence and real-time status indicators positively influence the perception of increased productivity in individual and team performance.

In the context of digital games as *social presence* **emerging technologies**, De Kort, IJsselstijn and Poels (2007) discussed the development of the Social Presence in Gaming Questionnaire (SPGQ) against the background of the social psychology of telecommunications by Short, Williams and Christie (1976).

Figure 3 presents a summary model of the elements that contribute to the establishment of a digitally transformed social presence. This summary visual model is a synthesis of processes and technology that will aid in establishing a digital presence that mirrors the function of presence awareness in the physical world.

Figure 3. Elements contributing to digital presence

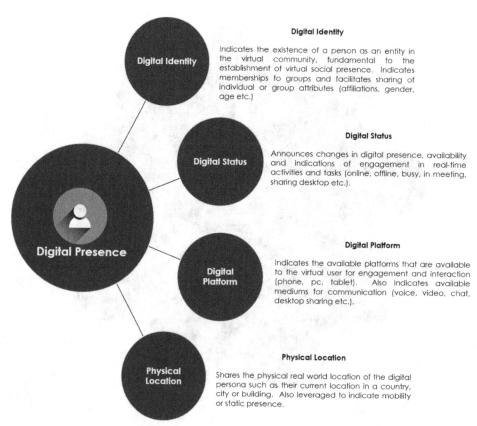

Digitally Transformed Persona via Emerging Technologies

H3: Digitally transformed multi-channel persona capabilities facilitated through a consolidated software client influence the perception of increased productivity in individuals.

H4: Enterprise-wide engagement through digitally transformed **emerging technologies** can increase engagement in innovation generating activities across the global automotive industry value chain.

When digitally transformed virtual groups are working in the Information Technology (IT) industry, they seek to communicate emotional information, in addition to factual information and data, similar to that found in face-to-face communication (Chmiel, et al., 2011).

Against the **background** of cross-disciplinary, inter-disciplinary and trans-disciplinary applications of electronic collaboration approaches and **emerging technologies** (Goosen, 2018b; Kock, 2013), Figure 4 proposes a model supporting the complementary interplay of digitally transformed synchronous and asynchronous communication achieved through **emerging technologies**. Building on the concepts of Kock (2005), as well as organizational information requirements, media richness and structural design (Daft & Lengel, 1986), the model visually describes the interplay of synchronous and asynchronous communication and collaboration channels in the establishment of a digitally transformed communication and collaboration experience for the end user. The resulting enhanced experience facilitates and promotes psychological arousal, perception, and increased motivation, while enhancing cognitive processes associated with the processing and analysis of data and information.

Figure 4. Model for enhanced synchronous and asynchronous digital communication enhancement

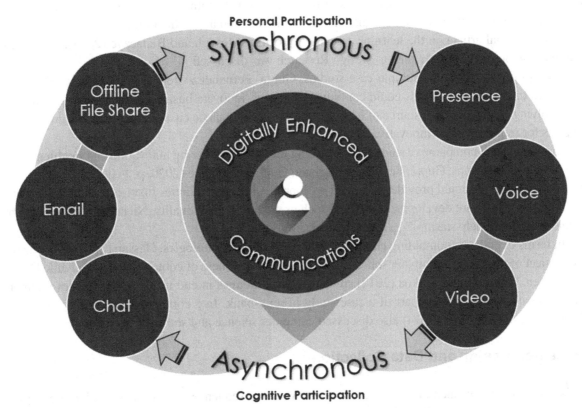

In the context of transactions on professional communication, Robert and Dennis (2005) provided a cognitive model of media choice against the **background** of the paradox of richness, while Dennis, Fuller and Valacich (2009) offered a theoretical and empirical overview of media synchronicity and media choice when choosing media for performance.

MAIN FOCUS OF THE CHAPTER

Issues, Problems and Challenges

This section of the chapter will present the authors' perspective on the **issues**, **problems**, **challenges**, etc., as these relate to the main theme of the book, on emerging technologies for innovation management in the software industry, and arguments supporting the authors' position. It will also compare and contrast with what has been, or is currently being, done as it relates to the specific topic of the chapter on emerging technologies for innovation and productivity management in the automotive industry in terms of the impact of digital transformation on communication and collaboration.

In the journal article on the learning sciences by Collins, Joseph and Bielaczyc (2004), theoretical and methodological **issues** related to Design Research was discussed.

Based on insights from multiple case studies, Gupta, Fernandez-Crehuet and Hanne (2020, p. 1) indicated that software startups could continuously foster "innovate business model value proposition by involving freelancers as a source of innovative ideas (that enhance customer perceived value) and as experts for implementing" innovative ideas.

In an empirical comparative study on freelancing models for fostering innovation and **problem** solving in software startups, Gupta, Fernandez-Crehuet, Gupta and Hanne (2020, p. 1) indicated that "freelancers and startups could provide each other with promising opportunities that lead to mutual growth, by improving software development metrics, such as cost, time, and quality. Niche skills processed by freelancers could help startups" to reduce uncertainties.

In terms of end user computing **challenges** and **emerging technologies**, Hassan (2007) investigated the impact of multi-level computer self-efficacy on the effectiveness of computer training, while Oinas-Kukkonen, Hohtari and Paekkoa (2012) studied new **challenges** in end user computing, development and *software engineering* as part of a case study of an e-bank. In a computing handbook, Gonzalez, Diaz-Herrera and Tucker (2014) also discussed computer science and *software engineering*.

Research Design and Data Collection

This research was planned and conducted in a progressive sequence of five phases. Figure 5 depicts the five phases that were followed within the structure of the research study. These five phases include the initial literature study, framework proposal, framework deployment, data gathering, and evaluation.

Figure 5. Five primary research phases engaged in this study

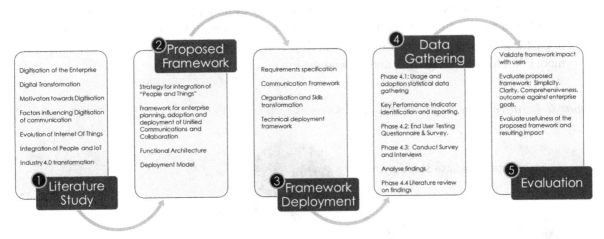

1. The initial phase involved a detailed review and analysis of scholarly and industry literature associated with the case study, with primary topics including digital transformation, influencing factors, Industry 4.0 and cyber-physical integration. As presented in the following **chapters**, it provided a pathway to establish and delimit the primary research question:

   a. An Empirical Study into the Impact on Innovation and Productivity towards the post-Covid-19 era: Digital Transformation of an Automotive Enterprise (Bolton, et al., 2021b);

   b. The Integration and Implementation of the Internet of Things Through Digital Transformation: Impact on Productivity and Innovation (Bolton, Goosen, & Kritzinger, 2021c); and

   c. The impact of unified communication and collaboration technologies on productivity and innovation towards promotion for the Fourth Industrial Revolution (4IR) (Bolton, Goosen, & Kritzinger, 2020b).

A review of the digitization of modern industry, as well as communication and collaboration, through the literature study, also served to place the primary research question in context.

2. A provisional framework was established and aligned with the primary subject of the research case study (General Motors) in the second research phase. Phase 2 was envisioned to facilitate the delivery of a strategy to integrate people with a digitally transformed enterprise. The framework was inclusive of a functional reference architecture and deployment model.

3. Phase 3 centered on the subsequent implementation and deployment of the framework and associated emerging technologies within the business enterprise of the iterative case study subject through a phased program as depicted in Figure 6.

4. This implementation established a foundation for data gathering and analysis of the resulting impact via the fourth phase. Phase 4 also focused on the aggregation of data for the purpose of evaluation as discussed in subsections describing data collection with regard to the interviews and secondary

sources, as well as **solutions** in terms of the emerging communication and collaboration technologies deployed and unified communication and collaboration production adoption and usage metrics.

5. The fifth and final phase of the study was focused on the evaluation of data and outcomes recorded from the empirical study, with discussion aligned to the research hypotheses. This evaluation of impact lead to the proposal of **future research directions** in terms of potential refinements of the model developed in stage two, and the **conclusion**.

Figure 6. Iterative process of case study development

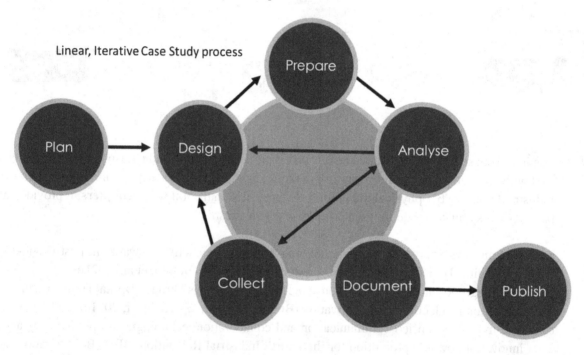

Research Instrument: Case Study

Case studies as a research method are used in many situations (Yin, 2011). A case study can be used to establish, review and contribute to the knowledge of an organization, group or individual and associated phenomenon, for example, social, technical or behavioral aspects. A vital component of this research was a case study on the observed effects that the introduction of emerging UC&C technologies had on General Motors, representing a large international automotive enterprise. Creswell (2007, p. 73) *defined* a case study as "a qualitative approach in which the investigator explores a bounded system (a case) or multiple bounded systems (cases) over time, through detailed, in-depth data collection involving multiple sources of information (e.g., observations, interviews" and documents), and reports a case description and case-based themes.

The case study was combined with other methods, incorporating sustainable and inclusive quality survey data obtained through research-informed practice (Goosen, 2018a), to establish and elaborate on the hypotheses associated with the research purpose of studying the impact of emerging unified communication and collaboration technologies on productivity and innovation management in automotive manufacturing, design and operations. Houghton, Casey, Shaw and Murphy (2013, p. 12) suggested that the quality of qualitative research cannot be "judged comparatively" with quantitative research methods that underscore the importance of validity and reliability.

The case study provided a tool through which the focus and refinement of the scope was established relating to the broader topic of **emerging technologies**' influence on productivity and innovation. The MAIN FOCUS of the study was a leader in the global automotive industry, with the observation of the subject pre- through post-implementation of the emerging technologies and features. The subject of the case study in this research (General Motors) represented an industry specific to that of an automotive Original Equipment Manufacturer (OEM). General Motors enterprise comprises of many business functions that are common across the industry (finance, marketing, IT, legal, Human Resources (HR), sales, manufacturing and product design) and represents an extensive global enterprise. The approach of combining case study and survey methods aligned to resolve some of the **challenges** that Yin (2009) highlighted about case study design. Yin (2009) also suggested that due to education and language diversity (Libbrecht & Goosen, 2015) and the richness of observed phenomenon associated with the real-life context of case studies, researchers must contend with more variables of interest than data points.

Figure 6 depicted the iterative process leveraged in the development of the research case study. Stemming from the originating case study plan, the case study design was iteratively revised and optimized throughout the deployment lifecycle. Optimization was largely driven by taking feedback and experience gained from analyzing the outcomes of individual case study deployment plans and collected data. Information gained from the iterative review of these elements across the phased technical deployment plan, summarized in Figure 8, was leveraged to continually improve and optimize the design as the study progressed.

This process was an important factor in the management of change throughout the case study lifecycle, as it progressed from envisioning of the E-UC&C framework, and the introduction through a limited 505 user pilot phase, through to complete deployment at enterprise scale inclusive of over 89,000 employees.

Data Collection: Survey

In the context of research, surveys are generally designed to produce statics relevant to a given population, facilitating the inference of characteristics by obtaining answers from a sample of respondents (Fowler, 2009). The premise of the survey process posited that by describing a sample group of respondents, the more extensive applicable population can be described. Application of this approach provided an efficient tool for the evaluation of observed phenomenon within an extensive group, such as the diverse population of over 110,000 employees, who were engaged in the emerging UC&C technologies deployment. Sapsford (2007) suggested that there are four primary elements involved in the central planning of a survey. These elements include the **problem** definition; sample selection (targeted respondent group); design and selection of measurements, and consideration of social and ethical responsibilities. This study was approved by the Ethical Clearance Committee of the College of Science, Engineering and Technology (CSET) of UNISA, to ensure that ethical **solutions** were produced, while maintaining ethical data management and research integrity (Goosen, 2018d) in the context of the community being engaged (Goosen, 2018c).

Figure 7 outlines the process and primary elements involved in the research survey design. The research design highlighted the iterative process involved in development of the research questions. The design of the defined **problem**, sample selection process, data measurement and ethical considerations were developed through an interactive process of feedback, enhancing the design of each component. The convergence of resulting designs in each of the primary elements of the survey resulted in a robust, complete and defined survey process and implementation plan.

Figure 7. Research survey design process

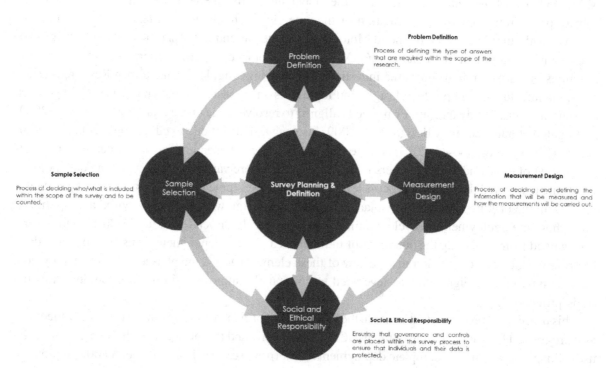

The research survey started in September 2017, following the deployment of a unified communication and collaboration framework and technologies portfolio across General Motors' global operations. The survey targeted participation across functions, representing all business functions and multiple geographies. General Motors has operations in over 300 office and manufacturing plant locations globally. The UC&C framework and emerging technologies are now deployed to over 110,000 employees.

The qualitative survey approach emphasized the importance of ensuring that no unnatural stimuli were introduced to the subjects during the process of data gathering. General Motors represents a highly distributed global organization, and employees are frequently engaged to participate in online digital surveys and questionnaires relating to business matters.

Care was taken within the scope of the survey design to ensure that the presentation and format of the study survey aligned aesthetically and was presented in a manner that was consistent with the prior experience of employees with online questionnaires. The design of the survey questions was focused on the **objective** of gathering data and establishing core categories, processes, concepts and behaviors affecting individuals, who had experienced the shift to the digitization of communication and collaboration through emerging technologies within the GM enterprise. The survey design was iteratively reviewed and modified through three cycles of pre-production publication to the target user group. An initial set of questions was developed and tested by a group of 20 business users in July 2016. Feedback from survey pilot user group and input from the GM corporate communications team were used for further refinement of the survey questions and answer options.

Two additional test surveys were implemented with iterative refinements, in August 2016, before publication to the target research survey group in September 2017. One of the critical **challenges** faced by the research team was the establishment of questions and answers that could be commonly interpreted and understood across a diverse scope of technical, administrative and business users, across multiple geographies and across many countries where English was a second language. The standard business language within GM is English, and the survey was presented in English.

The questions within the survey were designed to gain valuable insight and concepts arising from employee adoption and use of digital communication and collaboration facilitated via **emerging technologies** and capturing data relating to the employees' qualitative perspectives and perceptions of impact on their productivity (Goosen & Mukasa-Lwanga, 2017). The questions also sought to gather data to identify whether emerging UC&C technologies impacted (positively, negatively or not at all) their ability to engage and drive activity that contributed to the generation of innovation within the value chain of GM's business.

In a journal article on the security aspects of an empirical study into the impact of digital transformation via unified communication and collaboration technologies on the productivity and innovation of a global automotive enterprise, Bolton, Goosen and Kritzinger (2020a, p. 103) indicated that a "sample group of 2,000 employees, chosen as representative across all GM business functions and regions, were invited to participate in the survey."

The survey was designed to protect the anonymity of all participants, with no personal information collected or summarized in the results of the study. Alignment to General Motors business function was captured, along with the GM business region associated with each participant.

The survey consisted of a total of thirteen questions. Twelve questions were mandatory and required for registration of a complete submission, and one question relating to gender was optional. Individual survey questions and associated answer options is conveyed in Table 1. The qualtrics cloud platform was leveraged to develop, publish, administer and maintain the survey (http://www.qualtrics.com).

Data Collection: Interviews

The benefits of interviewing as a research method center on the capabilities of language to facilitate inquiry when human beings are the source of data for research (Seidman, 2013). When carried out via a structured approach, such as grounded theory, interviews can enrich research data. When provided with the opportunity to speak freely, people can convey a wealth of contextual information relative to the phenomenon being observed and explored. Seidman (2013) also highlighted the ability of humans to symbolize their experience through language. Nathaniel (2012) posited that the process of theory and hypothesis development relies on the existence of observable, predictable patterns.

Grounded theory is a method for establishing theory from data systematically obtained, with the resulting theories grounded in the perspectives of people (Gibson & Hartman, 2014). Grounded theory is one of the most widely used research methodologies and is applied across many disciplines, including marketing, business, architecture and sociology. Glaser and Strauss (2017, p. 4) suggested that the use of ground theory can "forestall the opportunistic use of theories that have dubious fit and working capacity".

Interviews were conducted between June and September 2016. The interview guide went through an iterative process with four revisions made to the guide based on experience gained through the initial interview process. Revisions to the interview guide focused on provoking more detail in responses focused on the core research questions.

Data Collection: Secondary Sources

To evaluate the findings of the survey and interview results, data from numerous sources were collated and reviewed. Data sources used to support validation included email and website communication developed and distributed in the process of service and technologies deployment to the end user community, end user training materials, pre-deployment and post-deployment support documentation, system and feature usage reporting and post-deployment operational support reports.

The data gathered and reviewed from the secondary sources served to corroborate findings established through the interview and survey research methods (Rubin & Babbie, 2009).

Table 1. Research survey question design and structure

	Question	Answer Options
1	Has Skype made it easier to communicate with work colleagues and business partners?	1. Much easier 2. About the same 3. More difficult
2	Please select the top 3 Skype features that you use most	1. Chat 2. Video call (peer-to-peer) 3. Skype call (peer-to-peer) 4. Video conference (more than 2 participants) 5. Voice conference (more than 2 participants) 6. Desktop Sharing 7. File Transfer
3	How often do you escalate a Skype chat to a voice call (Add a voice call to a chat session)?	1. Most of the time 2. About half of the time 3. Rarely
4	Has the flexible communication capabilities provided by Skype positively impacted your overall productivity?	1. Yes 2. About the same 3. No
5	How easy was it to adapt the Skype tool and use its features?	1. Very easy and intuitive 2. Easy for some features (i.e., chat) not for others 3. Somewhat difficult
6	In relation to communication, how would your productivity be impacted if the Skype client and service were removed?	1. Significantly decreased 2. Somewhat decreased 3. No impact 4. Somewhat increased 5. Significantly increased
7	What, in your opinion, is the most important benefit of Unified Communication and Collaboration (UC&C) technologies?	1. Ability to work on the move/remotely 2. Delivery of multiple features (chat, voice, video) in one tool 3. Multiple device support (PC, laptop, mobile phone, tablet)
8	Do you believe that UC&C technologies have helped	1. Significantly increased 2. Some increase 3. No increase
9	Do you believe that UC&C technologies, such as Skype, increase the ability of General Motors (GM) to drive innovation through collaboration?	4. Yes 1. No

Continued on following page

Table 1. Continued

	Question	Answer Options
10	Please select from the following Skype features those that you would like see to enabled at GM:	2. Conversation history 3. Mobile client integration with Outlook calendar 4. Scheduled Skype meetings 1. Voice mail
11	Please select the GM business function that your organization primarily supports	2. Global Brands, Sales, Service & Marketing 3. Global Communications 4. Global Connected Customer Experience 5. Global Human Resources 6. Global product Development, Purchasing & Supply Chain 7. Global Public Policy 8. Global Quality 9. GM Finance 10. GM Legal 11. It Shared Services 1. Operational Excellence
12	Please select the region that you currently work in	2. GME 3. GMI + China 4. GMNA 5. GMSA
13	Optional: Please identify your gender	1. Female 2. Male 3. I prefer not to disclose

SOLUTIONS AND RECOMMENDATIONS

This section of the chapter will discuss **solutions** and **recommendations** in dealing with the **problems** and **challenges** presented in the preceding section.

The elements contributing to digital presence detailed in Figure 3 are commonly found in unified communication and collaboration **solutions** and referred to in related literature. This model was leveraged in the development of a reference architecture for integrated digital presence functionality within the E-UC&C framework.

Solutions: Emerging Communication and Collaboration Technologies Deployed

Deployment of Emerging Communication and Collaboration Technologies

The scope of the UC&C technologies deployment within the General Motors use case included proactive pre-deployment communication and collaboration top end users. This communication focused on marketing new features, benefits, use-case examples and training materials. The purpose and intent of this communication was to educate the end users on how to leverage the emerging technologies, prepare them for the technologies' introduction and educate them on appropriate use-cases believed to deliver maximum benefits. Research and empirical studies, such as those by Hassan (2007) and Karahanna and Straub (1999), have indicated a positive relationship between perceived ease of use and end user acceptance of emerging technologies. Proactive training and education on the benefits of, for example, using vodcasts in their work environment, was focused on as a core component of the communication and collaboration strategy.

This component of the communication and collaboration strategy was important, as research had shown that users with a higher expectation of their ability to perform lead to the development of great sophistication (McQueen & Mills, 1998). Motivating users via the potential benefits of emerging UC&C technologies and providing proactive education on the features and operations of the UC&C technologies contributed to higher efficacy and thus the users were more likely to be confident in their ability to engage with and adopt the emerging technologies. The results of social research experiments indicate that there is a correlation between increased self-efficacy and proactive, positive reinforcement of an individual's potential capability (Bandura, 2014). Bandura (2014) also posited that changes in perceived self-efficacy mediate performance motivation.

Research by Oinas-Kukkonen, et al. (2012) suggested that well-planned documentation and organization of end user training are influential in the successful adoption of **emerging technologies**. Proactive training motivates individuals to use emerging technologies systems. Oinas-Kukkonen, et al. (2012) also highlighted the importance of continuity in training and communication until users have a sufficient degree of capability to operate emerging technologies independently. Communication to users was implemented via an interactive process over five phases to provide structure, continuity and iterative improvement of end user educational technologies and training materials. The strategy for communication to users involved pre-emptive and proactive communication to familiarize employees with the new services being introduced and motivate adoption by sharing benefits gained through the use of the emerging technologies.

Phase one of the communication initiative started with a pilot group of 505 users that were selected to test the technologies deployment and end user communication and collaboration. Phase three engaged an expanded pre-production pilot group of 8,000 users and leveraged a refined draft of the end user communication materials that were modified based on feedback and iterative review from the phase one pilot. Phase four involved the production of end user communication materials and distribution to all employees, comprising of primary artefacts consisting of web pages, wall posters, social media forums, a support portal, as well as video and print media - social media and mobile internet use are no longer only for teens and young adults (Lenhart, Purcell, & Smith, 2010). Phase five consisted of further feature enhancement and the roll-out of video and voice conferencing functionalities. This phase also included further iterative refinement of the original production materials with the addition of specific training and promotional content to support the voice and video specific features.

Figure 8 depicts the phased structure of the end user communication process aligned to the case study timeline. Detailed upfront development of the end-to-end communication strategy and plan was required to ensure the successful completion of the phased technologies deployment plan. The communication plan played a vital role in the iterative improvement of service and tailoring of end user communication and training to maximize adoption. Success within the case study centered on Key Performance Indicators (KPIs) associated with effective utilization and adoption, as opposed to KPIs that focused on technologies deployment and delivery. Low levels of adoption and use limit the effective capacity to evaluate the research hypotheses associated with increases in productivity and innovation.

Figure 8. Research study – five phased end user communication process

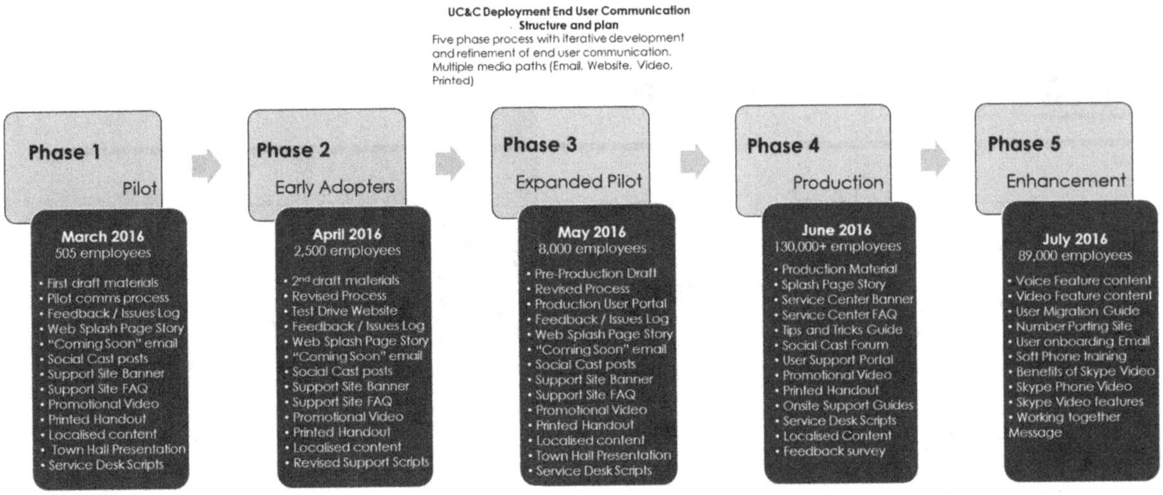

Unified Communication and Collaboration Production Adoption and Usage Metrics

When considering the adoption of **emerging technologies**, subscription versus use was considered. Stewart (1992) made the **recommendation** that subscription to emerging communication and collaboration technologies can be more of a function of organization structure and directives versus actual adoption. Seetaram and Petit (2012) highlighted the benefits of leveraging longitudinal data to empirical researchers, including the observation of change in an investigated entity over time. This research study leveraged service adoption and functionality usage metrics to assist in analyzing and detecting changes in usage versus subscription of the UC&C service and emerging technologies. This data also provided a valuable tool for comparative analysis during and post-deployment and complimentary qualitative data in the evaluation of complex causal observations uncovered within the case study, survey and interviews. Longitudinal data in research, such as subscription and feature use volume over time can contribute to the analysis and further understanding of causal factors in observed change (Dale & Mason, 2011).

The framework of UC&C technologies deployment in the research case study associated with General Motors specified the capturing and reporting of detailed metrics on adoption, feature use and end user **issues**. The volume metrics and data served to validate the General Motors business case and return on investment associated with the project. Usage data was collected from source systems within the deployed scope of the UC&C technologies portfolio and placed into two online dashboards. Reporting was developed within a data visualization tool, Tableau, providing the student and others with easy access to, and interpretation of, collected ICT data in a visual form.

Figure 9 presents the top-level dashboard that was developed within the scope of the research study. This central dashboard was leveraged by the IT project team in GM and provided the researcher with dynamic and near real-time feedback on deployment outcomes, such as end user adoption, service utilization and realization of financial benefits. The dashboard was developed in Sharepoint 2016 with access aligned to the key stakeholders identified within the IT management, operational and toll gate processes of the E-UC&C framework. Reports were created through the acquisition of system data into a Hadoop data repository with reporting through Microsoft Power Business Intelligence (BI) and Tableau.

Figure 9. Online adoption and feature volume usage metric dashboard

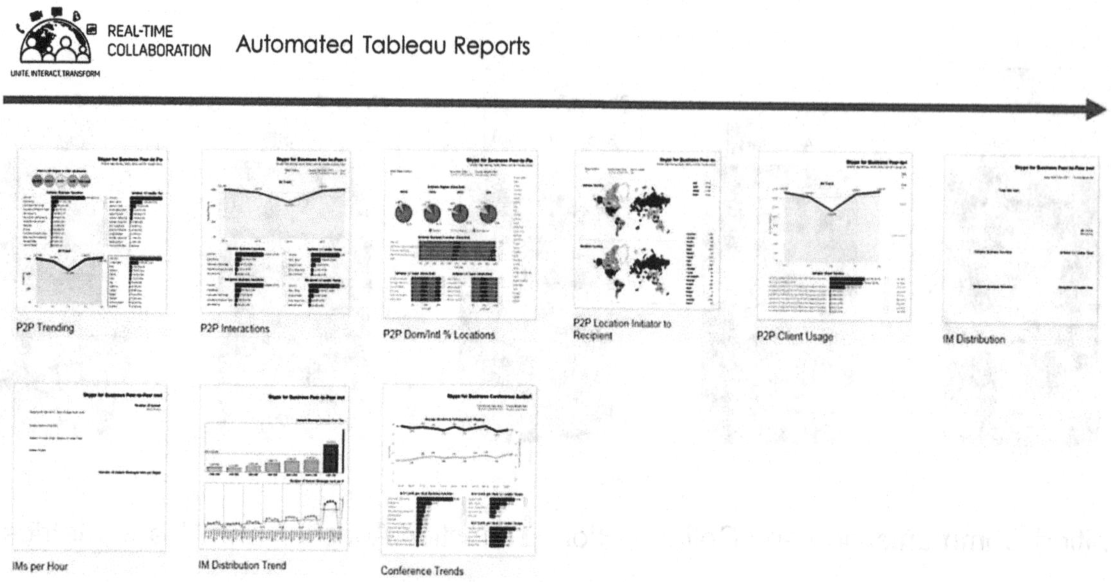

FUTURE RESEARCH DIRECTIONS

This section of the chapter will discuss **future** and **emerging trends** and provide insight about the future of the theme of the book on emerging technologies for innovation management in the software industry, from the perspective of the chapter focus on emerging technologies for innovation and productivity management in the automotive industry in terms of the impact of digital transformation on communication and collaboration. The viability of a paradigm, model, implementation **issues** of proposed programs, etc., may also be included in this section. **Future research directions** within the domain of the topic were mentioned earlier.

An example of what could be discussed here can be found in a chapter on end user computing challenges and technologies, in which Hassan (2007) discussed **emerging trends** with regard to tools and applications.

CONCLUSION

This section of the chapter will provide a discussion of the overall coverage of the chapter and concluding remarks.

The chapter provided a brief **introduction** to the research design and methodology employed within the empirical study, which served as a road map for completing a mainly qualitative dissertation from beginning to end (Dale-Bloomberg & Volpe, 2019). The focused subject of the integrated case study, General Motors, was presented, highlighting justification of the subject selection on the grounds of a unique position within the industry, global scale and the pending drive of GM towards IoT and Industry 4.0 digital transformation.

The introductory section also summarized the case study research **approach** and methods, leveraging a combination of literature review and case study-centered empirical investigation on the impact of digital transformation enabled by emerging UC&C technologies, as well as the possible contribution to theory (Ridder, 2016). The leverage of qualitative methods as a primary method for the research, combined with quantitative data analysis of system adoption and results, was reviewed, placing the focus in **justification** on the need for the production of data-rich observable and quantified metric-driven research data to explore the primary research question and developed hypotheses fully. The application of open coding methods (Yin, 2011) was applied within the research study to facilitate the process of investigation, conceptualization, comparative analysis and category specification of observed phenomena (Urquhart, 2013).

Sections in the chapter by Bolton, et al. (2021a) presented the theoretical framework for, and design of, the research study, highlighting the review of relevant scholarly literature as a foundational element in the establishing of critical concepts for in-depth research and construction of categories for explicit investigation. A summary of the application of evaluative categories in the assessment and exploration of the developed research hypotheses was presented, recognizing the individual creative license available to the researchers in establishing and interpreting their theoretical framework (Lamont-Strayhorn, 2013). The influence of the positions of Schneider (2006) and Fain (2017) on theory establishment highlighted the importance of theoretical development as essential within the process of scientific and technological knowledge.

The theoretical BACKGROUND associated with the research study was discussed, centered around arguments from Mioara (2012) on the necessity of knowledge and communication to society and people and the importance of these as foundational elements of societal and organizational life and as an influence on group behavior.

The primary ***research question*** was established, focused on the *extent to which emerging technologies for innovation and productivity management in the global automotive industry influence the impact of digital transformation on communication and collaboration.*

Three secondary research questions focused on the economic and technological forces influencing a shift towards digital transformation, the landscape of influencing **emerging technologies** and the subsequent impact experienced within the digital automotive industry.

The establishment and framework of *research variables* was discussed, highlighting the priority placed on transformation and digitization within the automotive industry. The importance in the independence of research variables was discussed (Stevens, 2009), focusing attention on situations of non-independence (Dattalo, 2013), active independence of variables (Gliner, Morgan, & Leech, 2009) and **issues** associated with multicollinearity in research (Parke, 2013). Dependent variables within the scope of the research were defined in the form of employee productivity and innovation.

The theoretical framework developed for the investigation and evaluation of the primary research question was presented. A framework for the digital transformation of communication and collaboration technologies was proposed, facilitating the modularization of the research questions and the establishment of four hypotheses that enabled the exploration and evaluation of these. A proposed model for the digital transformation of communication and collaboration technologies was presented, along with a model for the digital representation of presence and a model to support digitally enhanced synchronous and asynchronous communication and collaboration through emerging UC&C technologies.

The structure and process for data collection and analysis within the scope of the research design was summarized. A five-phased research design model was proposed and aligned to the execution and evaluation of the research through a literature review, framework design, framework deployment, data acquisition and evaluation. The primary instruments of research case study (Yin, 2011), research survey, participant interviews, technologies and service framework deployment and quantitative data collection were presented, along with the application of each within the research process.

Further details on how the empirical research was carried out can be obtained from a chapter on the impact of digital transformation via unified communication and collaboration technologies on productivity and innovation at a global enterprise (Bolton, Goosen, & Kritzinger, 2022) in the context of the development of new business models and consumer experience.

REFERENCES

Bandura, A. (2014). Exercise of Personal Agency Through the Self-Efficacy Mechanism. In R. Schwarzer (Ed.), *Self-Efficacy: Thought Control of Action* (pp. 3–38). Routledge.

Boisit, M. (1998). *Knowledge Assets: Securing Competitive Advantage in the Information Economy.* Oxford University Press.

Bolton, A., Goosen, L., & Kritzinger, E. (2016). Enterprise Digitization Enablement Through Unified Communication and Collaboration. *Proceedings of the Annual Conference of the South African Institute of Computer Scientists and Information Technologists.* 10.1145/2987491.2987516

Bolton, A., Goosen, L., & Kritzinger, E. (2020b). The Impact of Unified Communication and Collaboration Technologies on Productivity and Innovation: Promotion for the Fourth Industrial Revolution. In S. B. Buckley (Ed.), *Promoting Inclusive Growth in the Fourth Industrial Revolution* (pp. 44–73). IGI Global. doi:10.4018/978-1-7998-4882-0.ch002

Bolton, A., Goosen, L., & Kritzinger, E. (2021b). An Empirical Study into the Impact on Innovation and Productivity Towards the Post-COVID-19 Era: Digital Transformation of an Automotive Enterprise. In L. C. Carvalho, L. Reis, & C. Silveira (Eds.), *Handbook of Research on Entrepreneurship, Innovation, Sustainability, and ICTs in the Post-COVID-19 Era* (pp. 133–159). IGI Global. doi:10.4018/978-1-7998-6776-0.ch007

Bolton, A., Goosen, L., & Kritzinger, E. (2021c). The Integration and Implementation of the Internet of Things Through Digital Transformation: Impact on Productivity and Innovation. In P. Tomar (Ed.), Integration and Implementation of the Internet of Things Through Cloud Computing (pp. 85-112). IGI Global. doi:10.4018/978-1-7998-6981-8.ch005

Bolton, A. D., Goosen, L., & Kritzinger, E. (2021a). Unified Communication Technologies at a Global Automotive Organization. In M. Khosrow-Pour (Ed.), *Encyclopedia of Organizational Knowledge, Administration, and Technologies* (pp. 2592–2608). IGI Global. doi:10.4018/978-1-7998-3473-1.ch179

Bolton, A. D., Goosen, L., & Kritzinger, E. (2022). Impact of Digital Transformation via Unified Communication and Collaboration Technologies: Productivity and Innovation at a Global Enterprise. In *Impact of Digital Transformation on the Development of New Business Models and Consumer Experience (Approved for publication)*. IGI Global. doi:10.4018/978-1-7998-9179-6.ch014

Bolton, T., Goosen, L., & Kritzinger, E. (2020a, March 8). Security Aspects of an Empirical Study into the Impact of Digital Transformation via Unified Communication and Collaboration Technologies on the Productivity and Innovation of a Global Automotive Enterprise. Communications in Computer and Information Science, 1166, 99-113. doi:10.1007/978-3-030-43276-8_8

Brenny, S., & Hu, J. (2013). Social connectedness and inclusion by digital augmentation in public spaces. *8th International Conference on Design and Semantics of Form and Movement (DeSForm)*, 108-118.

Chmiel, A., Sienkiewicz, J., Thelwall, M., Paltoglou, G., Buckley, K., Kappas, A., & Hołyst, J. (2011). Collective emotions online and their influence on community life. *PLoS One, 6*(7), e22207. Advance online publication. doi:10.1371/journal.pone.0022207 PMID:21818302

Collins, A., Joseph, D., & Bielaczyc, K. (2004). Design Research: Theoretical and Methodological Issues. *Journal of the Learning Sciences, 13*(1), 15–42. doi:10.120715327809jls1301_2

Creswell, J. (2007). Qualitative Inquiry and Research Design: Choosing Among Five Approaches. London: Sage Publications Ltd.

Daft, R., & Lengel, R. (1986). Organizational information requirements, media richness and structural design. *Management Science, 32*(5), 554–571. doi:10.1287/mnsc.32.5.554

Dale, A., & Mason, J. (2011). Understanding Social Research: Thinking Creatively about Method (Illustrated ed.). London: Sage Publications Ltd.

Dale-Bloomberg, L., & Volpe, M. (2019). *Completing Your Qualitative Dissertation: A Road Map From Beginning to End*. London: Sage.

Dattalo, P. (2013). *Analysis of Multiple Dependent Variables*. Oxford University Press. doi:10.1093/acprof:oso/9780199773596.001.0001

De Kort, Y., IJsselstijn, W., & Poels, K. (2007). Digital Games as Social Presence Technology: Development of the Social Presence in Gaming Questionnaire (SPGQ). *Proceedings of PRESENCE*, (pp. 195-203).

Demerouti, E., Derks, D., Lieke, L., & Bakker, A. (2014). New ways of working: Impact on working conditions, work-family balance, and well-being. In C. Korunka & P. Hoonakker (Eds.), *The impact of ICT on quality of working life* (pp. 123–141). Springer. doi:10.1007/978-94-017-8854-0_8

Dennis, A., Fuller, R., & Valacich, J. (2009). Media Synchronicity and Media Choice: Choosing Media for Performance. In T. Hartmann (Ed.), *Media Choice: A Theoretical and Empirical Overview*. Routledge.

Ebadi, Y., & Utterback, J. (1984). The effects of communication on technological innovation. *Management Science, 30*(5), 572–585. doi:10.1287/mnsc.30.5.572

Fain, J. (2017). *Reading, Understanding and Applying Nursing Research*. F.A. Davis Company.

Fowler, F. (2009). *Survey Research Methods* (L. Bickman & D. Rog, Eds.; 4th ed.). Applied Social Research Methods Series. Sage Publications Ltd.

Gibson, B., & Hartman, J. (2014). *Rediscovering Grounded Theory*. Sage Publications Ltd. doi:10.4135/9781529799620

Glaser, B., & Strauss, A. (2017). The Discovery of Grounded Theory: Strategies for qualitative research. London: Routledge.

Gliner, J., Morgan, G., & Leech, N. (2009). Methods. In *Applied Settings: An integrated approach to design analysis* (2nd ed.). Routledge.

Gonzalez, T., Diaz-Herrera, J., & Tucker, A. (2014). *Computing Handbook: Computer Science and Software Engineering*. CRC Press. doi:10.1201/b16812

Goosen, L. (2004). *Criteria and Guidelines for the Selection and Implementation of a First Programming Language in High Schools*. Campus: North West University. Retrieved from http://hdl.handle.net/10394/226

Goosen, L. (2015). Educational Technologies for an ICT4D MOOC in the 21st Century. In D. Nwaozuzu, & S. Mnisi (Ed.), *Proceedings of the South Africa International Conference on Educational Technologies* (pp. 37 - 48). Pretoria: African Academic Research Forum.

Goosen, L. (2018a). Sustainable and Inclusive Quality Education Through Research Informed Practice on Information and Communication Technologies in Education. In L. Webb (Ed.), *Proceedings of the 26th Conference of the Southern African Association for Research in Mathematics, Science and Technology Education (SAARMSTE)* (pp. 215 - 228). Gabarone: University of Botswana.

Goosen, L. (2018b). Trans-Disciplinary Approaches to Action Research for e-Schools, Community Engagement, and ICT4D. In T. A. Mapotse (Ed.), *Cross-Disciplinary Approaches to Action Research and Action Learning* (pp. 97–110). IGI Global. doi:10.4018/978-1-5225-2642-1.ch006

Goosen, L. (2018c). Ethical Data Management and Research Integrity in the Context of e-Schools and Community Engagement. In C. Sibinga (Ed.), *Ensuring Research Integrity and the Ethical Management of Data* (pp. 14–45). IGI Global. doi:10.4018/978-1-5225-2730-5.ch002

Goosen, L. (2018d). Ethical Information and Communication Technologies for Development Solutions: Research Integrity for Massive Open Online Courses. In C. Sibinga (Ed.), *Ensuring Research Integrity and the Ethical Management of Data* (pp. 155–173). IGI Global. doi:10.4018/978-1-5225-2730-5.ch009

Goosen, L. (2019). Research on Technology-Supported Teaching and Learning for Autism. In L. Makewa, B. Ngussa, & J. Kuboja (Eds.), *Technology-Supported Teaching and Research Methods for Educators* (pp. 88–110). IGI Global. doi:10.4018/978-1-5225-5915-3.ch005

Goosen, L. (2021). Organizational Knowledge and Administration Lessons from an ICT4D MOOC. In M. Khosrow-Pour (Ed.), *Encyclopedia of Organizational Knowledge, Administration, and Technologies* (pp. 245–261). IGI Global. doi:10.4018/978-1-7998-3473-1.ch020

Goosen, L., & Mukasa-Lwanga, T. (2017). Educational Technologies in Distance Education: Beyond the Horizon with Qualitative Perspectives. In U. I. Ogbonnaya, & S. Simelane-Mnisi (Ed.), *Proceedings of the South Africa International Conference on Educational Technologies* (pp. 41 - 54). Pretoria: African Academic Research Forum.

Goosen, L., & Naidoo, L. (2014). Computer Lecturers Using Their Institutional LMS for ICT Education in the Cyber World. In C. Burger, & K. Naudé (Ed.), *Proceedings of the 43rd Conference of the Southern African Computer Lecturers' Association (SACLA)* (pp. 99-108). Port Elizabeth: Nelson Mandela Metropolitan University.

Gupta, V., Fernandez-Crehuet, J. M., Gupta, C., & Hanne, T. (2020). Freelancing Models for Fostering Innovation and Problem Solving in Software Startups: An Empirical Comparative Study. *Sustainability*, *12*(23), 10106. Advance online publication. doi:10.3390u122310106

Gupta, V., Fernandez-Crehuet, J. M., & Hanne, T. (2020). Fostering Continuous Value Proposition Innovation through Freelancer Involvement in Software Startups: Insights from Multiple Case Studies. *Sustainability*, *12*(21), 8922. Advance online publication. doi:10.3390u12218922

Hassan, B. (2007). The Impact of Multilevel Computer Self-Efficacy on the Effectiveness of Computer Training. In B. Hassan & S. Clarke (Eds.), *End User Computing Challenges and Technologies: Emerging Tools and Applications* (pp. 33–47). Information Science Reference. doi:10.4018/978-1-59904-295-4.ch003

Houghton, C., Casey, D., Shaw, D., & Murphy, K. (2013). Rigor in qualitative case-study research. *Nurse Researcher*, *20*(4), 12–17. doi:10.7748/nr2013.03.20.4.12.e326 PMID:23520707

Kahn, K. B. (2012). *The PDMA handbook of new product development*. John Wiley & Sons, Inc. doi:10.1002/9781118466421

Karahanna, E., & Straub, D. (1999). The psychological origins of perceived usefulness and ease-of-use. *Information & Management*, *35*(4), 237–250. doi:10.1016/S0378-7206(98)00096-2

Kock, N. (2005). Media richness or media naturalness? The evolution of our biological communication apparatus and its influence on our behavior toward e-communication tools. *IEEE Transactions on Professional Communication*, *48*(2), 117–130. doi:10.1109/TPC.2005.849649

Kock, N. (2013). *Interdisciplinary Applications of Electronic Collaboration Approaches and Technologies*. IGI Global. doi:10.4018/978-1-4666-2020-9

Lamont-Strayhorn, T. (2013). *Theoretical Frameworks in College Student Research*. University Press of America.

Lenhart, A., Purcell, K., & Smith, A. (2010). *Social Media & Mobile Internet Use Among Teens and Young Adults*. Pew Research Center. Retrieved August 10, 2017, from https://www.pewinternet.org/files/old-media/Files/Reports/2010/PIP_Social_Media_and_Young_Adults_Report_Final_with_toplines.pdf

Libbrecht, P., & Goosen, L. (2015). Using ICTs to Facilitate Multilingual Mathematics Teaching and Learning. In R. Barwell, P. Clarkson, A. Halai, M. Kazima, J. Moschkovich, N. Planas, & M. Villavicencio Ubillús (Eds.), *Mathematics Education and Language Diversity* (pp. 217–235). Springer. doi:10.1007/978-3-319-14511-2_12

Martinik, I. (2015). Rich-Media Technologies and Their Using in Crisis Management Communication. In J. Park, I. Stojmenovic, H. Y. Jeong, & G. Yi (Eds.), *Computer Science and Its Applications: Ubiquitous Information Technologies* (pp. 437–442). Springer. doi:10.1007/978-3-662-45402-2_66

McQueen, R., & Mills, A. (1998). End User Computer Sophistication in a Large Health Services Organization. In M. Khosrowpoue (Ed.), *Effective Utilization and Management of Emerging Information Technologies: Information Resources Management Association Conference* (pp. 263–276). Idea Group Publishing.

Miles, M., Huberman, M., & Saldana, J. (2014). *Qualitative Data Analysis: A Methods Sourcebook* (3rd ed.). Sage Publications Ltd.

Mioara, M. S. (2012). The impact of technological and communication innovation in the knowledge-based society. *Procedia: Social and Behavioral Sciences, 51*, 263–267. doi:10.1016/j.sbspro.2012.08.156

Nathaniel, A. K. (2012). An Integrated Philosophical Framework that fits Grounded Theory. In V. Martin & A. Gynnild (Eds.), *Grounded Theory: The Philosophy, Method, and work of Barney Glaser* (p. 193). Brown Walker Press.

Ngugi, J. K., & Goosen, L. (2021). Innovation, Entrepreneurship, and Sustainability for ICT Students Towards the Post-COVID-19 Era. In L. C. Carvalho, L. Reis, & C. Silveira (Eds.), *Handbook of Research on Entrepreneurship, Innovation, Sustainability, and ICTs in the Post-COVID-19 Era* (pp. 110–131). IGI Global. doi:10.4018/978-1-7998-6776-0.ch006

Oinas-Kukkonen, H., Hohtari, S., & Paekkoa, S. (2012). Organizing End-User Training: A Case Study of an E-Bank. In A. Dwivedi & S. Clarke (Eds.), *End-User Computing, Development, and Software Engineering: New Challenges* (pp. 335–354). IGI Global. doi:10.4018/978-1-4666-0140-6.ch016

Parke, C. (2013). *Essential First Steps to Data Analysis: Scenario based examples using SPSS*. Sage Publications Ltd. doi:10.4135/9781506335148

Raine, L., & Wellman, B. (2012). *Networked: The new social operating system*. MIT Press. doi:10.7551/mitpress/8358.001.0001

Ridder, H.-G. (2016). *Case Study Research: Approaches, Methods, Contribution to Theory*. Rainer Hampp Verlag.

Robert, L., & Dennis, A. (2005). Paradox of Richness: A Cognitive Model of Media Choice. *IEEE Transactions on Professional Communication, 48*(1), 10–21. doi:10.1109/TPC.2004.843292

Rubin, A., & Babbie, E. (2009). *Research Methods for Social Work*. Cengage. doi:10.1093/obo/9780195389678-0008

Sapsford, R. (2007). *Survey Research* (2nd ed.). Sage Publications. doi:10.4135/9780857024664

Schnieder, M. (2006). *Theory Primer: A Sociological Guide*. Rowman & Littlefield Publishers Inc.

Seetaram, N., & Petit, S. (2012). Panel Data Analysis. In L. Dwyer, A. Gill, & N. Seetraram (Eds.), *Handbook of Research Methods in Tourism: Quantitative and Qualitative approaches* (pp. 127–144). Edward Elgar. doi:10.4337/9781781001295.00013

Seidman, I. (2013). *Interviewing as Qualitative Research: A guide for researchers in education & the social sciences* (4th ed.). Teachers College Press.

Short, J., Williams, E., & Christie, B. (1976). *The Social Psychology of Telecommunications*. Wiley.

Skowron, M., Rank, S., Garcia, D., & Holyst, J. (2017). Zooming in: Studying Collective Emotions. In J. Holyst (Ed.), *Cyberemotions: Collective Emotions in Cyberspace* (pp. 279–304). Springer. doi:10.1007/978-3-319-43639-5_14

Stevens, J. (2009). *Applied Multivariate Statistics For The Social Sciences* (5th ed.). Routledge.

Stewart, C. M. (1992). Innovation is in the Mind of the User: A Case Study of Voice Mail. In U. E. Gattiker & R. S. Stollemmaier (Eds.), *Technology Mediated Communication* (Vol. 3, pp. 151–186). Walter de Gruyter. doi:10.1515/9783110860542.151

Taylor, S., Bodgan, R., & DeVault, M. (2016). *Introduction to Qualitative Research Methods: A Guidebook and Resource* (4th ed.). John Wiley & Sons Inc.

Urquhart, C. (2013). *Grounded Theory for Qualitative Research: A Practical Guide*. Sage Publications Ltd. doi:10.4135/9781526402196

Van Heerden, D., & Goosen, L. (2021). Students' Perceptions of e-Assessment in the Context of Covid-19: The Case of UNISA. In M. Qhobela, M. M. Ntsohi, & L. G. Mohafa (Ed.), *Proceedings of the 29th Conference of the Southern African Association for Research in Mathematics, Science and Technology Education (SAARMSTE)* (pp. 291-305). SAARMSTE.

Yin, R. K. (2009). *Case study research: Design and methods*. Sage Publications Ltd.

Yin, R. K. (2011). *Qualitative Research from Start to Finish*. The Guilford Press.

Chapter 4

An Integrative Model of Hardware Product Development in Startup Contexts:
A Qualitative Study

Khalid Khan
Karachi Institute of Economics and Technology, Pakistan

Faiza Khan
Karachi Institute of Economics and Technology, Pakistan

Trung Nguyen Quang
Thuongmai University, Vietnam

Anh Nguyen Duc
University of South-Eastern Norway, Norway

ABSTRACT

Hardware startups are increasingly popular due to recent advancements in hardware technologies. Nowadays, hardware product development involves the process innovation not only at the hardware level but also at software components. The scarcity of knowledge on hardware startup product development motivates the authors to carry out an empirical investigation on five hardware startup companies. They found some common good practices among hardware startups (i.e., process definition, evolutionary development process, and document management). They reveal several factors that are different from software startups, such as low priority of product quality, product pipeline, and unrecognized product platform. They proposed an integrative process model of hardware product development that shows the connections between human factors in the startups, their speed-prioritized development processes, and the consequence of hindered productivity in the later phases. The model has some implications for hardware startup founders to plan for the trade-off between team, speed, quality, and later productivity.

DOI: 10.4018/978-1-7998-9059-1.ch004

INTRODUCTION

With the Industry 4.0 revolution (Lasi et al., 2014), the adoption and development of hardware-related technologies, for instance, Internet-of-things (IoT), cyber-physical systems, and robotics are becoming mainstreams. According to Gartner's hype cycle, by 2020, hardware technologies will be in 95% of electronics for new product designs. According to Statistica (Statista, n.d.) report, in 2025, the total number of connected devices in the world will be approximately 75.44 billion devices. Being part of this development, a significant amount of hardware products has been developed and popularized by startup companies, including Fitbit, Gopro, and Jawbone, to name a few.

Hardware startups have not enjoyed much popularity in last three decades due to several issues, i.e. highly complexity, expensive production and long product development circles. Moreover, hardware products demands many physical quality attributes. Especially they are not fault-tolerant once they are released to the market. This has changed in last ten years with the production of hardware in the way they are similar to software development. Heavy upfront investment and heavy-duty market research is no more mandatory as the hardware design is now much easier to develop and iterations in prototyping become cheaper due to the technological advancements. The trend has attracted even the big software giants like Google, Microsoft and Facebook who are investing billions in hardware by acquiring companies like Dropcam[1], Skybox[2], and Oculus VR[3]. This must have given confidence to the budding hardware entrepreneurs across the world. Hence, we see lots of angel funding going into hardware startups in the recent years.

Startups, new companies with limited resources, short operational histories, and that are often looking for scalable business models, appear as a special context in which traditional product development approaches might not be directly applicable (Unterkalmsteiner, 2016). The global movement of startups calls for the attention of practitioners and researchers in the quest for development methodologies that are suitable to startups' business objectives, as well as their unique engineering environments (Unterkalmsteiner, 2016). Startups face with many challenges to survive in early stages, in which many are found to be related to engineering activities (Giardino, Bajwa, Wang et al, 2015). Startups adopt certain approaches to develop their products, and to some extent, have a direct impact on business objective and activities. For instance, empirical studies on software startups reveal common phenomena in the development of software products, such as agile development, evolutionary prototypes, customer involvement, technical debt, and the neglect of quality ((Ries, 2014); (Giardino, Bajwa, Wang et al, 2015); (Batova et al., 2016);(Bajwa et al., 2017);(Seppänen et al., 2017))

Nowadays hardware startups must deal with the development of a comprehensive system of both software and hardware components. For instance, in a GoPro[4] camera, it is not sufficient to have only hardware components that capture and store video, as the business' value also relies on software components that enable users to process the video. Hence, it is essential for them to consider both hardware and software engineering processes. With recent advances in hardware prototyping (i.e. 3D printing, and hardware development kits), the development of hardware-related products can be more agile and iterative ((Larman & Basili, 2003) (Rigby et al., 2016)). For instance, a higher development pace and greater flexibility is reported to be facilitated by using Agile methodologies in hardware projects at Ericsson (Statista, n.d.). However, in general, the complex nature of hardware products can impose many dependencies and constraints that burden the methodological adoption (Ronkainen & Abrahamsson, 2003).

To the best of our knowledge, the body of research examining the usefulness of hardware product development processes in the context of software startups is very limited. To address this research gap, we aimed to explore the state-of-practice of hardware-related product development. This research paper presents the results from a multiple-case study investigating five early-stage Pakistani startups. First, we analyzed well known high-tech startup models and prepared a holistic list of factors these models have proposed to make a startup successful. Later, we used the same list of factors to evaluate our cases of hardware startups.

The paper is organized as below. Section 1 introduces the importance and relevance of the topic. Section 2 presents related work. Section 3 is our research methodology. Section 4 presents our findings and Section 6 discusses and concludes the paper.

RELATED WORK

A startup can be defined as an organization that is challenged by youth and immaturity, with extremely limited resources, multiple influences, and dynamic technologies and markets (Klotins et al., 2015). As we will be discussing the impact of various hardware startup models in the context of software startup. First we will discuss hardware development in startups, than we will move to product development in software startup and later the hardware models used to extract the factors to make the software startup successful.

Hardware Development in Startups

Hardware startups are those startups that develop products with mixed hardware and software parts, including embedded systems, sensor devices, and advanced robotics (Berg & Birkeland, 2018). As seen from Figure 1, hardware startups are distinct from software startups, as they need to handle hardware design and development, and manufacturing in addition to software development. They also have to deal with production and logistics issues like packaging, shipping, and customs (Gokaram Narayana Murthy, 2016). Hardware startups need teams with boundary-spanning knowledge, including capabilities within software development, mechanical and electronics engineering, product design, and specific industry knowledge (e.g., experience from working with third parties) (Berg et al., 2018). This implies higher initial financial and human investments required for hardware startups (Berg & Birkeland, 2018). Research on development processes in hardware startups is rare, where exploration of state-of-practice is limited to a few studies (Berg et al., 2018).

Figure 1. Types of hardware startup
(Duc et al., 2019)

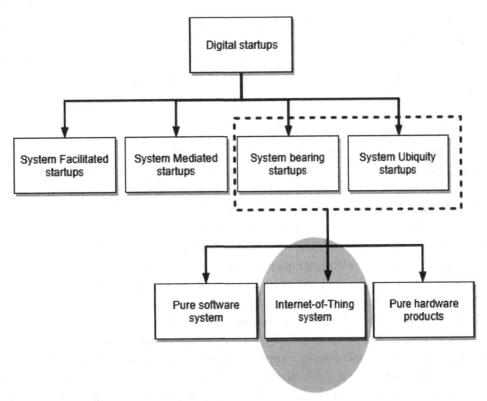

The adoption of Software Engineering paradigms for the development of hardware-related products is mentioned in recent publications (Larman & Basili, 2003). Zambonelli proposed a way to explore related engineering areas to identify a general model and methodology for Internet-of-Things software engineering (Zambonelli, 2016). Harrison et al. described engineering methods and tools for distributed component-based development of cyber-physical systems (Duc et al., 2019). Usländer et al. presented a methodology that combined service engineering and Agile development in Internet-of-Things context (Usländer & Batz, 2018). From the theoretical perspective, these studies often propose methods without empirical validation. Furthermore, the methods are not specifically discussed in the context of startups.

A broader view on the literature about embedded systems reveals possible adoptions of Software Engineering methodologies and tools in hardware-related development (Kaisti et al., 2013). Ronkainen et al. described challenges with hard real-time requirements, prototyping, documentation, and test-driven development in Agile hardware development(Abrahamsson et al., 2003). Greene reported a positive experience of applying Agile approaches in firmware development at Intel (Greene, 2004). Adopting XP practices, Santos et al. showed a successful software version created for control of a satellite camera (Dos Santos et al., 2007). Kaisti et al. conducted a systematic mapping study about the adoption of Agile methodology in embedded systems development (Duc et al., 2019). The authors suggested that Agile practices can be used in the embedded domain, but the practices need to be adapted to fit the strictly constrained field of embedded system development.

Software Startup Product Development

Entrepreneurial success is complex and depends on several interrelated factors. There exist a large amount of research on product development, particularly in software startup contexts (Berg & Birkeland, 2018). Giardino et al. (Bailetti, 2012) introduced a Greenfield startup model (GSM) for modelling technical debt in startups. The model also gives a direction and model for future research on software development in start-ups, strategies to speed up development initially. It focuses on early engineering activities, from idea conception to the ðrst open beta release of the product. It suggests that software start-ups need software engineering practices of same level or better then large companies. The model has seven main categories and causal relationships in the Greenðeld Start-up Model. Namely, Speed up development, Evolutionary Approach/define process, Product quality low priority, Team is the catalyst for development, Accumulated Technical debt, Initial growth hinder performance, and severe lack of resources. The model is centered on the central category, speed up development, which is the most interconnected node in the theory reñecting the fact that *"is the one [category] with the greatest explanatory power"*.

It is reported that a vast number of start-ups fails within 2 years due to self-structure (Kelly & Culleton, 1999). Operating in an evolving and uncertain environment, intense time pressure and relentless competition. Trying to transform the product to adjust according to the market demands with limited resources they have gathered/have. Research is required to investigate and support start-ups engineering services, guidance for decision making to avoid business failure choices. Software start-ups are product-oriented in the first period of development. Early results are often good but when software development and organization management increase in complexity it generally deteriorates overtime. The need for establishing initial repeatable and scalable processes cannot be postponed forever. A lot of efforts have been done to show how can current software development practices be useful for start-ups, the primary benefit of one size fits all SPIs often do not hold for start-ups which instead of promoting product quality minimize time to market.

A recent study from Klotins and colleagues reveals software engineering practices in startups (Maimbo & Pervan, 2005). Often start-ups focusing on a limited number of suitable functionalities, and adopting partial and rapid evolutionary development approaches, early-stage software start-ups operate at high development speed, aided by skilled and highly co-located developers. Through these development strategies, early-stage software start-ups aim to ðnd early product/market ðt within uncertain conditions and severe lack of resources.

It is found that driving characteristics of start-ups were uncertainty, lack of resources, and time-pressure (Bailetti, 2012; Berg et al., 2018; Duc et al., 2019). When bringing the ðrst product to market, start-ups' most urgent priority is releasing the product as quickly as possible to verify the product/market ðt, and to adjust the business and product trajectory according to early feedback and collected metrics. At this stage, start-ups often discard formal project management, documentation, analysis, planning, testing and other traditional process activities. The most signiðcant challenge for early-stage start-ups is ðnding the balance between being fast enough to enter the market early and controlling the amount of accumulated technical debt (Bailetti, 2012).

What follows from these findings are two software development objectives that need to be considered by early-stage start-ups and researchers seeking to improve state-of-the-art: (1) Integration of scalable solutions with fast iterations and minimal set of functionalities, (2) Empowerment of the team-members granting them the responsibility and autonomy to be involved in all activities of the development phases.

Important Factors for Startup Product Development

We have used six well known high-tech startup models to develop a list of factors that can be utilized for Software product development.

Start-up often lack the foundations required for success—a historical record of experience, infrastructure for process instantiation, improvement, repeatable and predictable practices. It can be challenging for a start-up to strictly adhere to the Capability Maturity Model. As a result, one must select and prioritize process issues and technologies according to the start-up's wants and available means. A start-up's capacity to stay alive hinges on it does this till the CMM can become pertinent and useful. They need tactics that help them function more efficiently and effectively at lower levels of maturity, where they must first flourish if they are to finally mature. Capability Maturity Model's chief objectives is to improve process and software quality (Paulk, 2002). The CMM also targets to improve process predictability as well as manageability. Start-ups embody a software industry segment that has been mostly ignored in process trainings, and it is possible that lessons derived from start-ups are also applicable to further developed organizations. Process maturity tends to encourage product quality and process predictableness and reliability. In contrast, a start-up company at times aims to lessen the time to market and other objectives might suffer.

Greenfield Startup Model (GSM) (Giardino, Paternoster, Unterkalmsteiner et al, 2015) aims to improve the understanding of the software development strategies employed by startups. The focus of the GSM model is to explain the priority of startups to release the product as quickly as possible. GSM model allows startups to verify product and market fit and help in shortening the time-to-market, by speeding up the development through low-precision engineering activities. The overall results suggests that startups are influenced with uncertainty, lack of resources, and time-pressure. Bringing the first product to market has its own challenges as the verification of the product/market fit can only be assessed after the reslease of the product. This mostly results in evolutionary prototyping as startups are pushed to discard formal project management and other traditional process activities.

The understanding of converting ideas into products while keeping the track of dynamic evolution of product-market fit is a complex need which is addressed in (Nguyen-Duc et al., 2015) as a conceptual model to capture the evolution of software startup activities over time is proposed. Hunter Gatherer cycle (HGC) depicts that a software startup can be characterized by: (1) The activities that occur in different situation (hunting activities or gathering activities) (2) The environment in which innovate ideas/ prototypes/ products will be tested (3) The speed of transitions between different phases of software startup. It is concluded that the current software development processes are not enough to understand and support software startup development because the local context of software and software development organizations has lot of impact.

The impact of ordinary activities on the evolution of product development (EPD) is analyzed in (Crowne, 2002). The study presented a detailed comparison of 90 diverse product development processes over a 15-year period. The paper concludes that focus should be shifted from aggregate entities to the practical realities of core organizational processes. It is also highlighted that fine-grained perspective leads to a set of better insights and higher-level of capabilities result in improved performance because of the stabilization in managerial attention. In (Baskerville et al., 2003), a model is presented that can analyze the evolution of product development (EPD) from startup to maturity. It is a three stage model: 1) Startup, 2) Stabilization, 3) Growth. For each stage certain symptoms are identified and counter actions are proposed. This can help is self-assessment as the benchmarking is made easy through this process.

Internet-speed software development (ISSD) proposed in (Baskerville et al., 2003) caters hostile environments having rapid requirement changes and unpredictable product complexity. Such environments require software development approaches that balance flexibility and disciplined methodology. In ISSD, software product quality becomes negotiable and development speed is paramount. Development costs become more aligned with operating costs. Quality becomes negotiable, a notion of quality-in-use where the exact quality requirements are a moving target in play with functionality and product availability. Second is project management, it differs from traditional project management in a way that there is no start and end of project. Thirdly, maintenance in Internet-speed development is sometimes merged into the specification-build-release cycle along with new functionality, or maintenance cycles become small project cycles (maintenance releases) interspersed with larger project cycles (functional releases). Lastly, human resource management differs in Internet-speed development. Team members are less interchangeable, and teams require people with initiative, creativity, and courage as well as technical knowledge, experience, and drive.

Software requirements analysis is a complex tasks especially for startups due to lack of resources and market analysis. In (), Grounded Theory (GT) is used to streamline requirement engineering for startups. The work presented a conceptual model to effectively perform requirements engineering. It also details out the processes and practices to for the same. Researches can use this model to propose new techniques and evaluate them against what is being done today.

As we are looking to create a holistic list of the factors that can influence a startup towards success, we have listed the factors on each model in Table 1.

Table 1. Important factors from the discussed models

Factors Presented in the Models	GSM	CMM	HGC	EPD	ISSD	GT
Rapid MVP development (P)	X	X	X	X	X	X
Evolutionary development process (P)	X	X	X		X	X
Low priority of product quality (P)	X	X	X	X	X	X
Team is the catalyst for development (P)	X	X		X		X
Accumulated Techincal debt/Learn and reuse (P)	X	X	X		X	X
Initial growth hinder performance (C)	X	X	X	X	X	X
Usaged of limited resources (C)	X	X	X	X	X	X
Remaining Flexiblility (P)		X	X		X	
Right Form of Process Definition (C)		X	X			X
Lean aproach for market research (P)			X	X	X	
Characteristics of startup founders (P)				X		X
Product platform is unrecognised (C)				X	X	
Product pipeline (P)			X	X	X	X
Documentation Management (P)				X	X	X

METHODOLOGY

We performed a qualitative study on five Pakistani startups. The study mainly bases on semi-structured interviews. In the sections below, we present our data collection and analysis, together with the descriptions of our investigated companies.

Data Collection and Analysis

Software engineering research is to a great extent concerned with investigating the development, operation, and maintenance of software products. The case study process is considered suitable for such multidisciplinary areas where existing theory may be inadequate (Kwanya & Stilwell, 2017), and so we have designed a case study protocol inspired by Pervan and Maimbo (Maimbo & Pervan, 2005) to guide the collection and analysis of data. The study is of exploratory nature as we seek to create knowledge by investigating events and actions of those who experience them. Semi structured interviews of selected participants fitted both the time-constraints and availability of hardware startups and is considered suitable for qualitative data analysis. Interviews allowed for a discoverable approach, as interviewees could express themselves more freely and provide their own perspectives on personal experiences related to the research topics. Before the interviews, we looked into the cases' business background, either through their company websites or other relevant incubator or accelerator websites. Additionally, most participants answered a simple questionnaire prior to interviews where they pulled out basic information about themselves and the company. These measures allowed for more efficient interviews as the first and second author possessed more knowledge about the case and could use less time on initial formalities. Initial company analysis allowed for a holistic understanding of each case and provided stronger evidence for the conclusions drawn from the interviews.

Interview Questions

Section 1: Business Background

Q.1.1: Describe your product?
Q.1.2: Describe your company? Brief history, current head counts, departments etc
Q.1.3: What is your software development methodology, processes, environment and tools

Section 2: Idea Visualization and Prototyping

Q.2.1: When did the idea came into your mind?
Q.2.2: How did you built the ðrst prototype?
Q.2.3: What was your learning from the prototyping?
Q.2.4: Is the initial idea and the current product same? In terms of product, ðnances, team etc
Q.2.5: When and where did you ðrst launch your product?

Section 3: Product Development and Launching

Q.3.1: When the actual development started?
Q.3.2: Were the customers involved during the product development?
Q.3.3: How the current product is different from the prototype?

Section 4: Challenges and Lessons Learnt

Q.4.1: What were the three biggest challenges?
Q.4.2: What would you do differently?

Section 5: Adoption of Paradigm

Q.5.1: Which is your preferable model for IoT software development such as water fall, agile etc?
Q.5.2: What are Agile practices you have used in your companies? Do they work?
Q.5.3: How do you balance between the speed of development and quality of the product?

The resulting model will explain the priorities of hardware startups, and why introducing process and specific methodologies is hard. The model will be the results of an early investigation of how hardware startups operate and point out opportunities for future research.

In the coming section, we will introduce five hardware startups companies that are used to analyze various models and consilidated factors.

Startup Case Description

We have evaluated the startup companies from Pakistan shown in Table 2.

Table 2. Startups case description

Startup	Year	Total Persons	Company and Product Description
Clique	2015	8 in total: CEO (1) CTO (1) Hw. Engineer (2) Sw. Engineer (3) Sale (1)	Clique is an IoT based startup that makes innovative products to make your life more convenient, secure, and affordable and energy efficient. The core value of the company is to make home a smart environment for living. This includes solutions for rooms, electronic devices, etc. The ambition of Clique is a connected smart home which is affordable, secure, convenient, maintainable and beautiful.The case reflects their experiene on two major products Smartic and Smart Board. The **Smartic** is a Plug n Play device that can be connected to any electrical device to automate it. It only automates one device and does not provide the dimming functionality like the Smart Board does. **Smart Board**, on the other hand, replaces the conventional switchboards in your home and automates all the electrical devices of the installed room.
Electroid	2015	14 in total: CEO (1) CTO (1) Hw. Engineers (4) Sw. Engineers (5) Sale (3)	Electroid is an Intelligent Home Automation System, which allows its user to control electric appliances remotely, using an Android app through both GSM and Wi-Fi. In addition to this, it also provides a number of other features including bill estimation, scheduling turn on/off of electrical appliances, security features, user profiles, data sync through web servers. It is a home automation software that gives end-users the power to control the power consumption of their digital appliances.
Eye Automate	2016	10 in total: CEO (1) CTO (1) CMO (1) Engineers (7)	Eye-Automate is a novel navigating device which aims to facilitate visually impaired individuals. The Eye-Automate device – employing eye-tracking to record eye movements and coverts the information into a digital data – will help the visually impaired to operate and control things like wheelchairs, computers and other household consumer devices with convenience. EyeAutomate is very helpful for disables and even for normal people too. And we are providing smart wheel chair and home automation with eye gaze.
Car Chabi	2016	18 in total: CEO (1) CTO (1) Engineers (13) Sale (3)	Car Chabi RACK Pro is a solution for automotive vehicles to remotely start the cars. RACK Pro offers a variety of solutions but most importantly Remote Starting of cars. Car Chabi device facilitates you by providing you an ease in accessing your car with a smartphone. Another core features of Car Chabi RACK Pro is Proximity. Ranges can be set by the user itself.Auto security is also one of the features worth mentioning which allows users to secure their cars from smartphones. With Car Chabi RACK Pro device, the cars will automatically be immobilized, once the phone gets disconnected from the car. In case of snatching or theft, the car will be immobilized after the time specified by the user. Auto Security makes the car more secure in the situations where you feel that the car is not safe.
Xgear	2014	15 CEO (1) CTO (1) Engineers (13)	Xgear is a predictive analytics platform for vehicles. It delivers real-time actionable insights to drivers and car owners for preemptive car maintenance and performance optimization. By collecting millions of data points and aggregating them, XGear is able to perform predictive analysis using machine learning to identify risks of certain events happening and informing drivers before they take place. XGear provides a mobile and web-based interface to drivers and corporations for monitoring and improving driving behavior, increasing fuel efficiency, pre-emptive car maintenance, geofencing, vehicle tracking, forensic audits and safer driving. The XGear dashboard provides an integrated system that provides real-time data to help organizations track close to 150 data points in each vehicle. Combined with external conditions, the data provides recommendation to enhance driver safety, reduce costs and improve productivity of the fleet.

We will analyze these startup companies by using the factors consolidated from five different startup models. By analyzing these models, we realized that different models has presented different factors as their areas are different from each other. We developed a holistic list of factors which gives an overall picture of the factors presented by individual model as shown in Table 1.

RESULTS

Findings from Cross-Case Analysis

The finding from the evaluation of the startup companies are given in table 3 which clearly shows that most of the areas were marked as important by the participating startups.

Table 3. Factors relevant in hardware startup product development

Startup Evaluation Factors	Car Chabi	Clique	Electroid	X Gear	Eye Automate
Team is the catalyst for development	Important	Important	Important	Important	Important
Appropriate Process Definition	Important	Important	Important	Important	Important
Evolutionary development process	Important	Important	Important	Important	Important
Document management	Important	Important	Important	Important	Important
Initial growth hinder performance	Moderate	Important	Important	Important	Important
Characteristics of startup founders (P)	Important	Important	Important	Moderate	N/A
Speed up development	Important	Important	Important	Moderate	Moderate
Usaged of limited resources (C)	Moderate	Moderate	Moderate	Moderate	Moderate
Rapid MVP development (P)	Trivial	Moderate	Trivial	Important	Moderate
Remaining Flexiblility (P)	Trivial	Important	Important	Moderate	Moderate
Accumulated Techincal debt/Learn and reuse (P)	Moderate	Important	Moderate	Trivial	Important
Lean aproach for market research (P)	Trivial	Trivial	Trivial	Trivial	Trivial
Product platform is unrecognised (C)	Trivial	Trivial	Trivial	Trivial	Trivial
Product pipeline (P)	Moderate	Important	Trivial	Important	Moderate
Low priority of product quality (P)	N/A	N/A	N/A	N/A	N/A

We conducted a focus group to categorize the factors into two groups (1) Factors Relevant and applicable in hardware startups and (2) Factors need to be adjusted.

Team is the Catalyst for Development

In new companies' engineers have enormous obligations. Honestly, limited HR, cause the colleagues to be dynamic in each part of the improvement procedure, from the deðnition of functionalities to the ðnal sending. Engineers handle both the improvement and are in the meantime in charge of showcasing and deals. The proactivity of the team significantly affects speed in a context of restricted resources. Anticipatory, change-oriented, and self-initiated team members are a necessity in the fast-changing, high-risk environment of startups. This factor applies to all startups as without the proper resources it not possible to build a product, all five startups owner/co-founders had or learned the skills required for their product. The team includes every members of the startups, from the founders to hired engineers.

Finding the right vendors as the manufacturing partners. Hiring good talent at a low wage that the startup can afford." (CEO of Clique)

"Team formation is key, also retaining team and the vision" (CEO of Car Chabi)

The startups in question realizes the important of a resource for a team and a team for a company. The team must not only be skilled with the required skillset for the project but also share the vision of the startup.

Appropriate Process Definition

Following the right hardware development process can ensure your new product or technology makes a successful impact on the architectural and technical dimensions of hardware products. in early-stage hardware startup, the product development process often relates the hybridization of the heavy-handed processes prescribed by the manufacturing/quality community, and the lightweight processes used by many design professionals. This includes also user-experience perspective, manufacturing, quality assurance plan, etc. In a process definition, the process manager, often the CTO of the startup plans to catch action and antique stream, and speak to this in different ways, including formal visualization, i.e. stream graphs or informal language. Albeit average formalisms of these sorts have oft refereed to impediments (equivocalness, inadequacy, familiarity, etc), the purposes behind characterizing a procedure may make explicit capture of hardware-related constraints. Furthermore, the process definition can make relevant regulations in the application domains visible to the lower-level of development.

The coding language selection is done by analyzing which languages will have the most developers support in the future and at current stage (CEO of Clique)

We develop the hardware, write the firmware and the build the apps around it. (CEO of Car Chabi)

We have adopted a hybrid model in which we are using two different software development life cycles at a time to ensure quality. We gather requirements and then make them refine and after implementing them we go for testing. After successful UAT we add new passed feature to product otherwise discard it and repeat the cycle again (CEO of Eye Automate)

Evolutionary Development Process

By releasing few sufficient functionalities incrementaly, the startup veriðes the reasonableness of the highlights and sees how to modify the product development path towards genuine clients' needs. The ðrst variant of the item is regularly a model containing essential functionalities created with the least conceivable exertion that approves basic features, enabling the startup's survival for the time being. Upheld by direct contact and perception of clients, mechanized criticism accumulation and investigation of item metrics, startups endeavor to ðnd what is important for clients. In cases Xgear, Eye automate and Electroid, the CEOs stating their early stages with the first MVPs with limited functionalities and later on had additions based upon customer feedback.

From the time of first prototype we have added numerous features to the first prototype. And then we launched first beta testing product that was delivered to the users without any mark up with terms and conditions. We asked about qualitative feedback from them. And using that feedback we ensured the quality of product and added value in the user experience. (CEO of Eye automate)

Prototype was just a very simple version of our system. It was nothing more than switching on/off of an energy saver using SMS from our mobile phone. But current product has a ton of features including controlling, grouping, timers, electricity consumption monitors, motion sensors, camera (CEO of Electroid)

Documentation Management

Document management is essential for keeping company information private and secure. Comparing to software development, realistic production of hardware products involves a wide range of documents:

1. Product Requirement Documents
2. Technical files for design, i.e. CAD, Gerbers,
3. Inspection guideline for Quality controls
4. Manufacturing and Service Agreement
5. Regulation and industry-specific constraints
6. Bills and contracts with suppliers

However, not all businesses maintain an ongoing document management process with their employees. It's essential for startup to maintain document for all processes and product development, this will aid them in future improvement and will make it easier for other/team members in become aware of different development aspects of the startups.

In our case, we keep a formal documentation management process since prototyping was done (CEO of Xgear)

... Rough drafts during prototyping, formally designing documentation where required (CEO of Eye-Automate)

In the other two cases, Xgear and Eye automate documented their entire process from idea to conceptualization, prototyping, production and manufacturing. Although they acknowledged the importance of the documentation, Car Chabi, Clique and Electroid have no clear evidence of in-depth document that has been done for their products.

Initial Growth Hinder Performance

The absence of consideration given in the ðrst stages to designing exercises enables new businesses to deliver code rapidly. In any case, if the startup endures, the underlying item turns out to be increasingly perplexing after some time, the quantity of clients increments, and the organization begins to develop. Under these conditions the need to control the underlying tumult powers the advancement group to restore the gathered specialized obligation, rather than concentrating on new clients' solicitations. Consequently, the underlying development thwarts execution regarding new functionalities conveyed to the clients. This has been a similar observation with existing findings in software startup context. Startups, in general, prioritized the growth in their early-stage, which somehow hinder their performance. However, as seen before, the definition of performance might varies and company performance might not necessarily mean the performance of their offered products.

Founders' Characteristics

Startups heavily depend on the personalities and characteristics of their co-founders. Also, it is important how the co-foudners can work as one team. There is harming struggle between new administrators and the organizers of the organization who may likewise be real investors. Individuals keep on seeking the organizers for item and thought authority, albeit new pioneers have been delegated to give these. Founders should either expect a standard official job, really acknowledge a subordinate position, or join the board as a non-executive director or chief.

The founders are integral part of the startups, but no evidence of micromanaging was found between the all five cases as resources employed belonged to friends or family circle.

Speed Up Development

The low consideration offered at first to building angles identified with item quality encourages the efðciency of cooperation. This allows startups to have a functioning but faulty product, which can be quickly introduced to the market, starting from a prototype implementation on day-one. The focus on speed is the same in our cases. However, this does not mean the scarification of the quality. Startups can be quick with their throw-away prototypes for the purpose of demonstration and funding attraction. However, evolutionary prototypes are typically developed with focus on their quality.

The first prototype was just a proof of concept and was built using minimum resources and quality control (CEO of Clique)

Very first prototype was just a simple device which turns on/off an energy saver through a simple SMS. This device consisted of Arduino & GSM module (CEO of Electroid)

Firstly we made a user interface that could interact with end-user easily and could be reliable. We ensured it by UAT. After quality assurance we implemented it on a robot. And made first prototype. (CEO of Eye-Automate)

So, for each company the product of the speed up development was recognized as faulty, but a needed release based on market entry. Each product was later evolved through UAT, quality assurance and feedback.

Usaged of Limited Resources

The idea of serious absence of assets portrays the vulnerability of improvement procedures in new businesses and it is made from three subcategories: time-deficiency, constrained HR and restricted access to expertise. Since new companies need to offer the item for sale to the public as fast as could be expected under the circumstances, the asset they are the most denied of is time. New companies work under a steady time weight, chiefly created by outside sources (financial specialist or investor weight, business weight) and now and again inside necessities, for example, inner due dates and demo introductions at occasions etc. In general, startups often operate in the conditions of lack of cash, hardware/ computing resource and HR/ management competence. In our case, all startups mention about this fact, however, they do not play an important role. We interpreter that the lack of initial resource occurs, but not significant enough to hinder key production and marketing activities in their early stages. For instance:

We think in the beginning it is important to hire good talent at the wage that the startup can afford. (CEO of Clique)

Insufficient Funds and Finding Investors was a challenge. But we found the way to solve it lately (CEO of Xgear)

Some of electrical components were unavailable in Pakistani market. We had to import them from china but still there was a hurdle of NOC every time. Gradually, we moved away from these component (CEO of Electroid)

Rapid MVP Development

Achieving speed in hardware startups is not as straightforward as adopting Agile practices or rapid prototyping in software startups. Almost all startups immediately built a physical prototype to elicit requirements and achieve rapid business experimentation. They usually followed an evolutionary approach, performing incremental improvements on an early low-resolution prototype. Rapid prototyping is important to obtain customer feedback, however it can be problematic in the hardware context. Hardware startups usually have a significant focus on non-functional requirements because of the many challenges and regulations associated with complex systems development and the general hardware ecosystem. Hardware startups' need for speed could also be the trade-off for product quality.

Table 4. Factors that are different in hardware startups

Elements	Variant
Remaining Flexiblility	Hardware startups might be rigid and stick to their production plan, rather than chaning their course of actions easily
Accumulated Techincal debt/Learn and reuse	Technical debt is formally formed at feature-level and evolve from one iteration to the other. This is not bug fixes or patches like in software startups
Lean aproach for market research	Startups perform market research in early stages, could be a parallel process with product research and development
Product platform is unrecognised	Product platform is highly relevant to software product, which take place differently in hardware context
Product pipeline	Product pipeline is often kept empty so startups can focus on a single hardware product. This differs from software variants that can be forked from a mainstream software development.
Low priority of product quality	Hardware startups aim at integrate both speed and quality focus on their development process

Remaining Flexibility

The flexibility is described as the startup's capacity to change their course of action. Frequently, start-ups can't anticipate or control the outer conditions driving such changes. These conditions frequently require a quick and opportune reaction. Rethinking a procedure each time the procedure parameters change can be restrictively moderate and exorbitant. A characterized however adaptable procedure is the most ideal approach to expand progression while encouraging adjustment. Adaptability incredibly encourages dealing with procedure exemptions and deviations; an adaptable procedure definition can give a viable model to the ideal consequences of sporadic executions, without hindering the treatment of unpredictable circumstances.

Accumulated Technical Debt/Learn and Reuse

New features are implemented in small, iterative cycles to perform rapid business experimentation, with minimal effort on quality assurance and documentation practices. Software features are implemented with a minimal amount of functionality. As the documentation would need to be updated for every change made to the code base, developers rely on their own knowledge instead of updating formal documentation. Since hardware startups rarely have the capacity to produce many prototypes, problem space testing becomes a challenging endeavor. The evolutionary approach increases the chance of feature creeps. Restricted resources and need for rapid development speed lead to the accumulation of technical debt. Xgear and Car chabi added feature in small iterative cycles, where the product was launched with fewer feature, which were later on increased.

The current technology being used by Clique is at the cutting edge whereas the first prototype was basically made by copying what was already created by hobbyists and tinkerers on the internet. The idea has evolved and gotten more refined with time and failures. (CEO of Clique)

...Current product is advanced now and includes other features that consumers wanted (CEO of Car Chabi)

Initially it was just an analogue to digital converter and a small circuit to measure RPM, temperature and speed and other gauges. The current product is far more versatile now the device and give insight in case of an accident what factor caused it, features like weather condition, road conditions, traffic conditions how they affect the car performance. Predictive analysis for when the parts requires maintenance. There also a mobile app that help monitor and improve driving behavior, increase fuel efficiency so on and so forth (CEO of Xgear)

Instead of creating the whole product and complicating the usage for end-user, these startups introduced the products with minimal usable features and evolved the product through versioned feedback accommodation and enhancements.

Lean Approach for Market Research

One of the main reasons for startup failure is that they face the problem of having little or no market for the products they create. Hence, market research is an essential activity startups perform in their early stage.

There is not enough convincing value suggestion or convincing event for the buyer to make a buying commitment in fact. Good sellers will tell you that you need to find buyers "burn hair" or "extreme suffering" to take orders in the challenging conditions today. The timing of the market is wrong. You may be in front of your market for a few years and you are not ready for your specific answer now.(CEO of Clique)

All of our cases have sufficient market research behind launching their products as home automation devices, vehicle performance analytics, vehicle security as well as sight-controlled wheelchair. All are in accordance to the need for them in market locally and internationally

Home automation devices need to help reduce electricity usage (CEO of Clique/electroid)

Vehicle performance analytics or accident analytics need (CEO of Xgear)

Mobility needs for fully paralyzed patients (CEO of Eye-automate)

The startups in question found the pain areas of their surroundings and addressed them in their products. Another reason the startup lacks time is that during the extensive product development life cycle the society might find a way to solve the pain area your product is focusing as necessity is the mother of invention.

Product Platform Is Unrecognized

The Product is requested on a wide range of stage blends without clear cost support. Labor and gear use heighten in item improvement without expanding efficiency of highlights and bug fixes. Different regions of the organization appear to be ill-equipped to help the new stage mixes. The software component that is the mobile application are developed for android and MS windows initially and later the iOS version was introduced for all the five cases. Product platform is highly relevant to software product, which take place differently in hardware context.

Product Pipeline

The company cannot meet demand for information on future product developments. It offers instead mundane and uninteresting announcements on minor product enhancements. There are many ideas for new products, but no effective way to decide between them and assign resources. These also help to avoid feature creeps or wide product portfolio at the early stage. This way startups can focus on normally one hardware product. This is different for software cases that variant of the key software products can be created and experienced in early stages. The product pipeline at the current stages is empty for four startups except for eye automatic, which plan to design and market wheelchair according to the disability needs as the initial product was for people who are entire disable except for sight/eyes control. Car Chabi and Xgear initially had pipeline for the product to move forward with more feature and advancements. Currently all of the five cases are stagnant with no further advancement plans.

Product Quality Low Priority

Product quality can be seen from multiple non-functional requirements, i.e. User Experience, Product Design, Robustness, Performance, Reliability, etc. Over time understanding state of UX is frequently the most imperative credit to consider for client disclosure of developmental methodologies in perspective on the constrained HR and time deficiency, introduced in. Overall, the hardware startups aims at combining spend and quality of their product in an integrative process. They employed both various quality assurance activities in development and production. However, it becomes clear that hardware startups lack both strategies and mindsets for achieving the long-term quality of the product during the prototyping and development phases.

An Integrative View on Hardware Product Development

The integrative process model on hardware product development captures the commonalities among hardware startup cases and differ from the model of software startups development (Giardino, Paternoster, Unterkalmsteiner et al, 2015). The common themes presenting in the previous section are connected in our model, as shown in Figure 2. The arrows represent the network of causal relationship between themes. The network is centered around the team, founders' characteristics and rapid MVP. It can be expected that the human factors are the main input for the product development. There is an influence from the founder's personalities and their behaviors to the rest of the team. In hardware startups, teams share common practices, which are appropriate processes, evolutionary development, document management and speed-up development. This differs from software startup processes that take ease on documents, emphasize the agility of both business and product development. Hardware development still requires some sort of procedure in place due to the involvement of physical components. Hardware product development also aims at quickly achieving MVPs. However, functional MVPs covers essential quality attributes, and hence, a balance between the speed and quality assurance is often a part of evolutionary MVP development process.

Not as severe as software business, hardware startups often require a certain level of initial capital. However, they still operate in the constraints of financial and human resources, which impact their team and development approaches. Eventually, The focus on speed, the limited resource and the characteristics of the founders contribute to the quick growth of product and business in the early phase, but later hinder the productivity in the later phase.

Figure 2. An integrative model of hardware product development in startup companies

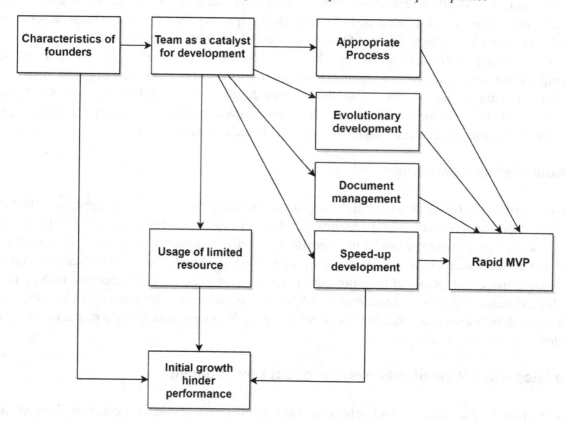

THREATS TO VALIDITY

In qualitative research, the validity must be addressed to enable the reliability, creditability and the replication of research. To ensure the validity of this study, we followed the validity guidelines in conducting case studies. Construct validity ensures that the operational measures that are studied really represent what the researcher have in mind and what is investigated according to the research questions. To assure that the interview questions were suitable for answering our research questions, we reused the interview protocol from previous research that has been published. Interviewees were key people, often founders of the startups, with sufficient insight into business- and technical-related aspects. External validity refers to the extent to which the findings are generalizable beyond the context studied. For qualitative studies, the intention is to enable analytical generalization where the results are extended to cases, which have common characteristics. All of our startups are from Pakistan, mainly consisting of early-stage small-size entrepreneurial teams. They are also mostly self-funded and acquiring some key competence from the start. The cases were reflected on theoretical factors in literature. However, it would be safe to repeat the study in different contexts, i.e. Europe, US, etc. Reliability refers to the extent that data and the analysis are dependent on the specific researchers. To decrease the risk of biased interpretations, several meetings were conducted among authors to discuss quotes and their meaning. Additionally, we compared findings to related literature examining similarities, contrasts, and explanations.

CONCLUSION

Startups create items blended with physical equipment and programming parts, requiring skill experts within a wide scope of tech fields. Notwithstanding programming advancement equipment, startups manage creation and coordination issues, factors suggesting higher beginning budgetary and human ventures are required for both types of startups thou software startups need a lesser initial budget. Hardware startups are comparable to software startups, as many software engineering methods and processes nowadays can be adopted in the development of hardware systems. In this study, we aim at understanding the methodological commonalities among hardware startup companies. The knowledge is built on the comparison with what is known in software startup product development.

Our observations on five case studies reveal important factors for all hardware startups, which are team is the catalyst for development, appropriate process definition, evolutionary development process and document management. We also reveal several factors that are different from software startups, such as low priority of product quality, product pipeline and unrecognized product platform.

We proposed the integrative model of hardware startup product development, highlighting the connections between human factors in the startups and their adopted speed-prioritized development processes, practices, a circumstance of constrained operation and the consequence of hindered productivity in the later phases.

The model has some implications for hardware startup founders who plan for their long-term product development. Startup founder should consider the tradeoff between early growth and sustainable product development. Perhaps, a strategy for developing rapid MVPs as the milestones for acquire funding and providing foundations for further evolutionary MVPs would be the key for early-stage success. Our process model also suggests a set of transferrable methods and techniques from software engineering to hardware product development. In the startup context, this suggests a lightweight approach to manage hardware-related procedures, relevant regulations and project documents. From our findings, future research on startups can propose processes, techniques, practices, and tools that support the development of MVPs in hardware startup context.

REFERENCES

Abrahamsson, P., Warsta, J., Siponen, M. T., & Ronkainen, J. (2003). New directions on agile methods: a comparative analysis. *25th International Conference on Software Engineering*, 244–254. 10.1109/ICSE.2003.1201204

Bailetti, A. J. (2012). What technology startups must get right to globalize early and rapidly. *Technology Innovation Management Review*, 2(10), 5–16. doi:10.22215/timreview/614

Bajwa, S. S., Wang, X., Duc, A. N., & Abrahamsson, P. (2017). Failures to be celebrated: An analysis of major pivots of software startups. *Empirical Software Engineering*, 22(5), 2373–2408. doi:10.100710664-016-9458-0

Baskerville, R., Ramesh, B., Levine, L., Pries-Heje, J., & Slaughter, S. (2003). Is "Internet-speed" software development different? *IEEE Software*, 20(6), 70–77.

Batova, T., Clark, D., & Card, D. (2016). Challenges of lean customer discovery as invention. *2016 IEEE International Professional Communication Conference (IPCC)*, 1–5. 10.1109/IPCC.2016.7740514

Berg, V., & Birkeland, J. (2018). *Exploring Empirical Engineering Approaches in Startup Companies: The Trilateral Hardware Startup Model*. NTNU.

Berg, V., Birkeland, J., Pappas, I. O., & Jaccheri, L. (2018). The Role of Data Analytics in Startup Companies: Exploring Challenges and Barriers. *Conference on e-Business, e-Services and e-Society*, 205–216. 10.1007/978-3-030-02131-3_19

Crowne, M. (2002, August). Why software product startups fail and what to do about it. Evolution of software product development in startup companies. In *IEEE International Engineering Management Conference* (*Vol. 1*, pp. 338-343). IEEE.

Dos Santos, D., da Silva, I. N., Modugno, R., Pazelli, H., & Castellar, A. (2007). Software Development Using an Agile Approach for Satellite Camera Ground Support Equipment. In *Advances and Innovations in Systems, Computing Sciences and Software Engineering* (pp. 71–76). Springer. doi:10.1007/978-1-4020-6264-3_14

Duc, A. N., Khalid, K., Lønnestad, T., Bajwa, S. S., Wang, X., & Abrahamsson, P. (2019). How do startups develop internet-of-things systems: a multiple exploratory case study. *Proceedings of the International Conference on Software and System Processes*, 74–83.

Giardino, C., Bajwa, S. S., Wang, X., & Abrahamsson, P. (2015). Key challenges in early-stage software startups. *International Conference on Agile Software Development*, 52–63.

Giardino, C., Paternoster, N., Unterkalmsteiner, M., Gorschek, T., & Abrahamsson, P. (2015). Software development in startup companies: The greenfield startup model. *IEEE Transactions on Software Engineering*, 42(6), 585–604. doi:10.1109/TSE.2015.2509970

Giardino, C., Wang, X., & Abrahamsson, P. (2014). Why early-stage software startups fail: a behavioral framework. *International conference of software business*, 27–41. 10.1007/978-3-319-08738-2_3

Gokaram Narayana Murthy, R. (2016). *Production ramp-up of a hardware startup: developing inventory management strategies and establishing a framework for vendor selection*. Massachusetts Institute of Technology.

Gralha, C., Damian, D., Wasserman, A. I. T., Goulão, M., & Araújo, J. (2018). The evolution of requirements practices in software startups. *Proceedings of the 40th International Conference on Software Engineering*, 823–833. 10.1145/3180155.3180158

Greene, B. (2004). Agile methods applied to embedded firmware development. *Agile Development Conference*, 71–77. 10.1109/ADEVC.2004.3

Hokkanen, L., Kuusinen, K., & Väänänen, K. (2015). Early product design in startups: towards a UX strategy. *International Conference on Product-Focused Software Process Improvement*, 217–224. 10.1007/978-3-319-26844-6_16

Hokkanen, L., & Väänänen-Vainio-Mattila, K. (2015). UX work in startups: current practices and future needs. *International Conference on Agile Software Development*, 81–92. 10.1007/978-3-319-18612-2_7

Kaisti, M., Rantala, V., Mujunen, T., Hyrynsalmi, S., Könnölä, K., Mäkilä, T., & Lehtonen, T. (2013). Agile methods for embedded systems development-a literature review and a mapping study. *EURASIP Journal on Embedded Systems*, *2013*(1), 15. doi:10.1186/1687-3963-2013-15

Kelly, D. P., & Culleton, B. (1999). Process improvement for small organizations. *Computer (Long. Beach. Calif)*, *32*(10), 41–47.

Klotins, E., Unterkalmsteiner, M., & Gorschek, T. (2015). Software engineering knowledge areas in startup companies: a mapping study. *International Conference of Software Business*, 245–257. 10.1007/978-3-319-19593-3_22

Kwanya, T., & Stilwell, C. (2017). Scholarly collaboration amongst researchers in Kenya: a social network analysis. *Proceedings of the 4th Multidisciplinary International Social Networks Conference*, 5. 10.1145/3092090.3092096

Larman, C., & Basili, V. R. (2003). Iterative and incremental developments. a brief history. *Computer (Long. Beach. Calif)*, *36*(6), 47–56. doi:10.1109/MC.2003.1204375

Lasi, H., Fettke, P., Kemper, H.-G., Feld, T., & Hoffmann, M. (2014). Industry 4.0. *Business & Information Systems Engineering*, *6*(4), 239–242. doi:10.100712599-014-0334-4

Maimbo, H., & Pervan, G. (2005). Designing a case study protocol for application in IS research. PACIS 2005 Proc., 106.

Nguyen-Duc, A., Seppänen, P., & Abrahamsson, P. (2015). Hunter-gatherer cycle: a conceptual model of the evolution of software startups. *Proceedings of the 2015 International Conference on Software and System Process*, 199–203. 10.1145/2785592.2795368

Paulk, M. (2002). Capability maturity model for software. Encyclopedia of Software Engineering. doi:10.1002/0471028959.sof589

Ries, E. (2014). *Lean Startup: Schnell, risikolos und erfolgreich Unternehmen gründen*. Redline Wirtschaft.

Rigby, D. K., Sutherland, J., & Takeuchi, H. (2016). Embracing agile. *Harvard Business Review*, *94*(5), 40–50.

Ronkainen, J., & Abrahamsson, P. (2003). Software development under stringent hardware constraints: Do agile methods have a chance? *International Conference on Extreme Programming and Agile Processes in Software Engineering*, 73–79. 10.1007/3-540-44870-5_10

Salvato, C. (2009). Capabilities unveiled: The role of ordinary activities in the evolution of product development processes. *Organization Science, 20*(2), 384–409. doi:10.1287/orsc.1080.0408

Seppänen, P., Tripathi, N., Oivo, M., & Liukkunen, K. (2017). How are product ideas validated? *International Conference of Software Business*, 3–17. 10.1007/978-3-319-69191-6_1

Statista. (n.d.). https://www.statista.com/statistics/471264/iot-number-of-connected-devices-worldwide/

Unterkalmsteiner, M. (2016). Software startups—a research agenda. *e-Informatica. Software Engineering Journal, 10*(1).

Usländer, T., & Batz, T. (2018). Agile Service Engineering in the Industrial Internet of Things. *Futur. Internet, 10*(10), 100. doi:10.3390/fi10100100

Zambonelli, F. (2016). *Towards a general software engineering methodology for the Internet of Things.* arXiv Prepr. arXiv1601.05569.

ENDNOTES

[1] www.dropcam.com
[2] https://skybox.xyz/en
[3] https://www.oculus.com/
[4] https://gopro.com/en/us/

Chapter 5
Value Proposition Innovation in Startups:
Value Proposition Identification and Prioritization

Varun Gupta

(iD) https://orcid.org/0000-0003-2824-3402
University of Alcala, Spain

Chetna Gupta
Jaypee Institute of Information Technology, India

Luis García Piedrabuena
University of Alcala, Spain

ABSTRACT

In highly dynamic situations, entrepreneurs build value propositions in resource-constrained conditions. The activity is set up as a series of experiments, with each one aimed at validating value proposition-related assumptions with customers. Validation entails interactions between potential customers and the startup team utilizing prototypes, which leads to the confirmation of current assumptions as well as the discovery of new insights that lead to more experiments. The main features of the value proposition identification model are highlighted in this chapter, and a novel value prioritizing approach is proposed.

INTRODUCTION

Startups are transient businesses that are always trying to find a scalable and repeatable business model. Once such model is achieved, the changes in business model becomes more stable. To formulate an effective business model, the main activity is to design an effective value proposition. Value proposition denotes the benefits that the product is intended to offer to the customers, helping them address their pains. To formulate such a value proposition, the startup team performs series of experimentations in

DOI: 10.4018/978-1-7998-9059-1.ch005

markets to evaluate their assumptions regarding value proposition. The goals of such experiments are to investigate the market in order to build a business strategy that best matches with market realities rather than being based solely on speculation. Continuous interactions with customers, for example, assist startups in testing their assumptions, also known as value proposition hypotheses, refining existing hypotheses, and finally identifying the one that best suits customer needs. Customers will prefer to acquire the firm's product over their competitor's products because of value proposition innovation, innovation which involves creating new value propositions or refining existing ones (Morris et al., 2005; Johnson et al., 2008). The limited resources of startups and highly uncertain markets limit their ability to foster innovations. Innovation by taking support from innovation ecosystem (also called as open innovation) is thus a key for market success. The importance of freelancers and academia as open innovation partners has been well documented in recent years (Gupta et al., 2020a; Gupta et al., 2020b; Gupta et al., 2020c; Gupta et al., 2020d; Gupta et al., 2020e; Gupta et al., 2021a). Their skills might be used by the startup to both construct and innovate an innovative value proposition. The main activity that affects the startup's success and competitive advantage is value proposition identification and ranking of identified values.

The major parts of the value proposition identification model are highlighted in this chapter, and a methodology for benefit prioritization is proposed.

ESSENTIAL ELEMENTS OF VALUE PROPOSITION IDENTIFICATION MODEL

The value proposition innovation approach includes tasks such as gathering product value proposition ideas, validating those ideas, implementing those ideas, and eventually making the product available to customers on the market. The most important job is determining an accurate value proposition, or the benefits that a product is expected to provide to its customers in order to increase customer value. These benefits should be validated in the sense that none of the underlying assumptions about the product value proposition should be merely hypotheses, but rather something those potential buyers truly require. Such a process is actually a market experiment, with the startup team gathering initial ideas, interacting with customers using prototypes (Gupta et al., 2021b) to validate these ideas, as well as uncovering additional insights about customer needs, and finally identifying the product value proposition. The process of determining the product value proposition is structured as a customer experiment with the goal of accurately detecting customer expectations about the product. The following properties should be present in the value proposition identification model.

1. **Incorporating Non-Functional values:** Customers frequently state their functional requirements but rarely the non-functional benefits they require. To find non-functional benefits that will improve customer experience, the startup team must apply their tactical expertise, observations of consumers' interactions with prototypes, and knowledge of the customer working domain (where goods will be adopted). The product's security features are one example of non-functional benefits. Finger authentication, passwords, authentication mechanisms, and so forth are examples of this. These are unspoken requirements that no user will declare because users can only specify functional requirements. It will be of no value to have a system that performs all operations but may be accessed by anyone. If an ATM machine completes your transaction but also allows anyone to access your account, it is of no benefit to you. As a result, we must consider the attacker and identify the weaknesses that are the most typical targets of attackers in order to safeguard them.

The security need list must be applied and updated on a regular basis. As a result, a product value proposition that only provides functional benefits may reduce the real product value because the lack of non-functional value reduces functional utility.

2. **Prioritizing Benefits:** Because of their limited resources, the startup team's contacts with customers may result in the identification of several benefits that cannot be realized in the product. Furthermore, client expectations change over time, so it's a good idea to start with the basics and then deliver updated versions of products based on customer feedback. The startup team must be able to rate the identified benefits because they are of high priority. Various characteristics, such as business values, such as customer happiness, relevance to users, involved hazards, dependence limitations, and so on, can be used to determine priority. In the startup setting, requirement engineering is still in its infancy (Gupta et al., 2020a), which implies that the startup team has limited access to scholarly literature. The startup team can defer the execution of lower priority benefits and thus the associated risks by prioritizing the benefits.

3. **Risk Estimation:** Future difficulties that could result in a loss or jeopardize the project's success, but have not yet occurred, are referred to as risks. Such dangers may or may not materialize. However, one should be prepared to deal with such ambiguities. As a result, comprehensive risk management must be in place to address the many hazards that may arise and to take appropriate measures as necessary. This means that, based on the research of similar but past ventures, the value proposition identification model should be able to inform the startup team about the risks associated with the identified benefits.

4. **Reuse:** Reuse means "the reapplication of a variety of kinds of knowledge about one system to another similar system in order to reduce the effort of value proposition identification task with a new project". For instance, the startup team could identify the benefits but based on historical project, the model could suggest which other benefits could be of interest for current project.

5. **Support for Experimentation:** The model should make it simple for the startup team to conduct additional experiments. This may be accomplished if the model is adaptable enough to be updated with new information and allows historical values to be analyzed to anticipate future outcomes that drive future decision-making.

PROPOSED VALUE PROPOSITION IDENTIFICATION MODEL

The proposed model helps startup team to rank the identified and validated benefits within their resources. The prioritization requires the active support of strategic partnerships with the freelancers and academia. Their support helps them to is possible take advantage of their experiences and tactical knowledge in driving the ranking of benefits. The factors employed for ranking includes the following (Table 1):

- **Customer Value:** This signifies difference between the advantage provided to the customers by the product and involved price.
- **Dependency Constraints:** From implementation point of view, there could be set of benefits that are good to be implemented together as a cluster. This means that the benefits that are very dependent on each other should be implemented together.
- **Risks:** This signifies the business problems that could happen if the benefit is not implemented.

Table 1. Benefit priority matrix

S.No.	Benefits	Customer Value	Dependency Constrains	Business Risks	Final Value
1	B1				
2	B2				
3	B3				
...	...				
X	BX				

The main idea behind this method is that benefits need to be prioritized against multiple factors. The important criteria are customer value because if product enhances customer value, then only customers are going to buy the product. Startup team must also select the benefits that are dependent on other benefits. This is because, if dependent benefits are implemented in future, their implementation will enhance efforts for their implementation and testing, for instance, ripple effects and technical debt.

Finally, involved business risks should be considered. For instance, if a benefit is not implemented then it may lead to negative impacts to business. This may happen because of competitor positioning. There could be some benefits that could help to target the "non-users" or tackle the future moves of the competitor.

The price is also the main element of customer value so efforts should be made to optimise this parameter. Involvement of academia and freelancers helps to provide their expertise about the prioritization factors based on their understanding of customer domain. For instance, freelancers can be employed both as customer knowledge agents and as the persons responsible for implementing the value propositions (Gupta et al., 2021). The startup team can do open innovation with freelancers and experts from academia institutions for following prioritization factors (Table 2):

Table 2. Prioritization criteria knowledge sources.

S. No.	Prioritization Criteria	Knowledge Source	Main Driver
1.	Customer Value	Freelancers	Close Proximity with customers.
		Startup Team	Interactions with customers.
		Academia	Close proximity with customers.
2.	Dependency Constrains	Freelancers.	Implementation knowledge and skills.
		Startup Team	
		Academia (Technical Domain)	
3.	Business Risks	Freelancers	Firm specific knowledge based on their previous association with companies as freelancer or full time employee.
		Startup Team	Increased familiarity of industry.
		Academia (Business Domain)	Increased understanding of industry.

The prioritization involves ranking the three criterias with customer value being weighted more than others. The division of weight depends on the startup, industry, and product innovation levels. The values provided by freelancers and those in academia needs to be merged with the startup team and could be achieved through consensus buildings. In case of conflict, same could be validated by designing a small experimentation and validating it with customers using prototypes.

The algorithm works as follows:

Vx: Average value allocated to individual benefit against single criteria.
Vy: Prioritization criteria weight (sum of all column weights is 100).

The difference between Vx and Vy is normalised value of benefit against selected criteria. This is given as:

$$Vdiff = Vy - Vx$$

Similarly, we compute Vdiff for the benefit for each column. This process is repeated for all benefits. Finally, the sum of all normalized values for each benefit for three criteria is used to determine the benefit's final ranking. The following formula is used to calculate this:

$$Vfinal = Vdiff1 + Vdiff2 + \ldots\ldots + Vdiffn.$$

Higher the value of Vfinal, higher the priority. So, to find priorities follow the algorithm shown in Box 1.

Box 1.

Algorithm: Priority (Benefit_number, Customer_value, Dependency Constrains, Business_Risks)
1. Fill the matrix as shown in table1.
2. For each Benefit, **DO:**
    a) For each column, calculate the value of Vdiffi.
    b) Calculate the value of Vfinal.
3. Arrange benefits in decreasing order of the Vfinal.

CONCLUSION

A startup team's ability to construct an effective value proposal is required for value proposition innovation. This does, however, need the startup team selecting a set of benefits as part of the value proposition that are most important to the customers. The proposed ranking method could be improved with Artificial Intelligence (AI) algorithms to assist the startup team in making accurate predictions based on past data, thereby expediting future experiments.

REFERENCES

Gupta, V., Fernandez-Crehuet, J. M., Gupta, C., & Hanne, T. (2020c). Freelancing models for fostering innovation and problem solving in software startups: An empirical comparative study. *Sustainability*, *12*(23), 10106. doi:10.3390u122310106

Gupta, V., Fernandez-Crehuet, J. M., & Hanne, T. (2020b). Freelancers in the software development process: A systematic mapping study. *Processes (Basel, Switzerland)*, *8*(10), 1215. doi:10.3390/pr8101215

Gupta, V., Fernandez-Crehuet, J. M., & Hanne, T. (2020d). Fostering continuous value proposition innovation through freelancer involvement in software startups: Insights from multiple case studies. *Sustainability*, *12*(21), 8922. doi:10.3390u12218922

Gupta, V., Fernandez-Crehuet, J. M., Hanne, T., & Telesko, R. (2020a). Requirements engineering in software startups: A systematic mapping study. *Applied Sciences (Basel, Switzerland)*, *10*(17), 6125. doi:10.3390/app10176125

Gupta, V., Fernandez-Crehuet, J. M., Hanne, T., & Telesko, R. (2020e). Fostering product innovations in software startups through freelancer supported requirement engineering. *Results in Engineering*, *8*, 100175. doi:10.1016/j.rineng.2020.100175

Gupta, V., & José María Fernández-Crehuet, J. M. (2021a). Divergent Creativity for Requirement Elicitation Amid Pandemic: Experience from Real Consulting Project. *Tenth International Workshop on Creativity in Requirements Engineering (CreaRE'21). The 27th International Working Conference on Requirement Engineering: Foundation for Software Quality (REFSQ 2021)*.

Gupta, V., Rubalcaba, L., Gupta, C., & Gupta, V. (2021b). Multimedia Prototyping for Early-Stage Startups Endurance: Stage for New Normal? *IEEE MultiMedia*, *28*(4), 107–116. doi:10.1109/MMUL.2021.3122539

Johnson, M. W., Christensen, C. M., & Kagermann, H. (2008). Reinventing your business model. *Harvard Business Review*, *86*(12), 57–68.

Morris, M., Schindehutte, M., & Allen, J. (2005). The entrepreneur's business model: Toward a unified perspective. *Journal of Business Research*, *58*(6), 726–735. doi:10.1016/j.jbusres.2003.11.001

Chapter 6
Ambidexterity, Knowledge Management, and Innovation in Technology Development Zones:
The Case of Turkey

Şükran Sirkintioğlu Yildirim
(iD) https://orcid.org/0000-0002-3578-4074
Kastamonu University, Turkey

Özlem Atay
(iD) https://orcid.org/0000-0002-2563-825X
Ankara University, Turkey

ABSTRACT

This chapter searches how knowledge management and innovation activities, which enable an advantageous position for firms over their opponents, influence ambidexterity and business performance. These enable firms to gain an advantage over their competitors, concerning ambidexterity and organizational performance. The population for this study comprises firms, operating in technology development zones in Ankara, Turkey. According to the sectoral distribution of the enterprises in the technology development zones, the majority operate in the software sector. No sampling methods were used because the sensus method was adopted. Three hundred sixty high-tech enterprise top managers form the basis of this empirical research. In this study, structural equation modeling was used for testing research model. As a result of the structural equation modeling, it was understood that firms' knowledge management and innovation usage preferences have a positive impact on ambidexterity and organizational performance. This outcome is important for firms to gain a competitive advantage.

DOI: 10.4018/978-1-7998-9059-1.ch006

INTRODUCTION

In today's world of intense competition, firms seek to reduce their costs as much as possible while striving to increase their productivity and quality. Therefore, managers have to control many contrasting situations concurrently to sustain the business. The rapid advancement of technology and globalization has brought a new dimension to the competition and firms are attaching more importance to notions such as novelty, creativity, and speed because they pave the way for knowledge as a strategic value. Firms need to implement innovation activities to manage chaos and also enable sustainability.

Nowadays, the concept that is creating a difference between firms is knowledge and the human factor that builds knowledge. Creating, sharing, using, and managing knowledge within firms becomes part of the organizational culture. The fact that knowledge can become a competitive weapon for firms in a globalized world and that capital-intensive firms are replaced by knowledge-intensive firms shows how important knowledge management is for firms. Yet firms can encounter an insufficient knowledge level; there can be a gap between the available knowledge level of firms and the required knowledge level needed to produce new products, processes, or services. Firms need creative studies to close this gap. At this point, the important thing for a firm is the quality and amount of knowledge and how it will be utilized to carry out innovation activities. Because, firms increase their creativity and performance by integrating knowledge management and knowledge processes (Shahzad, Bajwa, Siddiqi, Ahmid and Sultani, 2016).

Creating knowledge is an essential point for creating innovation processes, and innovation management is a critical issue for enterprises. When considered from this aspect, the long-term success of any enterprise is mainly to discover new skills while developing current skills also (Raisch, Birkinshaw, Probst and Tushman, 2009).

Firms need to take advantage of their basic knowledge and as well explore new opportunities by opening doors to new information (Cantarello, Martini and Nosella, 2012). Ambidexterity also handles the innovation and knowledge management that interacts with it as well as the variables affecting ambidexterity. The main feature of successful firms can balance explorative and exploitative strategies (Chang and Hughes, 2012). Anzenbahcer and Wagner (2019: 572) highlighted "the ability to balance exploratory and exploitative activities has become more and more crucial for firms in today's increasingly globalized business environment in the face of rapid technological change". Ambidextrous firms can balance and manage exploitation and exploration knowledge (Raisch et al., 2009).

A resource-based approach is a tool by which firms gain an advantage over their competitors by using their internal resources (Barney, 1991). With the resource-based approach, it was tried to explain why some companies are more successful and gain a sustainable competitive advantage (Khan and Zaman, 2020). This study adopts a resource-based approach and a knowledge-based approach and aims to research how knowledge management and innovation activities, which enable an advantageous position for firms over their opponents, influence ambidexterity and business performance. This chapter answer these research questions: whether knowledge management and innovation activities affect ambidexterity and performance of the firm? In this chapter, the relationship between ambidexterity, innovation, knowledge management and firm performance will be examined.

BACKGROUND

Knowledge Management and Innovation

Knowledge management practices in firms encompass a series of strategies and initiative activities used for the generation, transfer, apply and storage of knowledge (Donate andPablo, 2015). Managing knowledge fruitfully increases the innovation capacity of firms (Darroch and McNaughton, 2002; Donate andGuadamillas, 2011). Nonaka (1994) argued that knowledge creation in firms is the basis of innovation and competition. Thus, knowledge management helps firms launch new products and services.

In knowledge-based economies, knowledge is a necessary resource to carry out efficient management policies and practices for firms. Thanks to knowledge management, firms gain innovation-making skills, raise productivity, and consequently achieve a competitive advantage in the medium to long term (Kremp and Mairesse, 2004). Firms aim to develop more innovation activities and create value with their improving knowledge. Subramaniam and Youndt (2005) described innovation as knowledge management processes concerned with defining and using ideas and an opportunity to create new products/services. In this manner, knowledge management is seen as the core of the innovation process and organizational harmony in terms of firms (Earl, 2001).

There are many studies in the literature examining the relationship between knowledge management and innovation (Khan and Zaman, 2020; Hamdoun, Jabbour and Othman, 2018; Durmuş-Özdemir and Abdukhoshimov, 2018; Mardani, Nikoosokhan, Maradi and Doustar, 2018; Inkinen, Kianto and Vanhala, 2015; Donate and Pablo, 2015; Lai, Hsu, Lin, Chen and Lin, 2014; Yeşil, Koska and Büyükmeşe, 2013; Wang and Wang, 2012; Donate and Guadamillas, 2011; Lopez-Saez, and Castro Delgado-Verde, 2011). Ode and Ayavoo (2020) examined the relationship between knowledge management practices and firm innovation in companies operating in the service sector in developing countries. As a result of the study, knowledge management practices contribute to firm innovation both directly and indirectly. In a recent study conducted by Gürlek and Çemberci (2020), knowledge management efforts in firms turn into innovation performance and consequently into firms performance.

Innovation strongly depends on availability of the knowledge and its recombination leading to products or services in a way that delivers value to the customers. In a pandemic, there is plenty of information that could be converted into knowledge leading to successful commercialisation of innovations in the market. For small sized firms with limited resources, knowledge acquisition and its recombination could be effortful. However, in previous research the startups have used university libraries (Gupta et al., 2021a; Gupta et al., 2022a) and competitor peer startups (Gupta et al., 2021b) as their strategic knowledge partners and have relied on technology adoption for exploring market knowledge (Gupta et al., 2021b; Gupta et al., 2022b) to successfully innovate and survive.

H$_1$: Knowledge management will have a positive influence on innovation.

Innovation and Ambidexterity

Robert Duncan, for the first time, mentioned the 'ambidexterity' notion to define dual organization structures in the administration and organization literature in 1976 (as cited in Hodgkinson, Ravishandar and Aitken-Fischer, 2014). The notion, coming from the ability to use both the right and the left hand equally, then started to be used as a metaphor in the administration and organization literature (Lubatkin,

Şimşek, Ling and Veiga, 2006). Although it is hard to define the ambidexterity notion thoroughly, it is generally agreed that firms can gather their resources and skills to maintain sustainability and achieve success (O'Reilly and Tushman, 2013).

Wernerfelt (1984) emphasizes the significance of balancing the exploitation of existing resources of firms with a resource-based perspective. Subsequently, March (1991) later defined the ambidexterity notion in the literature aftermath of Duncan (1976). March asserted the need to balance explorative and exploitative strategies. These two strategies are considered two subdimensions of a whole. Duncan stressed that there has to be a unit to conduct explorative activities as well as a different unit to conduct exploitative activities for firms to overcome the possible problems of his dual structure. Firms can manage conflicting demands and cost efficiency by using these dual organization structures and therefore any department inside the business can focus on adapting to the changing environmental conditions, whereas another department can focus on alignment (Birkinsaw and Gibson, 2004).

In firms, exploitative activities and exploratory activities contend for scarce resources (Anzenbacher and Wagner, 2019). That is, firms should focus on balanced activities that can both follow and develop innovations and benefit from available skills (Raisch et al., 2009).

The firms that realize their innovation activities in a specific cycle become more talented at innovation making, unlike the firms balancing their exploitative and explorative strategies. Particularly, these firms become more successful in terms of their product innovation (Şimşek, Veiga, Lubatkin and Dino, 2005). While the firms achieving their ambidexterity activities in a cycle allocate more time for exploitative activities, explorative activities prevent explorative activities, and these firms enter into a time loop (Gupta et al., 2006). Technology-based firms, realizing their cyclical ambidexterity period, are more inclined to seek out product innovation, and this situation is considered as an incremental element in business performance (Atuahene-Gima, 2005). When firms give more importance to explorative activities to produce new products, they can produce new products as well as discover new technology (Şimşek et al., 2005). When firms realize their exploitative and explorative activities in a cycle, they avoid a competency trap that results in giving weight to exploitative activities and also a failure trap that results in giving extreme weight to explorative activities (Siggelkow and Levinthal, 2003). Competency and failure trap affect the innovation performance of firms.

Wu, Wood, Chen, Meyer and Liu (2020) investigated the relationship between ambidexterity and innovation on 74 Chinese multinational firms and 60 domestic enterprises. According to the results of the research, ambidexterity has a negative effect on innovation in domestic companies. But this effect is less in Chinese multinational enterprises.

H$_2$: Innovation will have a positive influence on ambidexterity.

Ambidexterity, Knowledge Management, and Firm Performance

Ambidexterity consists of different learning methods in firms requiring diverse strategies, contexts, and organizational mechanisms (Gupta et al., 2006). Businesses can choose from among ambidexterity strategies by using different learning methods. Whereas firms try to develop their available knowledge and competence using exploitative methods for the sake of developing the available activities, they seek new knowledge for explorative activities. At this point, knowledge management plays a vital role in determining whether firms will go toward exploitative strategies or explorative strategies (Filippini, Güttel and Nosella, 2012).

When the importance of knowledge management is acknowledged, it helps firms manage their exploitative and explorative activities and become competitive in a dynamic environment (Cepeda and Vera, 2007). Verona and Ravasi (2003) described knowledge management as organizational regulations encouraging exploitative activities to raise productivity and explorative activities encouraging innovation in firms. Lubatkin et al. (2006) claimed that knowledge management processes solve the conflict between exploitative and explorative innovations. Tushman and O'Reilly (1996) emphasized that efficient knowledge management in firms is necessary for the long-term performance of explorative and exploitative innovation.

Exploitative and explorative strategies, as two subdimensions of ambidexterity, were considered different and competing concepts before March's (1991) study. Later studies understood that these two strategies were not competing with each other and could be balanced and integrated owing to firms' scarce resources (Raisch et al., 2009). March claimed that firms do not need any selection between exploitative and explorative strategies; on the contrary, they should have the skill to manage these two strategies at the same time. When academics explain exploitative and explorative strategies, they make a connection between knowledge management and innovation. They assert that firms should have both strategies to increase their knowledge level. On the one hand, an exploitative strategy can be realized through research and practice of innovation within the confines of available knowledge. On the other hand, an explorative strategy means any research on entirely new information and the production of novelties for firms. Both strategies necessitate the integration of knowledge in the business (Taylor and Greve, 2006).

Cao, Gedajlovic and Zhang (2009) stressed that exploitative and explorative innovation can cause a conflict of resources and place demands on firms and there should be a balance between these two innovation strategies; however, balance can be realized with ambidexterity. Even though it is hard to conduct exploitative and explorative strategies together, one cannot disregard the positive effect of competitive advantage and long-term performance for business (Jansen, Von den Bosch and Volberda, 2005). Many studies concluded that knowledge management affects ambidexterity (Abazeed, 2020; Dezi, Ferraris, Papa and Vrontis, 2019; Soto-Acosta, Popa, Martinez-Conesa, 2018; Oehmichen, Heyden, Georgakakis and Volberda, 2016).

Firms should follow changes and implement them into their business strategies to keep up with the continuous and rapidly changing environmental conditions. They should also seek out new knowledge and skills that will protect their competitive positions while they develop their existing knowledge and skills (Floyd and Lane, 2000). Peng, Lin, Peng and Chen (2019) stressed; "when an organization performs exploration and exploitation actions, it not only improves its operational efficiency but also promotes innovative performance". Firms implement all these activities to achieve good performance.

Severgnini, Galdamez and Vieira (2019) investigated the relationship between ambidexterity and firm performance on 227 software companies. According to the results of this study, ambidexterity increases business performance. This result is similar to Gibson and Birkinshaw's (2004) study, but different from Gupta et al., (2006) and Cao et al., (2009) studies. In the literature, studies are suggesting that ambidexterity affects business performance in a positive direction (Mura, Micheli and Longo, 2020; Junni, Sarala, Taras and Tarba, 2013; O'Reilly and Tushman, 2013; Atuahene-Gima, 2005). Some studies have concluded that there is a negative effect (Wu and Ang, 2019; Wu, Ma, Liu, and Lei, 2019; Menguc and Auh, 2008; Ebben and Johnson, 2005; Van Looy, Martens and Debackere, 2005).

H_3: Ambidexterity will have a positive influence on firm performance.

METHODOLOGY

Sampling

The population of the research comprises the firms operating at Technology Development Zones (technopark) in Turkey/Ankara. The reason behind the selection of these firms is that they are established to carry out research and development activities and they are knowledge-intensive firms. The target group in this study is senior executives of the firms operating at Technology Development Zones. Senior executives have a significant role in the strategic decision-making process of the firms (Lubatkin et al., 2006). Because ambidexterity is a strategic choice for firms, senior executives are particularly preferred for this study. There is a total of 970 firms operating at five Technology Development Zones in Ankara. All the questionnaires were delivered by hand to the 360 firms that agreed to participate in the survey. When the sectoral distribution of the firms in these Technology Development Zones is examined, there are many more firms operating in the software sector. Following the software sector, the densest sectors are computer technology and electronics, respectively. These 360 firms were classified into six different sectors (see Figure 1). Wang and Rafiq (2014) emphasized that the firms that apply ambidexterity strategies should be in high-technology sectors. Because firms using high technology were preferred, the study becomes rational.

Figure 1. Distribution by sectors

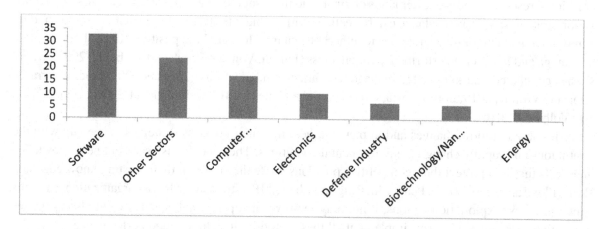

Method and Measuring Tools

The questionnaire used in this study was created from the preexisting scales found in the literature. The used research model was tested with structural equation modeling (SEM). The reason for using SEM is that structural equation modeling examines the relationship between observed and potential variables. SEM reveals unobtrusive connections (Yu, 2004, Reisinger and Turner, 2009). It is presumed that observed variables in the model measure potential variables. SEM can be used for different strategies in analyses. Jöreskog (1993) proposed a confirmatory modeling strategy, an alternative model strategy, and a model-developing strategy. In this study, a confirmatory modeling strategy was used because it tests the used model whether a data set is confirmed or not. Ambidexterity strategies were measured by 12 items (two dimensions), innovation by 21 items (four dimensions), knowledge management by 55 items (11 dimensions), and firms' performance by four items (one dimension). Information about the scales is given in Table 1.

Table 1. Information of scales

Variable	Number of Items	Source
Ambidexterity	12	Lubatkin et al. (2006)
Innovation	21	Lin, Chen and Shun (2010)
Knowledge Management	55	Lee and Choi (2003)
Firm Performance	4	Lichtenthaler (2009)

Findings

Dimension means, standard deviations, and skewness and kurtosis values of the variables in the questionnaire are given in Table 2. Whether the values show normal distribution or not can be understood through skewness and kurtosis values. If the values are between ±3, it shows a normal distribution (Shao, 2002). When the skewness and kurtosis values of variables are examined, one can see that the values are between ±3 and therefore the data show a normal distribution.

Table 2. Descriptive statistics

Scale	Means	Standard Deviation	Skewness	Kurtosis
Knowledge management	3,99	0,292	-0,377	0,199
Innovation	3,91	0,904	-0,253	-0,178
Ambidexterity	4,14	0,496	-0,233	-0,261
Performance	3,51	0,829	-0,482	-0,076

Whether the data belonging to the scale are suitable for analysis, Kaiser-Meyer-Olkin (KMO) test and also Bartlett's Sphericity (BS) test are applied to whether the data are suitable for factor analysis. Field (2013) stated that the sub-limit of the KMO value should be 0,50. The KMO value is 0,869, and the BS significance value shows that it is suitable for factor analysis. After it was understood that the data were suitable for factor analysis, they were passed to factor analysis. As a result of the analysis, 14 factors were obtained, they can be seen in Table 3.

Table 3. Exploratory factor analysis

Variables	Dimensions	Number of Items	Adjusted R Squared	Cronbach Alpha
Knowledge Management	Cooperation-Trust	9	13,290	0,86
	Learning	7	6,754	0,87
	Centralization	3	57,484	0,86
	T- Type Skill	5	42,071	0,79
	InformationTechnology Support	5	23,420	0,85
	Externalization	7	28,412	0,83
	Internalization	4	18,372	0,84
Innovation	Product Innovation	4	53,865	0,768
	Process Innovation	3	50,239	0,849
	Organizational Innovation	5	33,105	0,827
	Marketing Innovation	4	46,433	0,861
Ambidexterity	Exploitative Activities	4	60,415	0,650
	Explorative Activities	3	63,256	0,670
Performance	Performance	4	37,700	0,887

At the end of the factor analysis, the knowledge management scale was gathered under seven subdimensions. Because formalization, socialization, and integration subdimensions' (18 statements) factor load were under 0,500 (Nunnally, 1978), they were excluded from the scale. Cooperation and confidence dimensions were gathered under the same factor, and they were named as factor cooperation-confidence. The innovation scale was gathered under four dimensions. Because factor loads of four statements were under 0,500, they were excluded from the scale. The ambidexterity scale was gathered under two dimensions. Because factor loads of the five statements were under 0,500, they were excluded from the scale. And the scale belonging to business performance was gathered under a single factor.

Confirmatory Factor Analysis

Confirmatory factor analysis measures the relationship between potential variables and observed variables in the model. Statistical Package for the Social Sciences (SPSS) and Analysis of Moment Structures (AMOS) programs was applied for confirmatory factor analysis and goodness-of-fit values belonging to the model were computed. The goodness-of-fit values belonging to the measuring model can be seen in Table 4.

Table 4. Confirmatory factor analysis results

Fit Index	1. Degree CFA	2. Degree CFA	Goodness-fit Indexes*	Acceptable Fit
χ^2/sd	1,427	1,342	≤ 3	$\leq 4-5$
GFI	0,817	0,848	$0,95 \leq$ GFI ≤ 1	$0,90 \leq$ GFI $< 0,95$
CFI	0,921	0,943	$0,95 \leq$ CFI ≤ 1	$0,90 \leq$ CFI $< 0,95$
RMSEA	0,034	0,031	RMSEA $\leq 0,05$	$0,05 <$ RMSEA $< 0,10$
SRMR	0,052	0,058	SRMR < 0.05	$0,06 <$ SRMR $< 0,08$
RMR	0,036	0,041	RMR $\leq 0,05$	$0,05 <$ RMR $\leq 0,10$

When confirmatory factor analysis was employed, some of the goodness of fit values belonging to the model were under acceptable values. As a result of adjustments, a total of seven statements from the knowledge management variable, one statement from the ambidexterity variable, three statements from the innovation activities variable, and one statement from the business performance variable were excluded.

In the aftermath of modifications, goodness-of-fit values took place in the acceptable values (Table 4: 2. Degree CFA). First of all, we examined the chi-square (χ^2/ sd) goodness-of-fit test, as the most widely used index, and it was seen that the model was significant. However, because chi-square is highly sensitive to sample size, it is not sufficient alone to evaluate the fit between model and data. For this reason, other fit values were examined too. When the obtained index values were examined for the measuring model, the results were either good or acceptable: χ^2/sd value is under 3; RMSEA is under 0,05; CFI value is under 0,95; GFI value is near 0,95, and SRMR value is under 0,08. When the goodness of fit values was analyzed, it was seen that the relationships specified in the model and the data are acceptable

As a result of confirmatory factor analysis, the average variance extracted (AVE) and composite reliability (RE) values of each dimension were computed after goodness-of-fit values were between acceptable values (Table 5). Construct validity, in the meantime, was tested with AVE and CR. Hair, Black, Babin and Anderson (2009) claimed that the AVE value should be over 0,50 and the CR value should be over 0,70. Besides, the CR value should be over the AVE value in each dimension. When Table 5 is examined, AVE values of cooperation-confidence (AVE: 0,43), T-type skill (AVE: 0,46), externalization (AVE: 0,35), product innovation (AVE: 0,47), organizational innovation (AVE: 0,43), explorative activities (AVE: 0,48), and exploitative activities (AVE: 0,41) should be under 0,50 for all variables but Fornell and Larcker (1981: 46) impressed on "based on p_n (composite reliability) alone, the researcher may conclude that the convergent validity of the construct is adequate, even though more than 50% of the variance is due to error". The CR values should be over 0,70 for all variables. The model performs another circumstance for construct validity that the CR value should be higher than the AVE value for all variables.

Table 5. CR and AVE values

Variables	Dimensions	AVE	CR
Knowledge Management	Cooperation-Trust	0,43	0,87
	Learning	0,52	0,64
	Centralization	0,72	0,88
	T- Type Skill	0,46	0,81
	Information Technology Support	0,56	0,86
	Externalization	0,35	0,79
	Internalization	0,50	0,83
Innovation	Product Innovation	0,47	0,78
	Process Innovation	0,62	0,83
	Organizational Innovation	0,43	0,79
	Marketing Innovation	0,60	0,85
Ambidexterity	Exploitative Activities	0,48	0,73
	Explorotive Activities	0,41	0,73
Performance	Performance	0,72	0,91

Path Analysis

The existence of one-way causal relationships in the proposed model was tested by path analysis. Goodness-of-fit values were computed together with the path analysis. The χ^2/df, RMSEA, SRMR, RMR, CFI, and GFI values are given in Table 6 were within the acceptable range. In this manner, one can see that the set model is confirmed.

Table 6. Fit index values and goodness fit values for the structural model

Fit Index	Fit Index Values	Goodness-fit Indexes*	Acceptable Fit
x^2 değeri (p)		p > 0,05	-
χ^2/sd	1,356	≤ 3	≤ 4–5
GFI	0,847	0,95 ≤ GFI ≤1	0,90 ≤ GFI < 0,95
CFI	0,940	0,95 ≤ CFI ≤1	0,90 ≤ CFI <0,95
RMSEA	0,031	RMSEA ≤ 0,05	0,05 < RMSEA < 0,10
SRMR	0,058	SRMR < 0.05	0,06 < SRMR < 0,08
RMR	0,042	RMR ≤ 0,05	0,05 < RMR ≤0,10

When the index values are examined for the structural model (Table 6), it is seen that the results are good or acceptable. χ^2/sd value is under 3; RMSEA is under 0,05; CFI value is under 0,95; GFI is near 0,90 and SRMR value is under 0,08.

As a result of the analysis, the effect of knowledge management over innovation ($\beta1:0,98$) is positive and significant; the effect of innovation over ambidexterity ($\beta1:0,50$) is positive and significant; and the effect of innovation over business performance ($\beta1:0,64$) is positive and significant. Regression coefficients of ambidexterity, innovation activities, knowledge management, and business performance variables were computed within the context of the research scope to test the relations among them. Table 7 shows variables, regression coefficient, standard error values, and probability values.

Table 7. Path coefficients and significance levels of the predicted structural

Variables		Std.Regression Coefficient	Std. Error	Sig. Level
Innovation ←	Knowledge Management	0,563	0,208	<0,001
Ambidexterity ←	Innovation	0,741	0,097	<0,001
Performance ←	Ambidexterity	0,283	0,176	<0,001

*** p<0,001

As a result of regression analysis, we concluded that there is a positive effect of knowledge management over innovation; a positive effect of innovation over ambidexterity; and a positive effect of ambidexterity over business performance according to probability values. The most significant way to contribute can be decided along with standardized regression coefficients. When standardized coefficient numbers are examined, it is clear that the most contributing innovation activity to the model is ambidexterity. H_1, H_2 and H_3 hypotheses were accepted according to the analysis results.

FUTURE RESEARCH DIRECTIONS

Additional studies may obtain different results when comparing the firms operating at Technology Development Zones across Turkey and the world. Firms in different sectors using high technology can be used for future studies. Increasing studies in different sectors make it easier to compare results. Future studies can be designed by addressing cultural differences. A longitudinal sample collected at the point at different times will help support this research objective. Future studies could also take into consideration looking separately at different dimensions of exploration and exploitation strategies. The research population consists of the senior managers of the enterprises. However, other observation groups, such as customers, can be included in the research to fully understand the innovative activities of a business. A similar study could also be replicated in other industries such as manufacturing, aviation, food industry, and hospitality etc.

CONCLUSION

This study aimed was to research the effects of firms' ambidexterity and business performance by using knowledge management and innovation. As a result of the analysis within the context of a designated model, we concluded that there is a positive and significant effect of knowledge management over innovation; a positive and significant effect of innovation over ambidexterity; and a positive and significant effect of ambidexterity over business performance. After the model was put through the structural equation modeling linearity hypothesis, it was clear that going through innovation activities to ambidexterity has a greater impact compared with other ways.

Nonaka, Toyama and Konno (2000) asserted that there is a positive relationship between the efficient use of knowledge and innovation inside a business. Knowledge has become the most important resource today, and it is important to obtain, spread, evaluate, and store knowledge that is the keystone of innovation. Hargadon and Sutton (1997) claimed that new knowledge presents creative solutions and consequently paves the way for innovation for firms. Therefore, firms can adopt new competencies or they can develop their current competencies thanks to new knowledge. There are many studies in the literature examining the relationship between knowledge management and innovation (Ode and Ayavoo, 2020; Gürlek and Çemberci, 2020; Khan and Zaman, 2020; Hamdoun et al., 2018; Durmuş-Özdemir and Abdukhoshimov, 2018; Mardani et al. 2018; Inkinen et al., 2015; Donate and Pablo, 2015; Lai et al., 2014; Yeşil et al., 2013; Wang and Wang, 2012; Donate and Guadamillas, 2011; Castro et al., 2011). Innovation and knowledge management are significant for firms to develop new products as well as their current products. Firms undertake these activities to improve their performances.

Similar results were gained in comparisons with the studies in the literature. In the studies that support a positive effect of knowledge management over innovation, Lubatkin et al. (2006) claimed that knowledge management processes solve the conflict between exploitative and explorative innovations; similarly, Tushman and O'Reilly (1996) thought that efficient knowledge management in firms is necessary for long-term performance of exploitative and explorative strategies.

When examining the effect of ambidexterity over business performance, both He and Wong (2004) and O'Reilly and Tushman (2013) concluded that ambidexterity has a positive effect on business performance. There are studies in the literature that found similar results with this study. (Mura et al., 2020; Junni et al., 2013; Stettner and Lavie, 2013; Jansen, Van den Bosch and Volberda, 2006; Atuahene-Gima, 2005; Auh and Menguc, 2005; Gibson and Birkinshaw, 2004; Benner and Tushman, 2003; Lewin and Volberda, 1999; Tushman and O'Reilly, 1996). But some studies have concluded that there is a negative effect (Wu and Ang, 2019; Wu et al., 2019; Menguc and Auh, 2008; Ebben and Johnson, 2005; Van Looy et al., 2005).

Besides contributing to the literature, the study also has limitations. The results of this research cannot be generalized for all sectors. This research examined the firms operating at Technology Development Zones in Ankara (Turkey) province. The study covers only a limited area. Different regions can be selected as samples. Thus, studies embodying different regions can be compared.

In today's world of intense competition, firms pass through several transformations. These transformations give more weight to producing more qualified products/services and developing new strategies and innovation. The firms, giving more importance to innovation, use knowledge management more efficiently, and seek out new competencies while developing their existing competencies. The complexity and dynamism of the firms' environment can prevent their transformation from short- to long-term success. Thanks to ambidexterity, the firms have an opportunity to both transfer their present successes into the future and adapt to possible environmental changes that can be realized in the future at the same time (Jansen et al., 2005).

REFERENCES

Abazeed, R. A. M. (2020). Impact of strategic capabilities on organizational ambidexterity in thecommercial banks in Jordan: The mediating role of knowledge management. *Management Science Letters*, *10*, 1445–1456. doi:10.5267/j.msl.2019.12.023

Anzenbacher, A., & Wagner, M. (2020). The role of exploration and exploitation for innovation success: Effects of business models on organizational ambidexterity in the semiconductor industry. *The International Entrepreneurship and Management Journal*, *16*(2), 571–594. doi:10.100711365-019-00604-6

Atuahene-Gima, K. (2005). Resolving the capability rigidity paradox in new product innovation. *Journal of Marketing*, *69*(6), 61–83. doi:10.1509/jmkg.2005.69.4.61

Auh, S., & Menguc, B. (2005). Balancing exploration and exploitation: The moderating role of competitive intensity. *Journal of Business Research*, *58*(12), 1652–1661. doi:10.1016/j.jbusres.2004.11.007

Barney, J. (1991). Firm resources and sustained competitive advantage. *Journal of Management*, *17*(1), 99–120. doi:10.1177/014920639101700108

Benner, M. J., & Tushman, M. L. (2003). Exploitation, exploration, and process management: The productivity dilemma revisited. *Academy of Management Review*, *28*(2), 238–256. doi:10.5465/amr.2003.9416096

Birkinshaw, J., & Gibson, B. C. (2004). Building ambidexterity into an organization. *Sloan Management Review*, *45*, 47–55.

Cantarello, S., Martini, A., & Nosella, A. (2012). A multi-level model for organizational ambidexterity in the search phase of the innovation process. *Blackwell Publishing Ltd.*, *21*(1), 28–48. doi:10.1111/j.1467-8691.2012.00624.x

Cao, Q., Gedajlovic, E., & Zhang, H. (2009). Unpacking organizational ambidexterity: Dimensions, contingencies, and synergistic effects. *Organization Science*, *20*(4), 781–796. doi:10.1287/orsc.1090.0426

Cepeda, G., & Vera, D. (2007). Dynamic capabilities and operational capabilities: A knowledge management perspective. *Journal of Business Research*, *60*(5), 426–437. doi:10.1016/j.jbusres.2007.01.013

Chang, Y. Y., & Hughes, M. (2012). Drivers of innovation ambidexterity in small- to medium-sized firms. *European Management Journal*, *30*(1), 1–17. doi:10.1016/j.emj.2011.08.003

Cruz-González, J. & Amores-Salvadó, J. (2011). Technological innovation. An intellectual capital-based view. *Rand Management, 41*, 319-319.

Darroch, J., & Mc Naughton, R. (2002). Examining the link between knowledge management practices and types of innovation. *Journal of Intellectual Capital*, *3*(3), 210–222. doi:10.1108/14691930210435570

Dezi, L., Ferraris, A., Papa, A., & Vrontis, D. (2019). The role of external embeddedness and knowledge management as antecedents of ambidexterity and performances in Italian SMEs. *IEEE Transactions on Engineering Management*, 1–10.

Donate, M., & Pablo, J. S. (2015). The role of knowledge-oriented leadership in knowledge management practices and innovation. *Journal of Business Research*, *68*(2), 360–370. doi:10.1016/j.jbusres.2014.06.022

Donate, M. J., & Guadamillas, F. (2011). Organizational factors to support knowledge management and innovation. *Journal of Knowledge Management, 15*(6), 890–914. doi:10.1108/13673271111179271

Duncan, R. (1976). *The Ambidextrous organization: designing dual structures for innovation.* The Management of Organization.

Durmuş-Özdemir, E., & Abdukhoshimov, K. (2018). Exploring the mediating role of innovation in the effect of the knowledge management process on performance. *Technology Analysis and Strategic Management, 30*(5), 596–608. doi:10.1080/09537325.2017.1348495

Earl, M. (2001). Knowledge management strategies; toward a taxonomy. *Journal of Management Information Systems, 18*(1), 215–233. doi:10.1080/07421222.2001.11045670

Ebben, J. J., & Johnson, A. C. (2005). Efficiency, flexibility, or both? Evidence linking strategy to performance in small firms. *Strategic Management Journal, 26*(13), 1249–1259. doi:10.1002mj.503

Field, A. (2013). Discovering statistics using IBM SPSS statistics (4th ed.). Sage Publications.

Filippini, R., Güttel, W. H., & Nosella, A. (2012). Ambidexterity and the evolution of knowledge management initiatives. *Journal of Business Research, 65*(3), 317–324. doi:10.1016/j.jbusres.2011.04.003

Floyd, S. W., & Lane, P. J. (2000). Strategizing throughout the organization: Managing role conflict in strategic renewal. *Academy of Management Review, 25*(1), 154–177. doi:10.5465/amr.2000.2791608

Fornell, C., & Larcker, D. (1981). Evaluating structural equation models with unobservable variables and measurement error. *JMR, Journal of Marketing Research, 18*(1), 39–50. doi:10.1177/002224378101800104

Gibson, C. B., & Birkinshaw, J. (2004). The antecedents, consequences, and mediating role of organizational ambidexterity. *Academy of Management Journal, 47*(2), 209–226.

Gupta, A. K., Smith, K. G., & Shalley, C. E. (2006). The interplay between exploration and exploitation. *Academy of Management Journal, 49*(4), 693–706. doi:10.5465/amj.2006.22083026

Gupta, V., & Rubalcaba, L. (2021a). University libraries as open innovation partners: Harnessing hidden potential to foster global entrepreneurship. *Journal of Academic Librarianship.* Advance online publication. doi:10.1016/j.acalib.2021.102432

Gupta, V., Rubalcaba, L., & Gupta, C. (2022b). *Global Requirement Engineering through secondary market research: Lessons from real consulting project. IT Professional.* doi:10.1109/MITP.2022.3151005

Gupta, V., Rubalcaba, L., Gupta, C., & Pereira, L. (2022a). Library social networking sites for fostering startup business globalization through strategic partnerships. *Journal of Academic Librarianship,* 102504. Advance online publication. doi:10.1016/j.acalib.2022.102504

Gupta, V., Rubalcana, L., & Gupta, C. (2021b). Multimedia Prototyping for Early- Stage Startups Endurance: Stage for New Normal? *IEEE Multimedia.* doi:10.1109/MMUL.2021.3122539

Gürlek, M., & Çemberci, M. (2020). Understanding the relationships among knowledge-oriented leadership, knowledge management capacity, innovation performance and organizational performance. *Kybernetes, 49*(7), 33–52. doi:10.1108/K-09-2019-0632

Hair, J. F., Black, W., Babin, B., & Anderson, R. (2009). *Multivariate data analysis.* Prentice-Hall.

Hamdoun, M., Jabbour, C. J., & Othman, H. B. (2018). Knowledge transfer and organizational innovation: Impacts of quality and environmental management. *Journal of Cleaner Production, 193,* 759–770. doi:10.1016/j.jclepro.2018.05.031

Hargadon, A., & Sutton, R. I. (1997). Technology brokering and innovation in a product development firm. *Administrative Science Quarterly, 42*(4), 716–749. doi:10.2307/2393655

He, Z., & Wong, P. (2004). Exploration vs. exploitation: An empirical test of the ambidexterity hypothesis. *Organization Science, 15*(4), 481–494. doi:10.1287/orsc.1040.0078

Hodgkinson, I. R., Ravishandar, M. N., & Aitken-Fischer, M. (2014). A Resource-advantage perspective on the orchestration of ambidexterity. *Service Industries Journal, 34*(15), 1234–1252. doi:10.108 0/02642069.2014.942655

Inkinen, H. T., Kianto, A., & Vanhala, M. (2015). Knowledge management practices and innovation performance in Finland. *Baltic Journal of Management, 10*(4), 432–455. doi:10.1108/BJM-10-2014-0178

Jansen, J. J. P., Van den Bosch, F. A. J., & Volberda, H. W. (2005). Exploratory innovation, exploitative innovation, and ambidexterity: The impact of environmental and organizational antecedents. *Schmalenbach Business Review, 57*(4), 351–363. doi:10.1007/BF03396721

Jansen, J. P., Van den Bosch, F. A., & Volberda, H. W. (2006). Exploratory innovation, exploitative innovation and performance effects: Effects of organizational antecedents and environmental moderators. *Management Science, 52*(11), 1661–1674. doi:10.1287/mnsc.1060.0576

Jöreskog, K. G. (1993). Testing Structural Equation Models. In K. A. Bollen & J. S. Long (Eds.), *Testing Structural Equation Models* (pp. 294–316). Sage.

Junni, P., Sarala, R. M., Taras, V., & Tarba, S. Y. (2013). Organizational ambidexterity and performance: A meta-analysis. *The Academy of Management Perspectives, 27*(4), 299–312. doi:10.5465/amp.2012.0015

Khan, M. S., & Zaman, U. (2020). The effect of knowledge management practices on organizational innovation: Moderating role of management support. *Journal of Public Affairs,* 1–9.

Kremp, E., & Mairesse, J. (2004). Knowledge management, innovation and productivity: A firm-level exploration based on french manufacturing CIS3 data. National Bureau of Economic Research. 1237.

Lai, Y. L., Hsu, M. S., Lin, F. J., Chen, Y. M., & Lin, Y. H. (2014). The effects of industry cluster knowledge management on innovation performance. *Journal of Business Research, 67*(5), 734–739. doi:10.1016/j.jbusres.2013.11.036

Lee, H., & Choi, B. (2003). Knowledge management enablers, processes, and organizational performance: An integrative view and empirical examination. *Journal of Management Information Systems, 20*(1), 179–228. doi:10.1080/07421222.2003.11045756

Lewin, A. Y., & Volberda, H. W. (1999). Prolegomena on coevolution: A framework for research on strategy and new organizational forms. *Organization Science, 10*(5), 519–534. doi:10.1287/orsc.10.5.519

Lichtenthaler, U. (2009). Absorptive capacity, environmental turbulence, and the complementarity of organizational learning processes. *Academy of Management Journal*, *52*(4), 822–846. doi:10.5465/amj.2009.43670902

Lin, R. J., Chen, R., & Shun, C. K. K. (2010). Customer relationship management and innovation capability: An empirical study. *Industrial Management & Data Systems*, *110*(1), 111–133. doi:10.1108/02635571011008434

Lubatkin, M. H., Şimşek, Z., Ling, Y., & Veiga, J. F. (2006). Ambidexterity and performance in small-to medium-sized firms: The pivotal role of top management team behavioral integration. *Journal of Management*, *32*(5), 646–672. doi:10.1177/0149206306290712

March, J. G. (1991). Exploration and exploitation in organizational learning. *Organization Science*, *2*(1), 71–87. doi:10.1287/orsc.2.1.71

Mardani, A., Nikoosokhan, S., Moradi, M., & Doustar, M. (2018). The relationship between knowledge management and innovation performance. *The Journal of High Technology Management Research*, *29*(1), 12–26. doi:10.1016/j.hitech.2018.04.002

Menguc, B., & Auh, S. (2008). The asymmetric role of market orientation on the ambidexterity firm performance relationship for prospectors and defenders. *Industrial Marketing Management*, *37*(4), 455–470. doi:10.1016/j.indmarman.2007.05.002

Mura, M., Micheli, P. G., & Longo, M. (2020). Effects of performance measurement system uses on organisational ambidexterity and firm performance. *Academy of Management Proceedings*, *1*(1), 1–40. doi:10.5465/AMBPP.2020.13898abstract

Nonaka, I. (1994). A dynamic theory of organizational knowledge creation. *Organization Science*, *5*(1), 14–37. doi:10.1287/orsc.5.1.14

Nonaka, I., Toyama, R., & Konno, N. (2000). SECI, Ba and leadership: A unified model of dynamic knowledge creation. *Long Range Planning*, *33*(1), 5–34. doi:10.1016/S0024-6301(99)00115-6

Nunnally, J. C. (1978). *Psychometric theory* (2nd ed.). McGraw-Hill.

O'Reilly, C. A. III, & Tushman, M. L. (2013). Organizational ambidexterity: Past, present, and future. *The Academy of Management Perspectives*, *27*(4), 324–338. doi:10.5465/amp.2013.0025

Ode, E., & Ayavoo, R. (2020). The mediating role of knowledge application in the relationship between knowl-edge management practices and firm innovation. *Journal of Innovation and Knowledge*, *5*(3), 1–9. doi:10.1016/j.jik.2019.08.002

Oehmichen, J., Heyden, M. L. M., Georgakakis, D., & Volberda, H. W. (2016). Boards of directors and organizational ambidexterity in knowledge-intensive firms. *International Journal of Human Resource Management*, *28*(2), 283–306. doi:10.1080/09585192.2016.1244904

Peng, M. Y. P., Lin, K. H., Peng, D. L., & Chen, P. (2019). Linking organizational ambidexterity and performance: The drivers of sustainability in high-tech firms. *Sustainability*, *11*(14), 1–17. doi:10.3390u11143931

Raisch, S., Birkinshaw, J., Probst, G., & Tushman, M. L. (2009). Organizational ambidexterity: Balancing exploitation and exploration for sustained performance. *Organization Science, 20*(4), 685–695. doi:10.1287/orsc.1090.0428

Reisinger, Y., & Turner, L. (2009). Structural equation modeling with LISREL: Application in tourism. *Tourism Management, 20*(1), 71–88. doi:10.1016/S0261-5177(98)00104-6

Severgnini, E., Galdamez, E. V. C., & Vieira, V. A. (2019). The effects of exploration, exploitation, and ambidexterity on software firm performance. *Revista de Administração Contemporânea, 23*(1), 111–134. doi:10.1590/1982-7849rac2019170330

Shahzad, K., Bajwa, S. U., Siddiqi, A. F. I., Ahmid, F., & Raza Sultani, A. (2016). Integrating knowledge management (KM) strategies and processes to enhance organizational creativity and performance: An empirical investigation. *Journal of Modelling in Management, 11*(1), 154–179. doi:10.1108/JM2-07-2014-0061

Shao, A. T. (2002). *Marketing research: an aid to decision making.* South-Western/Thomson Learning.

Siggelkow, N., & Levinthal, D. A. (2003). Temporarily divide to conquer: Centralized, decentralized, and reintegrated organizational approaches to exploration and adaptation. *Organization Science, 14*(6), 650–669. doi:10.1287/orsc.14.6.650.24840

Şimşek, Z., Veiga, J. F., Lubatkin, M., & Dino, R. N. (2005). Modeling the multilevel determinants of top management team behavioral integration. *Academy of Management Journal, 48*(1), 69–84. doi:10.5465/amj.2005.15993139

Soto-Acosta, P., Popa, S., & Martinez-Conesa, I. (2018). Information technology, knowledge management and environmental dynamism as drivers of innovation ambidexterity: A study in SMEs. *Journal of Knowledge Management, 22*(4), 1–19. doi:10.1108/JKM-10-2017-0448

Stettner, U., & Lavie, D. (2013). Ambidexterity under scrutiny: Exploration and exploitation via internal organization, alliances, and acquisitions. *Strategic Management Journal, 35*(13), 1903–1929. doi:10.1002mj.2195

Subramaniam, M., & Youndt, M. A. (2005). The influence of intellectual capital on the types of innovative capabilities. *Academy of Management Journal, 48*(3), 450–463. doi:10.5465/amj.2005.17407911

Taylor, A., & Greve, H. R. (2006). Superman or the fantastic four? Knowledge combination and experience in innovative teams. *Academy of Management Journal, 49*(4), 723–740. doi:10.5465/amj.2006.22083029

Tushman, M. L., & O'Reilly, C. A. III. (1996). Ambidextrous organizations: Managing evolutionary and revolutionary change. *California Management Review, 38*(4), 8–30. doi:10.2307/41165852

Van Looy, B., Martens, T., & Debackere, K. (2005). Organizing for continuous innovation: On the sustainability of ambidextrous organizations. *Creativity and Innovation Management, 14*(3), 208–221. doi:10.1111/j.1467-8691.2005.00341.x

Verona, G., & Ravasi, D. (2003). Unbundling dynamic capabilities: An exploratory study of continuous product innovation. *Industrial and Corporate Change, 12*(3), 577–606. doi:10.1093/icc/12.3.577

Wang, C. L., & Rafiq, M. (2014). Ambidextrous organizational culture, contextual ambidexterity and new product innovation: A comparative study of UK and Chinese high-tech firms. *British Journal of Management, 25*(1), 58–76. doi:10.1111/j.1467-8551.2012.00832.x

Wang, Z., & Wang, N. (2012). Knowledge sharing, innovation and firm performance. *Expert Systems with Applications, 39*(10), 8899–8908. doi:10.1016/j.eswa.2012.02.017

Wernerfelt, B. (1984). A resource-based view of the firm. *Strategic Management Journal, 5*(2), 171–180. doi:10.1002mj.4250050207

Wu, J., & Ang, S. H. (2020). Network complementaries in the international expansion of emerging market firm. *Journal of World Business, 55*(2), 1–10. doi:10.1016/j.jwb.2019.101045

Wu, J., Ma, Z., Liu, Z., & Lei, C. K. (2019). A contingent view of institutional environment, firm capability, and innovation performance of emerging multinational enterprises. *Industrial Marketing Management, 82*, 148–157. doi:10.1016/j.indmarman.2019.01.018

Wu, J., Wood, G., Chen, X., Meyer, M., & Liu, Z. (2020). Strategic ambidexterity and innovation in Chinese multinational vs. indigenous firms: The role of managerial capability. *International Business Review, 29*(6), 1–8. doi:10.1016/j.ibusrev.2019.101652

Yeşil, S., Koska, A., & Büyükmeşe, T. (2013). Knowledge sharing process, innovation capability and innovation performance: An empirical study. *Procedia: Social and Behavioral Sciences, 75*, 217–225. doi:10.1016/j.sbspro.2013.04.025

Yu, C. (2004). *Structural Equation Model.* https://www.creative-wisdom.com/teaching/WBI/SEM.shtml

KEY TERMS AND DEFINITIONS

Dual Organization Structures: They are organizational structures that contain dynamic and stable structures.

Dynamic Capabilities: It is supported by the organizational routines and management skills of businesses.

Exploitative Strategies: Is a strategy of exploit.

Explorative Strategies: Is a explore strategy.

Knowledge-Intensive Firms: They are companies that find intangible solutions to customers' problems by using the knowledge of their employees.

Technology Development Zones: It is an organization that provides opportunities for entrepreneurs, academics and those who want to do research.

Technology-Based Firms: They are businesses that maintain the process of technological innovation.

ENDNOTE

[1]   This study is based on the Ph.D. dissertation under the title "The Choice of Strategic Ambidexterity in the Perspectives of Knowledge Management and Innovation: a Research in Ankara Technology Development Zones".

Chapter 7
Emerging Technologies Supporting Knowledge Management for Innovation Management

Kağan Okatan
https://orcid.org/0000-0002-0517-665X
Istanbul Beykent University, Turkey

ABSTRACT

This chapter explores the emerging technologies that have emerged in recent years and have a positive effect on productivity and innovation outputs, with the effect of 'knowledge management'. Digital technology has long seemed like a clear way to improve enterprise knowledge management. Knowledge and information represented digitally and placed on an intranet can be accessed by anyone in the organization at any time in the future. Document management systems, staff directories, and other repositories that define specialties are created and used in some cases. Today, knowledge management systems have become more effective, especially with the effect of 'internet of things' and 'artificial intelligence'. The purpose of this chapter is to demonstrate to academics, students, business professionals, and entrepreneurs how developing technologies have an impact on knowledge management and effective use of intellectual capital for innovation.

INTRODUCTION

The purpose of this book chapter is to discuss knowledge management, which is a supporting factor of innovation management, and emerging technologies that increase the effectiveness of knowledge management. In particular, we can think of this discussion on the axis of the software industry, which in general has focused on the software industry.

At this point, we can ask the following question:

DOI: 10.4018/978-1-7998-9059-1.ch007

- Why is knowledge management and developing technologies in this field important for innovation management in the software industry?
- What does knowledge management mean for the software industry?

As we begin to answer these questions, we see that:

- First of all, software development is one of the most knowledge-intensive jobs possible. Moreover, it requires you to have different kinds of constantly updated information about the software processes themselves, in addition to the products and services you are working on.

Not every software product and development process is the same in terms of their purpose and environment. This leads to the fact that a particular software development method cannot be applied to all software products. Software developers repeatedly create various processes for development, which causes software development to be inherently experimental; software engineers thus continually gain knowledge with every development project. Ideally, the knowledge gained will be applied to future projects to avoid reverberating mistakes and increase success, but software development teams often fall into not using and capitalizing on existing knowledge and constantly repeating previous mistakes. These shortcomings are similarly reflected in the difficulties of sharing knowledge with learners in the organization (Chugh, Chanderwal, Mishra, & Punia, 2019).

Any unused knowledge and experience are loss from the intellectual capital of the business. This loss is much more costly than any apparent monetary loss.

The biggest cost is the wasting the value of:

- Mistakes made for this experience,
- Difficulties overcome in the development of any product or service,
- Time spent for a notice of critical facilitation method and so on.

This is literally a 'memory waste'. At a time when knowledge is more valuable than gold, experiencing such memory loss is an unbearable cost not only for the software industry but for all industries. 'Implementing an effective knowledge management system' is a necessity rather than an option for any organization that is not only trying to be innovative but also wanting to survive.

LITERATURE REVIEW

Undoubtedly, knowledge represents a sustainable presence and competitive advantage for innovative companies. This is especially important for software industries that have to work in unpredictable environments. The knowledge we mean is generally explicit knowledge. It is difficult for us to always find the knowledge explicitly. In addition, with the advancement of technologies faster than ever and the dynamically changing demands of the market, existing knowledge management systems are losing their competence day by day. This situation has made it necessary to strengthen our knowledge management systems with emerging technologies day by day.

The software industry, by its nature, is a sector that requires knowledge to be processed and shared as quickly as possible, and it has also realized the need to manage knowledge in its field. This is emphasized more in innovative businesses. Information technology-based systems are required to support and develop a fast and effective knowledge management (knowledge creation, storage/retrieval, transfer and application). These systems also facilitate the creation of knowledge networks and improve interpersonal relationships among team members (Khalil & Khalil, 2020).

'Innovation capability based on knowledge management' is the positive difference arising from internal and external knowledge in the process of making changes in the existing products or services of organizations. The duality of knowledge contributes positively to innovation capability. Innovation capability is one of the notable contributions of knowledge management (Benitez, Castillo, Llorens, & Braojos, 2018).

KNOWLEDGE MANAGEMENT

What is our most important capital for innovation? Let us think of the answer to this question as something that happens with our human resources and even thanks to it. Let there be such a capital that it is more valuable than money, precious metals, our buildings, facilities and vehicles. May all we have on the path of innovation be thanks to it? Our knowledge capital has now become more important than our financial and physical capital.

Knowledge management is defined as access to expertise, knowledge and expertise that provides new capabilities, enables better performance, encourages development and innovation, and increases customer value.

Knowledge management is also a set of processes and systems of use aimed at changing the organizational pattern of computing and value. Awareness of research and development engineers involved in a project determines its success. Indeed, knowledge management is the most important part of research and development management for innovation. Systematic innovation is based on the actions of systematic knowledge creation (discovery of new knowledge) and knowledge use (use of existing knowledge).

Implicit knowledge is a type of knowledge best described as "we know more than we can say". Unobservable but existing knowledge is an important start in the innovation process and has a significant impact on the application for the innovation process. It is difficult to grasp from the minds as it is deeply rooted in the actions and experiences of the individual.

Where large amounts of knowledge are used for innovation, collaboration between cross-functional teams is essential. Unfortunately, the information in these "recipes" is not necessarily codified, but often remains within the routines and skills of innovation and operations teams.

Knowledge management can assist in accessing and codifying such confidential information. The experience and skill of the engineer is valuable knowledge for a research and development department. It is also very valuable knowledge for a technical or administrative personnel to know how to do a job in the fastest and most accurate way and in what way it was done before and in what way the results were obtained. Therefore, systematizing practical experience for storage and retrieval can reduce the gap between experts in our staff and novices or novices. Knowledge management plays an important role in facilitating collaboration.

The fact that knowledge is not explicitly available complicates knowledge sharing and application in the innovation process, because the innovation process contains many complex messages. Although most of the inputs of the process can be observed physically, it is necessary to use accumulated experience to obtain the best input combination. One of the most important issues for knowledge management is to embody this tacit knowledge.

Research and development, products, processes or services, etc. It is defined as discovering new knowledge about the market and then applying this knowledge to create new products, processes and services that meet market needs or to improve existing ones. Evaluating research and development performance is difficult because it is a complex construct. Research on research and development project success factors has shown that these projects are a set of factors that depend on personal experience and ensure the success of the project, so personal or team-owned knowledge is one of the main determinants of a research and development project. Success is the form of that knowledge (tacit or implicit) and knowledge management is the dynamic capabilities action crucial to innovation performance (Niu & Chang, 2018).

The act of managing knowledge also includes ensuring the functioning of the systematic learning process within the institution. The continuous input of knowledge we need to deliver the systematic innovation output is the result of continuous learning action. In summary, the systematic innovation process is a journey that includes systematic learning.

Systematic learning is to ensure that learning takes place in a structured way, not by chance. That is, every new teaching must establish a relationship with the existing. This requires organizations to actively manage their learning processes (Chirumalla, 2017).

The content of this management requires the continuity of certain actions. These are basically;

- Maintaining learning cycles in all organizational processes,
- Systematically disseminating new and existing information to an organization; and
- Application of knowledge wherever it can be used in the organization (Chirumalla, 2017).

The most important thing is that these actions are not carried out only once or in certain periods but are continuous. These actions must be from their regular business, like any other physical or financial action of the organizations. If we embarked on a systematic innovation journey, what we need to know is that knowledge is our raw material and we need to manage the knowledge in the best way for the best output.

Figure 1. Knowledge management process
(Barbosa, Gonçalves, Simonetti, & Leitão, 2009)

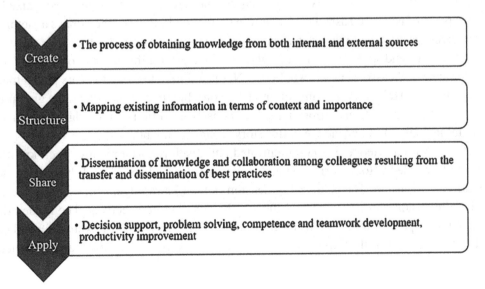

CREATE

Our starting point in the knowledge management process is to obtain as much knowledge as possible. This can only be achieved by contacting the knowledge as much as possible. It would be useful to expand on this theme a little more. Let us consider our own body as an example. There is as much information flow inside as possible through our internal organs and circulatory system. At this point, we can think of the interior of the body as the interior of any organization. There is a structure that provides the flow and formation of knowledge about everything that happens inside us. So, is this much knowledge enough for us to survive? What if we did not realize that we were in an area surrounded by tigers, for example, if we just turned inside and lived? Or what if we notice and interpret a truck with a broken brake on us? Answer: It is not possible for us to survive without external knowledge and interpretation.

Every organism lives in a certain eco-system and is in constant exchange of knowledge with this eco-system. This allows him to continue his life and develop some points.

Starting from this point; we have also understood two sources from which knowledge can arise:

- Our internal resources
- Our external resources

The inside of our business is a source of knowledge for us. Our intellectual capital stands alone in our business. This intellectual capital is what our employees have in mind, what is shared or not yet shared, projects we are working on or planning to work on, etc. It stands in the middle of the business as a treasure. But they can stand in different ways. Knowledge is generally found in our business in two forms:

- Explicit knowledge
- Tacit knowledge

We actually know more than what we say and what we make clear (Lu, Wang, & Mao, 2007). These things we know come out differently when the time comes, and we actually see how much knowledge and expertise has been accumulated over a very long time. Perhaps one of the best examples in this regard is Picasso's phrase '40 years plus 5 minutes';

Spanish painter Pablo Picasso was in a restaurant one day, when the waiter recognized him and handed him a piece of paper and asked him to draw a picture on it. Picasso then draws a picture within 5 minutes. He gives his drawing to the waiter and asks for a thousand dollars. Of course, the waiter finds this amount of money and states that it is not right for him to ask for this amount of money for a picture he drew in 5 minutes. Picasso's answer would be: 'Not just 5 minutes, but 40 years plus 5 minutes'.

You may have heard this story in many different versions, but they all have the same gist and premise. The ongoing work, experience and effort in humans constitutes serious knowledge. Of course, there is another capital in addition to knowledge in this story, which is 'talent'.

In this story, tacit knowledge was communicated and displayed as a picture. Tacit knowledge is a difficult type of knowledge to be formatted and communicated and accessed. It has both a 'technical' and a 'cognitive' dimension. The technical dimension of tacit knowledge; skill consists of craft, while the cognitive dimension consists of mental models, beliefs, and perspectives. The hidden dimension of knowledge has important implications for understanding the difficulty of expressing and conveying individual knowledge and skills. Explicit knowledge, on the other hand, is formal and systematic, easily transmitted and disseminated. Meanwhile, explicit knowledge is easily expressed and codified, so its management includes knowledge storage, dissemination, retrieval, use and preservation (Lu, Wang, & Mao, 2007).

At the end of the day, the real issue often comes down to how tacit knowledge is made explicit, externalized, and shared. Let us leave this to the sharing step for now.

We should also point out that knowledge does not only occur within our company. Especially in the present time. In the inside information, we gave our body as an example. If we continue with the example of our body, we need to talk about our sense organs. Our sense organs are our gateway to the outside. They constantly collect information from our environment. In order to receive maximum information from the outside, we must connect more tightly to the eco-system and open our receivers even more. Collaborations, joint projects, joint ventures, workshops, etc. strengthens our external exchange of information. The vigorous continuation of this information exchange takes us to the next step, 'open innovation'.

SYSTEMATIC LEARNING

The systematic learning approach typically emerges through external acquisitions, alliances, or joint development by firms. Understanding (learning) occurs through data collection and analysis processes. Managers use the information gathered to make decisions and take action. It is important to take a rational view of potential partners as an organization seeks to increase its competitiveness in technology areas through an acquisition or alliance. Too often, companies fail to realize the expected benefits from these strategies because the processes used to analyze the takeover candidate or potential partner are not systematic. This approach to learning about potential partners will lead the organization to collect rigorous data and analyze it, which should reduce uncertainty about potential outcomes. The underlying assumption is that the organization knows its environment and has the ability to gather and process information.

Google bought 55 companies between 2001 and 2009. In this process, Google has focused on ensuring that they fully understand the companies and technologies they have acquired. One way Google did this was by encouraging developers to build web applications using their own databases and APIs first. Therefore, as firms begin to partner with or contract with other firms to gain technology-related concerns:

- A clear understanding of how potential partners can integrate with each function of the organization. Managers should distribute the rigorous analysis obtained to each functional area.
- Have a group of experts within the organization who understand potential synergies and issues that blend people, processes, and resources from multiple companies. These professionals should be able to analyze and interpret data from both organizations to facilitate the adoption of best practices.
- If technology acquisition does occur, a clear set of guidelines should be prepared to interpret the potential for success.
- Guidelines to be strengthened and made more robust should be developed.

These lessons may be useful in the near future, but the firm needs to periodically review them based on the current and future environment. Most institutions emphasize one type of learning over the other.

Therefore, the question is what kind of learning will dominate. Various factors influence the precise mix of interpreters or systematic learning that the firm will use.

For example, we know that the impact of the firm's culture on knowledge sharing will consequently also influence the mix of learning styles of the firm's culture. Similarly, the size of a firm is also important because it is subject to greater influence from a smaller firm environment. For example, Pegasus Solutions is the Internet's leading hotel reservation company. The company has conducted internal and external studies to acquire technology. However, the learning method is almost entirely interpretive. The rapidly changing environment requires the firm to adapt quickly and continuously by seeking environmental changes. In contrast, a dominant firm in a field may rely on a systematic approach. The RFID (Radio Frequency Identification) technology discussed earlier initially had several different technologies competing with each other. However, Walmart used a systematic approach to analyze which technology to use. Because Walmart is such a dominant force in global retail, when it chose a technology based on its analytics, it became the standard for the industry (White & Bruton, 2011).

STRUCTURE

We cannot situate every piece of information created in separate corners. If we proceed in this way, we will get a construction site with bricks on each side, but we want to build a building. This phase includes building each new information on existing information, establishing a link between the new and the existing that is, mapping the information. This stage requires rethinking the rights and wrongs experienced in the past and analyzing the new information with this perspective. This means understanding how new learning will affect experienced right and wrong. This is important to us because it means systematic innovation, incrementally adding value, not wasting any learning. In the configuration phase, each information should be considered as a new cell that will integrate with existing cells.

Figure 2. From structuring to meaning

SHARE

The need for information that will flow into innovation and creativity processes in a meaningful way is that it flows through the veins to all organs of the enterprise. Knowledge needs to be dispersed relentlessly within the enterprise so that the information that is scattered everywhere creates a cycle by adding new information. Perhaps it would be appropriate to call it the 'information artery and vein'. This type of knowledge distribution system implies multi-directional information exchange.

Figure 3. Interaction of the organs

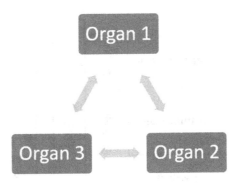

The relationship between the organs of the enterprise is multifaceted. The most important issue is that the knowledge is always available for the organ that needs it. Sharing also aims to ensure that no knowledge within the business remains idle. For an idea that we are considering but cannot act on at the moment, others may have the resources and complementary information to implement it. Sharing knowledge has a snowball effect. The important thing here is that we transform tacit knowledge into explicit knowledge. This will be done by externalizing the known.

Nonaka and Takeuchi introduced the 'SECI' (Socialization, Externalization, Combination, and Internalization) model, which is the cornerstone of knowledge creation and transfer theory. They proposed four ways in which types of knowledge can be combined and transformed, showing how knowledge is shared and created in the organization. This method is based on tacit and explicit types of knowledge (Nonaka, Umemoto, & Senoo, 1996)

Figure 4. Knowledge Management Creation
(Salim, Takeuchi, Nonaka, Toyama, & Othman, 2006)

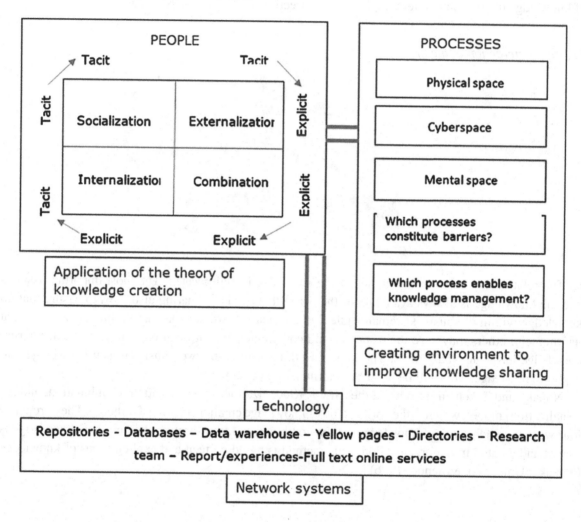

Socialization is the process of creating shared tacit knowledge through shared experiences. To begin socializing, we need to create a space of interaction where individuals share their experiences at the same time and place, thus creating common unexpressed beliefs or embodied skills (Nonaka, Umemoto, & Senoo, 1996).

Externalization is the process of turning tactical knowledge into explicit knowledge such as concepts and/or diagrams, often using metaphors, analogies and/or sketches. This phase is triggered by a dialogue aimed at creating concepts from tactical knowledge. Creating a new product concept is a good example of externalization (Nonaka, Umemoto, & Senoo, 1996).

Consolidation is the process of combining new and existing explicit knowledge into a systemic knowledge, such as a set of determinants for the prototype of a new product. More often than not, a newly created concept must be combined with existing explicit knowledge to embody it into something tangible (Nonaka, Umemoto, & Senoo, 1996).

This phase begins with connecting the different bodies of explicit knowledge. The aim is to deductively form a systemic, clear knowledge (Nonaka, Umemoto, & Senoo, 1996).

Internalization is the embedding of explicit knowledge into tacit knowledge, such as 'mastery'. This phase is triggered by "learning by doing or using". Clear information documented in text, audio or video formats facilitates the internalization process. Therefore, manuals are widely used for concise explicit knowledge, internalization. In addition, engineering case studies help novice engineers internalize explicit knowledge that has been externalized from master engineers' experience-based knowledge of design processes. In addition to providing such clear information to organizational members, it is equally important to expand the scope of direct experience and encourage them to experience it (Nonaka, Umemoto, & Senoo, 1996).

It would be more explanatory to illustrate this theory of knowledge creation with an example.

Fuji Xerox has defined its mission as "Building an Environment for the Creation and Effective Use of Knowledge". The leading copier manufacturer has developed an intranet-based information sharing system called "Z-EIS or Zen-in Engineering Information System". By the way, 'Zen-in' means everyone. They also built a "Zen-Design Room," or a meeting room, where designers and engineers from all stages of the design process come together to discuss three-dimensional, visualized drawings.

The development of information sharing and creation systems at Fuji Xerox began in the early 1990s when the company's R&D managers decided to solve the problem of long lead times due to design changes at the last stage of the development process. The engineers responsible for the final stage, closer to the users, had to wait for a prototype, and therefore, to solve the problem, the designers and engineers of the entire development process interacted with each other to discuss their search for solutions. They realized the importance of on-site experience or tacit knowledge of designers and engineers, which was only revealed in front of the prototypes. Thus, they tried to visit every part of the development phase and capture the on-site information (Socialization) there.

Meanwhile, they came up with the concept of "Zen-in Design" or "Design by All"; this means that "every engineer must participate in the entire design process, making comments or suggestions for better designs, while taking responsibility for each. Still, there was a problem with how to organize the captured information. For this purpose, an online engineering information sharing system was developed and named Z-EIS. Thus, designers and engineers began to express their on-site knowledge and enter the system (Externalization).

Because not every formulated information is good enough to be shared among all designers and engineers, middle managers of each development phase should only identify usable items that are officially registered in the Z-EIS. In addition to the knowledge in the field, three-dimensional graphical models, part specifications, market data, patent information and product management data were entered into Z-EIS. Therefore, 4,500 on-the-spot know-how is shared between 500 designers and 4,100 engineers, and approximately 50,000 questions are asked to Z-EIS each month (Combination).

For recorded knowledge to become truly important, it must be truly used and acted upon. Therefore, in order to use explanatory know-how effectively and efficiently, the most useful information is selected and compiled into a "quality assurance list", i.e., new 'clear information' to be used in design reviews. Thus, the explicit use of design and development know-how is used, adapted, and thus re-overlapped in the field (Internalization).

'Knowledge creation theory application' is a spiral, not a cycle. Therefore, the process of knowledge formation continues and re-socialization takes place. In the Zen-in Design Room, designers and engineers come together and interact with each other with enriched and embodied knowledge (Umemoto, 2002).

In knowledge management formation, the success of knowledge formation also depends on the processes and network services that will support it. Processes should provide an environment that fosters and encourages knowledge sharing. Another important factor in this type of environment is 'tools'. The most effective sharing of the resulting information depends on keeping it in the best and ready condition and being accessible.

The level of presence of information stores, databases, data warehouses, directories, customizable reporting infrastructure and the widest online services is directly proportional to the efficiency of information sharing. The presence of these network services is of vital importance in information management, especially in enterprises with large and separate work environments.

APPLY

Perhaps the most critical point where we will reap the fruits of knowledge management within the framework of systematic innovation will be our application to our innovation process. What will knowledge management give us? Organizational and systematic learning will connect us to building bricks upon bricks from day one in our innovation building. It will put information on information. As this information is structured, it will become the biggest resource for decision-making (understanding big data --> big knowledge). Knowledge management, which will be the biggest supporter of the problem solving and added value creation process. We cannot improve productivity without collective mind formation and sharing. Managing knowledge is making it grow like a snowball every day.

EMERGING TECHNOLOGIES SUPPORT KNOWLEDGE MANAGEMENT FOR INNOVATION

The fact that we call the era we live in as the 'information age' highlights how important 'information' is for business output and innovative value production. The literature now agrees on this importance. This importance is even higher for knowledge-intensive business areas. On the other hand, we have started to use the concept of 'knowledge-oriented economy' for business outcomes and general business life. This concept in the simplest way; it refers to the added value obtained as a result of meeting the innovative business outputs obtained with knowledge management with the consumer. Recent developments in the digital field have opened new horizons to many research fields such as engineering, computer science, electrical engineering, especially with the fourth industrial revolution, which is called Industry 4.0 in the literature. Industry 4.0 is a tool to move from a manufacturing paradigm where machines simply operationalize routines to digital manufacturing, where machines can communicate with each other and collaborate autonomously (Manesh, Pellegrini, Marzi, & Dabic, 2021). In particular, it makes significant contributions to the processes required for the use of in-house information for innovative outputs. We will talk about these new technologies later in this section.

Internet of Things (IoT)

The Internet of Things (IoT) applications have radically changed our lives by adding great value to the lives of both individuals and organizations. Today, billions of everyday objects are equipped with advanced sensors, wireless networks and innovative computing capabilities. This abundance has led to wearable devices, smart home applications, advanced healthcare systems, "smart cities" and industrial automation. After years of uncertainty, IoT is ready to move into mainstream business use: the number of businesses adopting IoT technologies is growing every day, and the number of IoT connected devices worldwide is estimated to reach 43 billion by 2023 (Sestino, Prete, Piper, & Guido, 2020). The data production speed caused by the rapid growth of big data produced by the Internet of Things will bring the capacity of the Internet to be exceeded in the near future. Thus, more than 90% of IoT big data will be processed and analyzed locally rather than in remote clouds. At this point, if more artificial intelligence applications come into play, the IoT service mode will gradually change from "Data as a Service" to "Knowledge as a Service". Knowledge is the true value of data that includes learning outcomes and models derived from IoT data (Lin, Wu, Liang, & Yang, 2019).

One of the biggest operational challenges for knowledge management systems is to access the real-time data necessary for optimal and effective decision making. From the moment it emerged, the Internet of Things has made a positive difference in providing high-volume and instant data communication, especially between computer systems, which are one of the basic components of information management systems. The Internet of Things (IoT), defined as the collection of smart devices capable of responding to environmental stimuli as well as storing and processing digital information and transmitting it to other agents (or users) via Internet protocols has big capability to improve knowledge processes (creating, structuring, sharing and applying knowledge as well as protecting / encoding / archiving / collecting) (Rot & Sobinska, 2018).

The next step in IoT technology is to explore how to share self-learned knowledge between smart IoT devices with minimal human intervention. Until now, users or systems have repeated the same procedure when using multiple IoT devices where similar or even the same knowledge is required.

For example, in a smart home, when an IoT device that provides personalized services (e.g., smart mirrors, smart doorbells, home robots, and other IoT devices) is newly installed at home, each family member repeatedly participates in facial recognition training. Also, multiple devices generate the same knowledge for face recognition and store the copy (Jang, Lee, Choi, & Son, 2019).

The most important issue here is that IoT devices can share the information they produce with other devices and areas that people reach. The issue that should draw our attention here is that IoT devices can manage an information creation process (Create, structure, share, apply) from start to finish.

This competency can certainly be applied to any major software development platform. Working on the codes and code explanations of the devices can make effective suggestions to the programmers, as well as suggesting them to review some codes.

IoT knowledge processes supports software industry in some major activities:

- Today, information flow is what we call 'big data'; provided directly from data obtained from objects and users.
- Analyzing the data provided simultaneously and saving it to cloud platforms.
- Content is always available online.
- There is no limitation for sharing information between people or objects (Meško, Suklan, & Roblek, 2017).
- Errors or improvement areas that occur in the operation of all kinds of software can be determined.

- When the data obtained during the software development phase is transferred to the software development interface, the software developer can be promptly guided with 'warnings' and 'suggestions'.
- The software developer can instantly share a solution he finds.

Artificial Intelligence

The main purpose of implementing a knowledge management system is for people in an organization to share business information, knowledge and experience. This sharing is done to produce new knowledge and turn it into innovative outputs. An efficient knowledge management system will increase productivity. It should be noted that effective knowledge management requires time, attention and energy to be spent on this task. It is often difficult to provide these at the highest level, at this point artificial intelligence applications provide a lot of advantages.

The functioning of artificial intelligence appears in two streams:

1. The "expert system" flow receives information from experienced people and this information is programmed into an "expert system" that can then be used by less experienced people doing the same task. An important feature that distinguishes such systems from information systems is that "expert systems" often ask the user questions and then draw conclusions, rather than asking users to know the right questions to ask. One strength of expert systems is the ability to explain their reasoning to users (Kingston, 2019).
2. The "machine learning" flow gains knowledge by searching a large "training set" of data for patterns and then recognizing those patterns as they repeat. The strengths of this approach are that it can identify patterns that even experienced people are unaware of, and it can do its job 24/7 because it does not need a human operator; the main weakness is that it is often difficult to decipher what the patterns mean (Kingston, 2019).

At this point, it is useful to review the prominent areas where artificial intelligence contributes to knowledge management:

1. Artificial intelligence simplifies the discovery of knowledge. An effective knowledge management program provides employees with the tools they need to engage in four key knowledge management practices:

    a. Creation,
    b. Structuring,
    c. Sharing,
    d. Application.

As the amount of information created and shared increases, the difficulty of discovering information increases in coordination. Artificial intelligence uses modern technologies to simplify the discovery of knowledge. AI-powered knowledge bases use new technologies such as semantic search, natural language processing, and machine learning to make it easy for employees to find the information they are looking for quickly and easily. Semantic search and natural language processing eliminate the need for Boolean searches, complex hierarchies, and detailed labeling and categorization. Instead, AI allows employees to search the knowledge base using natural language. It then infers and presents results based on search terms, synonyms, and implied context. Machine learning tracks both terms used and user behavior to predict what employees are searching for. Machine learning algorithms look at what employees are searching for, then predict what information they are looking for based on what information has satisfied other employees who have had similar queries in the past (Greene, 2021).

2. Artificial intelligence connects data from different sources.

Another major information management hurdle is that employees in different departments do not always capture and share information in the same way: Support teams capture and share information in a ticketing system. HR uses a secure intranet portal. Sales representatives manage their information in a CRM tool. Product teams use project management tools and so on. This creates another knowledge discovery problem: employees do not know where to look for the information they need. In many cases, they may not even have access to the means in which the information is stored. AI-powered tools help you consolidate information across multiple systems, making information accessible to all employees, wherever they are (Greene, 2021).

3. AI helps you keep your knowledge base content up to date.

We discussed how AI helps with knowledge discovery, but it is also useful in another problematic knowledge management process: Knowledge maintenance. It generally works like this: There is a lot of pressure to document information and upload it to a new company knowledge base. In the end, there is an enormous amount of information stored in your knowledge base, and that includes the fact that no one bothers to go back and update old information. Keeping outdated information in your knowledge base is detrimental to your knowledge management program. When employees find out-of-date information in your knowledge base and therefore make mistakes, they lose confidence in the system. Eventually, they stop using it altogether. Artificial intelligence solves this problem by reminding employees to regularly update the recorded information (Greene, 2021).

4. AI tools provide key knowledge management metrics.

How can you understand or, more importantly, demonstrate that your knowledge management program delivers the promised benefits? For most businesses, this is very difficult, if not impossible. An AI-powered knowledge management tool allows you to monitor metrics that show the precise impact of your knowledge management program on productivity and operational costs (Greene, 2021).

Artificial Intelligence contribute to knowledge management in software industry in some major activities:

- Knowledge distribution: Online databases can provide AIs with knowledge spanning different fields and application areas according to software.
- A well-built machine can extract from the actual data store, which increases with the number of interactions with users feeding new information into the algorithm. This means new information retrieval and therefore a larger data repository for customers or system users.

- The act of delivering (or transferring) knowledge is often performed by chatbots: artificial technologies based on NLP that analyze and interact with human language through a speech-like simulation environment during software development.
- The information caught from the software running on production can automatically be analyzed and fix or improvement areas can be automatically determined.

CONCLUSION

Much attention is drawn to the importance of knowledge management in this book chapter. The main purpose in this is that knowledge is very difficult to obtain but very easy to lose. It is essential that for us to be able to retain knowledge obtained with great difficulty. It is not enough just to hold it in our hands, we must put it into the knowledge creation life cycle for new knowledge creation. In fact, we can easily compare this situation to a snowball turning into an avalanche (in a positive sense, of course).

Knowledge management is a very important dimension of innovation management, especially innovation competence (Okatan & Alankuş, 2017). Weakness of this dimension definitely affects the innovation outputs negatively. What weapon do we have for innovation more powerful than knowledge? We do not need to think too much about that. Knowledge is the most important capital, especially for knowledge-intensive industries such as the software development industry. Your success in software development depends on your ability to manage information effectively and efficiently. As long as this knowledge stays in the brains of your employees, it has no meaning. The aim is to put the knowledge in the brains into the process for the creation of new knowledge and to make all kinds of information accessible. Obviously, this takes time, but the emerging technologies we discuss in this book chapter make this task much easier. They do not only simplify it but also broaden the content and quality of the task.

Undoubtedly, innovation increases with the sharing of knowledge, and this sharing is much more intense and accessible, especially in the open innovation method. The sharing of knowledge involves the two-way exchange of knowledge between firms themselves and their innovation ecosystems, specifically to promote internal innovation to achieve business objectives. Innovation and entrepreneurship are inseparable. In recent years, it has generally been new ventures that have brought into account notable innovations in the software industry. At this point, sharing of open innovation is very important especially for new enterprises. Entrepreneurial libraries also contribute greatly to an effective sharing. They can serve as hubs of entrepreneurial activity and market knowledge (Gupta & Rubalcaba, 2021). This makes them one of the strongest elements of the innovation ecosystem. As one of the current technologies that support innovation and knowledge management in the software industry, it is necessary to add university libraries, especially considering the technologies that have developed in recent years.

REFERENCES

Barbosa, J., Gonçalves, A., Simonetti, V., & Leitão, A. (2009). A Proposed Architecture for Implementing a Knowledge Management System in the Brazilian National Cancer Institute. *Brazilian Administration Review*, 6(3), 247–262. doi:10.1590/S1807-76922009000300006

Benitez, J., Castillo, A., Llorens, J., & Braojos, J. (2018). IT-enabled knowledge ambidexterity and innovation performance in small U.S. firms: The moderator role of social media capability. *Information & Management, 55*(1), 131–143. doi:10.1016/j.im.2017.09.004

Chirumalla, K. (2017). Clarifying the feedback loop concept for innovation capability: A literature review. In *Conference: XXVIII ISPIM Innovation Conference* (s. 1-19). Vienna: ISPIM.

Chugh, M., Chanderwal, N., Mishra, A. K., & Punia, D. K. (2019). The effect of knowledge management on perceived software process improvement: Mediating effects of critical success factors and moderating effect of the use of information technology. *VINE Journal of Information and Knowledge Management Systems, 49*(4), 546–567. doi:10.1108/VJIKMS-11-2018-0106

Greene, J. (2021, 1 1). *4 key benefits of adding AI to your knowledge management program.* Knowledge Management: https://www.atspoke.com/blog/knowledge-management/ai-helps-knowledge-management/

Gupta, V., & Rubalcaba, L. (2021). University libraries as open innovation partners: Harnessing hidden potential to foster global entrepreneurship. *Journal of Academic Librarianship, 102432*, 1–3. doi:10.1016/j.acalib.2021.102432

Jang, I., Lee, D., Choi, J., & Son, Y. (2019). An Approach to Share Self-Taught Knowledge between Home IoT Devices at the Edge. *Sensors (Basel), 19*(4), 833. doi:10.339019040833 PMID:30781639

Khalil, C., & Khalil, S. (2020). Exploring Knowledge Management in Agile Software Development Organizations. *The International Entrepreneurship and Management Journal, 16*(2), 555–569. doi:10.100711365-019-00582-9

Kingston, J. (2019). Artificial Intelligence, Knowledge Management and Human Vulnerability. In *Proceedings of the European Conference on the impact of Artificial Intelligence and Robotics* (pp. 198-204). Oxford: ECIAIR.

Lin, X., Wu, J., Liang, H., & Yang, W. (2019). Making Knowledge Tradable in Edge-AI Enabled IoT: A Consortium Blockchain-Based Efficient and Incentive Approach. *IEEE Transactions on Industrial Informatics, 15*(12), 6367–6378. doi:10.1109/TII.2019.2917307

Lu, I.-Y., Wang, C.-H., & Mao, C.-J. (2007). Technology Innovation and Knowledge Management in the High-tech Industry. *International Journal of Technology Management, 39*(1/2), 3–19. doi:10.1504/IJTM.2007.013437

Manesh, M. F., Pellegrini, M. M., Marzi, G., & Dabic, M. (2021). Knowledge Management in the Fourth Industrial Revolution: Mapping the Literature and Scoping Future Avenues. *IEEE Transactions on Engineering Management, 68*(1), 289–300. doi:10.1109/TEM.2019.2963489

Meško, M., Suklan, J., & Roblek, V. (2017). *The Impact of the Internet of Things to Value Added in Knowledge-Intensive Organizations.* In *Knowledge Management Strategies and Applications.* IntechOpen. doi:10.5772/63142

Niu, H.-J., & Chang, C.-J. (2018). A Novel Method Guiding IC Manufacturing R&D Direction: Perspective From Knowledge Integration Innovation. *International Journal of Innovative Computing, Information, & Control, 14*(4), 1371–1388.

Nonaka, I., Umemoto, K., & Senoo, D. (1996). From Information Processing to Knowledge Creation:A Paradigm Shift in Business Management. *Technology in Society*, *18*(2), 203–218. doi:10.1016/0160-791X(96)00001-2

Okatan, K., & Alankuş, O. B. (2017). Effect of Organizational Culture on Internal Innovation Capacity. *Journal of Organisational Studies and Innovation*, *4*(3), 18–50.

Rot, A., & Sobinska, M. (2018). The Potential of the Internet of Things in Knowledge Management System. In *Position Papers of the 2018 Federated Conference on Computer Science and Information Systems* (pp. 63-68). Poznań: Polskie Towarzystwo Informatyczne.

Salim, J., Takeuchi, H., Nonaka, I., Toyama, R., & Othman, M. S. (2006). Integrating Japanese Knowledge Creation Theory Into Knowledge Management Initiatives. *Knowledge Management International Conference & Exhibition (KMICE)*, 241-247.

Sestino, A., Prete, M. I., Piper, L., & Guido, G. (2020). Internet of Things and Big Data as enablers for business digitalization strategies. *Technovation*, *98*(102173), 1–9. doi:10.1016/j.technovation.2020.102173

Umemoto, K. (2002). Managing Existing Knowledge is Not Enough: Knowledge Management Theory and Practice in Japan. *Strategic Management of Intellectual Capital & Organizational Knowledge*, 463-476.

White, M. A., & Bruton, G. D. (2011). *The Management of Technology and Innovation: A Strategic Approach*. Thomson-Southwestern.

Chapter 8
Empirical Insights Into Software Startups

Varun Gupta
https://orcid.org/0000-0003-2824-3402
University of Alcala, Spain

Zoe Hoy
https://orcid.org/0000-0003-3377-2288
University of Portsmouth, UK

Chetna Gupta
Jaypee Institute of Information Technology, India

ABSTRACT

Software startups bring innovative products to the market. However, such innovation is at the cost of highly educated guesswork about customer expectations and quick decision making by persons responsible for strategic planning and implementation. It is therefore of interest to understand the challenges and practices faced by startups that aim to release something innovative in selected market segments. Hence, this chapter investigates the challenges faced by entrepreneurs of startups and the practices they follow to become successful. The specific challenges explored include (1) how startups handle software evolution, (2) challenges faced in releasing products to the market, and (3) the state of affairs of software engineering in startups. Results indicate that despite guidance and support in terms of well-known and documented development methods, practitioners find it difficult to implement and apply these in practice. They must quickly evolve their products to sustain in the market, and the market is highly uncertain, which makes the complete process highly probabilistic.

DOI: 10.4018/978-1-7998-9059-1.ch008

INTRODUCTION

Startups are the ventures laid by Entrepreneurs, which emerge newly in the marketplace and present a new idea. A startup is usually a temporary organisation that produces innovative products in the market (Blank, 2014). Product-oriented software practices help startups to be flexible and quickly adapt to the target market (Paternoster et al., 2014). The product must have a strong value proposition providing benefits to the customer and solving customer problems (Gupta & Fernandez-Crehuet, 2020). Software startups need to formulate business models and validate them before finalizing a more appropriate model to use in the future (Gupta et. al., 2020). The business model evolves through a series of interactions with customers (customer development) (Blank, 2014). Uncertainties are usually handled in startups by increasing the interactions with their customers (Gupta et. al., 2020) and producing products in the shortest possible time, often adopting agile principles (Paternoster et al., 2014).

The startup must overcome challenges they face and must focus on strengthening their customer base. Startups differ from mature organisations in that they usually have minimal resources and are under time pressures (Kemell et al., 2020). Rather than produce documentation startups prefer to use their limited resources for product development (Paternoster et al., 2014). Startups face challenges not only from other startups but also from well established companies, trying to release a better product than a startup. Keeping existing customers and attracting new customers is difficult under extreme competition situations. To become successful the startups must satisfy the customer requirements and must deliver quickly (Giardino et al., 2016; Souza et al., 2017; Chanin et al., 2017).

Paternoster et. al. (2014) conducted a systematic mapping study of software engineering work practices in startups. Their study found that agile methodologies were considered the most viable for startup processes as they support fast releases with a short lead time between idea and software deployment. Lean startup, a variant of agile considers the most-risky parts and provides a minimum viable product (MVP) (Paternoster et. al., 2014), the minimum amount needed to satisfy the customer needs, which is usable by the customer, and no more (Patton, 2014, p. 34). Another agile variant used for startups is Extreme Programming (XP) which has minimal documentation and processes. In summary, startups preferred light-weight software practices which support fast software iterations (Paternoster et. al., 2014).

Research on software practices of startups is still scare and further studies are needed (Kemell et al., 2020). This study contributes towards this gap with empirical results of software practices followed by three startup companies, addressing three research questions (RQ).

RQ1: How startups handle software evolution?
RQ2: What are the challenges faced in releasing product in the market?
RQ3: What is the state of affair of Software Engineering in start-ups?

METHODOLOGY

Telephone interviews were conducted with three startup organisations, selected using convenience sampling as they were already known to the first author. Table 1 presents demographic information about the three startups who participated in this study. Unstructured interviews were conducted to prevent bias and allow the startup entrepreneurs to drive the conversation. First informed consent was sought through e-mail followed by two rounds of interviews. The first round conveyed more details about the research and instructions to participate. The second round conducted the interviews. Each interview took an average one hour. Notes were taken throughout the interview and discussed at the end to ensure nothing was missing or misinterpreted. The data were categorized into three themes, each theme representing a research question. Anonymity was maintained for the startup companies which are referred to a case A, B and C.

Table 1. Demographic information about the three startups

Case Name	Location of Case	Other Locations	Software Product Portfolio
A	India	Global	Large
B	USA	Global	Large
C	UK	Global	Large

DATA COLLECTION

See Table 2.

Table 2. Interview results

Theme	Case A	Case B	Case C	Overall
RQ1. How startups handle software evolution?	There is an evolution that significantly takes place in the idea and the concept of building a startup. The idea upon which the startup was established evolves by the time its first product is launched.	There is evolution but only in the field of technical prospects of the project. The idea had evolved but there is not much significant evolution in the idea.	The idea evolves and a big change is seen whenever the idea is implemented. When the idea is in the production phase it changes.	Evolution was constricted with either the concept of startup or with the technical prospects. Evolution depended on the maturity level of the startup.
RQ2. What are the challenges faced in releasing product in the market?	The key challenges that were faced comprised of funding problems at different phases of the project and maintaining the speed so that they can move one step ahead of their competitors.	The key challenges that were faced comprised of funding and resources problems. It is never easy to gather correct resources in a limited period of time.	The key challenges that were faced comprised of funding at the right time to get the project working. Also gathering the right team in place was found difficult at the start of the startup.	Funding problems were identified by all three startup companies. One startup faced a problem of maintaining speed faster than their competitors and one startup faced the challenge of gathering the right team.
RQ3: What is the state of affair of Software Engineering in start-ups?	It always aims to have a high agility which is provided by using the most accurate and precise software models in practice. This doesn't mean that a single software model is used in practice. A mixture of principles is used which enhances the vulnerability of the software product.	It also aims to have high agility. Using more than one software model and their principles in different stages of the project is carried out. It is found very difficult to stick to a single software model.	The aim is again the same, to have high agility but the software model used is agile. The model is used in the project phases. But there are difficulties following the agile model as it is not easy to completely follow its principles.	Startup companies prefer not to use a single software model. It was found very hard to stick to any modern-day model so various other principles were also used.

RESULTS ANALYSIS

Research Q1

For a start-up company there prevails a highly competitive ecosystem, which they focus on to explore the highly innovative segments of the market. The software startups handle their software evolution by identifying ideas which they believe are innovative, continuously modifying ideas as per customer feedback and launches by competitors. The idea gets modified very frequently. In the evolution of the software startups, one of the most challenging features is the correct level of funding at different stages of the project so that its execution can be done smoothly without any time delay. Maintaining speed in terms of time to market is also an essential practice that is followed. Moving faster than your competitors is utmost required otherwise any company may lose the effectiveness of its newly launched product.

Research Q2

The parameters for selecting the project for the main market is firstly to categorize your project as either Mass or Bespoke. Before releasing any product, it is a pre-requisite to define which audience is to be targeted, and categorizing your project as either Mass or Bespoke, identifies not only the targeted audience but also about the size and requirements of the audience, which in turn helps to release a better product which touches upon the maximum requirements of the targeted audience. However, for startups with low funding, mass market development is usually uncommon practice.

There are several key challenges that are tackled while running a software startup. One of the most important challenges is to get the right team in place. Secondly right levels of funding to keep your project execution going must be ensured. Thirdly speed is a factor that can play a major role. Moving faster than your competitors is required because a slow and steady production rate may enhance your development quality but on release of the product it might not create a buzz in the market probably due to a similar release of product already being done. Further, high release speed ensures fast feedback and immediate modification of the software product.

Research Q3

Startups should generally have high agility so that they can change their direction quickly and according to the industry. The software models used highly affect the agility of the startups. Nowadays the startup does not use a single software model rather they prefer to follow principles of more than one software model, which actually provide them flexibility and agility. It is very hard for people to follow a single methodology or models for software. The best principles are taken out of the models which can fulfill the requirements of the undergoing phases to completion. Also, resources are never easy to find for a startup company. The deadlines are always taken care of as a software company but for startups it is required to release the first best product in hand that start-ups can launch to customers. That impact of the first launched product is required for a startup to carry on its further execution. Generally, the interviewed companies do not follow the principles strictly.

CONCLUSION

The research has been concluded on various parameters which includes handling the evolutions in software practices, selecting a main stream project for the main market and the challenges faced during different phases of the project and state of affair of software engineering in start-ups. Collectively in a highly competitive ecosystem, the software start-ups need to touch upon highly innovative segments of the market. The software models that are used are not a single model but a mixture of principles that help them to maintain their agility. It is observed that the companies need to reach out to their targeted audience and it is most important to define a targeted audience.

Therefore, before selecting a project it is necessary to categorize the project as Bespoke or Mass so that the targeted audience is set and now company can focus on fulfilling the maximum requirements of the targeted audience. Also, there are a handful of challenges that the start-up companies face which includes the funding problem and the resource allocation problem. Also there are challenges faced in gathering the correct team and moving faster than the competitors in market. Moving faster than your competitors is utmost required otherwise any company may lose the effectiveness of its newly launched product. Also resources are never easy to find for a startup company. The deadlines are always taken care of as a software company but for startups it is required to release the first best product in hand that startups can launch to customers.

REFERENCES

Blank, S. (2014, March 4). *Why Companies are Not Startups*. Steve Blank. https://steveblank.com/2014/03/04/why-companies-are-not-startups/

Chanin, R., Pompermaier, L., Fraga, K., Sales, A., & Prikladnicki, R. (2017). Applying Customer Development for Software Requirements in a Startup Development Program. *2017 IEEE/ACM 1st International Workshop on Software Engineering for Startups (SoftStart)*.

Giardino, C., Paternoster, N., Unterkalmsteiner, M., Gorschek, T., & Abrahamsson, P. (2016). Software Development in Startup Companies: The Greenfield Startup Model. IEEE Transactions on Software Engineering, 42(6), 585-604.

Gupta, V., & Fernandez-Crehuet, J. M. (2020). Online feedback management tools for early-stage start-ups: Hidden treasures in the Rocky Mountains. IT Professional, 23(5), 67-72.

Gupta, V., Fernandez-Crehuet, J. M., Hanne, T., & Telesko, R. (2020). Requirements Engineering in Software Startups: A Systematic Mapping Study. Applied Sciences, 10(6125), 1-19=.

Kemell, K. K., Ravaska, V., Nguyen-Duc, A., & Abrahamsson, P. (2020). Software startup practices – Software development in startups through the lens of the essence theory of software engineering. In M. Morisio, M. Torchiano, & A. Jedlitschka (Eds.), *Product-Focused Software Process Improvement. PROFES 2020. Lectures Notes in Computer Science* (Vol. 12562, pp. 402–418). Springer. doi:10.1007/978-3-030-64148-1_25

Paternoster, N., Giardino, C., Unterkalmsteiner, M., & Gorschek, T. (2014). Software development in startup companies: A systematic mapping study. In Information and Software Technology (Vol. 56). Academic Press.

Patton, J. (2014). *User story mapping: Discover the whole story, build the right product.* O'Reilly.

Souza, R., Malta, K., & Almeida, E. (2017). Software Engineering in Startups: A Single Embedded Case Study. *2017 IEEE/ACM 1st International Workshop on Software Engineering for Startups (SoftStart).* 10.1109/SoftStart.2017.2

Chapter 9
Use of Framework Synthesis to Identify the Factors Considered for Five Popular Prioritisation Approaches

Zoe Hoy

https://orcid.org/0000-0003-3377-2288

University of Portsmouth, UK

ABSTRACT

Software requirement prioritisation is an important task that ultimately determines whether the software is successful and achieves customer satisfaction. Startups use agile methodologies to develop software, as it adapts to requirement changes well and delivers software quickly in short increments, called sprints. However, there is little research about the practices of agile requirement re-prioritisation, the activity to reprioritise requirements at the start of each sprint. This research contributes to this gap by identifying the factors considered for five popular prioritisation approaches and compares them to the agile requirement re-prioritisation process. The results show that the approaches studied do not address all factors of the agile requirement re-prioritisation process. The planning game covers five of the factors whereas analytical hierarchy process covers three of the factors. This may influence the choice of approach used for agile requirement re-prioritisation. This study contributes important insights for requirement prioritisation literature and practice.

INTRODUCTION

Startups use agile software development (Gupta, Fernandez-Crehuet, Hanne, & Telesko, 2020; Lim, Bentley, & Ishikawa, 2020; Nurdiani, Jabangwe, & Petersen, 2016) to deliver innovative software solutions (Gupta et. al., 2020). Agile engages stakeholders, supports requirements changes and delivers software quickly (Luong, Sivarajah, & Weerakkody, 2021).

DOI: 10.4018/978-1-7998-9059-1.ch009

Requirements prioritisation is an important activity for a software project. Requirements need to be prioritised which are high value and innovate the software (Gupta et al., 2020), but the activity is also challenging. The right balance must be achieved among competing requirements to ensure that the software meets the customer's needs (Svensson et al., 2011). Most software projects have a large number of requirements, so there is a need to prioritise which requirements to include in each sprint due to limited resources such as time and money (Hudaib, Masadeh, Qasem & Alzaqebah, 2018).

For agile, the requirements are held in a product backlog. The product backlog is dynamic as it reflects the continuous re-prioritisation of the requirements. Uncertainties in the form of requirement changes, are addressed with the focus on business value, incremental deliveries of the software and continuous re-prioritisation of the requirements (Racheva, Daneva, Herrmann, & Wieringa, 2010a). For agile software development, the product owner is responsible for managing and prioritising the product backlog (Bass, 2013). Racheva, Daneva, Sikkel, Wieringa. and Herrmann (2010b) found that developers are often delegated this client decision-making role, particularly for small client organisations or startups who may not have IT domain knowledge and cannot afford an IT consultant to act on their behalf.

Prioritising requirements is an ongoing activity for agile software development, as re-prioritisation of the requirements (Racheva et al., 2010a) occurs at the start of each sprint, to reflect the changing client's needs. Sprints are short software development cycles, typically 2-4 weeks in duration, where the customer/product owner is a member of the team (van Waardenburg & van Vliet, 2013).

There are many approaches which can be used to prioritise requirements. Achimugu, Selamat, Ibrahim and Mahrin (2014) identified 49 approaches. The article has been well cited and reports the top five most cited and used approaches as Analytic Hierarchy Process (AHP), Quality Functional Deployment (QFD), planning game, binary search tree, and $100 allocation. These five popular approaches have been selected for this study.

AHP is a robust, rigorous and proven method to evaluate alternatives (Das & Mukherjee, 2008; de Felice & Petrillo, 2010). Complex decisions are presented in a hierarchical structure, with the goal at the first level, criteria in the second level and sub-criteria in the third level (Acharya, Sharma & Gupta, 2018). This reduces complex decisions to a number of pair-wise comparisons, to provide the best alternative (de Felice & Petrillo, 2010). The large number of pairwise comparisons makes the process unsusceptible to judgement error (Karlsson, Wohlin, & Regnell, 1998). A ratio scale is used to rank the alternatives by their relative weights (de Felice & Petrillo, 2010; Dabbagh, Lee & Parizi, 2016), which provides a useful assessment of the requirements (Karlsson et al., 1998). The AHP approach can be used in combination with the QFD approach (Das & Mukherjee, 2008; de Felice & Petrillo, 2010; Akao, 2014). Akao (2014) used AHP to calculate the degree of importance weightings for each of the demanded quality items. The degree of importance weightings, reflects the importance of the requirements.

QFD is an approach to assure that the customers' needs are incorporated into a new software product (Akao & Mazur, 2003). The software product specification (hows) are based on the customers' needs (whats) and analysis of competitors (whys) (de Felice & Petrillo, 2010). QFD has been used around the world since 1966 (Akao & Mazur, 2003). An importance rating is calculated for each requirement. Those with a higher importance rating are prioritised as more important.

The planning game is easy and quick to use, and scalable for a large number of requirements (Ahl, 2005). The business value of the requirements and project constraints are considered (Maurer & Martel, 2002) when prioritising requirements, providing a balance between the customers' needs and the expertise and experience of the development team members (Maurer & Martel, 2002). Karlsson, Thelin,

Regnell, Berander and Wohlin (2007) found the planning game quicker to prioritise requirements and more accurate, when compared to pairwise approaches like AHP.

Ahl (2005) conducted an experiment to compare five prioritisation approaches; $100 test, AHP, binary search tree, planning game and planning game with AHP. The results showed that binary search tree was the best prioritisation approach having the benefits of scalability; to handle a medium/large number of requirements, ease of use and accuracy. These benefits were also reported by Saghir and Mustafa (2016) and Hudaib et al. (2018).

For the $100 allocation approach, stakeholders allocate $100 to candidate requirements (Chatzipetrou, Rovegård., & Wohlin, 2010). Requirement priorities are on a ratio scale, showing the relative importance between the requirements (Solinski & Petersen, 2016). The ratio scale enables the stakeholders' dollar allocations to be evaluated, to detect whether there is disagreement between the stakeholders or whether there are clusters of stakeholders with similar views (Riņķevičs & Torkar, 2013). When there is disagreement between the stakeholders, a knowledge of specific needs for a group of stakeholders, can help the product owner to make an informed decision when they prioritise the product backlog (Sverrisdottir, Ingason, & Jonasson, 2014). The approach is fast, easy to use, perceived to provide accurate results (Ahl, 2005; Hudaib, et al., 2018) and is scalable for a medium number of requirements (Hudaib et al., 2018).

Cristiano, Liker and White (2001) claim that benefits are more notable for smaller companies. Ettlie and Johnson (1994) claim that smaller companies have a greater focus on the customer and on process improvement, whereas large companies may suffer from a rigid organisation and functional silos. This means that the benefits of the five popular approaches may be more remarkable for smaller companies and startups.

Racheva et al. (2010a) claim that very little is known about the practices of agile re-prioritisation. They have contributed towards this gap by developing a conceptual model for agile requirements re-prioritisation. However, a limitation acknowledged by the authors is that it is a first proposal for the conceptual model, developed from literature (Racheva et al., 2010a) and therefore cannot explain how requirements prioritisation decision-making takes place. This study will contribute further in this area by identifying the factors considered when prioritising requirements for five popular prioritisation approaches. This research also compares these factors to the agile requirements re-prioritisation process to see how well these popular approaches support the agile process.

The need to increase knowledge of these agile re-prioritisation practices has motivated the following research questions (RQ):

RQ1: What factors do the five popular prioritisation approaches consider when prioritising requirements?
RQ2: How well do the five popular prioritisation approaches support the agile requirements re-prioritisation process?

The structure of this paper is as follows. First a best-fit framework is chosen for the agile requirements re-prioritisation process. Then factors considered by the five popular prioritisation approaches are identified and compared with the requirements re-prioritisation process. Before there are conclusions and a reflection on the contribution to knowledge.

CHOOSING A BEST FIT FRAMEWORK

To choose the agile re-prioritisation process for this study various frameworks are evaluated to determine the best fit framework. The methodology used to develop each framework is critically evaluated, to choose a framework developed by a robust methodology, and relevant for the agile requirements re-prioritisation process. The factors of the chosen agile re-prioritisation process are introduced in section 2.2 and used as themes for the data analysis.

Choosing a Framework for Agile Requirements Re-Prioritisation

Various frameworks have been reported in literature for requirements prioritisation. In the conceptual model developed by Al-Ta'ani and Razali (2013), two criteria are identified for requirements prioritisation; project constraints, which includes schedule, budget and scope, and requirements nature, which includes visibility, business value, dependencies and complexity. However, there are two limitations for this study, firstly more details were needed about the research methodology. For example, the search terms used, and criteria for the included studies and the steps followed to conduct the content analysis. These details are needed so that a researcher can replicate the study and achieve the same results (Saunders, Lewis, & Thornhill, 2016). Secondly, in order to ensure the validity of the study, the articles included must be fit for purpose (Denyer, & Tranfield, 2011). It was not clear how the quality of the included articles was assured as the details of the method for this were not evident in the reported study.

Al-Ta'ani and Razali (2016) developed another framework in a later study, which included the same two criteria for requirements prioritisation as their earlier study, i.e. project constraints and requirements nature. This framework was specifically developed for agile requirements prioritisation. However, this study had limited details of the methodology followed. For example, it was stated that grounded theory was used (Al-Ta'ani & Razali, 2016), but very limited details of the method were provided to enable the study to be replicated (Saunders et al., 2016).

A study by Moisiadis (2002) identified a framework for prioritising requirements, but not for agile requirements prioritisation. Agile requirements prioritisation is very different to plan-driven development (Racheva et al., 2010a). Agile has a product owner role and requirements are re-prioritised for every iteration of the software development.

The Conceptual Model B developed by Racheva et al. (2010a) was chosen as the best-fit framework for this research as it was specifically developed for agile requirements prioritisation. It was based on the description of 22 requirements prioritisation approaches listed in Racheva et al. (2010a)'s Table 1, with a clearly described method that used quality criteria to ensure the quality of literature sources included in the study. A limitation of the conceptual model, acknowledged by the authors, is that it has not been empirically validated (Racheva et al., 2010a). However, this limitation was not of a concern for this study, which compared the model to literature sources written by the creators of five popular prioritisation approaches. Any new factors not addressed by the best-fit framework would be analysed using thematic analysis.

Factors of the Chosen Framework

The best-fit framework considers six factors when prioritising requirements; business value, risk, effort estimation, learning experience, external change, and project constraints (Racheva et al., 2010a).

The business value for each story is determined by the client or product owner (Achimugu et al., 2014) and used to prioritise the requirements in the product backlog. The business value assigned reflects the product owner's tacit knowledge about the requirement and their learning experience, especially during the re-prioritisation of requirements (Racheva et al., 2010b). Racheva et al. (2010b) also identified that negative value can be used instead of business value. Negative value considers the potential lost business value of not implementing the requirement, instead of the business value to be gained by implementing the requirement.

The development team determines the risk (Achimugu et al., 2014) and effort for each requirement and provides this information to the product owner/clients for their decision making (Racheva et al., 2010a). In the planning game, requirements are assigned one of three risk categories, category one is for requirements which the development team are very confident they can estimate precisely, category two is for requirements which they are confident they can estimate reasonably well, and category three is for requirements which they cannot estimate (Beck, 2000). This risk reflects the perceived level of uncertainty with the estimation for each individual user story (Racheva et al., 2010a). Requirements are prioritised for the next release based on their business value, risk and the team's velocity (Beck, 2000).

The size or effort to implement requirement can be expressed in story points and estimated using planning poker cards (Grenning, 2002). The requirement is described to the agile team and questions are asked by the team members to gain further clarification as needed. Each team member has a deck of planning poker cards and holds up one card to the other team members, which they perceive represents the effort to implement the requirement. The team members then compare cards and discuss the reasons for their choice. Further estimation rounds continue until consensus is reached for the effort needed.

The factor learning experience is where the client uses their knowledge and experience in the agile software project to assess the business value for requirements (Racheva et al., 2010a).

The factor external changes could impact requirements prioritisation, for example Racheva et al. (2010a) claim that external changes from the project's or company's context, could influence which requirements are prioritised.

The output from requirements prioritisation is a prioritised product backlog, which is an input for the sprint (iteration) planning meeting. The sprint planning meeting is held at the start of each software development cycle (Racheva et al., 2010a. The purpose of the meeting is to prioritise which requirements from the prioritised product backlog should be included in the next sprint. Constraints such as the velocity, the available capacity which the agile team have for a single sprint are considered (Rosenberger & Tick, 2021). Requirements are chosen for the next sprint and moved into the sprint backlog, ensuring that the velocity is not exceeded.

RESEARCH METHOD

The framework synthesis approach was chosen as a published conceptual model was available to compare with the five popular approaches. Framework synthesis is a highly structured method to synthesize qualitative data (Carroll, Booth, & Cooper, 2011). A distinct factor of framework synthesis is the framework of best-fit, which is used (Barnett-Page & Thomas, 2009). Themes are identified from the framework and used as codes (Carroll et al., 2011) to guide the data extraction and synthesis of the findings (Shaw, Holland, Pattison., & Cooke, 2016).

Framework synthesis is a pragmatic method (Carroll et al., 2011) following both a deductive and inductive approach. A deductive approach is followed as it builds on the existing framework (Carroll et al., 2011). Then an inductive approach is followed to analyse new topics, which may emerge from the data (Barnett-Page & Thomas, 2009; Carroll et al., 2011) that cannot be mapped to the themes is performed. In framework synthesis, thematic analysis is used to analyse any new topics that may emerge (Carroll, Booth, Leaviss, & Rick, 2013). This is a popular approach for synthesis in software engineering (Cruzes & Dybå, 2011a) and provides a structured approach to develop themes from recurring patterns (Cruzes & Dybå, 2011b).

One limitation of framework synthesis is its reliance on a suitable best fit framework being identified (Carroll et al., 2011). As recommended by Carroll et al. (2013) the [1]BeHEMoTH strategy was used to find a suitable framework. Search terms included prioritization process and prioritisation process to represent the behaviour of interest and context (BeH) and the term framework was used to represent Models or Theories (MoTH). For exclusions (E), studies were manually excluded from the research results, which did not include a model for the requirements prioritisation process.

The model developed by Racheva et al. (2010a) was the best-fit framework chosen for this research in section 2.1, as it was developed by a robust methodology and focused on agile software development. The factors for the model described in section 2.2 were the themes: business value, risk, effort estimation, learning experience, external change, and project constraints (Racheva et al., 2010a).

A second limitation of framework synthesis is whether the author correctly interpreted themes consistently with their original intended meaning (Carroll et al., 2011). However, as Racheva et al. (2010a) provided a detailed description for each factor in the model, this limitation is minimal.

The literature sources selected were those written by the creators of five popular prioritisation approaches; Leffingwell and Widrig (2000) for $100 allocation, Saaty (2003; 2008) for AHP, Hibbard (1962) for binary search tree, Beck (2000) for planning game and Akao (2014) and Kamisawa (1994) edited by Akao for QFD. These original sources were chosen to prevent bias from any variations published on the approaches. These texts were analysed to identify sentences or paragraphs describing the prioritisation process, which were then compared to the themes. The five steps for thematic synthesis (Cruzes & Dybå, 2011b) were used to analyse any new factors, that emerged from the data (Barnett-Page & Thomas, 2009; Carroll et al., 2011).

RESULTS AND DISCUSSIONS

In this section, the factors considered by five popular prioritisation approaches are presented and then compared to the factors of the agile requirements re-prioritisation process.

For RQ1, Table 1 identifies the factors considered by the five popular prioritisation approaches. Five factors were reported in literature for the planning game, three were reported for AHP, one was reported for QFD and no factors were identified for binary search tree and $100 allocation.

Table 1. Comparison of the approaches against the factors of the re-prioritisation process

Factors Identified in Literature for the Approaches (ü)	AHP	Binary Search Tree	Planning Game	QFD	$100 Allocation
Business Value	ü		ü	ü	
Risk	ü		ü		
Effort	ü		ü		
Learning experience			ü		
Project constraints			ü		

For RQ2 the factors considered by the five approaches were compared to the factors considered by the agile requirements re-prioritisation process. Literature for the five popular approaches did not consider the factor external change, hence this factor was excluded from Table 1. Also, no new factors emerged from the analysis of the five popular approaches, therefore no new factors were added to Table 1.

For RQ2, Table 1 shows that the five approaches studied do not address all factors of the agile requirements re-prioritisation process. The planning game covers five of the factors of the re-prioritisation process. AHP covers three of the factors. Although AHP literature (Saaty, 2003; 2008) did not report on project constraints, project constraints could be chosen as a criterion. For AHP, stakeholders choose the criteria to prioritise the requirements against (Saaty, 2008).

The factor business value was not identified in the literature for $100 allocation or binary search tree. However, it is likely that stakeholders consider business value for '$100 allocation' as they allocate more dollars to the requirements, which are more important (Leffingwell & Widrig, 2000). Requirements of higher importance could be considered to have higher business value. It is also likely that business value is considered for binary search tree, while determining the placement of each candidate requirement on the binary search tree. For example, those requirements on the right-hand side of the tree are more important than those requirements on the left-hand side of the tree (Hibbard, 1962). The right side of the tree could be considered to have a higher business value.

CONCLUSION

For RQ1, Table 1 provides an understanding of factors, which the five popular approaches consider. Five factors were reported in literature for the planning game, three were reported for AHP, one was reported for QFD and no factors were identified for binary search tree and $100 allocation. Although, the factor business value was not identified in the literature for $100 allocation or binary search tree, it is likely that stakeholders consider business value for $100 allocation as they allocate more dollars to the requirements, which are more important. It is also likely that business value is considered for binary search tree, while determining the placement of each candidate requirement on the tree.

For RQ2, the factors from the agile requirements re-prioritisation process were compared with the factors considered by the five popular approaches. The results confirm five of the factors identified in the agile requirements re-prioritisation process, the sixth factor external change, was not reported in the literature for the five popular approaches. The planning game covers five of the factors whereas AHP covers three of the factors. QFD only covered one factor and both the binary search tree and £100 allocation approaches did not report any of the factors. This may influence the choice of approach used for agile requirements re-prioritisation.

Table 1 shows the planning game fits the requirements re-prioritisation process the best. The planning game (Beck, 2000) identified five factors of the agile re-prioritisation process, except external change. The suitability of the planning game approach for agile software development is supported by Wood, Michaelides and Thomson (2013) who claim that the activity customer planning, which includes the planning game is positively related to the performance of agile software development teams.

Although, the Binary search tree and $100 allocation approaches did not support any of the factors listed in Table 1, they have numerous benefits, including being fast and easy to use. These benefits could support startups and smaller companies, which are more adaptive and have a greater focus on the customer and process improvement.

As little is known about the practices of agile re-prioritisation our study has contributed towards this gap, with insights that are important for requirements prioritisation literature and practice. Further research is needed to explore these five popular approaches in startups using agile software development.

REFERENCES

Acharya, V., Sharma, S. K., & Gupta, S. K. (2018). Analyzing the factors in industrial automation using analytic hierarchy process. *Computers & Electrical Engineering*, *71*, 877–886. Advance online publication. doi:10.1016/j.compeleceng.2017.08.015

Achimugu, P., Selamat, A., Ibrahim, R., & Mahrin, M. N. (2014). A systematic literature review of software requirements prioritization research. *Information and Software Technology*, *56*(6), 568–585. doi:10.1016/j.infsof.2014.02.001

Ahl, V. (2005). *An experimental comparison of five prioritization methods – Investigating ease of use, accuracy and scalability* (Unpublished master's dissertation). http://www.diva-portal.org/smash/get/diva2:833611/FULLTEXT01.pdf

Akao, Y. (2014). The method for motivation by Quality Function Deployment (QFD). *Nang Yan Business Journal*, *1*(1), 1–9. doi:10.2478/nybj-2014-0001

Akao, Y., & Mazur, G. H. (2003). The leading edge in QFD: Past, present and future. *International Journal of Quality & Reliability Management*, *20*(1), 20–35. doi:10.1108/02656710310453791

Al-Ta'ani, R. H., & Razali, R. (2013). Prioritizing requirements in agile development: A conceptual framework. *Procedia Technology*, *11*, 733–739. doi:10.1016/j.protcy.2013.12.252

Al-Ta'ani, R. H., & Razali, R. (2016). A Framework for Requirements Prioritisation Process in an Agile Software Development Environment: Empirical Study. *International Journal on Advanced Science, Engineering and Information Technology*, *6*(6), 846–856. doi:10.18517/ijaseit.6.6.1375

Barnett-Page, E., & Thomas, J. (2009). Methods for the synthesis of qualitative research: A critical review. *BMC Medical Research Methodology*, *9*(1), 59–69. doi:10.1186/1471-2288-9-59 PMID:19671152

Bass, J. M. (2013). Agile Method Tailoring in distributed Enterprises: Product Owner Teams. *Proceedings of IEEE 8th International conference on Global Software Engineering (ICGSE)*, 154-163. 10.1109/ICGSE.2013.27

Beck, K. (2000). *Extreme Programming Explained*. Addison-Wesley.

Carroll, C., Booth, A., & Cooper, K. (2011). A worked example of "best fit" framework synthesis: A systematic review of views concerning the taking of some potential chemopreventive agents. *BMS Medical Journal Methodology*, *11*(29), 1–9. doi:10.1186/1471-2288-11-29 PMID:21410933

Carroll, C., Booth, A., Leaviss, J., & Rick, J. (2013). "Best fit" framework synthesis: Refining the method. *BMS Medical Journal Methodology*, *13*(37), 1–16. doi:10.1186/1471-2288-13-37 PMID:23497061

Chatzipetrou, P., Rovegård, P., & Wohlin, C. (2010). Prioritization of issues and requirements by Cumulative Voting: A compositional data analysis framework. *36th EUROMICRO Conference on Software Engineering and Advanced Applications*. 361-370. 10.1109/SEAA.2010.35

Cristiano, J. J., Liker, J. K., & White, C. C. (2001). Key factors in the successful application of Quality Function Deployment (QFD). *IEEE Transactions on Engineering Management*, *48*(1), 81–95. doi:10.1109/17.913168

Cruzes, D. S., & Dybå, T. (2011a). Research synthesis in software engineering: A tertiary study. *Information Systems*, *53*(5), 440–455. doi:10.1016/j.infsof.2011.01.004

Cruzes, D. S., & Dybå, T. (2011b). Recommended Steps for Thematic Synthesis in Software Engineering. *2011 International Symposium on Empirical Software Engineering and Measurement*, 275-284. 10.1109/ESEM.2011.36

Dabbagh, M., Lee, S. P., & Parizi, R. M. (2016). Functional and non-functional requirements prioritization: Empirical evaluation of IPA, AHP-based, and HAM-based approaches. *Soft Computing*, *20*(11), 4497–4520. doi:10.100700500-015-1760-z

Das, D., & Mukherjee, K. (2008). Development of an AHP-QFD framework for designing a tourism product. *International Journal of Services and Operations Management*, *4*(3), 321–344. doi:10.1504/IJSOM.2008.017297

de Felice, F., & Petrillo, A. (2010). A multiple choice decision analysis: An integrated QFD – AHP model for the assessment of customer needs. *International Journal of Engineering Science and Technology*, *2*(9), 25–38. https://www.ajol.info/index.php/ijest/article/view/63849

Denyer, D., & Tranfield, D. (2011). Producing a Systematic Review. In D. A. Buchanan & A. Bryman (Eds.), *The SAGE Handbook of Organizational Research Methods* (pp. 671–689). Sage.

Ettlie, J. E., & Johnson, M. D. (1994). Product development benchmarking versus customer focus in applications of Quality Function Deployment. *Marketing Letters*, *5*(2), 107–116. doi:10.1007/BF00994101

Grenning, J. W. (2002). *Planning Poker or how to avoid analysis paralysis when release planning*. https://wingman-sw.com/papers/PlanningPoker-v1.1.pdf

Gupta, V., Fernandez-Crehuet, J. M., Hanne, T., & Telesko, R. (2020). Requirements engineering in software startups: A systematic mapping study. *Applied Sciences (Basel, Switzerland), 10*(6125), 1–19. doi:10.3390/app10176125

Hibbard, T. N. (1962). Some combinatorial properties of certain trees with applications to searching and sorting. *Journal of the Association for Computing Machinery, 9*(1), 13–28. doi:10.1145/321105.321108

Hudaib, A., Masadeh, R., Qasem, M. H., & Alzaqebah, A. (2018). Requirements Prioritization Techniques Comparison. *Modern Applied Science, 12*(2), 62–80. doi:10.5539/mas.v12n2p62

Kamisawa, N. (1994). The use of prioritization in quality deployment at the planning and design stages. In S. Mizuno & Y. Akao (Eds.), *QFD The customer-driven approach to quality planning and deployment* (pp. 108–134). Asian Productivity Organization.

Karlsson, J., Wohlin, C., & Regnell, B. (1998). An evaluation of methods for prioritizing software requirements. *Information and Software Technology, 39*(14-15), 939–947. doi:10.1016/S0950-5849(97)00053-0

Karlsson, L., Thelin, T., Regnell, B., Berander, P., & Wohlin, C. (2007). Pair-wise comparisons versus planning game partitioning – experiments on requirements prioritisation techniques. *Empirical Software Engineering, 12*(1), 3–33. doi:10.100710664-006-7240-4

Leffingwell, D., & Widrig, D. (2000). *Managing Software Requirements: A unified approach*. Addison-Wesley.

Lim, S. L., Bentley, P. J., & Ishikawa, F. (2020). Reaching the Unreachable A method for early stage software startups to reach inaccessible stakeholders within large corporations. *2020 IEEE 28th International Requirements Engineering Conference*, 376-381. 10.1109/RE48521.2020.00051

Luong, T. T., Sivarajah, U., & Weerakkody, V. (2021). Do agile managed information systems projects fail due to a lack of emotional intelligence? *Information Systems Frontiers, 23*(2), 415–433. doi:10.100710796-019-09962-6

Maurer, F., & Martel, S. (2002). Extreme Programming: Rapid development for web-based applications. *IEEE Internet Computing, 6*(1), 86–90. doi:10.1109/4236.989006

Moisiadis, F. (2002). The fundamentals of prioritising requirements. *Systems Engineering, Test & Evaluation Conference*, 1-12. https://pdfs.semanticscholar.org/7395/4e283497f15c6b0d7d2ef615afbd1587450c.pdf

Nurdiani, I., Börstler, J., & Fricker, S. A. (2016). The impacts of agile and lean practices on project constraints: A tertiary study. *Journal of Systems and Software, 119*, 162–183. http://ddo.org/10.1016/j.jss.2016.06.043. doi:10.1016/j.jss.2016.06.043

Racheva, Z., Daneva, M., Herrmann, A., & Wieringa, R. (2010a). A conceptual model and process for client-driven agile requirements prioritization. *4th International Conference on Research Challenges in Information Science*, 287-298. 10.1109/RCIS.2010.5507388

Racheva, Z., Daneva, M., Sikkel, K., Wieringa, R., & Herrmann, A. (2010b). Do we know enough about requirements prioritization in agile projects: insights from a case study. *2010 18th IEEE International Requirements Engineering Conference*, 147-156. 10.1109/RE.2010.27

Riņķevičs, K., & Torkar, R. (2013). Equality in cumulative voting: A systematic review with an improvement proposal. *Information and Software Technology, 55*(2), 267–287. doi:10.1016/j.infsof.2012.08.004

Rosenberger, P., & Tick, H. J. (2021). Agile enhancement of critical PMBOK V6 processes. *Journal of Modern Project Management, 9*(1), 190–203. doi:10.19255/JMPM02613

Saaty, T. L. (2003). Decision making with the AHP: Why is the principal eigenvector necessary. *European Journal of Operational Research, 145*(1), 85–91. doi:10.1016/S0377-2217(02)00227-8

Saaty, T. L. (2008). Decision making with the analytic hierarchy process. *International Journal of Services Sciences, 1*(1), 83–98. doi:10.1504/IJSSCI.2008.017590

Saghir, S., & Mustafa, T. (2016). Requirements Prioritization Techniques for Global Software Engineering. *Pakistan Journal of Engineering, Technology & Science, 6*(1), 42-63. http://journals.iobmresearch.com/index.php/PJETS/article/view/1143

Saunders, M., Lewis, P., & Thornhill, A. (2016). *Research Methods for Business Students* (7th ed.). http://lib.myilibrary.com/Open.aspx?id=819487

Shaw, R. L., Holland, C., Pattison, H. M., & Cooke, R. (2016). Patients' perceptions and experiences of cardiovascular disease and diabetes prevention programmes: A systematic review and framework synthesis using the Theoretical Domains Framework. *Social Science & Medicine, 156*, 192–203. doi:10.1016/j.socscimed.2016.03.015 PMID:27043372

Solinski, A., & Peterson, K. (2014). Prioritizing agile benefits and limitations in relation to practice usage. *Software Quality Journal, 24*, 447-482. doi:10.1007/s11219-014-9253-3

Svensson, R. B., Gorschek, T., Regnell, B., Torkar, R., Shahrokni, A., Feldt, R., & Aurum, A. (2011) Prioritization of quality requirements: State of practice in eleven companies. *2011 IEEE 19th International Requirements Engineering Conference*, 69-78. https://ieeexplore.ieee.org/stamp/stamp.jsp?arnumber=6051652

Sverrisdottir, H. S., Ingason, H. T., & Jonasson, H. I. (2014). The role of the product owner in scrum – comparison between theory and practices. *Procedia: Social and Behavioral Sciences, 119*, 257–267. doi:10.1016/j.sbspro.2014.03.030

van Waardenburg, G., & van Vliet, H. (2013). When Agile meets the enterprise. *Information and Software Technology, 55*(12), 2154–2171. doi:10.1016/j.infsof.2013.07.012

Wood, S., Michaelides, G., & Thomson, C. (2013). Successful extreme programming: Fidelity to the methodology or good teamworking? *Information and Software Technology, 55*(4), 660–672. doi:10.1016/j.infsof.2012.10.002

ENDNOTE

[1] "BeHEMoTH (Be – Behaviour of interest, H – Health context, E – exclusions, MoTH – Models or Theories)" Carroll et al. (2013).

Chapter 10
Awareness Without Actions:
A Qualitative Study on Risk Management in Nordic Software Startups

Quang-Trung Nguyen
ThuongMai University, Vietnam

Thananya Phromwongsa
University of Southern Denmark, Denmark

Sharanka Shanmugalingam
University of Southern Denmark, Denmark

Victor Steenfeldt Laursen
University of Southern Denmark, Denmark

Indira Nurdiani Jabangwe
University of Southern Denmark, Denmark

Anh Nguyen-Duc
ⓘ https://orcid.org/0000-0002-7063-9200
University of South-Eastern Norway, Norway

ABSTRACT

The success and survival of software startup companies depend on the decision-making of entrepreneurs. Risk perception and management is an important part of making both business and product-related decisions. In contrast to the popularity of research on risk management in the context of established organizations, there is relatively limited research on risk management in early-stage startup companies. In this work, the authors aim at understanding the perception and practices of managing risks in software startups. They interviewed CEOs and CTOs of nine early-stage software startups in Denmark and Norway. The results revealed an awareness of common types of risks among software startups. However, risks are not measured or managed by any established approaches. They found that startup founders do not believe in risk management methods and prioritize other tasks on their to-do list. The findings have direct implications for startup founders in their early stages in Nordic countries.

DOI: 10.4018/978-1-7998-9059-1.ch010

INTRODUCTION

A process innovation can be seen as the implementation of a new improved way of working, including the management of product development projects. While improvement always involve a certain level of risk, for many decades, risk management has been an integral part of project management (Boehm, 1989, 1991). Risk is a future uncertain event or condition that, if it occurs, has a positive or negative effect on project performance (IEEE Guide, 2004). Managing risk is an important aspect of increasing the success of process innovation in software industry. According to the report of the Chaos Report 2014, 16% of software development projects are successful; the other projects are completed untimely, poorly, or require more financial costs than was planned earlier (The Standish Group, 2014). According to a Microsoft Corporation study, if effective risk management is taken into account, there is a 50-75% chance of completing the software development project successfully (McConnell, 1997).

Research and application of risk management techniques, methods and tools is widespread. Their application is evident in various contexts of software development, such as, ERP (Aloini, Dulmin, & Mininno, 2007), global software projects (Munch, 2011), and Agile projects (Nyfjord, Kajko-Mattsson, 2008). While risk management is often seen as parts of standards (ISO 27005, ISO 31000) and frameworks (RMF), the implicit context of risk management is often in established organizations with the ability to implement strategies and processes.

Risk is an essential phenomenon in the startup context. Starting up a new venture is a high-risk activity with the majority of startups collapsing within the first two years of their creation (Much, 2011). As startup companies typically rely on a single product or service, unexpected incidents occurred during the development of the products or services might have a severe consequence on the whole business (Giardino, Unterkalmsteiner, Paternoster, Gorschek, & Abrahamsson, 2014). Startup founders are risk takers inherently, but they want to have a better ability to assess risk better than other people.

In the context of software startups, risk management looks unconventional, because startups might involve a much higher risk than traditional businesses. Moreover, startup context implies different types of risks relating to entrepreneurial activities that can have a direct impact on the engineering parts of the startup. Yet, perhaps even more so than in traditional contexts, evaluating and managing risk in the software startup context might be a key factor for success.

Similar to the understanding of Software Engineering Knowledge area in Software Startups (Berg, Birkeland, Nguyen-Duc, Pappas, & Jaccheri, 2018), we propose research about the application of Risk Management in software startup contexts. Being able to efficiently model and analyze risks in startups, we will be able to develop intelligent systems that support startups in making informed well-calculated decisions.

In the first step, risk and the context for risk management should be understood. In this paper, we aim to study the use of risk management, where software startups located in Denmark and Norway is our target. To accomplish the aim of the study, we performed a qualitative study of ten start-ups. To address the major question "How do software startup manage risk", we propose the following Research questions (RQs):

- RQ1: What types of risks are perceived in early-stage software startups?
- RQ2: How do software startups manage these risks?

The paper is structured as follows: Section 2 presents the fundamentals of software startups, risk and risk management, Section 3 presents the methods used in the study, as well as the threats to the validity of the study. Section 4 presents the research results. Section 5 contains a discussion of the ðndings and the impact they might have. Lastly, the conclusion of the paper is written in Section 6.

BACKGROUND

This section contains an overview of existing studies on software startups and startup's risk and a brief description of risk and risk management.

Managerial Perspectives of Software Startups

Startups have been a hype in different disciplines, societies and industries. Startups and their activities, including product development, is a part of an entrepreneurial process in which the characteristics, experience, and skills of entrepreneurs are determining factors for their successes (Klein & Bullok 2006; Kuratko 2005; Shane & Venkataraman, 2000; Simpeh, 2011). Startup development is a mix of the process of developing the business itself, and the development and deployment of its key products or services (Nguyen-Duc, Seppanen, & Abrahamsson, 2015). Other lines of research explore if and how the software engineering paradigm can benefit startups by increasing the success rate of products, sustainable development practices and methods, increasing quality and reducing costs (Bajwa et al. 2017; Berg et al. 2018, Giardino et al. 2016; Klotins et al. 2019). Much of the insights from engineering startup products relate to managerial matter, assuming project-oriented approaches.

Figure 1. Three different lens on software development in startups

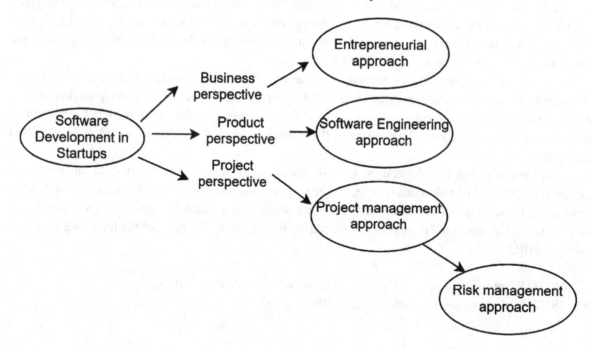

Startups typically adopt any things that might work to support their first needs, following the "Just do it" motto. They often do not adopt long-term plans (Nguyen-Duc, Seppanen, & Abrahamsson, 2015). On a daily basis, many startups are found to have various problems, i.e. technical debts and human resources due to weak project management (Giardino et al., 2016). Many perceive rigid project management as a "waste of time" that hinders development speed since the uncertainty makes formal scheduling pointless (Giardino et al., 2016). However, in the same work, the authors also acknowledge the need for project management, especially when the company faces team changes, i.e. growth or shift focus to business concerns (Giardino et al., 2016).

There are different project management approaches observed in different startup stages (Klotins et al., 2019). As start-ups progress through the life-cycle, metrics become more specific, attached to high-level business milestones, and consider both internal and external aspects jointly. The authors suggest that start-ups need to set clear goals and metrics to assess their performance from the very beginning objectively (Klotins et al., 2019). Managing project activities in a startup context does not separate from business development. For the startup, it is useful to fail often and quickly, as failures early in the project are inexpensive and provide crucial knowledge. The knowledge gained by the failures is then used to change the company in some way, i.e., to pivot (Bajwa et al., 2017). Pivot, as a strategic change in business direction, has a significant impact on engineering and project activities. As seen in Figure 1, we investigate risk management from the angle of project management, with the specific topic of early stage software startups.

Risks Factors in Software Development

Risk is defined as a possibility of loss, the loss itself, or any characteristic, object, or action that is associated with that possibility (Kuratko, 2005). In a software project, risk implies "the impact to the project which could be in the form of diminished quality of the end product, increased costs, delayed completion, loss of market share, or failure" (Alberts & Dorofee, 2010). It is long recognized in software projects that successful project managers are also good risk managers (Boehm, 1991).

Risk management is the management of that risk. The risks that might impact a project or company should be identified in order to be managed. Once a company has a list of identified risks, it can assess the risks to determine which events will have the largest impact, if they occur, and which events are most likely to happen. With these assessments, the company can prioritize the risks so that they can work effectively to mitigate and avoid negative effects (Larson & Gray, 2017). It can also be that project managers are not aware of terms such as risk identification, risk assessment, risk management planning, or risk monitoring, but they are actually practicing them (Boehm, 1991).

The area of software development risks is a large and quite distinct research domain that has grown much since the very first work on software project risks (Boehm, 1989, 1991). Several lists of software projects risks have been proposed that highlight factors such as communication, management, human, and organizational factors (Addison & Vallabh, 2002; Boehm, 1991; Han & Huang, 2007). Masso et al. conducted a systematic literature review on risk management in software life cycles and reported various risk management activities across specific processes of the projects, i.e. verification process, maintenance process, system analysis process and design process (Masso et al., 2020).

Perceived Risks in Software Startups

A startup can be defined as an organization that is challenged by youth and immaturity, with extremely limited resources, multiple influences, and dynamic technologies and markets (Bajwa et al., 2017). In this age of new business models, globalization and rapid growth in businesses across the globe and effective risk management has become critical factors for the success of businesses. Awareness and understanding of risks in startups are essential. Todeschini et al. (2017) found that start-ups have different ways of understanding the concept of risk management and a lack of familiarity with the concept of risk management. Although they have a lack familiarity, the managers of the start-ups are interested in risk management because of its benefits because the companies often have to deal with decisions regarding risks. Gelderen et al. (2005) studied risks from 517 startups and found a strong concern of market risks among entrepreneurs. The authors also mentioned about the importance of risk management, as the effective use of risk reduction techniques will lead to lower perceived risk.

METHODOLOGY

This section describes the methods used in this research project and identifies any threats to validity. The overall approach used to find the answer to the research questions is qualitative and exploratory. This method is chosen as we can get more in-depth answers to the problem. This method was chosen to understand how risk management is implemented in their natural environment. Risk is a considerable problem at the beginning of every software life cycle. We selected a startup as the unit of analysis and adopted a purposive sampling strategy to recruit cases (Palinkas et al., 2015). There is often difficulty in identifying a real startup case among other similar phenomena, such as pure software startups, SMEs or part-time startups. Therefore, we clearly defined the criteria for our case selection:

- A startup that has at least two full-time employees, so product development is not an individual activity;
- A startup that has at least six months of operation, so their experience can be relevant;
- A startup that has released at least one MVP, so its engineering practices are a relevant topic; and
- Software as their core value

Data Collection

We sent invitations for reviews to several companies in our professional networks. We also reached out to software companies in our regions. We chose to interview startups to get in-depth answers to each question and be able to discuss the topic. Semi-structured interviews are a common approach to collecting relevant insights into many phenomena in software engineering. The advantage of semi-structured interviews is that it allows improvisation and exploration of the objects studied. The interview subjects were primarily chosen based on availability, and they are all located in Odense (Denmark), Trondheim and Oslo (Norway). The data collection process was conducted between September 2018 and December 2019. Detailed information about the study participants can be found in Table 1.

Table 1. Interview subject profiles

Id	Role	Startup Age	# staffs	Startup Domain	Locations
S1	Founder	24 months	3	Computer vision	Odense
S2	CTO	12 months	3	Scheduling system	Odense
S3	Lead developer	12 months	3	Scheduling system	Odense
S4	CEO	24 months	2	Business networking	Odense
S5	Developer	24 months	8	Payment solution	Odense
S6	CEO	12 months	2	Healthcare platform	Trondheim
S7	CEO	23 months	3	Digital news platform	Trondheim
S8	CTO	30 months	12	Educational platform	Trondheim
S9	CEO	8 months	6	Data analytic	Oslo

The goal of the interview was to gather information to understand the use of risk management in start-up companies. The data in this study has been collected through semi-structured interviews. The interview was done face-to-face with one or more representatives from each startup. The role of the representative was chosen based on the availability of their resources. All of the interviews were recorded and notes were taken during the interviews.

Box 1.

Part 1: Warm-up
• Tell us about your company
• How does the startup idea come to your mind?
• What is your key product? How is it developed?
Part 2: Risk identification
• How do you define risks?
• What kind of risks did you face in your early stages?
• Do you have a list of identified risks? What does the list contain?
• How does your company prioritize risk?
Part 3: Risk management
• How do you handle risk?
• How would you describe "Risk Management"?
• Do you use any risk management techniques or processes?
• How did risk management help control the start-up phase?
• Would it have been different if you had not used risk management?

Data Analysis

After the data had been collected through interviews, the recordings were transcribed. Following the qualitative data analysis from Runeson et al. (2012), the transcriptions were first studied in detail. After this, we brought out the interesting quotes from the transcripts and gave each of them one or more codes. A code is a label assigned to a part of the text "representing a certain theme, area, construct, etc" (Runeson et al., 2012). The codes were also formulated during this process based on the themes, areas, etc. that exist in the transcripts, as mentioned in (Runeson et al., 2012). When a sentence was interesting but did not fit an existing code, we assigned it a new one, which could then be used in other parts of the texts.

Examples of coded quotes are shown in Figure 1. After the transcripts had been coded, the next step was to conclude (Runeson et al., 2012). This was done by grouping the coded quotes by their codes and examining the similarities and differences between the statements. From this, we extracted a conclusion.

Figure 2. Example of coded quotes and labels

Question	Quote	Code
How do you handle risk?	We could enter the market with an initial version that is copied by a larger player that has more resources.	Example of risk
How do you handle risk?	We could be taken by surprise by someone else.	Example of risk
List of risks	Risk in that someone else could steal our idea.	Example of risk
Do you know risk management?	When you are in a start-up I think your, or our, focus is very narrow.	Expectation of startups
Do you know risk management?	We have to launch a product. It is actually the only thing i think about right now.	Expectation of startups
Do you know risk management?	We do not not care about it, but we are kind of wearing blinkers	Expectation of startups
How do you handle risk?	There is always a risk that it goes wrong	Knowledge about risks and RM
Do you know risk management?	Risk management processes is not an expression i have heard before	Knowledge about risks and RM
List of risks	I do not have a list.	List of risks

Threats to Validities

The section covers the validity threats as well as the measures taken in an attempt to mitigate them. The validity threats are classified as suggested by Petersen and Gencel (2013).

- *Theoretical validities*: In this study, the primary threat to theoretical validity is the interpretation of "Risk". The researchers have primarily had an understanding of risk as described in Section 2. The understanding of risk varied highly among the interview subjects as described in Section 4. This threat to validity is mitigated by asking the interview subjects about their definition of risk. This might not completely remove the threat, but it should reduce its impact of it.
- *Descriptive validities*: Descriptive validity describes how accurately we are able to capture and describe the objective truth (Nyfjord & Kajko-Mattsson, 2008). The primary threat to descriptive validity in this study is the poor collection of data. The data collection, i.e. the interviews, were performed by researchers with extremely limited experience, and therefore, skill, in conducting interviews. The lack of skill among the interviewers might have contributed to issues with the data collection, e.g., the interviewers might not ask all the relevant questions.
- *Interpretative validities:* Interpretative validity, also called Conclusion validity (Runeson et al., 2012) is concerning the researcher's ability to draw correct conclusions from the data. A researcher might have expectations of a specific outcome, which can influence the conclusions that the researcher draws. Another factor that threatens the Interpretative validity is the experience and knowledge of the researcher. If the researcher is not skilled in qualitative data analysis that may influence the results. In this project, we attempted to mitigate the influence that the bias of each individual researcher by having all researchers check the coding performed.

- *Generalization validities:* Generalizability validity is concerning the extent to which the results are representative of a larger population and represent the actual industrial practices (Klotins et al., 2019). They are all located in Denmark and Norway.

RESULTS

The main findings of our research are the following:

RQ1: What Types of Risks Are Perceived in Early Stage Software Startups?

It is different from one start-up to another whether they have considered the concept of risk. The alternative terms that were used in the interviews are "problem", "challenge", "difficulty", "unknown", "concern" etc. All the interview subjects were able to explain and give examples of different types of risks they experienced through their startups. Even though none of the companies kept a formal list of identified risks, the interview subjects were able to reflect on the events that might threaten their business. For example:

Among the most significant risks to early-stage startups are financial issues. Most of the startups are bootstrap, with their own savings or 3F funding model (Friend-Family-Fools). Running out of cash, cash-burning rate, insufficient usage of money, and difficult constraints when receiving funding are all relevant problems. [Financial risks]: *"The problem is we started in 2009 we started with Innovation Norway. We quit our jobs, we focused a hundred percent on this [00:08:47] and we didn't get any funding so development stuck up."* (S9)

"How much money do we have to put in compared to the outcome?" (S4)

Startups have a lot to do in the quest for their markets. When come to market risks, the possible problems are the market size, consumer behaviors, and shifts in market features. [Market risks]: *"It [the current market] has some significant challenges in regards to a small population and huge geographical area. That makes it difficult..."* The market risks might not come from the market itself, as the startups might also target the wrong market, or make a product that does not really serve the targeted market, leading to a product-market mismatch.

Interview subjects mentioned different concerns with their teams, i.e. lack of necessary competence in their teams, challenges of growing teams, internal communication across team functionalities, etc. [Team risks]: *"Since we have limited resources, we could not do further development of the IOS because of focus, etc. We have to stay on the web because that was the biggest platform for us. I am not going to say it was a wrong decision, but we should have thought harder to keep developing for the IOS as well."*

As known in previous studies, startups typically perform several pivots with changed elements in their business models. Business risks involve pitfall on the journey of business development. [Business risks]: *"There is a risk that we do not reach our goal before we run out of money."* (S1)

The methodology is the usage of methods, practices, and tools that are not appropriate and cause damage to the startups. This is always expected as startups have limited operating history, and all the methods or practices need time to be selected and matured. [Methodology risks]: *"I think at least if you look back and try to learn, I know this is difficult but for start-ups to think about coding and testing from day one. I think you can say, [00:43:17] effort and frustration because you end up a lot of rework because you didn't think about all those things."* (S7)

Product risks are the problems within the product itself that make it less useful in acquiring customers, markets, achieving funding and serving for future product development. Product risks can be an indirect consequence of methodology risks, financial risks or team risks. [Product/ service risks]: *"Things that make our users unhappy are risks, I think"* (S4). *"Our cloud provider went down a couple of days ago"* (S3)

Proposition 1: Startups are aware of risks regarding to their finance, market, business, team, methodology and products

Financial risks are probably the type of risks that are better understood and controlled. Startups who are able to mention their financial numbers are also aware of gain and loss in term of money. Other categories of risks we do not find evidence on how they are quantified and controlled in practice. For instance, for business risks, the interviewee (S9) could mention a number of pivots and the reasons why they changed their course of action. However, it is often a post-mortem reflection and they did not plan or analyze them beforehand. Methodology risks are also reflected after the team had much wasted time and effort. In S7, it is even not possible to understand the impact of introducing new practices or methods to the team performance. We can see only three interview subjects that we're able to mention measurable risks. [Measurable risks]*"How large a probability there is for something to go wrong."* (S1). *"When a company has large expenses and not a lot of money."* (S6)

Proposition 2: Startup founders are mostly aware of uncertainties, but not measurable risks

Table 2. Types of risks from our cases

Id	Risk Examples	Immeasurable Risks	Measurable Risks
S1	X	X	X
S2	X	X	-
S3	X	X	-
S4	X	X	-
S5	X	X	-
S6	X	X	X
S7	X	X	-
S8	X	X	-
S9	X	X	X

RQ2: How Do Software Startups Manage These Risks?

Among interviewee, there are only two subjects who have knowledge about risk management. For instance: *"Yes, we had it during our study theoretically but not in practice" [...] ... I do not have any specific names of any methods"* (S1). One start-up uses a kind of informal risk management.

The rest of the cases have not heard about the term *"risk management"*. They also mentioned that they did not use risk management in their company. When asked, interviewee said that adoption of risk management might be wasting their time and efforts.

- *"We had to do with risk portfolio assessment tasks in relation to business analyses etc. We used those a lot in the beginning. [...] The tools and analyses we use today are our gut feeling, because [risk management] is such a waste of time"* (S4)
- *"There is also a risk in spending time on acquainting oneself with risk"* (S1)
- *"We will look at it [Risk management] when the time comes"* (S5)

As all the interview subjects mentioned, the companies do not use risk management, as they are very new with little operation history. They do not have enough time and resources, and first and foremost they focus on product-oriented activities. They aim at delivering their services and products as soon as possible, without much investment on methodology in general. As mentioned by startup S9:

- *"It is already time consuming to think about possible upcoming risks"* (S9)

S4 did make use of risk management in the early stage of their company but stopped as it was not worth the time.

- *"Our approach to risk is trial and error, where we instead of making a pipeline to Australia, [...] and sending 100 students, we send 3 students" (S4). This shows that they are aware that risks might occur and will perform small scale experiments in order to identify risks.*

S2 mentions: *"We pretty much follow that start-up philosophy where you have to pump out as much code as possible as fast as possible"* (S2) S5 said: *"When you are in a start-up then I think your, or our, focus is very narrow. [...] We have to launch a product [...] It is actually the only thing we think about right now."* (S5)

While they might not use a formal process, we also investigated other risk management activities the start-ups might apply. The first step of risk management is risk identification [6]. Therefore, we asked if they had a list of identified risks. To this S1 & S2 responded that they did not have a list. This shows that risks are not prioritized and risk identification activities have not been formally done.

Proposition 3: Startups do not perform formal risk management approaches due to their perceived wasted time and efforts

DISCUSSIONS

In this section, we offer our thoughts regarding the observations from our cases. This is organized into a discussion on why risk management is overlooked and the comparison to related work.

Why Risk Management Is Overlooked?

A possible reason that start-ups do not use risk management processes is a lack of familiarity. Three of the interviewed start-ups had no knowledge about what risk management was, and the two interviewees that had encountered risk management in their education had no hands-on experience. Another reason mentioned was that the risk management process is too time-consuming compared to the benefits. One start-up tried to implement risk management but abandoned it, and instead, they focused more on their own gut feeling and a trial-and-error process. The lack of risk management is also reasoned by the need to launch the product as soon as possible. Two of the start-ups are focused on the development of the product and they just want to launch it and those are their highest priority. Determining the reasons behind the lack of risk management in start-ups could be the subject of future work. We propose a framework that captures the reasons for the lack of risk management adoptions in early-stage software startups, as shown in Figure 3.

Figure 3. Fishbone diagram of lack of adoption of risk management in startups

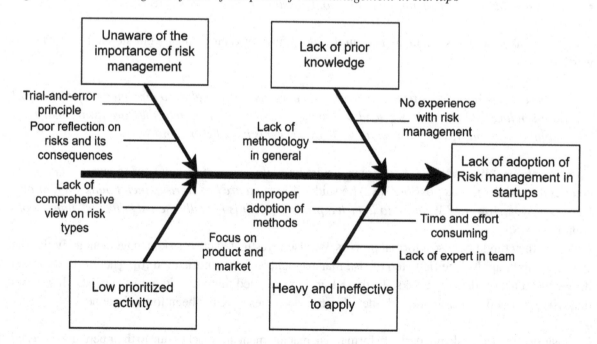

Comparison to Related Work

Todeschini et al. (2017) had a similar research problem to us. The findings of this research were reasonably similar to ours, as the start-ups they contacted had a lack of familiarity with the risk management tools. In our case, there were some interviewees that had some knowledge of risk management, but they were not able to explain this concretely, as they have not practiced it in real life. The difference between our study in relation to this study is that this study suggested a risk management method that was adapted to start-up companies. This was not done in our study, as we have lack of knowledge of using Risk Management methods in practice. We only have theoretical knowledge of this concept. Gelderen et al.(2005) investigated a sample of 517 entrepreneurs. One of the findings was the significance of the perceived risk of the market in comparison to other types of risks. The authors also mentioned the importance of risk management, as the effective use of risk reduction techniques will lead to lower perceived risk. Our observations from the nine cases showed a different perception of risk and risk management. Unterkalmsteiner et al. (2016) discussed several research areas in software startups, in which the authors suggest identifying the critical aspects of startup development risks that are suitable for simulation. The area would study, model, and quantify various aspects related to risk management in software startups, with the goal of providing tools, based on process simulation, that control risk.

CONCLUSION

Risk management is an interesting topic in software startup companies, where a lot of uncertainties and risks are expected. We conducted a qualitative study on nine early-stage software startups in Denmark and Norway. Two major topics were explored, namely risk identification and risk management. We found that startups were aware of risks regarding to their finance, market, business, team, methodology and products, however, they do not measure or analyze these risks. Furthermore, software startups do not perform any formal risk management approaches due to their perceived wasted time and efforts. These findings might not be generalized for a larger population, however, they could be useful for startups companies in Nordic countries, which share similar environmental contexts with our cases. We believe that the insights from this study would be helpful for people who are doing or want to start their software business. For future work, we will explore if there is any impact on startup performance when risk management is used versus when it is not. Another research goal is to explore the consequence of unmanaged risks to project and startup success.

REFERENCES

Addison, T., & Vallabh, S. (2002). Controlling software project risks: An empirical study of methods used by experienced project managers. *Proceedings of the 2002 Annual Research Conference of the South African Institute of Computer Scientists and Information Technologists on Enablement through Technology*, 128–140.

Alberts, C., & Dorofee, A. (2010). *Risk Management Framework* (CMU/SEI-2010-TR-017). Retrieved April 19, 2022, from the Software Engineering Institute, Carnegie Mellon University website: https://resources.sei.cmu.edu/library/asset-view.cfm?AssetID=9525

Aloini, D., Dulmin, R., & Mininno, V. (2007). Risk management in ERP project introduction: Review of the literature. *Information & Management, 44*(6), 547–567. doi:10.1016/j.im.2007.05.004

Bajwa, S. S., Wang, X., Nguyen Duc, A., & Abrahamsson, P. (2017). "Failures" to be celebrated: An analysis of major pivots of software startups. *Empirical Software Engineering, 22*(5), 2373–2408. doi:10.100710664-016-9458-0

Berg, V., Birkeland, J., Nguyen-Duc, A., Pappas, I. O., & Jaccheri, L. (2018). Software startup engineering: A systematic mapping study. *Journal of Systems and Software, 144*, 255–274. doi:10.1016/j.jss.2018.06.043

Boehm, B. W. (1989). *Software Risk Management*. IEEE Computer Society Press. doi:10.1007/3-540-51635-2_29

Boehm, B. W. (1991). Software risk management: Principles and practices. *IEEE Software, 8*(1), 32–41. doi:10.1109/52.62930

Giardino, C., Paternoster, N., Unterkalmsteiner, M., Gorschek, T., & Abrahamsson, P. (2016). Software Development in Startup Companies: The Greenfield Startup Model. *IEEE Transactions on Software Engineering, 42*(6), 585–604. doi:10.1109/TSE.2015.2509970

Giardino, C., Unterkalmsteiner, M., Paternoster, N., Gorschek, T., & Abrahamsson, P. (2014). What Do We Know about Software Development in Startups? *IEEE Software, 31*(5), 28–32. doi:10.1109/MS.2014.129

Han, W.-M., & Huang, S.-J. (2007). An empirical analysis of risk components and performance on software projects. *Journal of Systems and Software, 80*(1), 42–50. doi:10.1016/j.jss.2006.04.030

IEEE Guide Adoption of PMI Standard - A Guide to the Project Management Body of Knowledge, IEEE Std 1490-2003 (Revision of IEEE Std 1490-1998), pp. 1–194, May 2004, . doi:10.1109/IEEESTD.2004.94565

Klein, P. G., & Bullock, J. B. (2006). Can Entrepreneurship Be Taught? *Journal of Agricultural and Applied Economics, 38*(2), 429–439. doi:10.1017/S107407080002246X

Klotins, E., Unterkalmsteiner, M., Chatzipetrou, P., Gorschek, T., Prikladniki, R., Tripathi, N., & Pompermaier, L. (2019). A progression model of software engineering goals, challenges, and practices in start-ups. *IEEE Transactions on Software Engineering*, 1–1. doi:10.1109/TSE.2019.2900213

Kuratko, D. F. (2005). The Emergence of Entrepreneurship Education: Development, Trends, and Challenges. *Entrepreneurship Theory and Practice, 29*(5), 577–597. doi:10.1111/j.1540-6520.2005.00099.x

Larson, E., & Gray, C. (2017). *Project Management: The Managerial Process* (7th ed.). McGraw Hill.

Masso, J., Pino, F. J., Pardo, C., García, F., & Piattini, M. (2020). Risk management in the software life cycle: A systematic literature review. *Computer Standards & Interfaces, 71*, 103431. doi:10.1016/j.csi.2020.103431

McConnell, S. (1997). *Software project survival guide: how to be sure your first important project isn't your last.* Microsoft Press.

Munch, J. (2011). Risk Management in Global Software Development Projects: Challenges, Solutions, and Experience. *2011 IEEE Sixth International Conference on Global Software Engineering Workshop,* 35–35. doi:10.1109/ICGSE-W.2011.35

Nguyen-Duc, A., Seppänen, P., & Abrahamsson, P. (2015). Hunter-gatherer Cycle: A Conceptual Model of the Evolution of Software Startups. *Proceedings of the 2015 International Conference on Software and System Process,* 199–203. 10.1145/2785592.2795368

Nyfjord, J., & Kajko-Mattsson, M. (2008). Outlining a Model Integrating Risk Management and Agile Software Development. *2008 34th Euromicro Conference Software Engineering and Advanced Applications,* 476–483. 10.1109/SEAA.2008.77

Palinkas, L. A., Horwitz, S. M., Green, C. A., Wisdom, J. P., Duan, N., & Hoagwood, K. (2015). Purposeful Sampling for Qualitative Data Collection and Analysis in Mixed Method Implementation Research. *Administration and Policy in Mental Health, 42*(5), 533–544. doi:10.100710488-013-0528-y PMID:24193818

Petersen, P., & Gencel, C. (2013). Worldviews, research methods, and their relationship to validity in empirical software engineering research. In *2013 Joint Conference of the 23rd International Workshop on Software Measurement and the 8th International Conference on Software Process and Product Measurement* (pp. 81–89). IEEE 10.1109/IWSM-Mensura.2013.22

Runeson, P., Høst, M., Ohlsson, M. C., Regnell, B., Wohlin, C., & Wesslen, A. (2012). *Experimentation in Software Engineering.* Springer Science & Business Media.

Runeson, P., Host, M., Rainer, A., & Regnell, B. (2012). *Case Study Research in Software Engineering: Guidelines and Examples* (1st ed.). Wiley Publishing. doi:10.1002/9781118181034

Shane, S., & Venkataraman, S. (2000). The Promise of Entrepreneurship as a Field of Research. *Academy of Management Review, 25*(1), 217–226. doi:10.5465/amr.2000.2791611

Simpeh, K. N. (2011). *Entrepreneurship theories and Empirical research: A Summary Review of the Literature.* Undefined.

The Standish Group. (2014). *The Standish Group report chaos—Project smart.* https://www.projectsmart.co.uk/white-papers/chaosreport.pdf

Todeschini, B. V., Boelter, A. S., de Souza, J. S., & Cortimiglia, M. N. (2017). Risk Management from the Perspective of Startups. *European Journal of Applied Business and Management, 3*(3), 3. https://nidisag.isag.pt/index.php/IJAM/article/view/263

Unterkalmsteiner, M., Abrahamsson, P., Wang, X., Nguyen-Duc, A., Shah, S., Bajwa, S. S., Baltes, G. H., Conboy, K., Cullina, E., Dennehy, D., Edison, H., Fernandez-Sanchez, C., Garbajosa, J., Gorschek, T., Klotins, E., Hokkanen, L., Kon, F., Lunesu, I., Marchesi, M., … Yagüe, A. (2016). Software Startups – A Research Agenda. *E-Informatica Software Engineering Journal, 10.*

van Gelderen, M., Thurik, R., & Bosma, N. (2005). Success and Risk Factors in the Pre-Startup Phase. *Small Business Economics, 24*(4), 365–380. doi:10.100711187-004-6994-6

Chapter 11
COVID's Scholarly Literature and Innovation in Startups

Varun Gupta

(iD) https://orcid.org/0000-0003-2824-3402

University of Alcala, Spain

Chetna Gupta

Jaypee Institute of Information Technology, India

Lawrence Peters

Software Consultants International Limited, USA & Universidad Politecnica de Madrid, Madrid, Spain

Leandro Pereira

(iD) https://orcid.org/0000-0002-4920-0498

ISCTE, University Institute of Lisbon, Lisboa, Portugal

ABSTRACT

The importance of scholarly literature on startup capacities to stimulate innovation in pandemic times is highlighted in this chapter. The scholarly literature can help startups looking for opportunities or solutions in the face of a pandemic, but knowledge acquisition from secondary materials may be limited due to the growing number of publications, retractions, and preprints. The growing number of publications and venues makes it more difficult for entrepreneurs to get the information they need, analyse it, and then use collective intelligence to turn it into useful business knowledge. Retractions may steer startups in the incorrect direction, resulting in a waste of financial resources. Preprints are non-peer reviewed research articles that may provide some direction to startups but should not be relied upon entirely. The solutions to these issues are finally provided. Addressing these concerns could make scholarly literature beneficial to startups, allowing the global community to respond to the pandemic as a whole.

DOI: 10.4018/978-1-7998-9059-1.ch011

INTRODUCTION

The Coronavirus disease (COVID-19) has impacted all countries globally and the time when society is expected to return to normal is uncertain. However, coronavirus has united the global community in leveraging their coordinated efforts in finding solutions to a myriad of problems created by the pandemic. The startups are known to be the providers of innovations and have a promising role to play during the pandemic. This has been evident with European Union (EU) granting €166 million to the 36 startups under the European Innovation Council (EIC) Accelerator Pilot program to tackle the coronavirus pandemic[4]. The pandemic results in high levels of uncertainty in the business environment which makes it harder for startups to make rational decisions. The liabilities of small ness and newness also limit their abilities to innovate. The open innovation is thus a key for knowledge capture which could be made from public institutions, publishing agencies, customers, academia and much more. Each of these elements of open innovation has tried to contribute to coordinated efforts to put a united response to the pandemic. For instance, publishing institutions provided enhanced publishing opportunities to the researchers in terms of fast track reviews, waivers of Article Processing Charges (APC) and free access to the readers. The objective was to promote the corona virus related knowledge dissemination in a timely and cost effective manner across the innovation ecosystem. This knowledge could help startups to identify business trends, solutions to corona virus, survival strategies and much more. Thus, the scholarly literature has the great potential to support startups in exploring the markets with their existing or new business ideas. The acquisition of knowledge through the scholarly literature could assist startups in limiting their primary research efforts conducted with clients through onsite co-located meetings, which would otherwise be hampered by pandemic restrictions (Gupta and Fernandez-Crehuet, 2021a; Gupta et al., 2021b). Startups have higher failure rates mostly due to knowledge related issues (e.g., inadequate cost estimation and control, inadequate skills, collecting accurate market knowledge, lacking development and management skills and so forth). Startups have historically had a high failure rate due to these factors even though they may have breakthrough innovations. Costing and scheduling tend to be the primary culprits mostly due to the lack of management training of the startup's leaders. Scholarly literature could help startups acquire the needed business related knowledge thereby increasing their success rates and more in contributing to corona virus related solutions.

The scholarly literature is growing and has witnessed an increased number of research publications during the pandemic. The number of venues is growing, for example, the number of Journals, conferences, and workshops has increased. On the one hand, this growing number is an indication of increased contribution of experts and increased motivation to respond to the pandemic. On other hand, the increased number of such venues makes the process of knowledge acquisition much harder. For instance, startups with their limited resources may find the increased costs to search scholarly literature expensive. Searches for meaningful research across scholarly literature will be higher due to increased volumes of publications across multiple venues. This article reports three issues associated with scholarly literature that require urgent attention to make it more value to the startup community. This includes the growing number of publications, retractions, and Preprints.

SUPPORT OF SCHOLARLY LITERATURE FOR STARTUPS

Scholarly literature has provided good support to provide solutions during the pandemic. The disseminated research can be acquired by startups to make their business decisions, including diversification in industries with innovative products to provide a response to the pandemic. To achieve this, the scholarly literature during pandemic have made lot of innovations in their processes and services which include the following:

- Fast peer review of submitted articles related to the pandemic.
- Free publication of pandemic related articles under open access.
- Free dissemination of pandemic related research to the readers.
- Increased specialised sections, for instance special sections and special issues related to pandemic research.
- Launch of new venues like Journals, Conferences and Workshops to disseminate pandemic related research.

ISSUES WITH SCHOLARLY LITERATURE DURING COVID

Despite of the support of scholarly literature to startup community, there are three main issues that should be addressed. This includes growing the number of publications, retractions, and Preprints.

1. **Growing Number of Publications, Venues, and Retractions:** The number of submissions made to the journals, conferences as well as to preprint platforms grew quantitatively during coronavirus. The number of retractions of corona virus related articles were also reported in the news (*Heidi Ledford & Richard Van Noorden, Nature 582, 160, 2020*). Further, the number of venues is also growing, for instance, more special sections dedicated to corona virus related research, new journals addressing pandemic related issues, new workshops, and conferences. This makes it harder for startups to identify the information they are looking for and to do collective intelligence across the bifurcated knowledge accessed through different venues. The efforts invested in identifying the venues, filtering unwanted information, and selecting only meaningful research articles comprises transaction costs of knowledge acquisition. With limited resources, startups will find it harder to acquire knowledge across diverse and vast scholarly literature due to higher transaction costs.

One main difficulty is to filter out the contributions that are less valuable. Although there are fewer, there are some contributors that are simply looking for an opportunity to increase their publication repertoire by participating in the epidemic related research. In other words, there are some (although tiny) contributions to published pandemic research, with authors' contributions going outside their research expertise fields. This however is too hard and effortful to be identified. Recently, we observed with two research papers that one article was authored by approx. 52 authors and another (but the shorter one with 4 pages) by 11 authors, with both articles published by leading venues. This makes us believe that research funders should not consider "the number of quality publications" but rather "the number quality *ethical* publications" as the measure of quality publication. However, identifying the ethical publications may not be that easier, for instance, it will be almost impossible to categorise above two papers under such category although it seems very obvious to every researcher. Although it seems unethical to have long list of authors in a short paper, yet it is harder to challenge such occurrences. These behaviours could supplement the need for the open research method as the reward mechanism (*Ralitsa Madsen, Nature 586, 200, 2020*).

The contributions made by researchers that are far away from their research domains as the representation of interdisciplinary and diversified research in coronavirus related domains, had increased the traffic over diverse publication venues, which had enhanced the efforts of the reviewers and increased the chances of false positives. The Rapid Reviews: COVID-19 journal (*Vilas Dhar & Amy Brand, Nature 584, 192, 2020*) have been facing increased review load because of ever increasing the coronavirus related preprints.

The increased coronavirus related publications had made it hard to identify the quality research that actually had the ability to make real impacts in the society. The support offered by the publisher should be used honestly, leaving space to the researchers (former category) that are working hard to make a real difference in the corona virus related research.

2. Pre-Print Facility

The coronavirus was the unprecedented situation which resulted in panic everywhere, mostly because no one knew exactly how to react. Doctors and Scientists had been working hard to provide research solutions to the coronavirus. The academic publishers also offered their support by providing a facility to fast track peer review (and hence publication) of the corona virus related research and making it freely available to the readers. The Outbreak Science Rapid PREreview (see *Michael A. Johansson & Daniela Saderi Nature 584, 192; 2020*) is a commendable effort in the direction of making corona virus related preprints publicly available and subjecting them to rapid reviews by independent reviewers.

Preprints are usually useful to get early feedback from the research community as their peer review by an academic journal takes a long time. During the coronavirus era, the fast review process established by almost every journal provides an opportunity to the researchers to publicly share the "rigorously reviewed" research. This had utmost advantage over unrefereed preprints in terms of reputation, credibility and reach among research communities. If the quality of the research is "perceptually" high in the mind of the researcher, then publishing as a preprint does not make much sense because it could be reviewed quickly in leading journals. Further, the number of venues (including preprint platforms) accepting corona virus related research are too diverse that makes it hard for researchers to select suitable research solutions and adapt it as per their research requirements.

Preprint facility (referred and unreferred) for coronavirus research could turn out to be a bad idea as the lifesaving solutions should not be driven by preprints. The accuracy of the research resulting from preprints could be less trustworthy because of their unreferred nature or unsystematically conducted reviews.

PROPOSED SOLUTIONS

The following solutions may be useful in leveraging scholarly literature to increase the value of it for entrepreneurs.

1. **Uniform Indexing:** For pandemic-related research, the various publication platforms might employ standard keywords, article kinds, and research article formats. About the contributors' profiles, further information might be gathered from Open Researcher and Contributor ID (ORCID), Scopus, and Web of Science ID. After then, the data might be utilized to rate the articles. Startups looking for research solutions in a specific domain can find searching bibliographic databases with standardised search techniques and standard criteria, such as research kinds, much easier.

2. **Pre-Print Facility:** The pre-prints should not be made public until the audience has assessed them and a level of reliability has been established. The trustworthiness value could be enhanced if their solutions provide real value to startups. For example, an empirical study that has been adopted by startups and found to be helpful to them should be given a higher ranking, indicating that it has made a genuine contribution to the startup community.

By addressing these challenges, scholarly literature may become more useful to startups, allowing the entire global community to respond to the pandemic.

REFERENCES

Dhar, V., & Brand, A. (2020). Coronavirus: Time to re-imagine academic publishing. *Nature, 584*(7820), 192–192. doi:10.1038/d41586-020-02330-4 PMID:32782373

Gupta, V., & Fernandez-Crehuet, J. M. (2021). *Divergent Creativity for Requirement Elicitation Amid Pandemic: Experience from Real Consulting Project.* http://ceur-ws. org

Gupta, V., Rubalcaba, L., Gupta, C., & Gupta, V. (2021). Multimedia Prototyping for Early-Stage Startups Endurance: Stage for New Normal? *IEEE MultiMedia, 28*(4), 107–116. doi:10.1109/MMUL.2021.3122539

Johansson, M. A., & Saderi, D. (2020). Open peer-review platform for COVID-19 *preprints. Nature, 579*(7797), 29–29.

Ledford, H., & Van Noorden, R. (2020). High-profile coronavirus retractions raise concerns about data oversight. *Nature, 582*(7811), 160. doi:10.1038/d41586-020-01695-w PMID:32504025

Madsen, R. (2020). Funders must mandate and reward open research records. *Nature, 586*(7828), 200. doi:10.1038/d41586-020-02395-1 PMID:32788703

Chapter 12
IT Technologies in Mechanical Engineering:
Impact of IT Technologies on the Engineering Industry

Anastasia Sergeevna Samoylova

Federal State Autonomous Educational Institution of Higher Education, Moscow Polytechnic University, Russia

Ekaterina Olegovna Bobrova

Federal State Budgetary Educational Institution of Higher Education Lomonosov, Moscow State University, Russia

Valentina Valentinovna Britvina

Federal State Autonomous Educational Institution of Higher Education, Moscow Polytechnic University, Russia

Galina Pavlovna Konyukhova

Moscow State University of Technology, Russia

ABSTRACT

This work is devoted to the implementation of IT technologies in the engineering industry. The chapter presents a model of the Autodesk Inventor Pro + project, which is a prototype of the CAD system Autodesk Inventor Professional, based on the programming of a gear wheel, which makes it possible to increase the profitability of production in mechanical engineering. The chapter also presents theoretical assumptions for optimizing the assembly and made a server for generating a research report, which will determine the existence of this part.

DOI: 10.4018/978-1-7998-9059-1.ch012

INTRODUCTION

Mechanical engineering is part of the sector of the economy responsible for a large share of scientific and technological growth in the federal economy. This economic area includes a fairly wide spectrum of activities - the development of machines, equipment, instruments; production of consumer goods. Many technological processes for processing, assembling, repairing and testing products are used i n mechanical engineering. Increasing productivity and innovative product quality always requires a deep researching of production processes. It should be consider that mechanical engineering occupies a significant share of blank production processes, for example, small-scale metallurgy that produces rolled metal, casting, forgings, and stamping. The efficiency of mechanical engineering is ensured by such important sub-sectors: electronic and radio industries, instrument making, machine tool building, tool production, bearing production, etc. The production process in mechanical engineering can be conditionally divided into stages: blank production, processing of parts and assembly of nodes and products.

The modernization of the engineering industry is characterized by the continuous improvement of construction of product and their production technology. Various technological production methods are used, depending on the official purpose and operating conditions of products, their structural features and the technical requirements imposed on them. Difficult tasks of choosing a method for obtaining a workpiece and determining its dimensions, choosing a variant of the technological process of machining a part with the selection of equipment, tooling and calculating cutting conditions at all stages of this process appear in front of the mechanical engineering technologist.

Computer technologies in production began to be used relatively recently, but have already been able to significantly facilitate the labor of workers and improve the quality of production. Despite the generally accepted opinion, the use of computer technology is sent not so much at automating production, but at changing the projection and production technology itself, which in itself significantly reduces the time needed to create products, reduces costs for the entire life cycle of the product, and also improves its quality. They are used not only for automating machine tools and equipment, but also for designing a product layout. This is primarily applicable to complex engineering parts. From computer technology, it is required to create an accurate and detailed layout of the manufactured part, first of all, this provides great opportunities for creating better products in a shorter time.

The object of this work is the introduction of innovative IT technologies in the area of mechanical engineering (Gavrilyuk, 2021; Sazhina & Gavrilyuk, n.d.). Now, in our modern time, the modernization of mechanical engineering processes is proceeding slowly. One of the reasons for this slowdown is the deficit of specialists with the competencies to introduce IT technologies into production. Even with modern equipment, production efficiency is not very high. From the above, we can define the main goal of the work - this is to increase the influence of IT technologies in real production. The task of the work is the automation of a design bureau in the domain of industry.

To increase the profitability of production, the economic efficiency of the enterprise, the modernization of production should develop in two directions. The first direction is the training of new innovative personnel, for example, such as "engineers-constructors-technologists-programmers" to ensure a new production structure. The second direction is to increase the share of IT technologies in engineering processes for the transition to Industry 4.0. The percentage of implementation of such technologies will increase not only the level of rivalry among enterprises and the speed of information processing, but will also reduce the cost of production. So, the relevance of the work is expressed by the increase in the logistics of companies and the transition to the fourth industrial revolution, which will transfer the engineering industry to artificial intelligence.

DEVELOPMENT, IMPLEMENTATION AND PROPOSALS

In industrial practice, there are no products that are the creative creation of one implementer. As known, the design and technology bureaus are working on the development of future production.

Designers and technologists begin to interact at the early stages of production organization. It is about a pre-production technology that discusses the initial technical tasks, research and development activities that allow the selection of more efficient and cost-effective equipment at a later stage. Until the 50s of the 20th century, the engineering industry managed with mechanized operations, both in the processing of parts and in the assembly of products. However, with a large number of inventions of more complex mechanisms, such as airplanes, cars, conveyors, steamboats, parts of complex configuration were required, which are very difficult to manufacture by hand. So since 1949 the third industrial revolution has come. This year," Parsons" was the first company to think about solving the problem of production efficiency of parts with a complex mathematical model. An example of such a product was a blade and the introduction of numerical control (CNC) into a machine tool turned out to be a strategically important step in the development of the engineering industry. So the development of the industry has moved to the 3rd stage of technology development - Industry 3.0.

To a present date, European and Russian companies are paying more attention to the technological problems of production - this is a reduction in the participation of a person in the manufacture of a part. In other words, since 2000, the main theme of research and development in the industry has been the automation of the technological route. Such developmental research requires not only changes in the design of machines, but also the introduction of smart technologies - IT technologies, where the most obvious solutions are:

- Introduction of virtual reality
- Automated preparation of the machine for work: all parts of the machine are moved by the intelligent system of the machine. The person only has access to the tool selection
- Energy saving: due to very high productivity and low energy consumption per part.
- Reducing the main time of manufacturing a part due to simultaneous processing along 4-8 axes (depending on the country of manufacture and the brand of the machine)

However, production managers, with all their efforts, decide only 50% of the organization of production, and the reason for this is the lack of attention to the design part of manufacturing parts. With simple mathematical operations, you can see that the introduction of smart systems into the design system can increase the operation of the complex by 50%, and, consequently, increase all the technical and economic indicators of the company. So, we can conclude that the influence of IT technologies has a positive effect on the economics of mechanical engineering.

As an example, the work proposes to consider a particular example of the manufacture of a gear, for which a project was created, which is based on the implementation of macro programs in the American system CAD Autodesk Inventor – Inventor Autodesk Pro+ (Petrakova & Samoilova, 2020; Samoilova, 2020).

The program consists of three parts (fig. 1).

Figure 1. Algorithm for constructing a gear with an involute profile

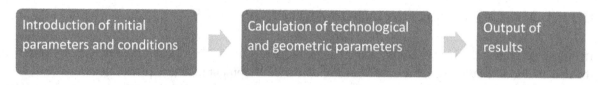

The introduction of initial parameters begins with the choice of names, which are entered in the table "User parameters", where each value is assigned either a Latin letter or a Latin short word. The specified variables are written to the program using the "Dim" code or by writing the original formula, drop-down list or selection list. Also, a special function in Ilogic "Form" can be a good option for entering a condition, where you can not only create a window for entering a value, but also explain the technological function of a variable (Fig. 1).

The calculation of technological and geometric parameters is one of the largest programming blocks. This part consists of two operations. The first operation is the selection and verification of formulas, both geometric and technological. The restoration algorithm of gear wheel includes nine technological formulas, starting with the selection of material (Samoilova & Sharipzyanova, 2017) and ending with the reduction gear setting. One of which serves as a test by comparing the variable with the two nearest intervals. It's about the center distance, which is one of the main quantities in the design of the gear. It is responsible for the size of the gear, and also carries information about the process of its engagement. But the choice of the value of the center distance from the interval is complicated by the process of sampling from the values of the state standard (GOST) set using experiments.

Figure 2. Part of the automated algorithm of design of gears.

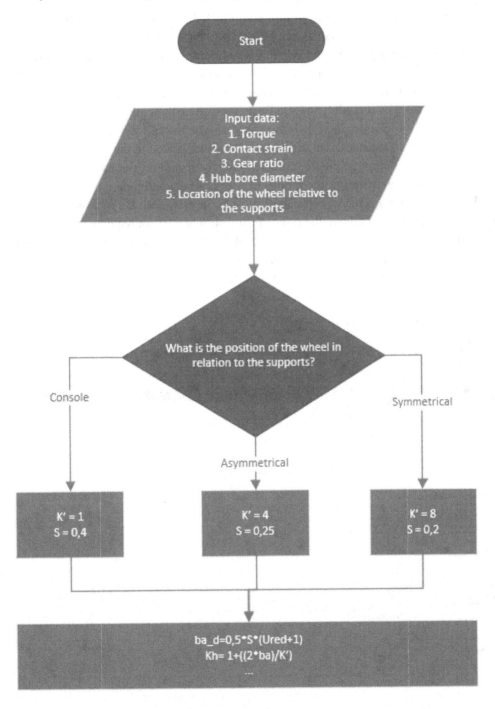

The second part of the program is the calculation of geometric quantities. These include: gear and gear wheel diameters, hub diameter and length, disc and ring gear thickness, gear and pinion tooth top diameter, and gear wheel and gear cavities diameter. This is a list of basic materials, but if you do not know, for example, the material of a gear and gear or one of the objects, then the calculation becomes more complicated by about 2-3 times. The program, which is presented in action, is complicated by the choice of a fixing coefficient, which in turn complicated the calculation by 3 times. The algorithm (Fig. 2) shows that the value of variables can be obtained by a combination of $3! = 3 \cdot 2 \cdot 1 = 6$, that is, on a given segment of the algorithm, the value of the variables can change by a maximum of 6 times.

For understanding, we note that this part of the algorithm is not even ½ the size of the program, which makes it multidimensional. It should also be noted one of the difficult parts of the program and the choice of center distance according to GOST using a system of inequalities. To solve such a problem, a sorting of two arrays was used, the satisfying value of which was entered into an empty array at the end and later, for the convenience of interface design, was presented in the form of a drop-down list.

The method for calculating geometric parameters was created on the basis of the interconnection of such a technological parameter as the prongs of a gear wheel and pinion. This block ends with the output of the final user parameters. Their names must be inserted into the measurement values instead of numbers, if this action is not done, the restructuring simply will not happen.

The last structure of the algorithm is called "Result Output". In this block, parameter values are displayed using a form, with explanations and the name of the SI system. If the engineer-constructor needs to export these parameters to Word, they can either generate a report using Ilogic's Export Materials feature.

Figure 3. Ilogic dialog window. Data export.

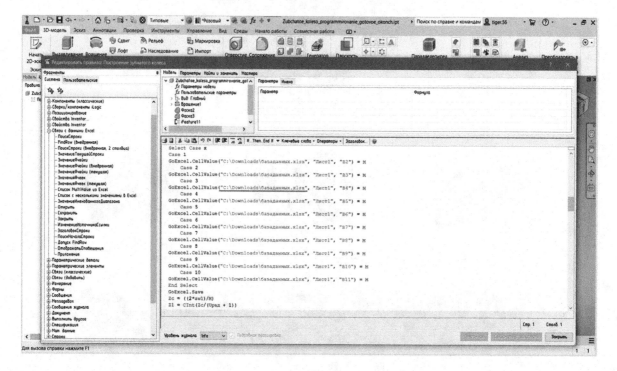

The data has been exported based on the function above. Since we need statistics on the design of the part, in this case a gear wheel is an example, it was customary to loop the program using the "For" statement, while setting the required number of cycles (Fig. 3). As an experiment, let's set 10 program passes. For the necessary variables, a data export block is now being created, where the template will be the following algorithm (Table 1)

Box 1.

```
   Table-window of the algorithm for recording export data in EXCEL
for x = от 1 до 10
   …
select case X
Case 1
GoExcel . CellValue (" the path to the file ", " sheet number in EXEL", " number content EXEL") = parameter in database
Case 2
GoExcel . CellValue ("C:\Downloads\ database .xlsx", " Sheet 1", "C3") = aw1
…
End select
   GoExcel . save
```

The template prescribes the automation of the program and after that a block with a selection is created, the "Select" command, the variables for each cycle and for each result are transferred using the "GoExcel.CellValue" command to an EXEL cell in a specific sheet, as shown in Table 1.

Figure 4. Exported data from the Ilogic program.

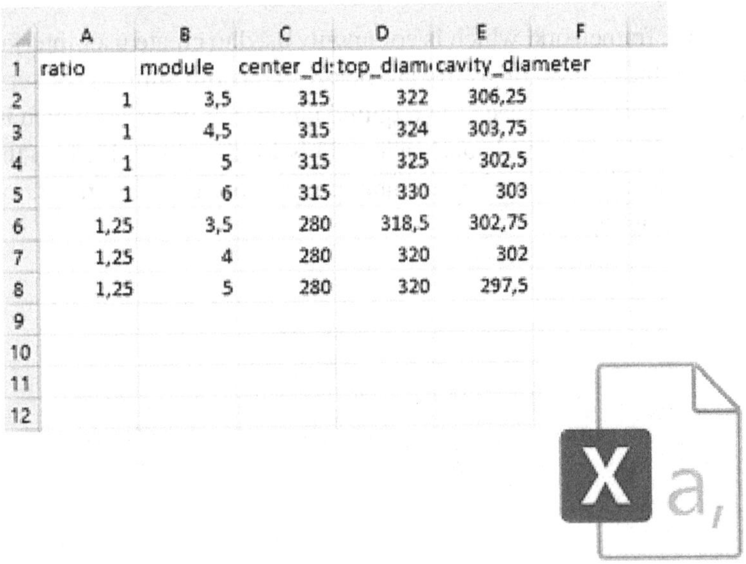

	A	B	C	D	E	F
1	ratio	module	center_di	top_diam	cavity_diameter	
2	1	3,5	315	322	306,25	
3	1	4,5	315	324	303,75	
4	1	5	315	325	302,5	
5	1	6	315	330	303	
6	1,25	3,5	280	318,5	302,75	
7	1,25	4	280	320	302	
8	1,25	5	280	320	297,5	
9						
10						
11						
12						

After the calculation, the command produces the following result (Fig. 4) Each cell has its own name, the values of the variables are reflected, which allows you to further build a diagram by compiling elementary dependencies. In order to determine the reality of the dependencies obtained, it was decided to create a server (Logachev et al., 2020) that would generate a report based on the data received from Autodesk Inventor.

Figure 5. Main software code

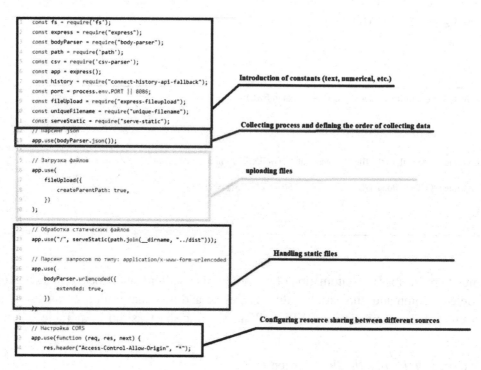

The Vue.js progressive framework, which is commonly used to create user interfaces, was chosen as the main application. But these days, this software platform has full support for server-side rendering. It is known that to create a server, you need the required number of libraries, which include data and all static variables, a general server assembly and an assembly for the client. Each of these files is written to a separate file, and in the common server assembly programming environment, a link is made to the source data and libraries (Fig. 5).

Figure 6. Report generation technology. Ready server with printing.

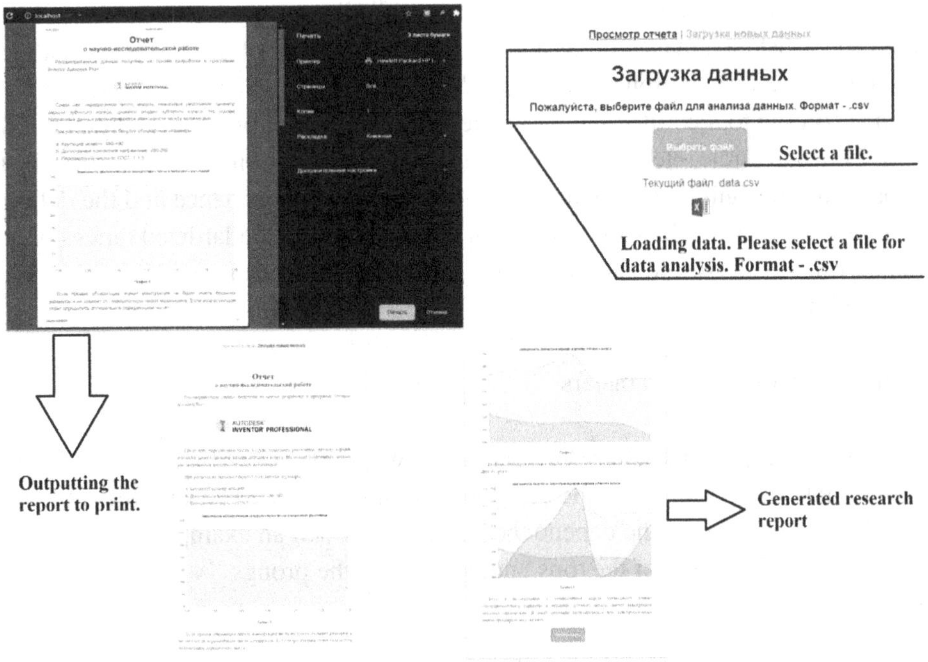

After registering all libraries, a server is created (Fig. 6) with a specific interface, where the computer requests another file extension - csv. instead of xlsx. To understand all the files that are built in the Vue. js framework, you can download and view without additional settings using the txt extension. Taking into account the factor indicated earlier, to build a report, the text of the EXEL file must be left in the cells, but with the transformation of information.

As all the necessary conditions are met, it is necessary to upload the file to the created server and the report will be generated by itself with notes and notes about the experiments in the details of the machine (Fig. 6), and it can also be printed.

RESEARCH WORK

On the basis of the developed program in Inventor Autodesk, ready-made data were obtained (Fig. 4), which allow us to draw conclusions about the storage of a particular mechanism. In this work, the gear wheel is an element of a horizontal reduction gear, so the indicators that were recorded in the computer's memory in advance can tell the designer the probability of a successful assembly of the mechanism. Several parameters were noted during the preparation of the research report:

1. The stability of the center distance for various technological and design parameters in the design of the gear transmission of a spur reducer (Konyukhova & Britvina, 2013; Samoilova et al., 2021).

The center-to-center distance is responsible for the dimensions of the device being designed: the greater the center-to-center distance, the larger the overall dimensions of the reducer housing. The stability of the center distance makes it possible to manipulate, first of all, the gear module, which is fully responsible for the configuration of the gear. This means that for different sizes, we can choose its variable pattern according to the following parameters: the number of prongs, the height of the prongs, the diameter of the ledge circle, etc. So, the main result of digitalization is the parameterization of the design of the part, the configuration of which is expressed by the dependence and the definition of design and technological variables. It is also important to note that the standardized ranges of engineering calculation values established by the international organization for metrology ISO have been introduced into the macro program.

2.   Dependences of geometric parameters

To determine new research topics, it is necessary to draw up new dependencies in the form of graphic elements. This was taken into account in the development of the server. The structure of the report contains a separate block for studying the dependence of graphs. Such an example in the research section is the dependence of the diameters of the tops and bottoms of the prongs

Figure 7. Dependence of the diameters of the tops and bottoms of the gear

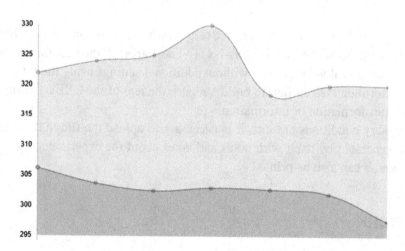

During automatic design, the following graph was built (Fig. 7). Let us turn to the formulas for calculating the diameters of the circumference of the cavities and the tops of the gear

$$D_{peaks} = d_{div} + 2 \cdot m \Leftrightarrow D_{hollow} = d_{div} - 2,5 \cdot m$$

Subtract the second equation from the first, assuming both diameters are equal, then we get the following expression:

$$0 = (d_{div} - d_{div}) - (2 \cdot m - 2,5 \cdot m) \rightarrow -2 \cdot m + 2,5 \cdot m = 0,5 \cdot m$$

this expression says that the line responsible for the functions of the diameter of the tops and the diameter of the troughs intersects at a certain point 0.5·m, and they cannot be parallel. If suddenly such a graph turns out, then there are two solutions: recalculation of all technological and design parameters or continuation of the program cycle to the point of intersection of two straight lines.

Changing the modulus of the gear wheel has a very strong effect on the dimensions of the involute gear: first of all, a large modulus is responsible for the increase in size, however, in the above graph, it is assumed that there are more dependencies. The program shows that the bigger the center distance, the bigger the module of the gear. This information assumes, with increasing design parameters, large housing dimensions, where the cause will be, first of all, the size of the gear. The graph is not stable, since each time it corresponds to the center distance. The explanation for this nature of the function will be the lack of verification of the comparison of the inter-axle interaction in comparison with the GOST with the experimental equation.

As a result, we can conclude that the more parameters will be exported from the macro program to the database, the more dependencies and relationships can be determined, which means that it will be possible to determine and calculate dependencies that were not paid attention to before. At this moment, from Figure 4, you can calculate the number of possible charts that can be inserted into the report (Formula 1)

$$C_n^k = \frac{n!}{(n-k)! \cdot k!} \tag{1}$$

Need calculate the possible number of combinations and dependencies between the parameters:

$$!\,_6^2 = \frac{5!}{(5-2)! \cdot 2!} = \frac{5 \cdot 4 \cdot 3!}{3! \cdot 2!} = \frac{5 \cdot 4}{1 \cdot 2} = \frac{20}{2} = 10 \tag{2}$$

So, a base consisting of 5 variables can allow an engineer to create a maximum of 10 graphs, among which 30% will be new dependencies formula (2).

The final stage of the study is the calculation of the efficiency indicator for the implementation of IT technologies, which will be expressed as a reduction in the work of an engineer in a design office, and in order to determine this, it is necessary to know how much time it takes to develop a software product. In practice, programmers identify the following significant quantities that affect the complexity:

- Task type (K1). This coefficient reflects the number of teams depending on the type of task. Table 1 shows the limits of coefficient changes.

Table 1.

Task Type	Coefficient Change Limits
Accounting task • Information collection system • Registration • Documentary turnover: capital turnover and other simple operations • Accounting, etc.	from 1400 to 1500
Tasks of operational management: • System for collecting and updating economic information • Collection of accounting data and their updating (wages, calculation of cost and production rate, profitability of production, etc. indicators) • Linking processes that are carried out by different production units, etc..	from 1501 to 1700
Tasks of strategic management • Resource allocation • Task selection • Development of ready-made solutions, etc.	from 1701 to 3000
Planning Tasks • Implementation of the development perspective into the software product • Options for rational use of resources • Definition of competitiveness • Options for improving the financial situation	from 3001 to 3500
Multivariate problems are problems that have several strategies and solutions.	from 3501 to 5000
Complex tasks - solving systems of interrelated tasks	from 5000 to 5500

- Novelty and complexity of the program (C). When writing program code, the developer must understand the degree of novelty of the program, which can be divided into 4 groups:
- Group A - the development of fundamentally new tasks, that is, tasks that have a complex organizational and technological model and are difficult to formalize.
- Group B - development of original programs. Such programs include unique improvements to existing codes that have already been introduced into production.
- Group C - development of programs using standard solutions. This group considers the solution of problems of an applied nature, that is, the tasks of a typical design solution - architectural, construction, design, engineering and technological solutions for multiple use.
- Group D - one-time typical task. Solution of problems of group B only for a specific production.

The complexity of the program from the point of view of information technology reflects the relationship between time and the amount of memory consumed, respectively, the less memory a program occupies, the higher its data processing speed. This technique considers three categories of complexity: 1 - optimization algorithms and system modeling, 2 - tasks of accounting, reporting and statistics, 3 - any standard algorithms; and two programming language level categories: high level(Lisp, JavaScript, Python, Ruby, SQL, VBA etc.) and low level(C, C++, Java, C#, Perl etc.)

Depending on the choice of the complexity of the task, the values of the coefficient of novelty C are selected, which is presented in Table 2.

Table 2.

Programming Language Level and Task Complexity Category	Novelty Coefficient			
	A	B	C	D
High level language of program				
1	1,38	1,26	1,15	0,69
2	1,3	1,19	1,08	0,65
3	1,2	1,1	1	0,6
Low level language of programming				
1	1,58	1,45	1,32	0,79
2	1,48	1,37	1,24	0,74
3	1,38	1,26	1,15	0,69

- Task change (C) – task change coefficient. This coefficient is directly related to the complexity and category of the task. Changing the task involves changing the code by no more than 30%, if the volume of the program is changed by more than 50%, then this is a product of group B.

Table 3 proposes to consider the following values of the task change factor.

Table 3.

Programming Language Level and Task Complexity Category	Task Change Factor			
	A	B	C	D
High level language of program				
1	1,5	1,38	1,36	1,5
2	1,41	1,3	1,28	1,3
3	1,35	1,24	0,93	1,2
Low level language of programming				
1	1,5	1,48	1,5	1,5
2	1,5	1,4	1,44	1,39
3	1,35	1,32	1,08	1,2

- Programmer qualification (K2). It is known that a set of professional skills play an important role in the development of any product. The methodology and practice states that the higher the qualification of the programmer, the faster the work goes. The paper presents the value of the coefficient of qualification of work, depending on its length of service.

Table 4.

Programmer Experience	The Value of the Developer Qualification Factor
Up to two years	0,8
from 2 to 3 years	1
from 3 to 5 years	1,1-1,2
from 5 to 10 years	1,2-1,3
over 10 years	1,3-1,5

Knowing all the above variables, you can calculate the development time, which is expressed by the following dependence:

$$T_{dev} = \frac{Q \cdot B}{50 \cdot K}$$

Calculate the development time of a software product Autodesk Inventor Pro+:

$$T_{dev} = \frac{3501 \cdot 1,15}{50 \cdot 0,8} = \frac{4026,15}{40} = 100,65375 \approx 100,65$$

So the development of the Autodesk Inventor Pro + program will take 100.65 hours. To check the effectiveness of the introduction of a software product in a design bureau, let's consider the statistics of the time spent on creating drawings of parts for 1 designer for all enterprises, taking into account that it takes about 2.7 hours for one drawing of a spur gear according to the standards.

$$T'_{dev} = 19! \cdot 2,7 = 121\ 645\ 100\ 408\ 832\ 000 \cdot 2,7 = 328\ 441\ 771\ 103\ 846\ 400$$

hours will be required in order to make drawings of all variants of a spur involute gear.

RESULTS

The main role of the introduction of automation systems is to increase the level of efficiency, mobility and facilitate the work of employees. Due to these changes, the level of competitiveness in the market is increasing, and the resource base is being used powerfully. The most striking example is the introduction of Inventor Autodesk Pro+. Economic diagnostics showed that IT technologies reduce labor intensity by 15 orders of magnitude. This research is a weighty argument for the introduction of macroprogramming in the design office. It is worth noting the universality of the methodology: this algorithm allows you to describe the economic component in more than 90% of cases.

The development also has a good technical core. It realizes as part of a task received from a Russian mechanical engineering plant, so the data used in the calculations is real research material: when developing a task, namely designing a conveyor for assembling four modifications of bridges weighing from 6 to 12 tons, the developers faced the problem of low productivity when design operation, which accordingly slowed down the work of the entire product assembly system (Shakizada et al., 2021; Zueva, 2019).

The designed service within the framework of the study will allow us to consider more than 10 unique dependencies, which make it possible to expand the scientific overview of machine parts, as well as to allow the existence of designed products.

The main result of this work will be the introduction of this product not only in Russian, but also in European production.

REFERENCES

Gavrilyuk, A.V. (2021). Intellectual property in the digital economy: Theoretical and practical aspects. *Intelligence. Innovation. Investment, 2*, 20-33.

Konyukhova, G.P., & Britvina, V.V. (2013). Mathematical statistics in physical culture. *Theory and Practice of Physical Culture,* (11), 60.

Logachev, M. S., Voronin, I. V., Britvina, V. V., Tishchenko, S. A., & Altukhov, A. V. (2020). LAN Monitoring. *International Journal of Advanced Trends in Computer Science and Engineering*, 9, 4216–4222. doi:10.30534/ijatcse/2020/07942020

Petrakova, E. A., & Samoilova, A. S. (2020). Using iLogic technology in Autodesk Inventor to create a parametric 3D gear model and conduct research. *Scientific and Technical Bulletin of the Bryansk State University, 1*. www.ntv-brgu.ru/ntv-bgu-2020-01-10

Samoilova, A. S. (2020). Creating programs in Inventor Autogesk. International Competition for Scientific Achievements of Students, International Center for Scientific Cooperation. *Science and Education*, (8), 35–41.

Samoilova, A. S., Britvina, V. V., Bobrova, E. O., Konyukhova, G. P., & Altukhov, A. V. (2021). The use of information technology and mathematical modeling in the development of aluminum alloy regimes. *Proceedings of the CEUR Seminar, 2843*.

Samoilova, A.S., & Sharipzyanova, G.K. (2017). Study of the deformation parameters of aluminum alloy V-1461. *Theory and Practice of Project Education, 4*(4).

Sazhina, M.A., & Gavrilyuk, A.V. (n.d.). Intellectual property in the innovation economy: Methodological aspects. *Scientific Research of the Faculty of Economics, 12*(36), 26-39.

Shakizada, N., Dzhazykbaeva, B., Mottaeva, A., Mottaeva, E., & Zueva, A. (2021). Growth of green finance at the global level in the context of sustainable economic development. *XXII International Scientific Conference "Energy Management of Public Utilities and Sustainable Energy Technologies" (EMMFT-2020), 244*. 7-10.

Zueva, A. S. (2019). Foreign work force in the Russian economy: Effects, risks and forecasts. *Journal of Migration Law, 2*, 39–40.

Chapter 13
Sixteen Limitations for Five Popular Requirements Prioritisation Approaches

Zoe Hoy

 https://orcid.org/0000-0003-3377-2288
University of Portsmouth, UK

ABSTRACT

Software is an essential commodity that ensures mobile phones to the controls of an aeroplane work. There will always be more requirements for software than there is time and budget to achieve them, hence the need for various prioritisation approaches to decide which requirements to include in the software. There are also constraints for startups, such as small teams and multiple influencers, which must be considered when choosing a prioritisation approach. The wrong approach can waste resources and cause customer dissatisfaction. There is limited research linked to the limitations of requirements prioritisation approaches; however, this research helps to address the research gap. For example, the main contribution identifies 16 limitations associated with five popular prioritisation approaches combined with a framework which identifies the relationships between these limitations. The five requirement prioritisation approaches studied were analytic hierarchy process (AHP), quality functional deployment (QFD), the planning game, binary search tree, and $100 allocation.

INTRODUCTION

Agile software development is popular among startup companies (Gupta, Fernandez-Crehuet, Hanne, & Telesko, 2020; Lim, Bentley, & Ishikawa, 2020; Nurdiani, Jabangwe, & Petersen, 2016), who quickly evolve software with a focus on innovation (Nguyen-Duc, Kemell, & Abrahamsson, 2021, p. 4). Agile requirements re-prioritisation is an ongoing activity, where the requirements for developed software are re-prioritised at the start of each software iteration to reflect the changing needs of the customer (Racheva, Daneva, Herrmann, & Wieringa, 2010, p.5). This activity is essential as requirements are not correct upfront. Also there will always be more customer requirements for the software than there is time and

DOI: 10.4018/978-1-7998-9059-1.ch013

budget (Kukreja, Boehm, Payyavula, & Padmanabhuni, 2012, p. 303), so prioritisation approaches help to decide which requirements to include in each iteration, to innovate the software (Gupta et al., 2020, p. 14). Selecting the right requirements is essential as it will determine which requirements are in the final product, and whether satisfaction is realised for all project stakeholders.

There are many approaches to prioritising requirements and Achimugu, Selamat, Ibrahim and Mahrin (2014, p. 572) identify 49 of them. Figure 6 in their study presented 22 most cited and used approaches. Resources for this research project were limited regarding cost and time, so a Pareto was produced for the number of citations for these 22 approaches, in order to determine the scope of this study. The Pareto principles helps to identify the vital few to focus on (Baudin, 2012, p. 28). When using the Pareto, a key issue is to ensure that the categories are defined properly. For example, when a defect has multiple problems several categories on the Pareto may be relevant. This was not a concern for this study as the categories were the prioritisation approaches and the frequency was the number of citations. Figure 1 shows five approaches covering 50% of the citations, therefore studying these five approaches would provide significant coverage. Achimugu et al. (2014, p. 474) alludes to these approaches being among the most used and eminent techniques. Therefore an exploration of the limitations for these five approaches would be appropriate for this study.

Figure 1. Pareto for the number of citations

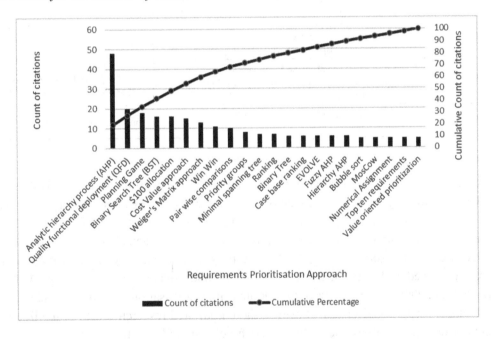

These five approaches are consistent with other studies presented in Table 1. They were among the seven approaches identified in studies by Svensson, Gorschek, Regnell, Torkar, Shahrokni, Feldt, and Aurum (2011), Pergher and Rossi (2013), and by Kaur and Bawa (2013), and listed among the 17 approaches identified by Kukreja, Boehm, Payyavula and Padmanabhuni (2012). AHP, cumulative voting ($100 allocation) and Planning Game list these among the top cited approaches identified by Sher, Jawawi, Mohamad and Barbar (2014, p. 36). AHP, cumulative voting ($100 allocation), Planning Game and Binary Search Tree are among the ten prioritisation approaches studied by Yousuf, Bokhari and Zeyauddin (2016, p. 3969). The five popular prioritisation approaches are Analytic hierarchy process (AHP), quality functional deployment (QFD), planning game, binary search tree, and $100 allocation.

Table 1. Literature sources which identified prioritisation approaches

Number of Approaches	Method	Source
49	Systematic literature review between 1996 and 2013, quality criteria used to filter the results. Clear traceability between the academic literature and the study results.	Achimugu et al. (2014)
7	It was not stated how the 7 approaches were determined.	Kaur and Bawa (2013)
17	A literature review was conducted, but as it was not described, it was not clear how the list of 17 approaches were derived. The list itself was in alphabetical order, so it was not possible to determine the order of those most cited.	Kukreja, Boehm, Payyavula and Padmanabhuni (2012)
7	It was not stated how the 7 approaches were determined.	Pergher and Rossi (2013)
59	Systematic literature review between 1990 and 2014. Academic sources were not identified to support the prioritisation approaches listed. Some technical aspects were identified, however there were no descriptions for the technical aspects to clarify what they represented.	Sher, Jawawi, Mohamad, & Barbar (2014)
5	It was not stated how the 5 approaches were determined. They were not used by the 11 companies interviewed.	Svensson, Gorschek, Regnell, Torkar, Shahrokni, Feldt, and Aurum (2011)
10	It was not stated how the 10 approaches were determined.	Yousuf, Bokhari & Zeyauddin (2016)

Prioritisation approaches have different processes and can produce a different set of prioritised requirements. Therefore, choosing the right approach is important as the wrong approach can waste resources and cause customer dissatisfaction (Soni, 2014, p. 2349). There are also constraints for startups, such as small teams and multiple influencers which must be considered when choosing a suitable approach (Nguyen-Duc, Kemell, & Abrahamsson, 2021). The prioritisation approaches have limitations when used, for example whether they are scalable, easy to learn and use and accurate (Santos, Albuquerque, & Pinheiro, 2016, p. 909). An awareness of limitations with prioritisation approaches could help inform software developers with this decision. However, there is limited research linked to the limitations of requirements prioritisation approaches. This research helps to address this gap by identifying limitations for five popular approaches. The five requirements prioritisation approaches studied were Analytic hierarchy process (AHP), quality functional deployment (QFD), the planning game, binary search tree, and $100 allocation.

Research Questions

The need to gain a knowledge of these limitations has motivated the following research questions (RQs):

RQ1: What limitations are reported in recent academic literature for five popular requirements prioritisation approaches?

RQ2: Are there any dependencies between the limitations?

RQ3: Which of the five approaches have fewest reported limitations?

The structure of this paper is as follows. The five popular prioritisation approaches are introduced. Then grounded theory is used to identify current reported limitations, presenting a comparison with previous related works. Before there are conclusions and a reflection on the contribution to knowledge.

RELATED WORK

In this section the five prioritisation approaches are introduced, and limitations identified from a well cited prior study (Achimugu et al., 2014) are presented, which this study extends.

Five Popular Prioritisation Approaches

AHP is a pairwise comparison technique, created by Saty (1977) where stakeholders can choose the criteria. The criteria are compared to each other and assigned a weighting. Requirements incorporating user stories are then compared against the criteria and an overall priority is calculated (Saaty, 2008, p. 88).

QFD by Akao and Mizuno (Akao & Mazur, 2003, p. 20), whose chart shows the relationship between the customer's requirements or demand and the supporting technical requirements or characteristics (Kamisawa, 1994, p. 115). Weightings are calculated and used to prioritise each of the customer requirements listed down the left-hand side of the quality chart. Those requirements with a higher value are more important that those with a lower value.

In the planning game, user stories feature requirements (Beck, 2000, p. 90). The development team estimate the effort to implement each story and the customer determines the value of each story. Stories are then prioritised for the next release based on the effort and the value to the customer. Effort to implement each story can be estimated using planning poker cards (Grenning, 2002). The story is described and questions are asked by the development team if clarification is needed. Each team member has a deck of planning poker cards and holds up a card, which represents the number of days they believe is needed to implement the story. Teams then use consensus to agree the effort.

The binary search tree introduced by Hibbard (1962, p. 13), organises the requirements in a tree structure. A single node at the top of the tree represents the most important requirement. Requirements to the left of each node are less important, those to the right of each node are more important. For example, the first comparison is made with the node at the top of the tree, if the requirement is more important the second comparison is made with the node on the right. If the requirement is more important move right, if it is less important move left. The comparisons continue until the end of a tree is reached, which is known as a leaf.

For the $100 allocation technique (Leffingwell & Widrig, 2000), a virtual $100 is given to each of the stakeholders, who then determine how to distribute it among the requirements. Requirements with a higher dollar value are more important than those with a lower dollar value.

Limitations for the Five Prioritisation Approaches

Achimugu et al. (2014, p. 569) claimed there was no existing systematic literature review, for the limitations of prioritisation approaches. Their systematic literature review between 1996 and 2013 has contributed towards this research gap and identified the limitations shown in Table 2, for the five prioritisation approaches. As the publication date was between 1996 and 2013 the limitations of the prioritisation approaches may not reflect the limitations experienced today.

Another limitation of their study was the limited search terms used: 'limitation' and 'shortcomings' (Achimugu et al., 2014, p. 570). Other terms may have been used in literature to describe the limitations.

This study helps towards addressing this research gap by researching literature about limitations, with wider search terms.

Table 2. Limitations of prioritisation approaches

Prioritisation Approach	Limitations Identified for the Approach
$100 test ($100 allocation)	1) Does not support large number of requirements
analytic hierarchy process	1) Time consuming when large number of requirements. 2) Not scalable[1]
binary search tree	1) Simple ranking without identifying any priorities
planning game	1) Not scalable when large number of requirements
quality function deployment	1) For small subsystems 2) Does not support inconsistencies 3) Not scalable

Source: Achimugu et al. (2014, p. 581).

RESEARCH METHOD

This section describes the search procedure followed, an application of grounded theory using an online library portal to access data sources, and steps followed to corroborate coding and analysis. Five files were generated from the search results, each containing direct quotes of sentences or paragraphs about limitations for five popular prioritisation approaches. These files were analysed using grounded theory method, a systematic way to create a theory from the data. When compared to a systematic literature review, the grounded theory method was chosen because as a theory, it is linked to the data to create a robust theory, which will last over time (Glaser & Strauss, 1967, p. 4).

Grounded theory follows an inductive approach exploring people and processes. This was relevant for this research which studies the limitations experienced by people when using five popular requirements prioritisation approaches. Grounded theory is also suitable when researching new areas (van Waardenburg, & van Vliet, 2013, p. 2155). With limited research on the approach limitations (Achimugu et al., 2014, p. 569) this research area is new and therefore leverages Urquhart's (2013) interpretation of the Glaser strand.

Grounded Theory Method requires a proficient use of theoretical codes (Glaser, 1992, p. 29) to identify connections between what is known and new discoveries of the unknown (Seyle, 1956, cited by Glaser, 1992, p. 29). The constant concurrent comparison of the data; i.e. where a code attached to some data is compared to the same code attached to some other data, was used to check that codes were being used in a consistent and proficient way (Urquhart, 2013, p. 192).

The literature review was not conducted until a draft limitations framework was created. This ensured the researcher had no preconceived ideas about the data (Urquhart, 2013, p. 16). Literature was only used to identify the research gap. This mitigated a limitation that the researcher's assumptions can affect their interpretation of the data (Charmaz, 2014, p. 30). Urquhart (2013, p. 38) supports this limitation stating that it is important not to impose any preconceptions the researcher has on the data.

In grounded theory, sampling continues until theoretical saturation has been reached where there is nothing new to be found (Glaser & Strauss, 1967, p. 61). As there is limited literature on limitations, all of the academic journal articles and conference papers which met the inclusion criteria were analysed. Three grounded theory steps described by Urquhart (2013) were then followed to provide an in-depth exploration of the limitations; open coding, selective coding, and theoretical coding.

Search Process

A search of academic literature was conducted, to identify sentences and paragraphs describing limitations for five popular requirements prioritisation approaches, to address RQ1.

The search string was [prioritisation approach search terms] AND [limitation search terms] AND priorit*.

The search period was January 2012 to December 2016, for peer reviewed, PDFs available in English. Search options were selected, to find all my search terms, search within the full text of the articles, and apply equivalent subjects. The University linking databases were used. Other institutions have different subscription and access levels.

To locate the limited research in this area. A thesaurus was used for the word 'limitation', to generate the list of limitation search terms, which included limitation, constraint, disadvantage, drawback, restriction, condition, barrier, failing, shortcoming, weak point, inability, flaw, defect, deficiency, failure, weakness, obstacle, challenge. The terms used for [prioritisation approach search terms] are noted in Table 3.

Table 3. Prioritisation approach search terms

Prioritisation Technique	Prioritisation Approach Search Terms
$100 allocation	"$100 test" OR "cumulative voting" OR "$100 allocation"
analytic hierarchy process	"analytic hierarchy process" NOT "hierarchy AHP" NOT "fuzzy AHP". The acronym AHP was excluded from the search terms as it had many other meanings, which included AHP proteins, Aluminium hypophosphite etc. NOT "hierarchy AHP" and NOT "fuzzy AHP" were included in the search terms as these AHP variants had a lower number of citations in the study by Achimugu et al (2014), so were excluded from the paper. With 2536 initial results, the term "software development" was added to ensure the resulted focused on software development.
binary search tree	"binary search tree"
planning game	"planning game"
quality function deployment	QFD OR "quality function deployment" OR "house of quality" OR HOQ. As 'House of quality' is considered a core part of the QFD approach (Li, Ming, Jin, & Wang, 2014, p 29) literature about QFD often refers to the House of quality and its abbreviation HOQ, so they were included as search terms. With 1348 initial results the term "software development" was added to ensure the results focused on software development

The papers were filtered against the inclusion and exclusion criteria in Table 4.

Table 4. Inclusion and exclusion criteria

Inclusion Criteria	Exclusion Criteria
Peer reviewed Journal articles/conference papers	Not yet published, for example In Press
PDFs available	Access restricted
Published in English	Only abstract available
Published between January 2012 and December 2016	Outside of the research scope, describes no limitations for the prioritisation approach

The academic journal articles and conference papers from the search results were scanned for limitations of five popular prioritisation approaches. Direct quotes of sentences or paragraphs about the limitations were copied into a separate file for each prioritisation approach.

Figure 2. The study selection process

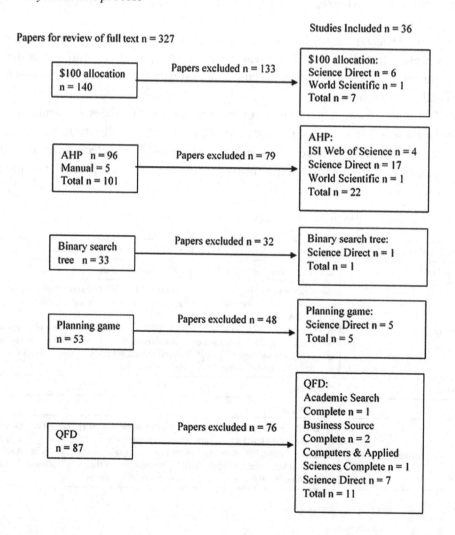

208

After the study selection process in Figure 2, there were twenty-two literature sources for AHP, one for binary search tree, five for planning game, eleven for QFD and seven for $100 allocation.

Grounded Theory Method

Open Coding

The first step of the grounded theory method is open coding, where each paragraph or sentence describing a limitation is explored and assigned codes. Figure 3 is an extract from the first step, where the codes were developed by the researcher, inspired from the data itself (Urquhart, 2013, p. 108).

Figure 3. Extract from open coding for $100 allocation

"Not suitable for large number of requirements" (Achimugu, Selamat, Ibrahim, & Mahrin, 2014, p. 582).

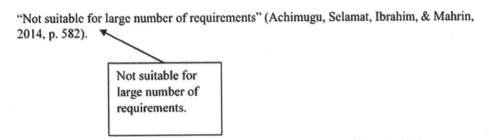

Not suitable for large number of requirements.

"This method proposes to use the hierarchical cumulative voting technique (HCV)" (Barney, Mohankumar, Chatzipetrou, Aurum, Wohlin, Angelis, 2014, p. 23). "Participants from the studies generally did not enjoy using the HCV method, with many finding the process to make the numbers

Technique disliked.

sum to 1000 frustrating" (Barney, Mohankumar, Chatzipetrou, Aurum, Wohlin, Angelis, 2014, p. 35).

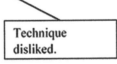

Frustrating to use.

Selective Coding

In the second step, the open codes were grouped into themes and assigned selective codes, to scale up the coding (Urquhart, 2013, p. 49). Table 5 is an extract of the selective coding for the $100 allocation technique, which shows how the open codes 'Technique disliked' and 'Frustrating to use' from Figure 3 have been scaled up to the selective code 'Usability'.

Table 5. Extract from selective coding for $100 allocation

Selective Code	Open Code
Usability	Technique disliked, frustrating to use, hard to use with large number of requirements, hard to use, time consuming, Complicated when a large amount of items to compare

Theoretical Coding

In the third step, the data was analysed to identify the relationships between the selective codes (Urquhart, 2013, p. 16). These were initially captured as hand written theoretical memos then paraphrased in section 4 and illustrated in the limitations framework. For example, the area highlighted in Figure 4 shows there is a relationship between the number of requirements and usability of the prioritisation approach. The open codes in Table 5 show that the $100 allocation approach is complicated and hard to use when there is a large number of requirements to compare. This shows that the number of requirements impacts on the usability of the prioritisation approach. The selective codes were integrated into a single integrative diagram (Urquhart, 2013, p. 114) to gain a holistic view of the overall limitations for the five popular requirements prioritisation approaches.

RESULTS AND DISCUSSION

The comprehensive search has generated sixteen limitations for the five prioritisation approaches. These are presented in Table 6 and are discussed below.

Table 6. Limitations for five popular prioritisation approaches

	AHP	BST	PG	QFD	$100
Usability	✓	✓	✓	✓	✓
Number of requirements	✓		✓	✓	✓
Cost	✓				
Customer Availability			✓		
Knowledge			✓	✓	✓
Remote Team Communication			✓		
Quality of Requirements	✓			✓	
Judgement Error	✓			✓	✓
Validity	✓	✓			✓
Conflicting Priorities	✓				✓
Priority rank updates problem	✓	✓	✓		
Consideration of other perspectives				✓	
Requirements Interdependencies	✓			✓	
Conflicting Requirements				✓	
Priority Value		✓	✓		
Graphical Expression				✓	

AHP analytic hierarchy process
BST binary search tree
PG planning game
QFD quality function deployment
$100 allocation

Usability was a limitation for all five approaches. The approaches were hard to use. For example, for QFD "team members had difficulty in assigning measures of priority to a list of customer preferences" (Büyüközkan, & Çifçin, 2012, p. 30). The approaches were also frustrating to use. For example, users of $100 allocation found making the numbers sum to 1000 frustrating (Barney, Mohankumar, Chatzipetrou, Aurum, Wohlin, Angelis, 2014, p. 35).

Number of requirements was identified as a limitation for AHP, Planning Game, QFD and $100 allocation. The included studies did not identify this limitation for binary search tree. This view is supported by Kakar (2015, p. 58) who describes a study by Ahl (2005) and a study by Bebensee et al. (2010), which both support the ability of the binary search tree approach to scale up for a large number of requirements. The literature showed a relationship between usability and the number of requirements; usability was impacted when there was a large number of requirements. For example, for AHP "they have to perform a huge number of comparisons when the project scale is increased" (Chaves-González & Pérez-Toledano, 2015, p. 2). Babar, Ghazali, Jawawi, Shamsuddin, and Ibrahim (2015, p. 179) describe how the number of requirements can be impractical. For example, for the Planning Game "the current techniques are not suitable for the prioritisation of a large number of requirements in projects where requirements may grow to the hundreds or even thousands" (Babar, Ghazali, Jawawi, Shamsuddin, & Ibrahim, 2015, p. 179).

Cost was a limitation for AHP. "AHP defines prioritisation criteria through a priority assessment of all the pairs of requirements. Hence its cost is quadratic with the number of requirements" (Tonella, Susi, & Palma, 2013, p. 173). This shows a relationship between cost and the number of requirements. This limitation was not identified in the search results for binary search tree, QFD, planning game and $100 allocation. However, cost could be a limitation for binary search tree as multiple comparisons are made until a leaf is reached. Each comparison made increases the cost of use. The limitation is not relevant for QFD, $100 allocation and planning game as comparisons are not made. However, in the planning game, story points are relative estimates, where each member of the team makes a relative comparison judgement based on their experience with previous stories. The cost limitation could be relevant for the planning game as effort is needed for the repeated rounds of estimation until consensus is achieved for each story.

Customer availability was a limitation for planning game. For agile software development the customer representative, called the product owner in Scrum, should make themselves available to the software team, to respond to questions about the requirements, provide feedback and maintain the prioritised backlog of requirements. When they are not available the team seek answers from other members of the team, which may not reflect the customer's needs (Yu & Petter, 2014, p. 916). The literature from the search results did not identify this limitation for AHP, binary search tree, QFD and $100 allocation, however Ramesh, Cao, and Baskerville (2010, p. 472) identify this limitation as requirements engineering risk for agile. Furthermore, their risk of inadequate user-developer interaction is critical due to the impact on the software. This shows a relationship between customer availability and the quality of requirements.

A limitation for the planning game was knowledge. For example, use of a prioritisation approach "assumes that customers have most of the information about what has to be developed and developers have most of the information about how to implement those features" (Torrecilla-Salinas, Sedeño, Escalona, & Mejías, 2015, p. 128). Although the limitation was not found for the other four approaches, knowledge about the requirements and how to implement them is essential. Ramesh, Cao, and Baskerville (2010, p. 471) identify this limitation as requirements engineering risk for agile. They further claim their risk 'issues with users' ability and concurrence among users' is more critical when following an agile, when compared to a traditional methodology due to the increased user interaction in agile. User interactions in agile is written in the *Manifesto for Agile Software Development* (2001) where individual and interactions are valued more than processes and tools. There is a relationship between knowledge and the number of requirements as the knowledge of the stakeholder needs helps to inform the number of requirements which are needed.

Remote team communication was a limitation for Planning Game. Stories are written on small index cards, not accessible to team members working in a remote location, hence software is often used to address this limitation (Dimitrijević, Jovanović, J., & Devedžić, 2015, p. 355). This shows a relationship between remote team communication and usability of the prioritisation approach.

Quality of requirements is a limitation for AHP and QFD, which highlights the dependency of the software on the requirements. For example, "A general criticism of systematic approaches to design decision and selection making, like QFD and AHP, is that the outcome is dependent on the criteria fed into the process (i.e. the customer and technical requirements)" (Nixon, Dey, & Davies, 2013, p. 157). Although raised against QFD and AHP, the criticism is for all systematic approaches; binary search tree, planning game and $100 allocation. The literature shows a relationship between knowledge of the requirements and the quality of the requirements. Knowledge of the customer's needs, helps to clearly communicate the requirements. This relationship is supported by Daneva, Damian, Marchetto, and

Pastor (2014, p. 2) who claim the quality of requirements can impact the productivity of the software development process. The quality from the output of the process is heavily dependent on the quality of the requirements to be prioritised. This shows a relationship between the quality of the requirements and the validity of the prioritised requirements.

A limitation for AHP, QFD and $100 allocation was judgement error, as the prioritisation of each requirement is subjective. For example, for AHP there is "uncertainty associated with the mapping of one's judgement to a number" (Leong, Tan, Aviso, & Chew, 2016, p. 51). The most common scale for AHP is 1-9. The uncertainty of mapping a judgement to a scale was also supported by Jessop (2014, p. 20) who claims "respondents find the 1-9 scale mentally taxing", and Wang (2012, p. 4415) who claims expressing preferences using a 1-5 scale is too demanding. Judgement error could also be present if stakeholders try to manipulate the prioritisation process. For example, for $100 allocation, if the stakeholder knows that other stakeholders will allocate dollars for the requirements they want, they could distribute their dollars on requirements which are only important to them (Riņķevičs, & Torkar, 2013, p. 269). This shows a relationship between judgement error and the validity of the prioritised requirements. Judgement error was not a limitation for the binary search tree or planning game. Binary search tree does not map a judgement to a number or use a numerical scale, instead the requirements are sorted in the order of importance (Hibbard, 1962, p. 23). For the planning game. Planning poker is a popular way to estimate the effort of stories (Grenning, 2002). Although each team member maps their judgement to a card, which they decide best represents the number of story points needed to implement the story, the process of using consensus to agree the effort could mitigate any judgement error. Gandomani, Wei, and Binhamid (2014, p. 175) claim the accuracy of the effort estimate is dependent on the expertise among the team members, which could introduce judgement error. Furthermore, Meyer (2014, p. 95) claim when a team member is an expert and the card they hold has a higher value than the others, the expert may find it difficult to argue, if they feel pressure by the majority who believe an alternative value is correct. However, a case study conducted by Gandomani, Wei, and Binhamid (2014, p. 180) concluded that planning poker was more accurate than experts' estimation, which would mitigate any potential judgement error.

A limitation for AHP, binary search tree and $100 allocation is validity. Issues were identified when a scale such as 1-5 was used. If multiple stakeholders assign a low number to a requirement, when the numbers are cumulated to determine the overall priority for each requirement, a low priority requirement could be compensated by the multiple stakeholders and become a higher priority requirement. For example, for AHP and $100 allocation "If priorities are given on a ratio scale, it is possible that lower priority items will be selected if their cumulative priority is higher" (Riņķevičs, & Torkar, 2013, p. 268). Although this limitation was not found for QFD, the approach also uses a 1-5 or 1-10 scale to determine customer importance, so it could also be relevant for QFD if voting from multiple stakeholders is used to determine the customer importance. This limitation was also not identified for planning game. As described above the use of planning poker is considered more accurate than experts' estimation, which would mitigate any potential validity issues. Achimumgu et al. (2014, p. 574) cited a study by Karlsson et al. (1998) which claimed "techniques like hierarchy AHP, spanning tree, binary search tree, priority groups produce unreliable results"), however they did not include this limitation against AHP or binary search tree in their research results table (Achimumgu et al. (2014, p. 581). Mon et al. (1994, cited by Leong, Tan, Aviso, & Chew, 2016, p. 42) support the view of unreliable results, claiming AHP is not precise. For example, "the ranking of the AHP is rather not precise since arbitrary values are used in pairwise comparison". This shows a relationship between validity and judgement error as subjective opinion could cause validity issues with the prioritised requirements.

A limitation for AHP and $100 allocation is conflicting priorities. When two or stakeholders have different priorities for a requirement, the prioritised requirements can impact on stakeholder satisfaction with the software shipped (Riņķevičs & Torkar, 2013, p. 268), which is a limitation for all of the prioritisation approaches. The product owner or equivalent is responsible for prioritising the product backlog and with the different needs from the different stakeholders determines the priority for each story (Bass, 2013, p. 154). There is a relationship between conflicting priorities and knowledge as the product owner uses their knowledge of the stakeholder needs to prioritise requirements that conflict.

A limitation for AHP, binary search tree and planning game was priority rank updates. Zaiden, Zaiden, Hussain, Haiti, Kia's, and Abdulnabi (2015, p. 19) claim 'rank reversal problem', is a limitation where any requirements added or deleted can change the ranking. Achimugu et al. (2014, p. 574) identify the same limitation but refer to it as 'rank updates issue'. They claim binary search tree and planning game suffer from this problem. When a story is added to the product backlog, the product owner determines its priority, which could cause other stories to move down the prioritisation order. When a story is deleted, the product owner could determine that some other stories are now a higher priority and update the backlog to reflect the change. Priority rank updates problems were not identified for QFD and $100 allocation. As there is no priority order between the requirements for QFD, when a requirement is deleted there is no impact. For $100 allocation, if a requirement was deleted which has a unique number of dollars assigned to it, then the ranking order would be updated. If there are multiple requirements with the same dollar value or no dollar value, the priority order is not identified, and therefore if these requirements were deleted it would have no impact on the overall ranking order.

A limitation for QFD is a consideration of other perspectives. Barney, Petersen, Svahnberg, Aurum, and Barney (2012, p. 652) claim "QFD considers customer and technical requirements in achieving the goals of the system to help prioritise the requirements. Unlike AHP where the stakeholders can determine the criteria to prioritise the requirements, QFD only assigns an importance rank. The literature did not identify this limitation for AHP, binary search tree, planning game or $100 allocation, however the limitation is also relevant for binary search tree and $100 allocation which also rank the requirements based on their perceived importance and without other perspectives. Ramesh, Cao and Baskerville (2010, p. 466) support this limitation and claim requirements are often prioritised on the single dimension of business value, focused on the time-to-market, without other perspectives. This shows a relationship between consideration of other perspectives and the validity of the prioritised requirements. The limitation is not relevant for planning game, as the developers discuss each story before estimating the effort, which could consider other perspectives.

A limitation for AHP and QFD is requirement interdependencies. For example, "In QFD, requirements are prioritised in an ordinal scale, and in AHP the requirements are classified by a pair cost-value. However, both kinds of methods do not support requirements interdependencies" (Chaves-González & Pérez-Toledano, 2015, p. 2; Chaves-González, Pérez-Toledano & Navasa, 2015a, p. 106; Chaves-González, Pérez-Toledano & Navasa, 2015b, p. 90). This limitation is also relevant for binary search tree and $100 allocation. For $100 allocation, requirements are ranked by dollar value and for binary search tree requirements are sorted by importance, rather than in requirement dependency order. This shows a relationship between requirement interdependencies and the validity of the prioritised requirements. For the planning game, there is a strong focus on communication among the team, which would identify any requirement dependencies.

A limitation for QFD was conflicting requirements. For example, when different stakeholders have conflicting requirements on a webpage (Escalona, Urbieta, Rossi, Garcia-Garcia, & Robles Luna, 2013, p. 3028), the QFD approach does not provide a way to manage this conflict (Chiou, Perng, & Tseng, 2012, p. 252). The literature did not identify this limitation for AHP, binary search tree, planning game and $100 allocation. With AHP, stakeholders establish their own criteria, which could include potential conflict. In binary search tree, when each requirement is discussed to determine its priority placement, conflicting requirements could be identified. The opportunity to identify conflicting requirements is limited for $100 allocation, as the stakeholders allocate dollars without discussion of the requirements. With the strong focus on communication in the planning game, any conflicting stories would be identified. There is a relationship between conflicting requirements and quality of requirements, as conflicting requirements could reduce the quality of the requirements.

A limitation for binary search tree and planning game is priority value. Achimugu et al. (2014, p. 581) claim binary search tree ranks the requirements, but does not assign priorities to the requirements. As the ranking order shows all of the requirements in order of importance, this could also be considered the priority order for the requirements. The same argument applies to AHP and $100 allocation. For QFD, there could be multiple requirements which have the same importance number and no priority order among them. With $100 allocation there is no priority order for multiple requirements with the same dollar value or no dollar value. Developers have the knowledge and decide which stories to include in each sprint from the prioritised product backlog. For example, they know whether there are requirement dependencies, unanswered questions about a story, and they have an awareness of potential impacts on architecture, so the limitation of not assigning a priority value is minimal. When priorities are used, there may not be a formal method to assign the priority value. For example, Torrecilla-Salinas, Sedeño, Escalona, and Mejías (2015, p. 129) claim "customers will establish "priorities", without proposing a concrete technique to do so". There is a relationship between the limitation priority rank updates and the limitation priority value. If there is no priority value for the requirements, there is a minimal impact on the priority rank updates limitation, after a change in ranking order. There is also a relationship between customer priority and requirement interdependencies as dependencies are considered by the developers before selecting stories for a particular sprint or software release.

Graphical expression was reported as a limitation for only QFD. When describing QFD Brace and Ekman (2014, p. 7) claim "the model does not provide a graphical expression and establishes a relationship between information pairs". This study disagrees with this limitation as the house shape of the QFD approach is a graphical expression of the requirements, as shown by ReVelle (2004).

This research between January 2012 and December 2016 included a two-year overlap with the research by Achimugu et al. (2014), January 2012 to December 2013. A comparison is made in Table 7 of this overlap period to determine whether the same sources were identified. In the second column, the first number, for example "3" represents the total number of sources found for each prioritisation approach. The numbers in brackets, for example "(80, 48, 88)" are the citation numbers reported in Achimugu et al.'s (2014) study. In the third column, the first number, for example "7" represents the total number of sources found for each prioritisation technique. The number in the brackets is the number of sources found in this research during the overlap period, which were not reported in Achimugu et al.'s (2014) study, for example "2".

Table 7. A comparison of the two-year overlap period of studies (2012-2013), column 2 is recorded from Achimuigu et al. (2014, p. 581) and column 3 from the findings of this research.

Prioritisation Technique	Limitation Sources Cited by Achimugu et al. (2014, p. 581) 1 Jan 1996-31 Dec 2013	Limitation Sources Found in this Research 1 Jan 2012-31 Dec 2016
$100 allocation	3 (80, 48, 88) 80 is 2005, 48 is 2008 and 88 is 2001 (p. 584).	7 (2 not reported in the overlap period)
analytic hierarchy process	3 (25,74,83) 25 is 1998 (p. 583), 74 is 2009 and 83 is 1997 (p. 584)	22 (8 not reported in the overlap period)
binary search tree	1 (74) 74 is 2009 (p. 584)	1 (0 not reported in the overlap period)
planning game	1 (74) 74 is 2009 (p.584)	5 (0 not reported in the overlap period)
quality function deployment	2 (89,54) 89 is 1992 and 54 is 2005 (p. 584)	11 (6 not reported in the overlap period)

Reasons why the sixteen sources were not report as limitations in the overlap period could include the search terms used. When applying Achimugu et al.'s (2014) search string, three of the sixteen sources would have been excluded due to the search terms used. Achimugu et al.'s (2014) study only included "limitations" OR "shortcomings" (Achimugu et al., 2014, p. 570). This study used a thesaurus to generate wider search terms, to expand the search to be more comprehensive. The "limitation" search terms for this study are described in section 3.1. Having wider search terms meant the findings could not be triangulated with Achimugu et al.'s (2014) findings, however, the wider search terms facilitated a comprehensive knowledge of reported limitations, between 2012 and 2016.

The remaining thirteen sources would have identified by using Achimugu et al.'s (2014) search string, but they were not used to support any limitations for the five prioritisation approaches studied. Further investigation found that two of the thirteen missed sources were cited elsewhere in Achimugu et. al. (2014)'s study (Kukreja, Payyavula, Boehm, & Padmanabhuni, 2013; Tonella, Susi, & Palma, 2013). These two sources had the term "requirements prioritization" in their article title. As a first stage of filtering the search results Achimugu et. al. (2014, p. 570) scrutinized the titles to determine relevant studies. It is therefore assumed that the two studies were included as they had "requirements prioritization" in their article title and that the remaining eleven sources, were excluded as they did not. "requirements" and "prioritization" were of importance as they were included in their search string (Achimugu et. al., 2014, p. 570). This study advances Achimugu et al.'s (2014, p. 581) study with additional limitations for five popular prioritisation approaches and dependencies among them.

While analysing the limitations, dependencies were reported among them. The dependencies were identified from the direct quotes of sentences or paragraphs about the limitations copied and analysed from the search results, and other secondary literature sources found by the author to support the logical connections. For example, the quality of the requirements limitation could impact the validity issues limitation. Therefore, this study also contributes a framework showing these dependencies, how the limitations can impact or influence other limitations. Figure 4 presents this holistic view (Urquhart, 2013, p. 114) of the limitations for the five popular prioritisation approaches. Although graphical expression identified in the literature for QFD was dismissed as a limitation, it will remain in the limitations framework where further research can determine whether this is a limitation experienced in the field.

Figure 4. Limitations framework

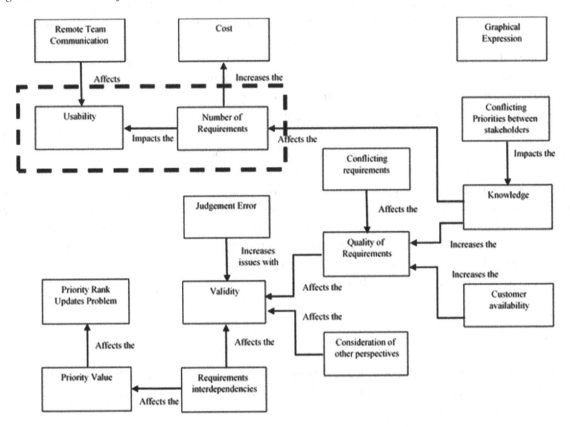

CONCLUSION

Where there are more customer requirements than there is time and budget, prioritisation approaches help decide which requirements to include, to innovate the software. Selecting the right approach to prioritise the requirements is important.

For RQ1, this study contributes sixteen limitations for five popular prioritisation approaches, see Table 6. With startups having high levels of uncertainty and small teams (Nguyen-Ducet al., 2021) a quicker approach to prioritise requirements might be more desirable. In Table 6, cost was reported as a limitation of the AHP approach. With all pairs of requirements assessed (Tonella, Susi, & Palma, 2013, p. 173) it requires much effort which could be difficult for a small team. The $100 allocation approach has fewer steps, which could facilitate quicker prioritisation decisions to adapt to uncertainty. The $100 allocation and the planning game approaches could both help manage the multiple influences of startups (Nguyen-Duc et al., 2021). Each key stakeholder or influencer could be allocated a virtual $100 to assign to the requirements ($100 allocation) or help determine the value of each story (planning game). The interaction of discussing user stories and asking questions, such as during the planning game, will help them make prioritisation decisions with a higher level of confidence (Gupta et al., 2020), which could help towards managing uncertainty prevalent in startups (Nguyen-Duc et al., 2021). The results could help software developers to understand the limitations of each approach and inform the approach they choose for requirements prioritisation.

For RQ2, Figure 4, shows the dependencies between the limitations of the five requirements prioritisation approaches. These dependencies could be used by product owners to mitigate the limitations for the current approach they are using. For example, Figure 4 shows that the quality of the requirements or user stories affects the validity of the requirements prioritised. Therefore, if the quality of the requirements was improved this could reduce validity issues. As the framework was developed from literature, the next step is to conduct empirical research to verify the model.

For RQ3, Table 6 gives product owners an awareness of the limitations for the current approach they are using. There were nine limitations for AHP and QFD, seven for the planning game, six for $100 allocation, and four for binary search tree. AHP and QFD had the highest number of limitations for the five popular approaches studied. If an approach with lots of limitations is currently being used, they might choose instead to use an approach with fewer limitations. Table 6 shows that the binary search tree approach has only four limitations, the lowest number of limitations for the five popular approaches studied. With the fewest limitations, this study shows that the binary search tree could be the best approach. However, an approach with a high number of limitations may be preferred if the benefits outweigh the limitations. Therefore, further research is needed to provide a balanced view, and also consider the benefits of these five popular approaches.

REFERENCES

Achimugu, P., Selamat, A., Ibrahim, R., & Mahrin, M. N. (2014). A systematic literature review of software requirements prioritization research. *Information and Software Technology*, *56*(6), 568–585. doi:10.1016/j.infsof.2014.02.001

Babar, M. I., Ghazali, M., Jawawi, D. N. A., Shamsuddin, S. M., & Ibrahim, N. (2015). PHandler: An expert system for a scalable software requirements prioritization process. *Knowledge-Based Systems*, *84*, 179–202. doi:10.1016/j.knosys.2015.04.010

Barney, S., Mohankumar, V., Chatzipetrou, P., Aurum, A., Wohlin, C., & Angelis, L. (2014). Software quality across borders: Three case studies on company internal alignment. *Information and Software Technology*, *56*(1), 20–38. doi:10.1016/j.infsof.2013.06.004

Bass, J. M. (2013). Agile Method Tailoring in distributed Enterprises: Product Owner Teams. *Proceedings of IEEE 8th International conference on Global Software Engineering (ICGSE)*, 154-163. 10.1109/ICGSE.2013.27

Baudin, M. (2012). Revisiting pareto in manufacturing: Revising your charts can provide clear communications to managers. *Industrial Engineering (American Institute of Industrial Engineers)*, *44*(1), 28–33. http://search.ebscohost.com/login.aspx?direct=true&db=asn&AN=70046451&site=eds-live

Beck, K. (2000). *Extreme Programming Explained*. Addison-Wesley.

Büyüközkan, G., & Çifçin, G. (2012). A new incomplete preference relations based approach to quality function deployment. *Information Sciences*, *206*, 30–41. doi:10.1016/j.ins.2012.04.010

Charmaz, K. (2014). *Constructing Grounded Theory* (2nd ed.). SAGE Publications.

Chaves-González, J. M., & Pérez-Toledano, M. A. (2015). Differential evolution with Pareto tournament for the multi-objective next release problem. *Applied Mathematics and Computation, 252*(1), 1–13. doi:10.1016/j.amc.2014.11.093

Chaves-González, J. M., Pérez-Toledano, M. A., & Navasa, A. (2015a). Software requirement optimization using a multiobjective swarm intelligence evolutionary algorithm. *Knowledge-Based Systems, 83*, 105–115. doi:10.1016/j.knosys.2015.03.012

Chaves-González, J. M., Pérez-Toledano, M. A., & Navasa, A. (2015b). Teaching learning based optimization with Pareto tournament for the multiobjective software requirements selection. *Engineering Applications of Artificial Intelligence, 43*, 89–101. doi:10.1016/j.engappai.2015.04.002

Chiou, C.-C., Perng, C., & Tseng, T.-F. (2012). Applying service science on systematic innovation for the convention and exhibition industry: The cases of world expo. *International Journal of Electronic Business Management, 10*(4), 247–260. http://search.ebscohost.com/login.aspx?direct=true&db=bth&AN=85717275&site=eds-live

Daneva, M., Damian, D., Marchetto, A., & Pastor, O. (2014, September). Empirical research methodologies and studies in requirements engineering: How far did we come? *Journal of Systems and Software, 95*, 1–9. doi:10.1016/j.jss.2014.06.035

Dimitrijević, S., Jovanović, J., & Devedžić, V. (2015). A comparative study of software tools for user story management. *Information and Software Technology, 57*, 352–368. doi:10.1016/j.infsof.2014.05.012

Escalona, M. J., Urbieta, M., Rossi, G., Garcia-Garcia, J. A., & Robles Luna, E. (2013). Detecting web requirements conflicts and inconsistencies under a model-based perspective. *Journal of Systems and Software, 86*(12), 3024–3038. doi:10.1016/j.jss.2013.05.045

Gandomani, T. J., Wei, K. T., & Binhamid, A. K. (2014). A case study research on software cost estimation using experts' estimates, wideband Delphi, and planning poker technique. *International Journal of Software Engineering and Its Applications, 8*(11), 173–182. doi:10.14257/ijseia.2014.8.11.16

Glaser, B. G. (1992). *Basic of Grounded theory Analysis: Emergence vs. forcing*. The Sociology Press.

Glaser, B. G., & Strauss, A. L. (1967). *The discovery of Grounded Theory: strategies for qualitative research*. Aldine Publishing Company.

Grenning, J. W. (2002). *Planning Poker or how to avoid analysis paralysis when release planning*. https://wingman-sw.com/papers/PlanningPoker-v1.1.pdf

Gupta, V., Fernandez-Crehuet, J. M., Hanne, T., & Telesko, R. (2020). Requirements engineering in software startups: A systematic mapping study. *Applied Sciences (Basel, Switzerland), 10*(6125), 1–19. doi:10.3390/app10176125

Hibbard, T. N. (1962). Some combinatorial properties of certain trees with applications to searching and sorting. *Journal of the Association for Computing Machinery, 9*(1), 13–28. doi:10.1145/321105.321108

Jessop, A. (2014). IPM: A decision aid for multiattribute evaluation using imprecise weight estimates. *Omega, 49*, 18–29. doi:10.1016/j.omega.2014.05.001

Kakar, A. K. (2015). Investigating the penalty reward calculus of software users and its impact on requirements prioritization. *Information and Software Technology, 65*, 56–68. doi:10.1016/j.infsof.2015.04.004

Kamisawa, N. (1994). The use of prioritization in quality deployment at the planning and design stages. In S. Mizuno & Y. Akao (Eds.), *QFD The customer-driven approach to quality planning and deployment* (pp. 108–134). Asian Productivity Organization.

Karlsson, J., Wohlin, C., & Regnell, B. (1998). An evaluation of methods for prioritizing software requirements. *Information and Software Technology, 39*(14-15), 939–947. doi:10.1016/S0950-5849(97)00053-0

Kaur, G., & Bawa, S. (2013). A survey of requirements prioritization methods. *International Journal of Engineering Research & Technology (Ahmedabad), 2*(5), 958–962. https://www.ijert.org/view-pdf/3492/a-survey-of-requirement-prioritization-methods

Kukreja, N., Boehm, B., Payyavula, S. S., & Padmanabhuni, S. (2012). Selecting an appropriate framework for value-based requirements prioritization. *2012 IEEE 20th International Requirements Engineering Conference*, 303-308. https://ieeexplore.ieee.org/stamp/stamp.jsp?arnumber=6345819

Leffingwell, D., & Widrig, D. (2000). *Managing Software Requirements: A unified approach*. Addison-Wesley.

Leong, Y. T., Tan, R. R., Aviso, K. B., & Chew, I. M. L. (2016). Fuzzy analytic hierarchy process and targeting for inter-plant chilled and cooling water network synthesis. *Journal of Cleaner Production, 110*, 40–53. doi:10.1016/j.jclepro.2015.02.036

Li, M., Jin, L., & Wang, J. (2014). Jin, L., & Wang, J. (2014). A new MCDM method combining QFD with TOPSIS for knowledge management system selection from the user's perspective in intuitionistic fuzzy environment. *Applied Soft Computing, 21*, 28–37. doi:10.1016/j.asoc.2014.03.008

Lim, S. L., Bentley, P. J., & Ishikawa, F. (2020). Reaching the Unreachable A method for early stage software startups to reach inaccessible stakeholders within large corporations. *2020 IEEE 28th International Requirements Engineering Conference*, 376-381. 10.1109/RE48521.2020.00051

Manifesto for Agile Software Development. (2001). http://agilemanifesto.org/

Meyer, B. (2014). *Agile!: The good, the hype and the ugly*. Springer International Publishing. doi:10.1007/978-3-319-05155-0

Nguyen-Duc, A., Kemell, K.-K., & Abrahamsson, P. (2021). The entrepreneurial logic of startup software development: A study of 40 software startups. *Empirical Software Engineering, 26*(5), 1–55. doi:10.100710664-021-09987-z

Nixon, J. D., Dey, P. K., & Davies, P. A. (2013). Design of a novel solar thermal collector using a multi-criteria decision-making methodology. *Journal of Cleaner Production, 59*, 150–159. doi:10.1016/j.jclepro.2013.06.027

Nurdiani, I., Jabangwe, R., & Petersen, K. (2016). Practices and challenges of managing requirements interdependencies in agile software development: a survey. *2016 International Conference on Engineering, Technology and Innovation/IEEE International Technology Management Conference*, 1-8. 10.1109/ICE/ITMC39735.2016.9025919

Pergher, M., & Rossi, B. (2013). Requirements prioritization in software engineering: A systematic mapping study. *2013 IEEE Third international workshop on Empirical Requirements Engineering*, 40-44. 10.1109/EmpiRE.2013.6615215

Racheva, Z., Daneva, M., Herrmann, A., & Wieringa, R. (2010). A conceptual model and process for client-driven agile requirements prioritization. *4th International Conference on Research Challenges in Information Science*, 287-298. 10.1109/RCIS.2010.5507388

Ramesh, B., Cao, L., & Baskerville, R. (2010). Agile requirements engineering practices and challenges: An empirical study. *Information Systems Journal, 20*(5), 449–480. doi:10.1111/j.1365-2575.2007.00259.x

ReVelle, J. B. (2004). *What is Quality Function Deployment (QFD)?* http://asq.org/learn-about-quality/qfd-quality-function-deployment/overview/overview.html

Riņķevičs, K., & Torkar, R. (2013). Equality in cumulative voting: A systematic review with an improvement proposal. *Information and Software Technology, 55*(2), 267–287. doi:10.1016/j.infsof.2012.08.004

Saaty, T. L. (1977). A scaling method for priorities in hierarchical structures. *Journal of Mathematical Psychology, 15*(3), 234–281. doi:10.1016/0022-2496(77)90033-5

Santos, R., Albuquerque, A., & Pinheiro, P. R. (2016). Towards the applied hybrid model in requirements prioritization. *Procedia Computer Science, 91*, 909–918. doi:10.1016/j.procs.2016.07.109

Sher, F., Jawawi, D. N. A., Mohamad, R., & Barbar, M. I. (2014). Requirements prioritization techniques and different aspects for prioritization: A systematic literature review protocol. *2014 8th Malaysian Software Engineering Conference*, 31-36. https://ieeexplore.ieee.org/stamp/stamp.jsp?tp=&arnumber=6985985

Soni, A. (2014). An evaluation of requirements prioritisation methods. *International Journal of Innovative Research in Advances Engineering, 1*(10), 2349-2163. https://www.academia.edu/11130987/IJIRAE_An_Evaluation_of_Requirements_Prioritisation_Methods

Svensson, R. B., Gorschek, T., Regnell, B., Torkar, R., Shahrokni, A., Feldt, R., & Aurum, A. (2011) Prioritization of quality requirements: State of practice in eleven companies. *2011 IEEE 19th International Requirements Engineering Conference*, 69-78. https://ieeexplore.ieee.org/stamp/stamp.jsp?arnumber=6051652

Tonella, P., Susi, A., & Palma, F. (2013). Interactive requirements prioritization using a genetic algorithm. *Information and Software Technology, 55*(1), 173–187. doi:10.1016/j.infsof.2012.07.003

Torrecilla-Salinas, C. J., Sedeño, J., Escalona, M. J., & Mejías, M. (2015, May). Estimating, planning and managing agile web development projects under a value-based perspective. *Information and Software Technology, 61*, 124–144. doi:10.1016/j.infsof.2015.01.006

Urquhart, C. (2013). *Grounded Theory for qualitative research: A practical guide*. Sage Publication Ltd. doi:10.4135/9781526402196

van Waardenburg, G., & van Vliet, H. (2013). When Agile meets the enterprise. *Information and Software Technology, 55*(12), 2154–2171. doi:10.1016/j.infsof.2013.07.012

Wang, Y.-M. (2012). Assessing the relative importance weights of customer requirements using multiple preference formats and nonlinear programming. *International Journal of Production Research, 50*(16), 4414–4425. doi:10.1080/00207543.2011.596848

Yousuf, M., Bokhari, M. U., & Zeyauddin, M. (2016). An analysis of software requirements prioritization techniques: A detailed survey. *2016 3rd International Computing for Sustainable Global Development,* 3966-3970. https://ieeexplore.ieee.org/abstract/document/7725002

Yu, X., & Petter, S. (2014). Understanding agile software development practices using shared mental models theory. *Information and Software Technology, 56*(8), 911–921. doi:10.1016/j.infsof.2014.02.010

Zaidan, A. A., Zaidan, B. B., Hussain, M., Haiqi, A., Kiah, M. L. M., & Abdulnabi, M. (2015). Multi-criteria analysis for OS-EMR software selection problem: A comparative study. *Decision Support Systems, 78,* 15–27. doi:10.1016/j.dss.2015.07.002

ENDNOTE

[1] Not scalable, refers to the difficulty in using the approach with a large number of requirements, for example, considering the number of decisions needed when using AHP, it may be problematic to use (Karlsson, Wohlin, & Regnell, 1998, p. 945).

Chapter 14
Technology–Based Innovation for Business Model Innovation

S Meenakshi Sundaram

GSSS Institute of Engineering and Technology for Women, India

Tejaswini R. Murgod

GSSS Institute of Engineering and Technology for Women, India

Sowmya M.

GSSS Institute of Engineering and Technology for Women, India

ABSTRACT

Innovation is the commercial application and successful exploitation of the idea. This means introducing something new into the business for improving or replacing business processes to increase efficiency and productivity. Development of entirely new and improved products and services for changing customer or consumer demands or needs, adding value to existing products, services, or markets is called business innovation. It is critical for any forward-thinking organization that technology plays a major role. Choosing technologies that will empower an organization is challenging. Today, technological innovations like internet-enabled mobile devices have allowed businesses to innovate news ways of doing things that were previously unthinkable. Innovation must be more than just technologically feasible and economically profitable. The successful exploitation of new ideas is crucial to a business being able to improve its processes, bring new and improved products and services to market, increase its efficiency, and most importantly, improve its profitability.

INTRODUCTION

Innovation is critical for any forward-thinking organization. This is where technology plays a major role. Choosing technologies that will empower an organization is challenging. Even a good development strategy needs to be implemented properly. Successful business leaders catapult growth and development with the help of an experienced technology partner. The pace of technological advancement is creating enormous potential to create and deliver better customer experiences through technology-enabled

DOI: 10.4018/978-1-7998-9059-1.ch014

process innovation. For instance, today, technological innovations like internet-enabled mobile devices have allowed businesses to innovate news ways of doing things that were previously unthinkable.

To innovate enough, start thinking about what kind of technology is actually required in order to be benefited with outcomes. Information technology (IT) innovation in an enterprise involves using technology in new ways to create a more efficient organization and improve alignment between technology initiatives and business goals. IT innovation can take many forms like turning business processes into automated IT functions, developing applications that open new markets, or implementing desktop virtualization to increase manageability and cut hardware costs. Many companies try to institutionalize the process of innovation by creating innovation teams from diverse segments of the company. Other firms rely on individual employees to flourish in an environment where innovation is encouraged.

Information and Communication Technologies (ICT) are emerging as a promising paradigm for creating a profound change in digitizing technologies (Chetna Gupta et. al., 2021). Technology innovation can take many forms, for instance, novel software implementing new algorithms and data processing models; or new hardware components (sensors, processors, components); or improved user interfaces offering seamless experiences; it can also happen at a higher level, in the form of new processes, business models, monetization engines, and so on. Management of technology and innovation must balance short-term efficiency with long-term effectiveness in the market if the firm is to add value and thrive in a changing environment. Strong dynamic capabilities are needed if the organization is going to be able to address the challenges of innovation and dynamic competition (Teece. D & Leih S. 2016). Business prototypes of varying degrees of fidelity and interactivity could be a powerful tool for early stage startups to validate their business model assumptions especially product value proposition (Varun Gupta et. al., 2021)

To bring in technology into business model entrepreneurs must involve themselves into research and development (R&D), generating new ideas, conducting experiments, designing and implementing new changes into the system. To achieve better performance appropriate strategy has to be followed. To bring in technology into business the first step of the entrepreneur must be recognizing the unanswered or unresolved customer needs. Before changing the business model the entrepreneurs must analyze the financial requirement, risk involved as well as opportunity that will be gained in the market. By considering the above factors business model can be modified or fully changed. The best tool must be selected for the business model as it depends on the nature of business and the competition. To successfully improve the business model the organization must think on setting up the values and establishing a network with all stakeholders.

To sustain in the competitive world the business model proposed must be innovative and should include new technological progress. Entrepreneurs must come up with new innovative ideas for products, services, marketing strategies through various experiments and should explicitly analyze the risk factor involved in it. Sustainable business development can contribute not only to the firm's growth but also for society and the economy as a whole.

Technology business model involves combined experimentation and production of products in consideration of the technological and scientific advancement which many technology firms belong to. Technology entrepreneurship searches solutions for problems through opportunity exploitation from emerging technologies, organization, management, and risk bearing. This is based on value creation and capture, target organizations, mechanism of delivery, and the interdependence of these mechanisms, which are interrelated through the business model. (Run Wang, 2021).

The business model innovation improves the current delivery system by creating a new offering system, which leads to a reconfiguration of the model by integrating with the technological ecosystem's capabilities in creating and exploiting new business opportunities. Business models expose the way enterprises are linked to various stakeholders and are involved in economic exchange with these stakeholders in creating value for the partners (Zott & Amit, 2007), as well as contribute to the successful commercialization of disruptive technologies (DaSilva et al., 2013). The value of technology alone will be less as values are emerged through commercializing using a business model (Chesbrough & Rosenbloom, 2002; DaSilva et al., 2013). That is, technological innovation requires business models in creating and bringing innovations to the market and creating an opportunity that satisfies the unsatisfied customer's need (Teece, 2010). Accordingly, looking for integrations among the economy and technology arises to be important to identify the most appropriate strategies (Roja & Năstase, 2014). Moreover, the intention should be tended to gain technological capability and personnel skills in developing innovation and being competitive (Khefacha & Belkacem, 2016). Therefore, it is crucial to look at the existing challenges and business model cases in improving performance (Kim & Min, 2015; Sabatier et al., 2010; Santos et al., 2015; Snihur & Tarzijan, 2018)

The innovative business model must be capable of producing new business ideas by combining the technology along with the business values so as to come up with solution to new customer requirements. There are three characteristics to be considered for technology with respect to the business model development. Technology supports business model through various supporting functions for a specific business model. Technology acts as the enabler for a business model and business model enables an innovative technology.

Trend Arena is a tool available to identify, evaluate and describe the future trend systematically. The Trend Arena tool analysis the database with text mining software and identifies the recent trend and real interest of the customers. These trend analyzed data can be used in the business model for strategic planning.

Smart Scouting is another tool analytical tool available which helps the entrepreneurs to identify the new technologies, market and monitor the status or progress of their competitors. The smart scouting tool helps to identify the unknown market or technologies and also displays the analyzed data in graphical view.

BACKGROUND

Need for Technology Support for Innovation

The dynamics of the technology that support business are rapidly changing, with the demand to streamline operations, reduce complexity and decrease costs. Technology Support Services is revolutionizing IT support for the future, with innovative, advanced technologies to help simplify the IT support management and dramatically expand and extend new value to business.

There are 5 essential innovations to transform IT support management which includes:

1. Automated IT device discovery and management
2. Augmented reality enhancement to remote technical support.
3. Support of Virtual Assistants to reduce call volume and wait times.
4. IT maintenance service request process streamlined with automation.

Enterprise IT environments are becoming more complex with the adoption of hybrid cloud and need for open-source support, while the demand for IT availability and related maintenance costs is on the rise. IT inventory and availability management, the task of identifying potentially thousands of data center devices along with warranty and support status for each of them can be overwhelming. Researching the latest updates, tracking inventory with spreadsheets can be time-consuming that the results are stale and inaccurate as soon as it is finished.

The road from disruption to recovery can be a long one. Checking hardware support information, describing the problem to a support representative or colleague, waiting for a field technician to arrive, hoping the technician will have the right parts with them to resolve the issue, the time really starts to add up. Today's customers are more connected than ever and likely to measure your customer service experience against not only the competitors, but also the best experiences they have had with other brands. So it's safe to say if a technical support issue isn't resolved in a timely manner, it can seriously damage the company's reputation.

In any technical support situation, time to resolution is critical. Traditionally, the IT administrator must first discover the error, meaning that the business likely feels the effects already. The administrator then has to spend time on the phone with the third-party maintenance provider while an operator manually entitles the call with the appropriate service and IT support information. At this rate, it could be days before the error is resolved. By automating complex service request tasks, Electronic Service Agents can help to streamline the entire service request process.

As more and more innovative technologies enter the market, it can be tricky to determine which ones are right for the unique IT environment. For unbiased recommendations about what to implement in the business, it all comes down to data. An estimated 41.6 billion Internet of Things (IoT) devices alone will generate 79.4 zetabytes i.e., 79.4 trillion gigabytes of data in 2025.

Technology Innovation — Trends and Opportunities

A number of actors - including systems integrators (Prencipe et al., 2003), entrepreneurs (Garud and Karnoe, 2003), or users (Von Hippel, 1988) - play a key role in trying to answer the long-standing question: What determines the direction of technology evolution? These actors will be driven by the cognitive frames they hold that connect perceived customer desires to the innovation agenda. Business models are not just statements of economic linkages but also cognitive devices; business models held in the minds of these actors influence technological outcomes. These cognitive business models exist even before the technology is designed and the products are built. At one extreme, the developer's business model could be something very simple and formed by the developer's own preferences concerning who the customer is and the method of customer engagement (Denyer et al., 2011; Haefliger et al., 2011) or, it may be driven by the current belief system of the company. At the other extreme, the actor may have a very rich and free-flowing view of the world, influenced by deep knowledge and understanding of social and technical possibilities and unencumbered by immediate external biases.

Technology is moving at an incredible pace. In this era where things like autonomous cars, personalized medicine, and quantum computing are becoming real, technologies like Artificial Intelligence, crypto-currencies, advanced automation, deep learning are reshaping the world. The years to come will bring impressive technological breakthroughs with a massive impact on our lives, markets, and societies. In the connected world, with the unprecedented level of information, knowledge, and ideas exchange, innovation is happening continuously, at scale, and in several forms.

It is driven by corporations, universities, startups, research scientists, or simply by thousands of creative individuals across the globe. Some of the most promising developments in the wider information technology spectrum are listed below:

1. Artificial Intelligence (AI)

In the recent times, AI is applied to areas like machine learning, deep learning, computer vision and Natural Language Processing. Computer vision is making huge steps, with massive applications in autonomous cars, navigation, robotics, pattern recognition, medical diagnosis, and more. Language Understanding has made tremendous progress as well, recently reached the levels of human understanding. Microsoft reports that the word error rate is 5.9% which is equal to human performance on the same input. Digital assistants become more and more intelligent, contextual, and proactive.

2. Natural User Interfaces

This is about the seamless experience like voice-driven interactions. It is also about natural dialogues and forms of communication combining multiple signals in meaningful, streamlined experiences. Conversational experiences will become richer, more natural, and effective. Effective voice authentication is in progress. PDAs will be able to retrieve older sessions, questions asked and answers served general patterns, and implicitly-stated preferences and interests.

3. Virtual Reality

Virtual reality (VR) technology is exploding. So are the opportunities for innovative experiences, use-cases, and products. Content creation for VR is a great opportunity with significant startup activity worldwide. VR startups are working across multiple domains and business scenarios, including E-commerce, gaming, social applications, learning and education, healthcare, online VR environments, and more.

4. Augmented Reality

Augmented reality is what we get when physical and digital worlds blend into a single experience. Typical examples are Microsoft HoloLens and Google Glass

5. Analytics and Visualization

Data availability has exploded and modern corporations have access to vast amounts of complex data, both internal and from the public domain. The breadth and depth of data available require new ways to summarize, visualize, and present data.

6. Blockchain

Blockchain is distributed, decentralized with immutable properties that make it the ideal way to store and track data across numerous domains and use cases. Recent applications include crypto-currencies and fin-tech.

7.   Robotics

With the progress in Artificial Intelligence it is possible to integrate cognitive services and dramatically increase Robot's capabilities for real-time decision making. In the near future, robots will have proactive behaviors, advanced context understanding, able to adapt to human sentiment, enforce 'personalities' and communication styles.

Technology as Vehicle for Innovation

Both innovation and technology are tightly interlaced. Two very notable ways technology propels innovation forward is that it boosts tinkering and experimentation, and that in itself accelerates innovation processes. Earlier experimentation with new technologies was only possible by multinational corporations or government-funded research labs. Today, affordable technology digital and others make it possible for most enterprises big and small to experiment with ideas and concepts in whole new ways, and also in reality instead of only in test labs.

For example, it's now possible to test products and services online at a very low cost, as well as test out updates, alterations and tweaks. Prototyping has become available to all through easy to use software and 3D printing. AI can simulate various market scenarios based on available real-life data. Virtual reality makes it possible to create completely new types of blueprints that actually make products and services come alive for real, and thus make them possible to evaluate prior to building or manufacturing them.

Digital technology and the new technologies that it enables (like AR, VR and AI) cut the traditional industrial age innovation process short. What used to take years of planning, testing, and executing can now be accomplished in months and sometimes even weeks.

One way of looking at technology as enhancer of human capabilities, is digital transformation, after having transformed domain after domain, has reached technology itself and is beginning to recursively transform technological evolution as we know it. This unlocks a great potential, but it also raises concerns as to what it means that technology and not only humans have control over technological progress.

Now, technological evolution has reached a point where it can help us overcome or at least circumvent cognitive short-comings. Where the human mind fails to display characteristics beneficial for driving change and creative thinking, technology can give us an extra push towards a greater innovative capacity.

Organizations that want to innovate must (in most cases) understand the seedbed that new technology creates for any market today. However new technology has changed the conditions in the market and with transformation of products and services. Understanding of technology is necessary for innovation is as an enabler

Technology and Innovation Challenges

Innovation must be socially desirable, economically profitable and technologically feasible. Technology, Innovation and Ventures capabilities should be brought together to support the clients' needs for sustainable growth. Approaches to anticipate the new trends, assess their potential, validate their enterprise-readiness, and exploit them responsibly should be enabled. Applied innovation in industries has enabled scaling, with certainty and trust, and with the power of data and intelligence built in

Innovation must be more than just technologically feasible and economically profitable. For an innovation to be sustainable, it must be socially desirable so as to benefit existing generations without prejudice for future ones while also protecting their environment. In a world of Volatility, Uncertainty, Complexity and Ambiguity, the purpose of an enterprise to equip customers with the right capabilities for them to transform themselves and address the key challenges like growing inequalities and climate change.

Innovation is centered on delivering short-term convenience over long-term benefit for humanity and the planet, and the benefits it brings are captured by a few private actors. Technological innovation creates options, choices and trade-offs. The digital transformation strategies should systematically account for the well-being of societies and their environment. Crises always highlight the limitations of an existing system and provide directions of rectification..

Achieving rapid changes to the operating model is not just a question of applying technology but also of aligning the teams and departments to a singular vision. Technological investments therefore go hand in hand with clear directives from leadership, to ensure that every department has a clear understanding of what is being done, why initiatives are being modified, and how this impacts their roles. Ambiguity, after all, is the parent of disconnection. Hence, technology's application needs to provide clarity across the firm so that KPIs, processes and outcome goals can be aligned to combat against frictions between departments. Silo-busting should be the consequence, and not the objective.

Enabling IT Innovation in Enterprises

A variety of megatrends, including the consumerization of IT, the explosion of big data and analytics, the rise of mobile and the cloud, plus the ongoing need to show operational efficiency, is driving enterprise technology leaders to push innovation across their organizations. We all know that changing the course of large organizations can be very difficult, but the 10 technology enablers listed below have shown how leaders of enterprises have successfully enable innovation in their organizations.

1. Embrace Software-as-a-Service (SaaS): Traditional innovation investment risks and costly proofs-of-concept can now often be avoided by choosing lower-cost online services that don't require huge up-front commitments.
2. Move aggressively to DevOps: DevOps, first and foremost, is a cultural rather than technological transformation. DevOps adoption often starts by assigning a leading evangelist and a small guerrilla force to create the links between developers and operations. The process might also include recruiting DevOps experts or outsourcing to accelerate adoption.
3. Support early-stage startups: Practically every week brings new enterprise application vendors with innovative ideas to support business. Some large enterprises avoid these small new vendors because they do not precisely align with existing internal processes or security concerns
4. Partner with users: Today's users have direct access to online tools that are often much better than the approved enterprise alternatives. Do not fight your users, collaborate with them. Help them with configuration and integration issues so they can be as productive as possible.
5. Try a bimodal approach to IT: This approach involves maintaining conservative, traditional IT methods in some areas while incorporating innovation and experimentation in others. The chal-

lenge is balancing the need for speed without compromising stability and security where it really matters.

6. Become a data-driven organization: IT systems generate a lot of data about application and server performance, customer behavior, network performance, and much more. Aggregating, analyzing, and making this data available across multiple technical and business silos can be the key to collaboration and making smarter technical and business decisions.

7. Embrace visibility: After systematically gathering data, make sure that it is continuously used. Monitor IT systems including costs, performance, and user behavior and ensure that data is available throughout the company in easy-to-understand formats. The more everyone knows about the technology and the business, the faster they can make better decisions.

8. Break the silos: Develop internal organization portals, integrate systems, and build processes to help break down the internal walls between different business units. Traditional silos helped organizations maintain accountability and responsibility, but innovation thrives when ideas and insights are cross-pollinated across multiple areas.

9. Drive user adoption: Innovation success is measured by user adoption. First, try to ensure that the mobile Apps or ERP used up to modern standards. Internal organization marketing should mimic the efforts of external vendors. It's important to get buy-in from stakeholders during planning and development, starting when the app is almost finished is far too late.

10. Create the culture: Corporate culture is often the key to successful innovation. Many traditional IT firms make innovation difficult by blaming the messenger instead of listening to the message and punishing failure without honest inquiry. High-trust cultures that are open to innovation no matter from where it comes from with promotion and rewarding risk-taking is expected.

Technology Innovation for Business Growth

Responsible innovation has been proposed as a broad theme where theoretical and practical analysis on how to make innovation responsible converges by taking into account the possible impacts of the innovation on individuals, institutions and society (Doorn. N & Gorman. E 2013, Koops, B. J. 2015). The successful exploitation of new ideas is crucial to a business being able to improve its processes, bring new and improved products and services to market, increase its efficiency and, most importantly, improve its profitability. Marketplaces, whether local, regional, national or global are becoming highly competitive. Competition has increased as a result of wider access to new technologies and the increased trading and knowledge-sharing opportunities offered by the Internet.

It is important to be clear about the difference between invention and innovation. Invention is a new idea. Innovation is the commercial application and successful exploitation of the idea. Fundamentally, innovation means introducing something new into the business. This could be improving or replacing business processes to increase efficiency and productivity, or to enable the business to extend the range or quality of existing products and/or services, developing entirely new and improved products and services, often to meet rapidly changing customer or consumer demands or needs adding value to existing products, services or markets to differentiate the business from its competitors and increase the perceived value to the customers and markets

Innovation can mean a single major breakthrough e.g. a totally new product or service. However, it can also be a series of small, incremental changes. Whatever form it takes, innovation is a creative process. The ideas may come from inside the business, e.g. from employees, managers or in-house research and development work. It can also be obtained from outside the business, e.g. suppliers, customers, media reports, market research published by another organization, or universities and other sources of new technologies. Success comes from filtering those ideas, identifying those that the business will focus on and applying resources to exploit them.

1. Benefits of Innovation

The benefits of introducing innovation include:

1. improve productivity
2. reduce costs
3. be more competitive
4. build the value of your brand
5. establish new partnerships and relationships
6. increase turnover and improve profitability

Businesses that fail to innovate run the risk of:

1. losing market share to competitors
2. falling productivity and efficiency
3. losing key staff
4. experiencing steadily reducing margins and profit
5. going out of business

2. Approaches to Innovation

Innovation in business can mean introducing new or improved products, services or processes. The following approached can be used to enhance business:

a. Analyze the marketplace

There's no point considering innovation in a vacuum. To move your business forward, study the marketplace and understand how innovation can add value to the customers.

b. Identify opportunities for innovation

Identify opportunities for innovation by adapting the product or service to the way the marketplace is changing. Innovation can be done by introducing new technology, techniques or working practices - perhaps using better processes to give a more consistent quality of product

CONCLUSION

Innovation is critical for any forward-thinking organization. This is where technology plays a major role. Choosing technologies that will empower an organization is challenging. Even a good development strategy needs to be implemented properly. Successful business leaders catapult growth and development with the help of an experienced technology partner. The pace of technological advancement is creating enormous potential to create and deliver better customer experiences through technology-enabled process innovation. To innovate enough, start thinking about what kind of technology is actually required in order to be benefited with outcomes.

Innovation must be socially desirable, economically profitable and technologically feasible. Technology, Innovation and Ventures capabilities should be brought together to support the clients' needs for sustainable growth. Approaches to anticipate the new trends, assess their potential, validate their enterprise-readiness, and exploit them responsibly should be enabled. This should be done through a future thinking and change making perspective.

Applied innovation in industries has enabled scaling, with certainty and trust, and with the power of data and intelligence built in. A network of numerous applied innovation exchanges support customer's innovation journey. Those who are benefited include employees, customers, and stakeholders alike. This also helps in building an agile and resilient model to help the business navigate challenging market conditions. Industries which think differently now can turn a crisis into an opportunity. A willingness to embrace innovation will help the organization to find those new opportunities. The need is that innovation must be spread across the entire organization.

Technology is moving at an incredible pace. In this era where things like autonomous cars, personalized medicine, and quantum computing are becoming real, technologies like Artificial Intelligence, crypto-currencies, advanced automation, deep learning are reshaping the world. A variety of megatrends, including the consumerization of IT, the explosion of big data and analytics, the rise of mobile and the cloud, plus the ongoing need to show operational efficiency, is driving enterprise technology leaders to push innovation across their organizations. We all know that changing the course of large organizations can be very difficult, but the 10 technology enablers listed below have shown how leaders of enterprises have successfully enable innovation in their organizations.

Innovation can mean a single major breakthrough e.g. a totally new product or service. However, it can also be a series of small, incremental changes. Whatever form it takes, innovation is a creative process. The ideas may come from inside the business, e.g. from employees, managers or in-house research and development work. It can also be obtained from outside the business, e.g. suppliers, customers, media reports, market research published by another organization, or universities and other sources of new technologies. Success comes from filtering those ideas, identifying those that the business will focus on and applying resources to exploit them.

REFERENCES

Bullinger, H-J., Nagele, R., Rueger, M., & Fischer, D. (2016). Business Model Innovation: From Technology Market to Market Success. *Proceedings of PICMET Technology Management for Social Innovation*, 1264-1270.

Chesbrough, H., & Rosenbloom, R. S. (2002). The role of business models in capturing value from innovation: Evidence from Xerox corporation's technology spin-off companies. *Industrial and Corporate Change, 11*(3), 529–555. doi:10.1093/icc/11.3.529

DaSilva, C. M., Trkman, P., Desouza, K., & Lindič, J. (2013). Disruptive technologies: A business model perspective on cloud computing. *Technology Analysis and Strategic Management, 25*(10), 1161–1173. doi:10.1080/09537325.2013.843661

Denyer, D., Parry, E., & Flowers, P. (2011). "Social", "open" and "participative"? Exploring personal experiences and organizational effects of enterprise 2.0 use. *Long Range Planning, 44*(5–6), 375–396. doi:10.1016/j.lrp.2011.09.007

Doorn, N., & Gorman, E. (2013). Early engagement and new technologies: Opening up the laboratory. Springer.

Garud, R., & Karnoe, P. (2003). Bricolage versus breakthrough: Distributed and embedded agency in technology entrepreneurship. *Research Policy, 32*(2), 277–300. doi:10.1016/S0048-7333(02)00100-2

Gupta, Gupta, & Stachowiak. (2021). Adoption of ICT-based Teaching in Engineering: An Extended Technology Acceptance Model Perspective. *IEEE Access.* doi:10.1109/ACCESS.2021.3072580

Gupta, V., Rubalcana, L., & Gupta, C. (2021). Multimedia Prototyping for Early-Stage Startups Endurance: Stage for New Normal? *IEEE MultiMedia, 28*(4), 107–116. Advance online publication. doi:10.1109/MMUL.2021.3122539

Haefliger, S., Monteiro, E., Foray, D., & Von Krogh, G. (2011). Social Software and Strategy. *Long Range Planning, 44*(5–6), 297–316. doi:10.1016/j.lrp.2011.08.001

Khefacha, I., & Belkacem, L. (2016). Technology-based ventures and sustainable development: Cointegrating and causal relationships with a panel data approach. *The Journal of International Trade & Economic Development, 25*(2), 192–212. doi:10.1080/09638199.2015.1048707

Kim, S. K., & Min, S. (2015). Business model innovation performance: When does adding a new business model benefit an incumbent? *Strategic Entrepreneurship Journal, 9*(1), 34–57. doi:10.1002ej.1193

Koops, B. J. (2015). The concept, approaches, and applications of responsible innovation. In B. J. Koops, I. Oosterlaken, H. Romijn, & J. van der Hoven (Eds.), *Responsible innovation 2: Approaches and implications* (pp. 1–15). Springer International Publishing. doi:10.1007/978-3-319-17308-5_1

Prencipe, A., Davies, A., & Hobday, M. (2003). *The Business of Systems Integration.* Oxford University Press. doi:10.1093/0199263221.001.0001

Roja, A., & Năstase, M. (2014, November 6–7). *Technology entrepreneurship and entrepreneurial strategies* [Conference session]. 8th International Management Conference Management Challenges for Sustainable Development, Bucharest, Romania.

Sabatier, V., Mangematin, V., & Rousselle, T. (2010). From recipe to dinner: Business model portfolios in the European biopharmaceutical industry. *Long Range Planning, 43*(2-3), 431–447. doi:10.1016/j.lrp.2010.02.001

Santos, J., Spector, B., & Van den Heyden, L. (2015). Towards a theory of business model innovation within incumbent firms. In N. Foss & T. Saebi (Eds.), *Business model innovation: The organizational dimension* (pp. 43–63). Oxford University Press. doi:10.1093/acprof:oso/9780198701873.003.0003

Snihur, Y., & Tarzijan, J. (2018). Managing complexity in a multi-business-model organization. *Long Range Planning*, *51*(1), 50–63. doi:10.1016/j.lrp.2017.06.010

Teece, D., & Leih, S. (2016). Dynamic capabilities and organizational agility: Risk, uncertainty, and strategy in the innovation economy. *California Management Review*, *58*(4), 13–35. doi:10.1525/cmr.2016.58.4.13

Teece, D. J. (2010). Business models, business strategy and innovation. *Long Range Planning*, *43*(2-3), 172–194. doi:10.1016/j.lrp.2009.07.003

Von Hippel, E. (1988). *The Sources of Innovation*. Oxford University Press.

Wang, R., & Chebo, A. K. (2021). The Dynamics of Business Model Innovation for Technology Entrepreneurship: A Systematic Review and Future Avenue. *Sage Journals, 11*(3).

Zott, C., & Amit, R. (2007). Business model design and the performance of entrepreneurial firms. *Organization Science*, *18*(2), 181–199. doi:10.1287/orsc.1060.0232

KEY TERMS AND DEFINITIONS

Ambiguity: There is a lack of clarity or awareness about situations.

Artificial Intelligence (AI): Is intelligence demonstrated by machines, as opposed to natural intelligence displayed by animals including humans. It is the study of "intelligent agents": any system that perceives its environment and takes actions that maximize its chance of achieving its goals.

Augmented Reality (AR): Is an interactive experience of a real-world environment where the objects that reside in the real world are enhanced by computer-generated perceptual information, sometimes across multiple sensory modalities, including visual, auditory, haptic, somatosensory, and olfactory.

Business Model: A business model describes how an organization creates, delivers, and captures value, in economic, social, cultural, or other contexts. The process of business model construction and modification is also called business model innovation and forms a part of business strategy.

Cognitive Devices: Devices like a Brain Computer Interface (BCI), sometimes called a brain–machine interface (BMI), is a direct communication pathway between the brain's electrical activity and an external device, most commonly a computer or robotic limb. BCIs are often directed at researching, mapping, assisting, augmenting, or repairing human cognitive or sensory-motor functions.

Complexity: Many different, interconnected factors come into play, with the potential to cause chaos and confusion.

Disruptive Technology: Disruptive technology is sometimes called disruptive innovation which is the name for a technology or innovation that changes the market by creating a new market. These new markets are small at first, which makes them uninteresting for established market players. If disruptive innovation is used, the market will grow at a high speed. Eventually, they will replace existing technology.

Innovation: Innovation is the practical implementation of ideas that result in the introduction of new goods or services or improvement in offering goods or services.

Natural-Language User Interface (LUI or NLUI): Is a type of computer human interface where linguistic phenomena such as verbs, phrases, and clauses act as UI controls for creating, selecting and modifying data in software applications.

Uncertainty: The present is unclear and the future is uncertain.

Value Creation: Business value creation is an informal term that includes all forms of value that determine the health and well-being of the firm in the long run. Business value expands concept of value of the firm beyond economic value (also known as economic profit, economic value added, and shareholder value) to include other forms of value such as employee value, customer value, supplier value, channel partner value, alliance partner value, managerial value, and societal value. Many of these forms of value are not directly measured in monetary terms.

Virtual Assistant: An intelligent virtual assistant (IVA) or Intelligent Personal Assistant (IPA) is a software agent that can perform tasks or services for an individual based on commands or questions. The term "chatbot" is sometimes used to refer to virtual assistants generally or specifically accessed by online chat.

Virtual Reality (VR): Is a simulated experience that can be similar to or completely different from the real world. Applications of virtual reality include entertainment (particularly video games), education (such as medical or military training) and business (such as virtual meetings). Other distinct types of VR-style technology include augmented reality and mixed reality, sometimes referred to as extended reality or XR.

Volatility: Change is rapid and unpredictable in its nature and extent.

APPENDIX

Paths to Business Model Innovation

Business model innovation demands neither new technologies nor the creation of brand-new markets: It's about delivering *existing* products that are produced by *existing* technologies to *existing* markets. As it often involves changes invisible to the outside world, it can bring advantages that are hard to copy. The challenge is defining what business model innovation actually entails. Without a framework for identifying opportunities, it is hard to be systematic about the process, which explains why it is generally done on an ad hoc basis. As a result, many companies miss out on inexpensive ways to improve their profitability and productivity. A framework helps managers take business model innovation to the level of a reliable and improvable discipline. Drawing on the idea that any business model is essentially a set of key decisions that collectively determine how a business earns its revenue, incurs its costs, and manages its risks, innovations to the model as changes to those decisions. Successful changes along these dimensions improve the company's combination of revenue, costs, and risks.

What Mix of Products or Services Should be offered? Uncertain demand is a challenge all businesses face and is in most cases their major source of risk. One way to reduce that risk is to make changes to your company's mix of products or services. In finance, if we have two portfolios offering a 20% return, we choose the less risky one, because it will create more value over time. The same is true with product portfolios. Companies looking to recalibrate their product or service mix have essentially options like focusing narrowly and searching for commonalities across products.

1. Focusing Narrowly

Focused business models are most effective when they appeal to distinct market segments with clearly differentiated needs. So if your business currently serves multiple segments, it may be best to subdivide into focused units rather than try to apply one model. The main drawback for a focused business is that it must rely on a single product, service, or customer segment—and it may omit key customer needs. People buy both bread *and* butter.

2. Searching for Commonalities Across Products

The success of Volkswagen owes much to a strategy whereby its cars share components. Although the strategy does not protect VW from general demand swings, it reduces demand variability for individual components, because shared components make it easy for VW to switch production at its plants from one model to another whenever the demand for car models shifts. Commonalities aren't just shared components among different products. They may also be the capabilities needed to serve various product, customer, and market segments.

Consequently, companies can add to their mix products or services that reflect new applications of their capabilities. For instance, in the late 1990s Amazon expanded from books into music, video, and games—all of which required the same logistics capabilities that books did. This allowed the company to cover the risk of failing to acquire enough share in any one of these categories with a potentially superior share in another.

Compilation of References

Rigby, D. K., Sutherland, J., & Takeuchi, H. (2016). Embracing agile. *Harvard Business Review, 94*(5), 40–50.

Zueva, A. S. (2019). Foreign work force in the Russian economy: Effects, risks and forecasts. *Journal of Migration Law, 2*, 39–40.

Ronkainen, J., & Abrahamsson, P. (2003). Software development under stringent hardware constraints: Do agile methods have a chance? *International Conference on Extreme Programming and Agile Processes in Software Engineering*, 73–79. 10.1007/3-540-44870-5_10

Klotins, E., Unterkalmsteiner, M., & Gorschek, T. (2015). Software engineering knowledge areas in startup companies: a mapping study. *International Conference of Software Business*, 245–257. 10.1007/978-3-319-19593-3_22

Berg, V., & Birkeland, J. (2018). *Exploring Empirical Engineering Approaches in Startup Companies: The Trilateral Hardware Startup Model*. NTNU.

Gokaram Narayana Murthy, R. (2016). *Production ramp-up of a hardware startup: developing inventory management strategies and establishing a framework for vendor selection*. Massachusetts Institute of Technology.

Berg, V., Birkeland, J., Pappas, I. O., & Jaccheri, L. (2018). The Role of Data Analytics in Startup Companies: Exploring Challenges and Barriers. *Conference on e-Business, e-Services and e-Society*, 205–216. 10.1007/978-3-030-02131-3_19

Zambonelli, F. (2016). *Towards a general software engineering methodology for the Internet of Things*. arXiv Prepr. arXiv1601.05569.

Duc, A. N., Khalid, K., Lønnestad, T., Bajwa, S. S., Wang, X., & Abrahamsson, P. (2019). How do startups develop internet-of-things systems: a multiple exploratory case study. *Proceedings of the International Conference on Software and System Processes*, 74–83.

Usländer, T., & Batz, T. (2018). Agile Service Engineering in the Industrial Internet of Things. *Futur. Internet, 10*(10), 100. doi:10.3390/fi10100100

Kaisti, M., Rantala, V., Mujunen, T., Hyrynsalmi, S., Könnölä, K., Mäkilä, T., & Lehtonen, T. (2013). Agile methods for embedded systems development-a literature review and a mapping study. *EURASIP Journal on Embedded Systems, 2013*(1), 15. doi:10.1186/1687-3963-2013-15

Gavrilyuk, A.V. (2021). Intellectual property in the digital economy: Theoretical and practical aspects. *Intelligence. Innovation. Investment, 2*, 20-33.

Lasi, H., Fettke, P., Kemper, H.-G., Feld, T., & Hoffmann, M. (2014). Industry 4.0. *Business & Information Systems Engineering, 6*(4), 239–242. doi:10.100712599-014-0334-4

Abrahamsson, P., Warsta, J., Siponen, M. T., & Ronkainen, J. (2003). New directions on agile methods: a comparative analysis. *25th International Conference on Software Engineering*, 244–254. 10.1109/ICSE.2003.1201204

Greene, B. (2004). Agile methods applied to embedded firmware development. *Agile Development Conference*, 71–77. 10.1109/ADEVC.2004.3

Dos Santos, D., da Silva, I. N., Modugno, R., Pazelli, H., & Castellar, A. (2007). Software Development Using an Agile Approach for Satellite Camera Ground Support Equipment. In *Advances and Innovations in Systems, Computing Sciences and Software Engineering* (pp. 71–76). Springer. doi:10.1007/978-1-4020-6264-3_14

Kelly, D. P., & Culleton, B. (1999). Process improvement for small organizations. *Computer (Long. Beach. Calif)*, *32*(10), 41–47.

Giardino, C., Wang, X., & Abrahamsson, P. (2014). Why early-stage software startups fail: a behavioral framework. *International conference of software business*, 27–41. 10.1007/978-3-319-08738-2_3

Hokkanen, L., & Väänänen-Vainio-Mattila, K. (2015). UX work in startups: current practices and future needs. *International Conference on Agile Software Development*, 81–92. 10.1007/978-3-319-18612-2_7

Hokkanen, L., Kuusinen, K., & Väänänen, K. (2015). Early product design in startups: towards a UX strategy. *International Conference on Product-Focused Software Process Improvement*, 217–224. 10.1007/978-3-319-26844-6_16

Bailetti, A. J. (2012). What technology startups must get right to globalize early and rapidly. *Technology Innovation Management Review*, *2*(10), 5–16. doi:10.22215/timreview/614

Sazhina, M.A., & Gavrilyuk, A.V. (n.d.). Intellectual property in the innovation economy: Methodological aspects. *Scientific Research of the Faculty of Economics, 12*(36), 26-39.

Statista. (n.d.). https://www.statista.com/statistics/471264/iot-number-of-connected-devices-worldwide/

Gralha, C., Damian, D., Wasserman, A. I. T., Goulão, M., & Araújo, J. (2018). The evolution of requirements practices in software startups. *Proceedings of the 40th International Conference on Software Engineering*, 823–833. 10.1145/3180155.3180158

Kwanya, T., & Stilwell, C. (2017). Scholarly collaboration amongst researchers in Kenya: a social network analysis. *Proceedings of the 4th Multidisciplinary International Social Networks Conference*, 5. 10.1145/3092090.3092096

Maimbo, H., & Pervan, G. (2005). Designing a case study protocol for application in IS research. PACIS 2005 Proc., 106.

Paulk, M. (2002). Capability maturity model for software. Encyclopedia of Software Engineering. doi:10.1002/0471028959.sof589

Salvato, C. (2009). Capabilities unveiled: The role of ordinary activities in the evolution of product development processes. *Organization Science*, *20*(2), 384–409. doi:10.1287/orsc.1080.0408

Crowne, M. (2002, August). Why software product startups fail and what to do about it. Evolution of software product development in startup companies. In *IEEE International Engineering Management Conference* (Vol. *1*, pp. 338-343). IEEE.

Baskerville, R., Ramesh, B., Levine, L., Pries-Heje, J., & Slaughter, S. (2003). Is "Internet-speed" software development different? *IEEE Software*, *20*(6), 70–77.

Petrakova, E. A., & Samoilova, A. S. (2020). Using iLogic technology in Autodesk Inventor to create a parametric 3D gear model and conduct research. *Scientific and Technical Bulletin of the Bryansk State University, 1*. www.ntv-brgu.ru/ntv-bgu-2020-01-10

Unterkalmsteiner, M. (2016). Software startups—a research agenda. *e-Informatica. Software Engineering Journal, 10*(1).

Giardino, C., Bajwa, S. S., Wang, X., & Abrahamsson, P. (2015). Key challenges in early-stage software startups. *International Conference on Agile Software Development*, 52–63.

Samoilova, A. S. (2020). Creating programs in Inventor Autogesk. International Competition for Scientific Achievements of Students, International Center for Scientific Cooperation. *Science and Education*, (8), 35–41.

Ries, E. (2014). *Lean Startup: Schnell, risikolos und erfolgreich Unternehmen gründen.* Redline Wirtschaft.

Samoilova, A.S., & Sharipzyanova, G.K. (2017). Study of the deformation parameters of aluminum alloy V-1461. *Theory and Practice of Project Education, 4*(4).

Logachev, M. S., Voronin, I. V., Britvina, V. V., Tishchenko, S. A., & Altukhov, A. V. (2020). LAN Monitoring. *International Journal of Advanced Trends in Computer Science and Engineering, 9*, 4216–4222. doi:10.30534/ijatcse/2020/07942020

Samoilova, A. S., Britvina, V. V., Bobrova, E. O., Konyukhova, G. P., & Altukhov, A. V. (2021). The use of information technology and mathematical modeling in the development of aluminum alloy regimes. *Proceedings of the CEUR Seminar, 2843.*

Konyukhova, G.P., & Britvina, V.V. (2013). Mathematical statistics in physical culture. *Theory and Practice of Physical Culture,* (11), 60.

Seppänen, P., Tripathi, N., Oivo, M., & Liukkunen, K. (2017). How are product ideas validated? *International Conference of Software Business*, 3–17. 10.1007/978-3-319-69191-6_1

Larman, C., & Basili, V. R. (2003). Iterative and incremental developments. a brief history. *Computer (Long. Beach. Calif), 36*(6), 47–56. doi:10.1109/MC.2003.1204375

Shakizada, N., Dzhazykbaeva, B., Mottaeva, A., Mottaeva, E., & Zueva, A. (2021). Growth of green finance at the global level in the context of sustainable economic development. *XXII International Scientific Conference "Energy Management of Public Utilities and Sustainable Energy Technologies" (EMMFT-2020), 244.* 7-10.

Abazeed, R. A. M. (2020). Impact of strategic capabilities on organizational ambidexterity in thecommercial banks in Jordan: The mediating role of knowledge management. *Management Science Letters, 10*, 1445–1456. doi:10.5267/j.msl.2019.12.023

Abdel-Hamid, T. K. (1989). The dynamics of software project staffing: A system dynamics based simulation approach. *IEEE Transactions on Software Engineering, 15*(2), 109–119. doi:10.1109/32.21738

Abidin, S. R. Z., Noor, S. F. M., & Ashaari, N. S. (2019). Low-fidelity Prototype Design for Serious Game for Slow-reading Students. *Learning, 10*(3).

Abrell, T., Pihlajamaa, M., Kanto, L., Vom Brocke, J., & Uebernickel, F. (2016). The role of users and customers in digital innovation: Insights from B2B manufacturing firms. *Information & Management, 53*(3), 324–335. doi:10.1016/j.im.2015.12.005

Acharya, V., Sharma, S. K., & Gupta, S. K. (2018). Analyzing the factors in industrial automation using analytic hierarchy process. *Computers & Electrical Engineering, 71*, 877–886. Advance online publication. doi:10.1016/j.compeleceng.2017.08.015

Achimugu, P., Selamat, A., Ibrahim, R., & Mahrin, M. N. (2014). A systematic literature review of software requirements prioritization research. *Information and Software Technology, 56*(6), 568–585. doi:10.1016/j.infsof.2014.02.001

Addison, T., & Vallabh, S. (2002). Controlling software project risks: An empirical study of methods used by experienced project managers. *Proceedings of the 2002 Annual Research Conference of the South African Institute of Computer Scientists and Information Technologists on Enablement through Technology*, 128–140.

Ahl, V. (2005). *An experimental comparison of five prioritization methods – Investigating ease of use, accuracy and scalability* (Unpublished master's dissertation). http://www.diva-portal.org/smash/get/diva2:833611/FULLTEXT01.pdf

Ahmad, T., & Van Looy, A. (2020). Business process management and digital innovations: A systematic literature review. *Sustainability*, *12*(17), 6827. doi:10.3390u12176827

Ahmed, S. Z. F., & Koubaa, M. B. (2013). Core competencies and phases of the organizational life cycle. *International Journal of Business and Management Studies*, *5*(1), 461–473.

Aitken, A., & Ilango, V. (2013). A comparative analysis of traditional software engineering and agile software development. *2013 46th Hawaii International Conference on System Sciences*, 4751–4760.

Akao, Y. (2014). The method for motivation by Quality Function Deployment (QFD). *Nang Yan Business Journal*, *1*(1), 1–9. doi:10.2478/nybj-2014-0001

Akao, Y., & Mazur, G. H. (2003). The leading edge in QFD: Past, present and future. *International Journal of Quality & Reliability Management*, *20*(1), 20–35. doi:10.1108/02656710310453791

Alberts, C., & Dorofee, A. (2010). *Risk Management Framework* (CMU/SEI-2010-TR-017). Retrieved April 19, 2022, from the Software Engineering Institute, Carnegie Mellon University website: https://resources.sei.cmu.edu/library/asset-view.cfm?AssetID=9525

Aloini, D., Dulmin, R., & Mininno, V. (2007). Risk management in ERP project introduction: Review of the literature. *Information & Management*, *44*(6), 547–567. doi:10.1016/j.im.2007.05.004

Al-Ta'ani, R. H., & Razali, R. (2013). Prioritizing requirements in agile development: A conceptual framework. *Procedia Technology*, *11*, 733–739. doi:10.1016/j.protcy.2013.12.252

Al-Ta'ani, R. H., & Razali, R. (2016). A Framework for Requirements Prioritisation Process in an Agile Software Development Environment: Empirical Study. *International Journal on Advanced Science, Engineering and Information Technology*, *6*(6), 846–856. doi:10.18517/ijaseit.6.6.1375

Altman, E. J., Nagle, F., & Tushman, M. (2015). *Innovating without information constraints: Organizations, communities, and innovation when information costs approach zero. In The Oxford Handbook of Creativity, Innovation, and Entrepreneurship*. Oxford University Press.

Alt, R., & Zimmermann, H.-D. (2001). Introduction to special section-business models. *Electronic Markets-The International Journal*, *11*(1), 1019–6781.

Ambler, S. (2002). *Agile modeling: Effective practices for extreme programming and the unified process*. John Wiley & Sons.

Anzenbacher, A., & Wagner, M. (2020). The role of exploration and exploitation for innovation success: Effects of business models on organizational ambidexterity in the semiconductor industry. *The International Entrepreneurship and Management Journal*, *16*(2), 571–594. doi:10.100711365-019-00604-6

Aramand, M. (2008). Software products and services are high tech? New product development strategy for software products and services. *Technovation*, *28*(3), 154–160. doi:10.1016/j.technovation.2007.10.004

Aßmann, U. (2015). *Part IV. 03*. The Lean Startup Process.

Atuahene-Gima, K. (2005). Resolving the capability rigidity paradox in new product innovation. *Journal of Marketing*, *69*(6), 61–83. doi:10.1509/jmkg.2005.69.4.61

Auh, S., & Menguc, B. (2005). Balancing exploration and exploitation: The moderating role of competitive intensity. *Journal of Business Research*, *58*(12), 1652–1661. doi:10.1016/j.jbusres.2004.11.007

Babar, M. I., Ghazali, M., Jawawi, D. N. A., Shamsuddin, S. M., & Ibrahim, N. (2015). PHandler: An expert system for a scalable software requirements prioritization process. *Knowledge-Based Systems*, *84*, 179–202. doi:10.1016/j.knosys.2015.04.010

Bailey, D. E., Leonardi, P. M., & Barley, S. R. (2012). The lure of the virtual. *Organization Science*, *23*(5), 1485–1504. doi:10.1287/orsc.1110.0703

Baiyere, A., Salmela, H., & Tapanainen, T. (2020). Digital transformation and the new logics of business process management. *European Journal of Information Systems*, *29*(3), 238–259. doi:10.1080/0960085X.2020.1718007

Bajwa, S. S., Wang, X., Duc, A. N., & Abrahamsson, P. (2016). How do software startups pivot? Empirical results from a multiple case study. *International Conference of Software Business*, 169–176. 10.1007/978-3-319-40515-5_14

Bajwa, S. S., Wang, X., Duc, A. N., & Abrahamsson, P. (2017). "Failures" to be celebrated: An analysis of major pivots of software startups. *Empirical Software Engineering*, *22*(5), 2373–2408. doi:10.100710664-016-9458-0

Bakalova, Z., Daneva, M., Herrmann, A., & Wieringa, R. (2011). Agile requirements prioritization: What happens in practice and what is described in literature. *International Working Conference on Requirements Engineering: Foundation for Software Quality*, 181–195. 10.1007/978-3-642-19858-8_18

Bandura, A. (2014). Exercise of Personal Agency Through the Self-Efficacy Mechanism. In R. Schwarzer (Ed.), *Self-Efficacy: Thought Control of Action* (pp. 3–38). Routledge.

Baran, A., & Zhumabaeva, A. (2018). Intellectual property management in startups—Problematic issues. *Engineering Management in Production and Services*, *10*(2), 66–74. doi:10.2478/emj-2018-0012

Barbosa, J., Gonçalves, A., Simonetti, V., & Leitão, A. (2009). A Proposed Architecture for Implementing a Knowledge Management System in the Brazilian National Cancer Institute. *Brazilian Administration Review*, *6*(3), 247–262. doi:10.1590/S1807-76922009000300006

Barczak, G., & Kahn, K. B. (2012). Identifying new product development best practice. *Business Horizons*, *55*(3), 293–305. doi:10.1016/j.bushor.2012.01.006

Bardhan, I. R. (2007). Toward a theory to study the use of collaborative product commerce for product development. *Information Technology and Management*, *8*(2), 167–184. doi:10.100710799-007-0013-y

Barnett-Page, E., & Thomas, J. (2009). Methods for the synthesis of qualitative research: A critical review. *BMC Medical Research Methodology*, *9*(1), 59–69. doi:10.1186/1471-2288-9-59 PMID:19671152

Barney, J. (1991). Firm resources and sustained competitive advantage. *Journal of Management*, *17*(1), 99–120. doi:10.1177/014920639101700108

Barney, S., Mohankumar, V., Chatzipetrou, P., Aurum, A., Wohlin, C., & Angelis, L. (2014). Software quality across borders: Three case studies on company internal alignment. *Information and Software Technology*, *56*(1), 20–38. doi:10.1016/j.infsof.2013.06.004

Basili, V. R., Heidrich, J., Lindvall, M., Münch, J., Seanian, C., Regardie, M., & Trendowicz, A. (2009). Determining the Impact of Business Strategies Using Principles from Goal-oriented Measurement. *Wirtschaftsinformatik*, (1), 545–554.

Bass, J. M. (2013). Agile Method Tailoring in distributed Enterprises: Product Owner Teams. *Proceedings of IEEE 8th International conference on Global Software Engineering (ICGSE)*, 154-163. 10.1109/ICGSE.2013.27

Batova, T., Clark, D., & Card, D. (2016). Challenges of lean customer discovery as invention. *2016 IEEE International Professional Communication Conference (IPCC)*, 1–5. 10.1109/IPCC.2016.7740514

Baudin, M. (2012). Revisiting pareto in manufacturing: Revising your charts can provide clear communications to managers. *Industrial Engineering (American Institute of Industrial Engineers)*, *44*(1), 28–33. http://search.ebscohost.com/login.aspx?direct=true&db=asn&AN=70046451&site=eds-live

Beck, K. (2000). *Extreme programming explained: Embrace change*. Addison-Wesley Professional.

Beck, K. (2000). *Extreme Programming Explained*. Addison-Wesley.

Benitez, J., Castillo, A., Llorens, J., & Braojos, J. (2018). IT-enabled knowledge ambidexterity and innovation performance in small U.S. firms: The moderator role of social media capability. *Information & Management*, *55*(1), 131–143. doi:10.1016/j.im.2017.09.004

Benner, M. J., & Tushman, M. L. (2003). Exploitation, exploration, and process management: The productivity dilemma revisited. *Academy of Management Review*, *28*(2), 238–256. doi:10.5465/amr.2003.9416096

Berg, V., Birkeland, J., Nguyen-Duc, A., Pappas, I. O., & Jaccheri, L. (2018). Software startup engineering: A systematic mapping study. *Journal of Systems and Software*, *144*, 255–274. doi:10.1016/j.jss.2018.06.043

Bhardwaj, S., Jain, L., & Jain, S. (2010). Cloud computing: A study of infrastructure as a service (IAAS). *International Journal of Engineering and Information Technology*, *2*(1), 60–63.

Birkinshaw, J., & Gibson, B. C. (2004). Building ambidexterity into an organization. *Sloan Management Review*, *45*, 47–55.

Bjarnason, E., Wnuk, K., & Regnell, B. (2011). A case study on benefits and side-effects of agile practices in large-scale requirements engineering. *Proceedings of the 1st Workshop on Agile Requirements Engineering*, 1–5. 10.1145/2068783.2068786

Blank, S. (2014, March 4). *Why Companies are Not Startups*. Steve Blank. https://steveblank.com/2014/03/04/why-companies-are-not-startups/

Blank, S. (2013a). *The four steps to the epiphany: Successful strategies for products that win*. BookBaby.

Blank, S. (2013b). Why the lean start-up changes everything. *Harvard Business Review*, *91*(5), 63–72.

Blank, S., & Dorf, B. (2012). *The startup owner's manual: The step-by-step guide for building a great company*. BookBaby.

Blank, S., & Euchner, J. (2018). The genesis and future of Lean Startup: An interview with Steve Blank. *Research Technology Management*, *61*(5), 15–21. doi:10.1080/08956308.2018.1495963

Boehm, B. W. (1989). *Software Risk Management*. IEEE Computer Society Press. doi:10.1007/3-540-51635-2_29

Boehm, B. W. (1991). Software risk management: Principles and practices. *IEEE Software*, *8*(1), 32–41. doi:10.1109/52.62930

Boisit, M. (1998). *Knowledge Assets: Securing Competitive Advantage in the Information Economy*. Oxford University Press.

Bolton, A., Goosen, L., & Kritzinger, E. (2021c). The Integration and Implementation of the Internet of Things Through Digital Transformation: Impact on Productivity and Innovation. In P. Tomar (Ed.), Integration and Implementation of the Internet of Things Through Cloud Computing (pp. 85-112). IGI Global. doi:10.4018/978-1-7998-6981-8.ch005

Bolton, T., Goosen, L., & Kritzinger, E. (2020a, March 8). Security Aspects of an Empirical Study into the Impact of Digital Transformation via Unified Communication and Collaboration Technologies on the Productivity and Innovation of a Global Automotive Enterprise. Communications in Computer and Information Science, 1166, 99-113. doi:10.1007/978-3-030-43276-8_8

Bolton, A. D., Goosen, L., & Kritzinger, E. (2021a). Unified Communication Technologies at a Global Automotive Organization. In M. Khosrow-Pour (Ed.), *Encyclopedia of Organizational Knowledge, Administration, and Technologies* (pp. 2592–2608). IGI Global. doi:10.4018/978-1-7998-3473-1.ch179

Bolton, A. D., Goosen, L., & Kritzinger, E. (2022). Impact of Digital Transformation via Unified Communication and Collaboration Technologies: Productivity and Innovation at a Global Enterprise. In *Impact of Digital Transformation on the Development of New Business Models and Consumer Experience (Approved for publication)*. IGI Global. doi:10.4018/978-1-7998-9179-6.ch014

Bolton, A., Goosen, L., & Kritzinger, E. (2016). Enterprise Digitization Enablement Through Unified Communication and Collaboration. *Proceedings of the Annual Conference of the South African Institute of Computer Scientists and Information Technologists*. 10.1145/2987491.2987516

Bolton, A., Goosen, L., & Kritzinger, E. (2020b). The Impact of Unified Communication and Collaboration Technologies on Productivity and Innovation: Promotion for the Fourth Industrial Revolution. In S. B. Buckley (Ed.), *Promoting Inclusive Growth in the Fourth Industrial Revolution* (pp. 44–73). IGI Global. doi:10.4018/978-1-7998-4882-0.ch002

Bolton, A., Goosen, L., & Kritzinger, E. (2021b). An Empirical Study into the Impact on Innovation and Productivity Towards the Post-COVID-19 Era: Digital Transformation of an Automotive Enterprise. In L. C. Carvalho, L. Reis, & C. Silveira (Eds.), *Handbook of Research on Entrepreneurship, Innovation, Sustainability, and ICTs in the Post-COVID-19 Era* (pp. 133–159). IGI Global. doi:10.4018/978-1-7998-6776-0.ch007

Borseman, M., Tanev, S., Weiss, M., & Rasmussen, E. S. (2016). Lost in the canvases: Managing uncertainty in lean global startups. *ISPIM Innovation Symposium*, 1.

Börsting, I., & Gruhn, V. (2018). Toward Rapid Digital Prototyping for Augmented Reality Applications. *2018 IEEE/ACM 4th International Workshop on Rapid Continuous Software Engineering (RCoSE)*, 12–15.

Bosch, J. (2009). From software product lines to software ecosystems. *SPLC*, 9, 111–119.

Bosch, J., Olsson, H. H., Björk, J., & Ljungblad, J. (2013). The early stage software startup development model: A framework for operationalizing lean principles in software startups. In *Lean Enterprise Software and Systems* (pp. 1–15). Springer. doi:10.1007/978-3-642-44930-7_1

Bowonder, B., Dambal, A., Kumar, S., & Shirodkar, A. (2010). Innovation strategies for creating competitive advantage. *Research Technology Management*, 53(3), 19–32. doi:10.1080/08956308.2010.11657628

Brenny, S., & Hu, J. (2013). Social connectedness and inclusion by digital augmentation in public spaces. *8th International Conference on Design and Semantics of Form and Movement (DeSForm)*, 108-118.

Brun, E. C. (2016). Start-up development processes in business incubators. *ISPIM Innovation Symposium*, 1.

Bullinger, H-J., Nagele, R., Rueger, M., & Fischer, D. (2016). Business Model Innovation: From Technology Market to Market Success. *Proceedings of PICMET Technology Management for Social Innovation*, 1264-1270.

Burke, A. E., Fraser, S., & Greene, F. J. (2009). Multiple effects of business plans on new ventures. *Journal of Management Studies*.

Büyüközkan, G., & Çifçin, G. (2012). A new incomplete preference relations based approach to quality function deployment. *Information Sciences*, *206*, 30–41. doi:10.1016/j.ins.2012.04.010

Bygstad, B., & Øvrelid, E. (2020). Architectural alignment of process innovation and digital infrastructure in a high-tech hospital. *European Journal of Information Systems*, *29*(3), 220–237. doi:10.1080/0960085X.2020.1728201

Cantarello, S., Martini, A., & Nosella, A. (2012). A multi-level model for organizational ambidexterity in the search phase of the innovation process. *Blackwell Publishing Ltd.*, *21*(1), 28–48. doi:10.1111/j.1467-8691.2012.00624.x

Cao, L., & Ramesh, B. (2008). Agile requirements engineering practices: An empirical study. *IEEE Software*, *25*(1), 60–67. doi:10.1109/MS.2008.1

Cao, Q., Gedajlovic, E., & Zhang, H. (2009). Unpacking organizational ambidexterity: Dimensions, contingencies, and synergistic effects. *Organization Science*, *20*(4), 781–796. doi:10.1287/orsc.1090.0426

Carmel, E. (1994). Time-to-completion in software package startups. *Proceedings of the Twenty-Seventh Hawaii International Conference on System Sciences*, *4*, 498–507. 10.1109/HICSS.1994.323468

Carroll, C., Booth, A., & Cooper, K. (2011). A worked example of "best fit" framework synthesis: A systematic review of views concerning the taking of some potential chemopreventive agents. *BMS Medical Journal Methodology*, *11*(29), 1–9. doi:10.1186/1471-2288-11-29 PMID:21410933

Carroll, C., Booth, A., Leaviss, J., & Rick, J. (2013). "Best fit" framework synthesis: Refining the method. *BMS Medical Journal Methodology*, *13*(37), 1–16. doi:10.1186/1471-2288-13-37 PMID:23497061

Cepeda, G., & Vera, D. (2007). Dynamic capabilities and operational capabilities: A knowledge management perspective. *Journal of Business Research*, *60*(5), 426–437. doi:10.1016/j.jbusres.2007.01.013

Cesaroni, F., & Piccaluga, A. (2013). Operational challenges and ST's proposed solutions to improve collaboration between IP and R&D in innovation processes. *California Management Review*, *55*(4), 143–156. doi:10.1525/cmr.2013.55.4.143

Chang, Y. Y., & Hughes, M. (2012). Drivers of innovation ambidexterity in small- to medium-sized firms. *European Management Journal*, *30*(1), 1–17. doi:10.1016/j.emj.2011.08.003

Chanin, R., Pompermaier, L., Fraga, K., Sales, A., & Prikladnicki, R. (2017). Applying customer development for software requirements in a startup development program. *2017 IEEE/ACM 1st International Workshop on Software Engineering for Startups (SoftStart)*, 2–5.

Chanin, R., Pompermaier, L., Fraga, K., Sales, A., & Prikladnicki, R. (2017). Applying Customer Development for Software Requirements in a Startup Development Program. *2017 IEEE/ACM 1st International Workshop on Software Engineering for Startups (SoftStart)*.

Charmaz, K. (2014). *Constructing Grounded Theory* (2nd ed.). SAGE Publications.

Chatzipetrou, P., Rovegård, P., & Wohlin, C. (2010). Prioritization of issues and requirements by Cumulative Voting: A compositional data analysis framework. *36th EUROMICRO Conference on Software Engineering and Advanced Applications*. 361-370. 10.1109/SEAA.2010.35

Chaves-González, J. M., & Pérez-Toledano, M. A. (2015). Differential evolution with Pareto tournament for the multiobjective next release problem. *Applied Mathematics and Computation*, *252*(1), 1–13. doi:10.1016/j.amc.2014.11.093

Chaves-González, J. M., Pérez-Toledano, M. A., & Navasa, A. (2015a). Software requirement optimization using a multiobjective swarm intelligence evolutionary algorithm. *Knowledge-Based Systems*, *83*, 105–115. doi:10.1016/j.knosys.2015.03.012

Chaves-González, J. M., Pérez-Toledano, M. A., & Navasa, A. (2015b). Teaching learning based optimization with Pareto tournament for the multiobjective software requirements selection. *Engineering Applications of Artificial Intelligence*, *43*, 89–101. doi:10.1016/j.engappai.2015.04.002

Chesbrough, H. (2010). Business Model Innovation: Opportunities and Barriers. *Long Range Planning*, *43*(2), 354–363. doi:10.1016/j.lrp.2009.07.010

Chesbrough, H., & Rosenbloom, R. S. (2002). The role of the business model in capturing value from innovation: Evidence from Xerox Corporation's technology spin-off companies. *Industrial and Corporate Change*, *11*(3), 529–555. doi:10.1093/icc/11.3.529

Cheung, M. (2019). *Live streamed vs freely streamed content's effect on the engagement of viewers*. Academic Press.

Chiou, C.-C., Perng, C., & Tseng, T.-F. (2012). Applying service science on systematic innovation for the convention and exhibition industry: The cases of world expo. *International Journal of Electronic Business Management*, *10*(4), 247–260. http://search.ebscohost.com/login.aspx?direct=true&db=bth&AN=85717275&site=eds-live

Chirumalla, K. (2017). Clarifying the feedback loop concept for innovation capability: A literature review. In *Conference: XXVIII ISPIM Innovation Conference* (s. 1-19). Vienna: ISPIM.

Chmiel, A., Sienkiewicz, J., Thelwall, M., Paltoglou, G., Buckley, K., Kappas, A., & Hołyst, J. (2011). Collective emotions online and their influence on community life. *PLoS One*, *6*(7), e22207. Advance online publication. doi:10.1371/journal.pone.0022207 PMID:21818302

Cho, J. (2008). Issues and Challenges of agile software development with SCRUM. *Issues in Information Systems*, *9*(2), 188–195.

Cho, Y., Kirkewoog, S., & Daim, T. U. (2018). Managing strategic intellectual property assets in the fuzzy front end of new product development process. *R & D Management*, *48*(3), 354–374. doi:10.1111/radm.12312

Christoforakos, L., & Diefenbach, S. (2018). Idealization Effects in UX Evaluation at Early Concept Stages: Challenges of Low-Fidelity Prototyping. *International Conference on Applied Human Factors and Ergonomics*, 3–14.

Chugh, M., Chanderwal, N., Mishra, A. K., & Punia, D. K. (2019). The effect of knowledge management on perceived software process improvement: Mediating effects of critical success factors and moderating effect of the use of information technology. *VINE Journal of Information and Knowledge Management Systems*, *49*(4), 546–567. doi:10.1108/VJIKMS-11-2018-0106

Cockburn, I. M., & MacGarvie, M. J. (2009). Patents, Thickets and the Financing of Early-Stage Firms: Evidence from the Software Industry. *Journal of Economics & Management Strategy*, *18*(3), 729–773. doi:10.1111/j.1530-9134.2009.00228.x

Cohn, M. (2004). *User stories applied: For agile software development*. Addison-Wesley Professional.

Collins, A., Joseph, D., & Bielaczyc, K. (2004). Design Research: Theoretical and Methodological Issues. *Journal of the Learning Sciences*, *13*(1), 15–42. doi:10.120715327809jls1301_2

Collins, J. C., & Porras, J. I. (1996). Building your company's vision. *Harvard Business Review*, *74*(5), 65.

Cooper, B., & Vlaskovits, P. (2010). *Entrepreneur's Guideto Customer Development*. Academic Press.

Cooper, R. G. (2019). The drivers of success in new-product development. *Industrial Marketing Management*, *76*, 36–47. doi:10.1016/j.indmarman.2018.07.005

Cooper, R. G., & Sommer, A. F. (2018). Agile–Stage-Gate for Manufacturers: Changing the Way New Products Are Developed Integrating Agile project management methods into a Stage-Gate system offers both opportunities and challenges. *Research Technology Management, 61*(2), 17–26. doi:10.1080/08956308.2018.1421380

Cremades, A. (2019, January 9). How Investors Decide To Invest In Startups. *Forbes.* https://www.forbes.com/sites/alejandrocremades/2019/01/09/how-investors-decide-to-invest-in-startups/

Creswell, J. (2007). Qualitative Inquiry and Research Design: Choosing Among Five Approaches. London: Sage Publications Ltd.

Cristiano, J. J., Liker, J. K., & White, C. C. (2001). Key factors in the successful application of Quality Function Deployment (QFD). *IEEE Transactions on Engineering Management, 48*(1), 81–95. doi:10.1109/17.913168

Croll, A., & Yoskovitz, B. (2013). *Lean analytics: Use data to build a better startup faster.* O'Reilly Media, Inc.

Cruzes, D. S., & Dybå, T. (2011a). Research synthesis in software engineering: A tertiary study. *Information Systems, 53*(5), 440–455. doi:10.1016/j.infsof.2011.01.004

Cruzes, D. S., & Dybå, T. (2011b). Recommended Steps for Thematic Synthesis in Software Engineering. *2011 International Symposium on Empirical Software Engineering and Measurement*, 275-284. 10.1109/ESEM.2011.36

Cruz-González, J. & Amores-Salvadó, J. (2011). Technological innovation. An intellectual capital-based view. *Rand Management, 41*, 319-319.

Curcio, K., Navarro, T., Malucelli, A., & Reinehr, S. (2018). Requirements engineering: A systematic mapping study in agile software development. *Journal of Systems and Software, 139*, 32–50. doi:10.1016/j.jss.2018.01.036

Dabbagh, M., Lee, S. P., & Parizi, R. M. (2016). Functional and non-functional requirements prioritization: Empirical evaluation of IPA, AHP-based, and HAM-based approaches. *Soft Computing, 20*(11), 4497–4520. doi:10.100700500-015-1760-z

Daft, R., & Lengel, R. (1986). Organizational information requirements, media richness and structural design. *Management Science, 32*(5), 554–571. doi:10.1287/mnsc.32.5.554

Dahle, Y., Nguyen-Duc, A., Steinert, M., & Reuther, K. (2020). Six pillars of modern entrepreneurial theory and how to use them. In *Fundamentals of Software Startups* (pp. 3–25). Springer. doi:10.1007/978-3-030-35983-6_1

Dal Lago, M., Corti, D., & Pedrazzoli, P. (2016). Turning a lean business model into a successful Start-up in the wearable technology sector: The case of Clara Swiss Tech. *Workshop on Business Models and ICT Technologies for the Fashion Supply Chain*, 111–122.

Dale, A., & Mason, J. (2011). Understanding Social Research: Thinking Creatively about Method (Illustrated ed.). London: Sage Publications Ltd.

Dale-Bloomberg, L., & Volpe, M. (2019). *Completing Your Qualitative Dissertation: A Road Map From Beginning to End.* London: Sage.

Daneva, M., Damian, D., Marchetto, A., & Pastor, O. (2014, September). Empirical research methodologies and studies in requirements engineering: How far did we come? *Journal of Systems and Software, 95*, 1–9. doi:10.1016/j.jss.2014.06.035

Darroch, J., & Mc Naughton, R. (2002). Examining the link between knowledge management practices and types of innovation. *Journal of Intellectual Capital, 3*(3), 210–222. doi:10.1108/14691930210435570

Das, D., & Mukherjee, K. (2008). Development of an AHP-QFD framework for designing a tourism product. *International Journal of Services and Operations Management, 4*(3), 321–344. doi:10.1504/IJSOM.2008.017297

DaSilva, C. M., Trkman, P., Desouza, K., & Lindič, J. (2013). Disruptive technologies: A business model perspective on cloud computing. *Technology Analysis and Strategic Management, 25*(10), 1161–1173. doi:10.1080/09537325.2013.843661

Dattalo, P. (2013). *Analysis of Multiple Dependent Variables*. Oxford University Press. doi:10.1093/acprof:oso/9780199773596.001.0001

Davis, M. M., Field, J., & Stavrulaki, E. (2015). Using digital service inventories to create customer value. *Service Science, 7*(2), 83–99. doi:10.1287erv.2015.0098

de Felice, F., & Petrillo, A. (2010). A multiple choice decision analysis: An integrated QFD – AHP model for the assessment of customer needs. *International Journal of Engineering Science and Technology, 2*(9), 25–38. https://www.ajol.info/index.php/ijest/article/view/63849

De Kort, Y., IJsselstijn, W., & Poels, K. (2007). Digital Games as Social Presence Technology: Development of the Social Presence in Gaming Questionnaire (SPGQ). *Proceedings of PRESENCE*, (pp. 195-203).

Demerouti, E., Derks, D., Lieke, L., & Bakker, A. (2014). New ways of working: Impact on working conditions, work-family balance, and well-being. In C. Korunka & P. Hoonakker (Eds.), *The impact of ICT on quality of working life* (pp. 123–141). Springer. doi:10.1007/978-94-017-8854-0_8

Dennis, A., Fuller, R., & Valacich, J. (2009). Media Synchronicity and Media Choice: Choosing Media for Performance. In T. Hartmann (Ed.), *Media Choice: A Theoretical and Empirical Overview*. Routledge.

Denyer, D., Parry, E., & Flowers, P. (2011). "Social", "open" and "participative"? Exploring personal experiences and organizational effects of enterprise 2.0 use. *Long Range Planning, 44*(5–6), 375–396. doi:10.1016/j.lrp.2011.09.007

Denyer, D., & Tranfield, D. (2011). Producing a Systematic Review. In D. A. Buchanan & A. Bryman (Eds.), *The SAGE Handbook of Organizational Research Methods* (pp. 671–689). Sage.

Devadiga, N. M. (2017). Software engineering education: Converging with the startup industry. *2017 IEEE 30th Conference on Software Engineering Education and Training (CSEE&T)*, 192–196.

Dezi, L., Ferraris, A., Papa, A., & Vrontis, D. (2019). The role of external embeddedness and knowledge management as antecedents of ambidexterity and performances in Italian SMEs. *IEEE Transactions on Engineering Management*, 1–10.

Dhar, V., & Brand, A. (2020). Coronavirus: Time to re-imagine academic publishing. *Nature, 584*(7820), 192–192. doi:10.1038/d41586-020-02330-4 PMID:32782373

Dimitrijević, S., Jovanović, J., & Devedžić, V. (2015). A comparative study of software tools for user story management. *Information and Software Technology, 57*, 352–368. doi:10.1016/j.infsof.2014.05.012

Dittrich, K., & Seidl, D. (2018). Emerging intentionality in routine dynamics: A pragmatist view. *Academy of Management Journal, 61*(1), 111–138. doi:10.5465/amj.2015.0010

Donate, M. J., & Guadamillas, F. (2011). Organizational factors to support knowledge management and innovation. *Journal of Knowledge Management, 15*(6), 890–914. doi:10.1108/13673271111179271

Donate, M., & Pablo, J. S. (2015). The role of knowledge-oriented leadership in knowledge management practices and innovation. *Journal of Business Research, 68*(2), 360–370. doi:10.1016/j.jbusres.2014.06.022

Doorn, N., & Gorman, E. (2013). Early engagement and new technologies: Opening up the laboratory. Springer.

Duncan, R. (1976). *The Ambidextrous organization: designing dual structures for innovation*. The Management of Organization.

Dunne, D. D., & Dougherty, D. (2012). Organizing for change, innovation, and creativity. In *Handbook of organizational creativity* (pp. 569–583). Elsevier. doi:10.1016/B978-0-12-374714-3.00022-7

Durmuşoğlu, S. S., & Barczak, G. (2011). The use of information technology tools in new product development phases: Analysis of effects on new product innovativeness, quality, and market performance. *Industrial Marketing Management*, *40*(2), 321–330. doi:10.1016/j.indmarman.2010.08.009

Durmuş-Özdemir, E., & Abdukhoshimov, K. (2018). Exploring the mediating role of innovation in the effect of the knowledge management process on performance. *Technology Analysis and Strategic Management*, *30*(5), 596–608. doi:10.1080/09537325.2017.1348495

Dzamashvili Fogelström, N., Gorschek, T., Svahnberg, M., & Olsson, P. (2010). The impact of agile principles on market-driven software product development. *Journal of Software Maintenance and Evolution: Research and Practice*, *22*(1), 53–80. doi:10.1002pip.420

Earl, M. (2001). Knowledge management strategies; toward a taxonomy. *Journal of Management Information Systems*, *18*(1), 215–233. doi:10.1080/07421222.2001.11045670

Ebadi, Y., & Utterback, J. (1984). The effects of communication on technological innovation. *Management Science*, *30*(5), 572–585. doi:10.1287/mnsc.30.5.572

Ebben, J. J., & Johnson, A. C. (2005). Efficiency, flexibility, or both? Evidence linking strategy to performance in small firms. *Strategic Management Journal*, *26*(13), 1249–1259. doi:10.1002mj.503

Edison, H. (2015). A Conceptual Framework of Lean Startup Enabled Internal Corporate Venture. In P. Abrahamsson, L. Corral, M. Oivo, & B. Russo (Eds.), *Product-Focused Software Process Improvement* (pp. 607–613). Springer International Publishing. doi:10.1007/978-3-319-26844-6_46

Ellingsen, S., Turnbull, S. E., Bassaget, J., Ryan, M., Evans, N., Burkholder, M., King, E., Cunningham, S., McCutcheon, M., & Healy, G. (2020). *Quibi disaster: How to lose $1.75 b on something you don't understand*. Screen Hub.

Escalona, M. J., Urbieta, M., Rossi, G., Garcia-Garcia, J. A., & Robles Luna, E. (2013). Detecting web requirements conflicts and inconsistencies under a model-based perspective. *Journal of Systems and Software*, *86*(12), 3024–3038. doi:10.1016/j.jss.2013.05.045

Ettlie, J. E., & Johnson, M. D. (1994). Product development benchmarking versus customer focus in applications of Quality Function Deployment. *Marketing Letters*, *5*(2), 107–116. doi:10.1007/BF00994101

Fain, J. (2017). *Reading, Understanding and Applying Nursing Research*. F.A. Davis Company.

Faraj, S., Jarvenpaa, S. L., & Majchrzak, A. (2011). Knowledge collaboration in online communities. *Organization Science*, *22*(5), 1224–1239. doi:10.1287/orsc.1100.0614

Fehlmann, T. M. (2008). New Lanchester theory for requirements prioritization. *2008 Second International Workshop on Software Product Management*, 35–40. 10.1109/IWSPM.2008.6

Feldman, M. S., Pentland, B. T., D'Adderio, L., & Lazaric, N. (2016). *Beyond routines as things: Introduction to the special issue on routine dynamics*. INFORMS.

Fernandes, J. M., & Afonso, P. (2018). Changing and pivoting the business model in software startups. *International Conference of Software Business*, 157–171. 10.1007/978-3-030-04840-2_11

Ferreira, J. J., Fernandes, C. I., & Ferreira, F. A. (2019). To be or not to be digital, that is the question: Firm innovation and performance. *Journal of Business Research*, *101*, 583–590. doi:10.1016/j.jbusres.2018.11.013

Fichman, R. G., Dos Santos, B. L., & Zheng, Z. (2014). Digital innovation as a fundamental and powerful concept in the information systems curriculum. *Management Information Systems Quarterly, 38*(2), 329–A315. doi:10.25300/MISQ/2014/38.2.01

Field, A. (2013). Discovering statistics using IBM SPSS statistics (4th ed.). Sage Publications.

Filippini, R., Güttel, W. H., & Nosella, A. (2012). Ambidexterity and the evolution of knowledge management initiatives. *Journal of Business Research, 65*(3), 317–324. doi:10.1016/j.jbusres.2011.04.003

Fine, C. H., & Whitney, D. E. (2002). *Is the make-buy decision process a core competence?* Fisher III, W. W., & Oberholzer-Gee, F. (2013). Strategic management of intellectual property: An integrated approach. *California Management Review, 55*(4), 157–183.

Fisler, L. (2012, October 9). Do You Need an OGSM? Use Strategic Planning to Boost Your Creative Career, by Linda Fisler. *Artists Network.* https://www.artistsnetwork.com/art-business/do-you-need-an-ogsm-use-strategic-planning-to-boost-your-creative-career-by-linda-fisler/

Fjeldstad, Ø. D., & Snow, C. C. (2018). Business models and organization design. *Long Range Planning, 51*(1), 32–39. doi:10.1016/j.lrp.2017.07.008

Floyd, S. W., & Lane, P. J. (2000). Strategizing throughout the organization: Managing role conflict in strategic renewal. *Academy of Management Review, 25*(1), 154–177. doi:10.5465/amr.2000.2791608

Flyverbom, M., Huysman, M., & Matten, D. (2016). *Sub-theme 63: digital transformations: technology, organization and governance in the algorithmic age.* Academic Press.

Folz, J. (2019). *Free and Open Source Software in India: Mobilising Technology for the National Good.* University of Manchester.

Fontão, A., Estácio, B., Fernandes, J., dos Santos, R. P., & Dias-Neto, A. C. (2018). Which factors affect the evangelist's support during training sessions in mobile software ecosystems? *Proceedings of the 12th European Conference on Software Architecture: Companion Proceedings,* 1–7. 10.1145/3241403.3241427

Fornell, C., & Larcker, D. (1981). Evaluating structural equation models with unobservable variables and measurement error. *JMR, Journal of Marketing Research, 18*(1), 39–50. doi:10.1177/002224378101800104

Foroutan, M., & Baski-Reeves, K. (2017). *Need for development and validation of a new product development (NPD) assessment and improvement tool: A review of literature.* Academic Press.

Fowler, F. (2009). *Survey Research Methods* (L. Bickman & D. Rog, Eds.; 4th ed.). Applied Social Research Methods Series. Sage Publications Ltd.

Frederiksen, D. L., & Brem, A. (2017). How do entrepreneurs think they create value? A scientific reflection of Eric Ries' Lean Startup approach. *The International Entrepreneurship and Management Journal, 13*(1), 169–189. doi:10.100711365-016-0411-x

Furqon, C., Sultan, M., & Wijaya, F. (2019). Business Development of Coffee Farmers Group Using Triple Layered Business Model Canvas. *Journal of Business & Economics Research, 4*(4), 163–170.

Furr, N., & Ahlstrom, P. (2011). Nail it then scale it: The entrepreneur's guide to creating and managing breakthrough innovation (Issue 658.421 FUR. CIMMYT.). Academic Press.

Furr, N., & Dyer, J. (2014). *The Innovator's Method: Bringing the Lean Start-Up Into Your Organization.* Harvard Business Review Press.

Gandomani, T. J., Wei, K. T., & Binhamid, A. K. (2014). A case study research on software cost estimation using experts' estimates, wideband Delphi, and planning poker technique. *International Journal of Software Engineering and Its Applications*, *8*(11), 173–182. doi:10.14257/ijseia.2014.8.11.16

García-Gutiérrez, I., & Martínez-Borreguero, F. J. (2016). The Innovation Pivot Framework: Fostering Business Model Innovation in Startups: A new tool helps entrepreneurs design business models by identifying the sources of competitive advantage embedded in an innovation. *Research Technology Management*, *59*(5), 48–56. doi:10.1080/08956308.2016.1208043

García-Muiña, F. E., Medina-Salgado, M. S., Ferrari, A. M., & Cucchi, M. (2020). Sustainability Transition in Industry 4.0 and Smart Manufacturing with the Triple-Layered Business Model Canvas. *Sustainability*, *12*(6), 2364. doi:10.3390u12062364

Gartner, I. (2011). *Gartner says worldwide mobile device sales to end users reached 1.6 billion units in 2010; smartphone sales grew 72 percent in 2010.* Academic Press.

Garud, R., & Karnoe, P. (2003). Bricolage versus breakthrough: Distributed and embedded agency in technology entrepreneurship. *Research Policy*, *32*(2), 277–300. doi:10.1016/S0048-7333(02)00100-2

Georgsson, A. (2011). *Introducing story points and user stories to perform estimations in a software development organisation. A case study at Swedbank IT.* Academic Press.

Gewirtz, D. (2014). *15 sites you know, that you may not know are based on Amazon Web Services.* ZDNet. https://www.zdnet.com/article/15-sites-you-know-that-you-may-not-know-are-based-on-amazon-web-services/

Ghezzi, A., Cavallaro, A., Rangone, A., & Balocco, R. (2015). A Comparative Study on the Impact of Business Model Design & Lean Startup Approach versus Traditional Business Plan on Mobile Startups Performance. *ICEIS*, (3), 196–203. doi:10.5220/0005337501960203

Giardino, C., Paternoster, N., Unterkalmsteiner, M., Gorschek, T., & Abrahamsson, P. (2016). Software Development in Startup Companies: The Greenfield Startup Model. IEEE Transactions on Software Engineering, 42(6), 585-604.

Giardino, C., Bajwa, S. S., Wang, X., & Abrahamsson, P. (2015). Key Challenges in Early-Stage Software Startups. In C. Lassenius, T. Dingsøyr, & M. Paasivaara (Eds.), *Agile Processes in Software Engineering and Extreme Programming* (pp. 52–63). Springer International Publishing. doi:10.1007/978-3-319-18612-2_5

Giardino, C., Paternoster, N., Unterkalmsteiner, M., Gorschek, T., & Abrahamsson, P. (2015). Software development in startup companies: The greenfield startup model. *IEEE Transactions on Software Engineering*, *42*(6), 585–604. doi:10.1109/TSE.2015.2509970

Giardino, C., Unterkalmsteiner, M., Paternoster, N., Gorschek, T., & Abrahamsson, P. (2014). What Do We Know about Software Development in Startups? *IEEE Software*, *31*(5), 28–32. doi:10.1109/MS.2014.129

Gibson, B., & Hartman, J. (2014). *Rediscovering Grounded Theory.* Sage Publications Ltd. doi:10.4135/9781529799620

Gibson, C. B., & Birkinshaw, J. (2004). The antecedents, consequences, and mediating role of organizational ambidexterity. *Academy of Management Journal*, *47*(2), 209–226.

Giessmann, A., & Legner, C. (2013). *Designing business models for platform as a service: Towards a design theory.* Academic Press.

Giessmann, A., Kyas, P., Tyrväinen, P., & Stanoevska, K. (2014). Towards a better Understanding of the Dynamics of Platform as a Service Business Models. *2014 47th Hawaii International Conference on System Sciences*, 965–974.

Giessmann, A., & Stanoevska-Slabeva, K. (2012). Business models of platform as a service (PaaS) providers: Current state and future directions. *Journal of Information Technology Theory and Application, 13*(4), 31.

Glaser, B., & Strauss, A. (2017). The Discovery of Grounded Theory: Strategies for qualitative research. London: Routledge.

Glaser, B. G. (1992). *Basic of Grounded theory Analysis: Emergence vs. forcing.* The Sociology Press.

Glaser, B. G., & Strauss, A. L. (1967). *The discovery of Grounded Theory: strategies for qualitative research.* Aldine Publishing Company.

Gliner, J., Morgan, G., & Leech, N. (2009). Methods. In *Applied Settings: An integrated approach to design analysis* (2nd ed.). Routledge.

Gonzalez, T., Diaz-Herrera, J., & Tucker, A. (2014). *Computing Handbook: Computer Science and Software Engineering.* CRC Press. doi:10.1201/b16812

Goosen, L. (2015). Educational Technologies for an ICT4D MOOC in the 21st Century. In D. Nwaozuzu, & S. Mnisi (Ed.), *Proceedings of the South Africa International Conference on Educational Technologies* (pp. 37 - 48). Pretoria: African Academic Research Forum.

Goosen, L. (2018a). Sustainable and Inclusive Quality Education Through Research Informed Practice on Information and Communication Technologies in Education. In L. Webb (Ed.), *Proceedings of the 26th Conference of the Southern African Association for Research in Mathematics, Science and Technology Education (SAARMSTE)* (pp. 215 - 228). Gabarone: University of Botswana.

Goosen, L., & Mukasa-Lwanga, T. (2017). Educational Technologies in Distance Education: Beyond the Horizon with Qualitative Perspectives. In U. I. Ogbonnaya, & S. Simelane-Mnisi (Ed.), *Proceedings of the South Africa International Conference on Educational Technologies* (pp. 41 - 54). Pretoria: African Academic Research Forum.

Goosen, L. (2004). *Criteria and Guidelines for the Selection and Implementation of a First Programming Language in High Schools.* Campus: North West University. Retrieved from http://hdl.handle.net/10394/226

Goosen, L. (2018b). Trans-Disciplinary Approaches to Action Research for e-Schools, Community Engagement, and ICT4D. In T. A. Mapotse (Ed.), *Cross-Disciplinary Approaches to Action Research and Action Learning* (pp. 97–110). IGI Global. doi:10.4018/978-1-5225-2642-1.ch006

Goosen, L. (2018c). Ethical Data Management and Research Integrity in the Context of e-Schools and Community Engagement. In C. Sibinga (Ed.), *Ensuring Research Integrity and the Ethical Management of Data* (pp. 14–45). IGI Global. doi:10.4018/978-1-5225-2730-5.ch002

Goosen, L. (2018d). Ethical Information and Communication Technologies for Development Solutions: Research Integrity for Massive Open Online Courses. In C. Sibinga (Ed.), *Ensuring Research Integrity and the Ethical Management of Data* (pp. 155–173). IGI Global. doi:10.4018/978-1-5225-2730-5.ch009

Goosen, L. (2019). Research on Technology-Supported Teaching and Learning for Autism. In L. Makewa, B. Ngussa, & J. Kuboja (Eds.), *Technology-Supported Teaching and Research Methods for Educators* (pp. 88–110). IGI Global. doi:10.4018/978-1-5225-5915-3.ch005

Goosen, L. (2021). Organizational Knowledge and Administration Lessons from an ICT4D MOOC. In M. Khosrow-Pour (Ed.), *Encyclopedia of Organizational Knowledge, Administration, and Technologies* (pp. 245–261). IGI Global. doi:10.4018/978-1-7998-3473-1.ch020

Goosen, L., & Naidoo, L. (2014). Computer Lecturers Using Their Institutional LMS for ICT Education in the Cyber World. In C. Burger, & K. Naudé (Ed.), *Proceedings of the 43rd Conference of the Southern African Computer Lecturers' Association (SACLA)* (pp. 99-108). Port Elizabeth: Nelson Mandela Metropolitan University.

Göthensten, V., & Hellström, A. (2017). *Finding product-market fit, How do software start-ups approach product-market fit?* Academic Press.

Graham, S. J., & Sichelman, T. S. (2016). *Intellectual Property and Technology Startups: What Entrepreneurs Tell Us', Technological Innovation: Generating Economic Results*. Emerald Group Publishing Limited.

Gralha, C., Damian, D., Wasserman, A., Goulão, M., & Araújo, J. (2018). The evolution of requirements practices in software startups. *2018 IEEE/ACM 40th International Conference on Software Engineering (ICSE)*, 823–833.

Greene, J. (2021, 1 1). *4 key benefits of adding AI to your knowledge management program*. Knowledge Management: https://www.atspoke.com/blog/knowledge-management/ai-helps-knowledge-management/

Grenning, J. W. (2002). *Planning Poker or how to avoid analysis paralysis when release planning*. https://wingman-sw.com/papers/PlanningPoker-v1.1.pdf

Grisold, T., Wurm, B., Mendling, J., & Vom Brocke, J. (2020). *Using process mining to support theorizing about change in organizations*. Academic Press.

Gupta, Gupta, & Stachowiak. (2021). Adoption of ICT-based Teaching in Engineering: An Extended Technology Acceptance Model Perspective. *IEEE Access*. doi:10.1109/ACCESS.2021.3072580

Gupta, V., & Fernandez-Crehuet, J. M. (2020). Online feedback management tools for early-stage startups: Hidden treasures in the Rocky Mountains. IT Professional, 23(5), 67-72.

Gupta, V., & Fernandez-Crehuet, J. M. (2021). *Divergent Creativity for Requirement Elicitation Amid Pandemic: Experience from Real Consulting Project*. http://ceur-ws. org

Gupta, V., & José María Fernández-Crehuet, J. M. (2021a). Divergent Creativity for Requirement Elicitation Amid Pandemic: Experience from Real Consulting Project. *Tenth International Workshop on Creativity in Requirements Engineering (CreaRE'21). The 27th International Working Conference on Requirement Engineering: Foundation for Software Quality (REFSQ 2021)*.

Gupta, V., Fernandez-Crehuet, J. M., Hanne, T., & Telesko, R. (2020). Requirements Engineering in Software Startups: A Systematic Mapping Study. Applied Sciences, 10(6125), 1-19=.

Gupta, A. K., Smith, K. G., & Shalley, C. E. (2006). The interplay between exploration and exploitation. *Academy of Management Journal, 49*(4), 693–706. doi:10.5465/amj.2006.22083026

Gupta, V., Fernandez-Crehuet, J. M., Gupta, C., & Hanne, T. (2020). Freelancing Models for Fostering Innovation and Problem Solving in Software Startups: An Empirical Comparative Study. *Sustainability, 12*(23), 10106. Advance online publication. doi:10.3390u122310106

Gupta, V., Fernandez-Crehuet, J. M., & Hanne, T. (2020). Fostering Continuous Value Proposition Innovation through Freelancer Involvement in Software Startups: Insights from Multiple Case Studies. *Sustainability, 12*(21), 8922. Advance online publication. doi:10.3390u12218922

Gupta, V., Fernandez-Crehuet, J. M., & Hanne, T. (2020b). Freelancers in the software development process: A systematic mapping study. *Processes (Basel, Switzerland), 8*(10), 1215. doi:10.3390/pr8101215

Gupta, V., Fernandez-Crehuet, J. M., Hanne, T., & Telesko, R. (2020a). Requirements engineering in software startups: A systematic mapping study. *Applied Sciences (Basel, Switzerland)*, *10*(17), 6125. doi:10.3390/app10176125

Gupta, V., Fernandez-Crehuet, J. M., Hanne, T., & Telesko, R. (2020e). Fostering product innovations in software startups through freelancer supported requirement engineering. *Results in Engineering*, *8*, 100175. doi:10.1016/j.rineng.2020.100175

Gupta, V., & Rubalcaba, L. (2021a). University libraries as open innovation partners: Harnessing hidden potential to foster global entrepreneurship. *Journal of Academic Librarianship*. Advance online publication. doi:10.1016/j.acalib.2021.102432

Gupta, V., Rubalcaba, L., & Gupta, C. (2022b). *Global Requirement Engineering through secondary market research: Lessons from real consulting project. IT Professional.* doi:10.1109/MITP.2022.3151005

Gupta, V., Rubalcaba, L., Gupta, C., & Gupta, V. (2021b). Multimedia Prototyping for Early-Stage Startups Endurance: Stage for New Normal? *IEEE MultiMedia*, *28*(4), 107–116. doi:10.1109/MMUL.2021.3122539

Gupta, V., Rubalcaba, L., Gupta, C., & Pereira, L. (2022a). Library social networking sites for fostering startup business globalization through strategic partnerships. *Journal of Academic Librarianship*, 102504. Advance online publication. doi:10.1016/j.acalib.2022.102504

Gürlek, M., & Çemberci, M. (2020). Understanding the relationships among knowledge-oriented leadership, knowledge management capacity, innovation performance and organizational performance. *Kybernetes*, *49*(7), 33–52. doi:10.1108/K-09-2019-0632

Gutbrod, M., Münch, J., & Tichy, M. (2017). How do software startups approach experimentation? Empirical results from a qualitative interview study. *International Conference on Product-Focused Software Process Improvement*, 297–304. 10.1007/978-3-319-69926-4_21

Haas, M., & Kunz, W. H. (2010). How to master the challenges of service mass customization–A persona-based approach. In *Handbook of Research in Mass Customization and Personalization: (In 2 Volumes)* (pp. 603–621). World Scientific.

Hacklin, F., Björkdahl, J., & Wallin, M. W. (2018). Strategies for business model innovation: How firms reel in migrating value. *Long Range Planning*, *51*(1), 82–110. doi:10.1016/j.lrp.2017.06.009

Haefliger, S., Monteiro, E., Foray, D., & Von Krogh, G. (2011). Social Software and Strategy. *Long Range Planning*, *44*(5–6), 297–316. doi:10.1016/j.lrp.2011.08.001

Hair, J. F., Black, W., Babin, B., & Anderson, R. (2009). *Multivariate data analysis*. Prentice-Hall.

Hamdoun, M., Jabbour, C. J., & Othman, H. B. (2018). Knowledge transfer and organizational innovation: Impacts of quality and environmental management. *Journal of Cleaner Production*, *193*, 759–770. doi:10.1016/j.jclepro.2018.05.031

Hanssen, G. K. (2012). A longitudinal case study of an emerging software ecosystem: Implications for practice and theory. *Journal of Systems and Software*, *85*(7), 1455–1466. doi:10.1016/j.jss.2011.04.020

Han, W.-M., & Huang, S.-J. (2007). An empirical analysis of risk components and performance on software projects. *Journal of Systems and Software*, *80*(1), 42–50. doi:10.1016/j.jss.2006.04.030

Hargadon, A., & Sutton, R. I. (1997). Technology brokering and innovation in a product development firm. *Administrative Science Quarterly*, *42*(4), 716–749. doi:10.2307/2393655

Harris, R. S., & Cohn, M. (2006). Incorporating learning and expected cost of change in prioritizing features on agile projects. *International Conference on Extreme Programming and Agile Processes in Software Engineering*, 175–180. 10.1007/11774129_19

Hassan, B. (2007). The Impact of Multilevel Computer Self-Efficacy on the Effectiveness of Computer Training. In B. Hassan & S. Clarke (Eds.), *End User Computing Challenges and Technologies: Emerging Tools and Applications* (pp. 33–47). Information Science Reference. doi:10.4018/978-1-59904-295-4.ch003

Hatzijordanou, N. (2019). *Towards Conducting Viable Competitor Analysis in Early-Stage Startups: A Design Science Approach*. Academic Press.

Haunts, S. (2014, December 19). *Advantages and Disadvantages of Agile Software Development*. https://stephenhaunts.com/2014/12/19/advantages-and-disadvantages-of-agile-software-development/

Häussler, C., Harhoff, D., & Müller, E. (2012). *To be financed or not...-The role of patents for venture capital-financing*. ZEW-Centre for European Economic Research Discussion Paper, 09–003.

Heeager, L. T., & Nielsen, P. A. (2018). A conceptual model of agile software development in a safety-critical context: A systematic literature review. *Information and Software Technology, 103*, 22–39. doi:10.1016/j.infsof.2018.06.004

Heirman, A., & Clarysse, B. (2007). Which tangible and intangible assets matter for innovation speed in start-ups? *Journal of Product Innovation Management, 24*(4), 303–315. doi:10.1111/j.1540-5885.2007.00253.x

Hernes, T. (2017). Process as the becoming of temporal trajectory. In *The Sage handbook of process organization studies* (pp. 601–607). SAGE Publications.

He, Z., & Wong, P. (2004). Exploration vs. exploitation: An empirical test of the ambidexterity hypothesis. *Organization Science, 15*(4), 481–494. doi:10.1287/orsc.1040.0078

Hibbard, T. N. (1962). Some combinatorial properties of certain trees with applications to searching and sorting. *Journal of the Association for Computing Machinery, 9*(1), 13–28. doi:10.1145/321105.321108

Hildenbrand, T., & Meyer, J. (2012). Intertwining lean and design thinking: Software product development from empathy to shipment. In *Software for people* (pp. 217–237). Springer. doi:10.1007/978-3-642-31371-4_13

Hodgkinson, I. R., Ravishandar, M. N., & Aitken-Fischer, M. (2014). A Resource-advantage perspective on the orchestration of ambidexterity. *Service Industries Journal, 34*(15), 1234–1252. doi:10.1080/02642069.2014.942655

Ho, J., Tian, F., Wu, A., & Xu, S. X. (2017). Seeking value through deviation? Economic impacts of IT overinvestment and underinvestment. *Information Systems Research, 28*(4), 850–862. doi:10.1287/isre.2017.0710

Hokkanen, L., Kuusinen, K., & Väänänen, K. (2016). Minimum Viable User EXperience: A Framework for Supporting Product Design in Startups. *Agile Processes, in Software Engineering, and Extreme Programming*, 66–78. doi:10.1007/978-3-319-33515-5_6

Hokkanen, L., & Leppänen, M. (2015). Three patterns for user involvement in startups. *Proceedings of the 20th European Conference on Pattern Languages of Programs*, 1–8. 10.1145/2855321.2855373

Hokkanen, L., Xu, Y., & Väänänen, K. (2016). Focusing on user experience and business models in startups: Investigation of two-dimensional value creation. *Proceedings of the 20th International Academic Mindtrek Conference*, 59–67. 10.1145/2994310.2994371

Holzer, A., & Ondrus, J. (2011). Mobile application market: A developer's perspective. *Telematics and Informatics, 28*(1), 22–31. doi:10.1016/j.tele.2010.05.006

Honig, B., & Karlsson, T. (2004). Institutional forces and the written business plan. *Journal of Management, 30*(1), 29–48. doi:10.1016/j.jm.2002.11.002

Honig, B., & Karlsson, T. (2013). An institutional perspective on business planning activities for nascent entrepreneurs in Sweden and the US. *Administrative Sciences, 3*(4), 266–289. doi:10.3390/admsci3040266

Houghton, C., Casey, D., Shaw, D., & Murphy, K. (2013). Rigor in qualitative case-study research. *Nurse Researcher, 20*(4), 12–17. doi:10.7748/nr2013.03.20.4.12.e326 PMID:23520707

Howard, J. (2007, November 7). On the Origin of Touchpoints. *Design for Service.* https://designforservice.wordpress.com/2007/11/07/on-the-origin-of-touchpoints/

Hudaib, A., Masadeh, R., Qasem, M. H., & Alzaqebah, A. (2018). Requirements Prioritization Techniques Comparison. *Modern Applied Science, 12*(2), 62–80. doi:10.5539/mas.v12n2p62

Hummel, M., & Epp, A. (2015). Success factors of agile information systems development: A qualitative study. *2015 48th Hawaii International Conference on System Sciences*, 5045–5054.

Hyrynsalmi, S., Mäkilä, T., Järvi, A., Suominen, A., Seppänen, M., & Knuutila, T. (2012). App store, marketplace, play! An analysis of multi-homing in mobile software ecosystems. *Jansen*, 59–72.

Iamratanakul, S. (2018). A conceptual framework of implementing business strategy for the NPD process. *Review of Integrative Business and Economics Research, 7*(1), 116.

Ide, M., Amagai, Y., Aoyama, M., & Kikushima, Y. (2015). A lean design methodology for business models and its application to IoT business model development. *2015 Agile Conference*, 107–111. 10.1109/Agile.2015.8

Idu, A., van de Zande, T., & Jansen, S. (2011). Multi-homing in the apple ecosystem: Why and how developers target multiple apple app stores. *Proceedings of the International Conference on Management of Emergent Digital EcoSystems*, 122–128. 10.1145/2077489.2077511

IEEE Guide Adoption of PMI Standard - A Guide to the Project Management Body of Knowledge, IEEE Std 1490-2003 (Revision of IEEE Std 1490-1998), pp. 1–194, May 2004, . doi:10.1109/IEEESTD.2004.94565

Inkinen, H. T., Kianto, A., & Vanhala, M. (2015). Knowledge management practices and innovation performance in Finland. *Baltic Journal of Management, 10*(4), 432–455. doi:10.1108/BJM-10-2014-0178

Jang, I., Lee, D., Choi, J., & Son, Y. (2019). An Approach to Share Self-Taught Knowledge between Home IoT Devices at the Edge. *Sensors (Basel), 19*(4), 833. doi:10.339019040833 PMID:30781639

Jansen, S., Finkelstein, A., & Brinkkemper, S. (2009). A sense of community: A research agenda for software ecosystems. *2009 31st International Conference on Software Engineering-Companion Volume*, 187–190.

Jansen, J. J. P., Van den Bosch, F. A. J., & Volberda, H. W. (2005). Exploratory innovation, exploitative innovation, and ambidexterity: The impact of environmental and organizational antecedents. *Schmalenbach Business Review, 57*(4), 351–363. doi:10.1007/BF03396721

Jansen, J. P., Van den Bosch, F. A., & Volberda, H. W. (2006). Exploratory innovation, exploitative innovation and performance effects: Effects of organizational antecedents and environmental moderators. *Management Science, 52*(11), 1661–1674. doi:10.1287/mnsc.1060.0576

Jansen, S., Brinkkemper, S., Hunink, I., & Demir, C. (2008). Pragmatic and opportunistic reuse in innovative start-up companies. *IEEE Software, 25*(6), 42–49. doi:10.1109/MS.2008.155

Jessop, A. (2014). IPM: A decision aid for multiattribute evaluation using imprecise weight estimates. *Omega, 49*, 18–29. doi:10.1016/j.omega.2014.05.001

Johansson, H. (2017). *Finding the Product/Market fit: Lean Canvas framework as a tool for establishing customer-validated market orientation in early-stage startup businesses*. Academic Press.

Johansson, M. A., & Saderi, D. (2020). Open peer-review platform for COVID-19 *preprints*. *Nature, 579*(7797), 29–29.

Johnson, M. W., Christensen, C. M., & Kagermann, H. (2008). Reinventing your business model. *Harvard Business Review, 86*(12), 57–68.

Jöreskog, K. G. (1993). Testing Structural Equation Models. In K. A. Bollen & J. S. Long (Eds.), *Testing Structural Equation Models* (pp. 294–316). Sage.

Joshi, S. (2019, October). *PaaS (Platform-as-a-Service)*. https://www.ibm.com/cloud/learn/paas

Joshi, A. (2009). Usability goals setting tool. *4th Workshop on Software and Usability Engineering Cross-Pollination: Usability Evaluation of Advanced Interfaces*.

Junni, P., Sarala, R. M., Taras, V., & Tarba, S. Y. (2013). Organizational ambidexterity and performance: A meta-analysis. *The Academy of Management Perspectives, 27*(4), 299–312. doi:10.5465/amp.2012.0015

Kahn, K. B. (2012). *The PDMA handbook of new product development*. John Wiley & Sons, Inc. doi:10.1002/9781118466421

Kakar, A. K. (2015). Investigating the penalty reward calculus of software users and its impact on requirements prioritization. *Information and Software Technology, 65*, 56–68. doi:10.1016/j.infsof.2015.04.004

Kamisawa, N. (1994). The use of prioritization in quality deployment at the planning and design stages. In S. Mizuno & Y. Akao (Eds.), *QFD The customer-driven approach to quality planning and deployment* (pp. 108–134). Asian Productivity Organization.

Käpyaho, M., & Kauppinen, M. (2015). Agile requirements engineering with prototyping: A case study. *2015 IEEE 23rd International Requirements Engineering Conference (RE)*, 334–343.

Karahanna, E., & Straub, D. (1999). The psychological origins of perceived usefulness and ease-of-use. *Information & Management, 35*(4), 237–250. doi:10.1016/S0378-7206(98)00096-2

Karlsson, J., Wohlin, C., & Regnell, B. (1998). An evaluation of methods for prioritizing software requirements. *Information and Software Technology, 39*(14–15), 939–947. doi:10.1016/S0950-5849(97)00053-0

Karlsson, L., Thelin, T., Regnell, B., Berander, P., & Wohlin, C. (2007). Pair-wise comparisons versus planning game partitioning – experiments on requirements prioritisation techniques. *Empirical Software Engineering, 12*(1), 3–33. doi:10.100710664-006-7240-4

Karlsson, T., & Honig, B. (2009). Judging a business by its cover: An institutional perspective on new ventures and the business plan. *Journal of Business Venturing, 24*(1), 27–45. doi:10.1016/j.jbusvent.2007.10.003

Kaur, G., & Bawa, S. (2013). A survey of requirements prioritization methods. *International Journal of Engineering Research & Technology (Ahmedabad), 2*(5), 958–962. https://www.ijert.org/view-pdf/3492/a-survey-of-requirement-prioritization-methods

Kawano, A., Motoyama, Y., & Aoyama, M. (2019). A LX (Learner eXperience)-Based Evaluation Method of the Education and Training Programs for Professional Software Engineers. *Proceedings of the 2019 7th International Conference on Information and Education Technology*, 151–159. 10.1145/3323771.3323789

Kemell, K. K., Ravaska, V., Nguyen-Duc, A., & Abrahamsson, P. (2020). Software startup practices – Software development in startups through the lens of the essence theory of software engineering. In M. Morisio, M. Torchiano, & A. Jedlitschka (Eds.), *Product-Focused Software Process Improvement. PROFES 2020. Lectures Notes in Computer Science* (Vol. 12562, pp. 402–418). Springer. doi:10.1007/978-3-030-64148-1_25

Khalil, C., & Khalil, S. (2020). Exploring Knowledge Management in Agile Software Development Organizations. *The International Entrepreneurship and Management Journal*, 16(2), 555–569. doi:10.100711365-019-00582-9

Khan, M. S., & Zaman, U. (2020). The effect of knowledge management practices on organizational innovation: Moderating role of management support. *Journal of Public Affairs*, 1–9.

Khefacha, I., & Belkacem, L. (2016). Technology-based ventures and sustainable development: Cointegrating and causal relationships with a panel data approach. *The Journal of International Trade & Economic Development*, 25(2), 192–212. doi:10.1080/09638199.2015.1048707

Kim, S. K., & Min, S. (2015). Business model innovation performance: When does adding a new business model benefit an incumbent? *Strategic Entrepreneurship Journal*, 9(1), 34–57. doi:10.1002ej.1193

Kingston, J. (2019). Artificial Intelligence, Knowledge Management and Human Vulnerability. In *Proceedings of the European Conference on the impact of Artificial Intelligence and Robotics* (pp. 198-204). Oxford: ECIAIR.

Kiznyte, J., Welker, M., & Dechange, A. (2016). Applying project management methods to the creation of a start-up business plan: The case of Blendlee. *PM World Journal*, 5(5), 1–24.

Klein, L. (2013). *UX for Lean Startups: Faster, Smarter User Experience Research and Design*. O'Reilly Media, Inc.

Klein, P. G., & Bullock, J. B. (2006). Can Entrepreneurship Be Taught? *Journal of Agricultural and Applied Economics*, 38(2), 429–439. doi:10.1017/S107407080002246X

Kleis, L., Chwelos, P., Ramirez, R. V., & Cockburn, I. (2012). Information technology and intangible output: The impact of IT investment on innovation productivity. *Information Systems Research*, 23(1), 42–59. doi:10.1287/isre.1100.0338

Klotins, E., Unterkalmsteiner, M., Chatzipetrou, P., Gorschek, T., Prikladniki, R., Tripathi, N., & Pompermaier, L. (2019). A progression model of software engineering goals, challenges, and practices in start-ups. *IEEE Transactions on Software Engineering*, 1–1. doi:10.1109/TSE.2019.2900213

Klotins, E., Unterkalmsteiner, M., & Gorschek, T. (2019). Software engineering in start-up companies: An analysis of 88 experience reports. *Empirical Software Engineering*, 24(1), 68–102. doi:10.100710664-018-9620-y

Knauber, P., Muthig, D., Schmid, K., & Widen, T. (2000). Applying product line concepts in small and medium-sized companies. *IEEE Software*, 17(5), 88–95. doi:10.1109/52.877873

Kock, N. (2005). Media richness or media naturalness? The evolution of our biological communication apparatus and its influence on our behavior toward e-communication tools. *IEEE Transactions on Professional Communication*, 48(2), 117–130. doi:10.1109/TPC.2005.849649

Kock, N. (2013). *Interdisciplinary Applications of Electronic Collaboration Approaches and Technologies*. IGI Global. doi:10.4018/978-1-4666-2020-9

Koops, B. J. (2015). The concept, approaches, and applications of responsible innovation. In B. J. Koops, I. Oosterlaken, H. Romijn, & J. van der Hoven (Eds.), *Responsible innovation 2: Approaches and implications* (pp. 1–15). Springer International Publishing. doi:10.1007/978-3-319-17308-5_1

Kraaijenbrink, J. (2012). *Three shortcomings of the business model canvas*. Kraaijenbrink Training Advies Atom.

Kraus, S., & Kauranen, I. (2009). Strategic management and entrepreneurship: Friends or foes? *International Journal of Business Science and Applied Management, 4*(1), 37–50.

Kremp, E., & Mairesse, J. (2004). Knowledge management, innovation and productivity: A firm-level exploration based on french manufacturing CIS3 data. National Bureau of Economic Research. 1237.

Kukreja, N., Boehm, B., Payyavula, S. S., & Padmanabhuni, S. (2012). Selecting an appropriate framework for value-based requirements prioritization. *2012 IEEE 20th International Requirements Engineering Conference*, 303-308. https://ieeexplore.ieee.org/stamp/stamp.jsp?arnumber=6345819

Kuratko, D. F. (2005). The Emergence of Entrepreneurship Education: Development, Trends, and Challenges. *Entrepreneurship Theory and Practice, 29*(5), 577–597. doi:10.1111/j.1540-6520.2005.00099.x

Kyriakou, V., Garagounis, I., Vasileiou, E., Vourros, A., & Stoukides, M. (2017). Progress in the electrochemical synthesis of ammonia. *Catalysis Today, 286*, 2–13. doi:10.1016/j.cattod.2016.06.014

Ladd, T. (2016). The limits of the lean startup method. *Harvard Business Review, 94*(3).

Lafley, A. G., & Martin, R. (2013). Instituting a company-wide strategic conversation at Procter & Gamble. *Strategy and Leadership, 41*(4), 4–9. doi:10.1108/SL-04-2013-0023

Lai, Y. L., Hsu, M. S., Lin, F. J., Chen, Y. M., & Lin, Y. H. (2014). The effects of industry cluster knowledge management on innovation performance. *Journal of Business Research, 67*(5), 734–739. doi:10.1016/j.jbusres.2013.11.036

Lamont-Strayhorn, T. (2013). *Theoretical Frameworks in College Student Research*. University Press of America.

Larson, E., & Gray, C. (2017). *Project Management: The Managerial Process* (7th ed.). McGraw Hill.

Lawton, G. (2008). Developing software online with platform-as-a-service technology. *Computer, 41*(6), 13–15. doi:10.1109/MC.2008.185

Ledford, H., & Van Noorden, R. (2020). High-profile coronavirus retractions raise concerns about data oversight. *Nature, 582*(7811), 160. doi:10.1038/d41586-020-01695-w PMID:32504025

Lee, H., & Choi, B. (2003). Knowledge management enablers, processes, and organizational performance: An integrative view and empirical examination. *Journal of Management Information Systems, 20*(1), 179–228. doi:10.1080/07421222.2003.11045756

Leffingwell, D., & Widrig, D. (2000). *Managing Software Requirements: A unified approach*. Addison-Wesley.

Lenarduzzi, V., & Taibi, D. (2016). MVP explained: A systematic mapping study on the definitions of minimal viable product. *2016 42th Euromicro Conference on Software Engineering and Advanced Applications (SEAA)*, 112–119.

Lenhart, A., Purcell, K., & Smith, A. (2010). *Social Media & Mobile Internet Use Among Teens and Young Adults*. Pew Research Center. Retrieved August 10, 2017, from https://www.pewinternet.org/files/old-media/Files/Reports/2010/PIP_Social_Media_and_Young_Adults_Report_Final_with_toplines.pdf

Leonardi, P. M. (2011). When flexible routines meet flexible technologies: Affordance, constraint, and the imbrication of human and material agencies. *Management Information Systems Quarterly, 35*(1), 147–167. doi:10.2307/23043493

Leong, Y. T., Tan, R. R., Aviso, K. B., & Chew, I. M. L. (2016). Fuzzy analytic hierarchy process and targeting for inter-plant chilled and cooling water network synthesis. *Journal of Cleaner Production, 110*, 40–53. doi:10.1016/j.jclepro.2015.02.036

Leonhardt, D., Haffke, I., Kranz, J., & Benlian, A. (2017). *Reinventing the IT function: the Role of IT Agility and IT Ambidexterity in Supporting Digital Business Transformation.* Paper presented at the ECIS.

Lewin, A. Y., & Volberda, H. W. (1999). Prolegomena on coevolution: A framework for research on strategy and new organizational forms. *Organization Science, 10*(5), 519–534. doi:10.1287/orsc.10.5.519

Libbrecht, P., & Goosen, L. (2015). Using ICTs to Facilitate Multilingual Mathematics Teaching and Learning. In R. Barwell, P. Clarkson, A. Halai, M. Kazima, J. Moschkovich, N. Planas, & M. Villavicencio Ubillús (Eds.), *Mathematics Education and Language Diversity* (pp. 217–235). Springer. doi:10.1007/978-3-319-14511-2_12

Lichtenthaler, U. (2009). Absorptive capacity, environmental turbulence, and the complementarity of organizational learning processes. *Academy of Management Journal, 52*(4), 822–846. doi:10.5465/amj.2009.43670902

Lim, S. L., Bentley, P. J., & Ishikawa, F. (2020). Reaching the Unreachable A method for early stage software startups to reach inaccessible stakeholders within large corporations. *2020 IEEE 28th International Requirements Engineering Conference*, 376-381. 10.1109/RE48521.2020.00051

Li, M., Jin, L., & Wang, J. (2014). Jin, L., & Wang, J. (2014). A new MCDM method combining QFD with TOPSIS for knowledge management system selection from the user's perspective in intuitionistic fuzzy environment. *Applied Soft Computing, 21*, 28–37. doi:10.1016/j.asoc.2014.03.008

Lima, M., & Baudier, P. (2017). Business model canvas acceptance among French entrepreneurship students: Principles for enhancing innovation artefacts in business education. *Journal of Innovation Economics Management, 2*(23), 159–183. doi:10.3917/jie.pr1.0008

Lindgren, E., & Münch, J. (2016). Raising the odds of success: The current state of experimentation in product development. *Information and Software Technology, 77*, 80–91. doi:10.1016/j.infsof.2016.04.008

Lin, R. J., Chen, R., & Shun, C. K. K. (2010). Customer relationship management and innovation capability: An empirical study. *Industrial Management & Data Systems, 110*(1), 111–133. doi:10.1108/02635571011008434

Lin, X., Wu, J., Liang, H., & Yang, W. (2019). Making Knowledge Tradable in Edge-AI Enabled IoT: A Consortium Blockchain-Based Efficient and Incentive Approach. *IEEE Transactions on Industrial Informatics, 15*(12), 6367–6378. doi:10.1109/TII.2019.2917307

Li, W., & Qiu, Z. (2006). State-of-the-art technologies and methodologies for collaborative product development systems. *International Journal of Production Research, 44*(13), 2525–2559. doi:10.1080/00207540500422080

Lobo, S., & Whyte, J. (2017). Aligning and Reconciling: Building project capabilities for digital delivery. *Research Policy, 46*(1), 93–107. doi:10.1016/j.respol.2016.10.005

Lubatkin, M. H., Şimşek, Z., Ling, Y., & Veiga, J. F. (2006). Ambidexterity and performance in small-to medium-sized firms: The pivotal role of top management team behavioral integration. *Journal of Management, 32*(5), 646–672. doi:10.1177/0149206306290712

Lucassen, G., Dalpiaz, F., van der Werf, J. M. E. M., & Brinkkemper, S. (2016). Improving agile requirements: The Quality User Story framework and tool. *Requirements Engineering, 21*(3), 383–403. doi:10.100700766-016-0250-x

Lu, I.-Y., Wang, C.-H., & Mao, C.-J. (2007). Technology Innovation and Knowledge Management in the High-tech Industry. *International Journal of Technology Management, 39*(1/2), 3–19. doi:10.1504/IJTM.2007.013437

Luong, T. T., Sivarajah, U., & Weerakkody, V. (2021). Do agile managed information systems projects fail due to a lack of emotional intelligence? *Information Systems Frontiers, 23*(2), 415–433. doi:10.100710796-019-09962-6

Lusch, R. F., & Nambisan, S. (2015). Service innovation. *Management Information Systems Quarterly, 39*(1), 155–176. doi:10.25300/MISQ/2015/39.1.07

Lyytinen, K., Yoo, Y., & Boland, R. J. Jr. (2016). Digital product innovation within four classes of innovation networks. *Information Systems Journal, 26*(1), 47–75. doi:10.1111/isj.12093

Madsen, R. (2020). Funders must mandate and reward open research records. *Nature, 586*(7828), 200. doi:10.1038/d41586-020-02395-1 PMID:32788703

Maher, J. H. (2015). *Software evangelism and the rhetoric of morality: Coding justice in a digital democracy.* Routledge. doi:10.4324/9780203762172

Malins, J., & Liapis, A. (2010). IT-based tools to support new product design: A case study of a design consultancy firm. In *Information Technology and Product Development* (pp. 65–79). Springer. doi:10.1007/978-1-4419-1081-3_4

Manesh, M. F., Pellegrini, M. M., Marzi, G., & Dabic, M. (2021). Knowledge Management in the Fourth Industrial Revolution: Mapping the Literature and Scoping Future Avenues. *IEEE Transactions on Engineering Management, 68*(1), 289–300. doi:10.1109/TEM.2019.2963489

Manifesto for Agile Software Development. (2001). http://agilemanifesto.org/

March, J. G. (1991). Exploration and exploitation in organizational learning. *Organization Science, 2*(1), 71–87. doi:10.1287/orsc.2.1.71

Mardani, A., Nikoosokhan, S., Moradi, M., & Doustar, M. (2018). The relationship between knowledge management and innovation performance. *The Journal of High Technology Management Research, 29*(1), 12–26. doi:10.1016/j.hitech.2018.04.002

Markerink, E. J. P. (2014). *Enhancing Organizational Creation, Product Development and Success Through the use of Lean Startup in Relation to the Information Technology Sector.* University of Twente.

Markides, C. (1997). Strategic innovation. *Sloan Management Review, 38*, 9–24.

Martinik, I. (2015). Rich-Media Technologies and Their Using in Crisis Management Communication. In J. Park, I. Stojmenovic, H. Y. Jeong, & G. Yi (Eds.), *Computer Science and Its Applications: Ubiquitous Information Technologies* (pp. 437–442). Springer. doi:10.1007/978-3-662-45402-2_66

Masso, J., Pino, F. J., Pardo, C., García, F., & Piattini, M. (2020). Risk management in the software life cycle: A systematic literature review. *Computer Standards & Interfaces, 71*, 103431. doi:10.1016/j.csi.2020.103431

Matharu, G. S., Mishra, A., Singh, H., & Upadhyay, P. (2015). Empirical study of agile software development methodologies: A comparative analysis. *Software Engineering Notes, 40*(1), 1–6. doi:10.1145/2693208.2693233

Maurer, F., & Martel, S. (2002). Extreme Programming: Rapid development for web-based applications. *IEEE Internet Computing, 6*(1), 86–90. doi:10.1109/4236.989006

Maurya, A. (2010). *Lean Canvas–How I Document my Business Model.* Http://Www. Ashmaurya. Com/2010/08/Businessmodelcanvas

Maurya, A. (2012). *Running lean: Iterate from plan A to a plan that works.* O'Reilly Media, Inc.

Maurya, A. (2016). *Scaling lean: Mastering the key metrics for startup growth.* Penguin.

McClure, D. (2019, February 19). *Startup Metrics for Pirates.* https://www.slideshare.net/dmc500hats/startup-metrics-for-pirates-long-version

McConnell, S. (1997). *Software project survival guide: how to be sure your first important project isn't your last.* Microsoft Press.

McGrath, R. G. (2010). Business models: A discovery driven approach. *Long Range Planning, 43*(2–3), 247–261. doi:10.1016/j.lrp.2009.07.005

McQueen, R., & Mills, A. (1998). End User Computer Sophistication in a Large Health Services Organization. In M. Khosrowpoue (Ed.), *Effective Utilization and Management of Emerging Information Technologies: Information Resources Management Association Conference* (pp. 263–276). Idea Group Publishing.

Meertens, L. O., Iacob, M.-E., & Nieuwenhuis, L. B. J. (2011). A method for business model development. *International Symposium on Business Modeling and Software Design,* 113–129.

Melegati, J., & Goldman, A. (2015). Seven patterns for software startups. *Proceedings of the 22nd Conference on Pattern Languages of Programs (PLoP'15), 20*(11).

Melegati, J., Goldman, A., Kon, F., & Wang, X. (2019). A model of requirements engineering in software startups. *Information and Software Technology, 109,* 92–107. doi:10.1016/j.infsof.2019.02.001

Mendling, J., Pentland, B. T., & Recker, J. (2020). *Building a complementary agenda for business process management and digital innovation.* Taylor & Francis. doi:10.1080/0960085X.2020.1755207

Mendling, J., Weber, I., Aalst, W. V. D., Brocke, J. V., Cabanillas, C., Daniel, F., ... Dustdar, S. (2018). Blockchains for business process management-challenges and opportunities. *ACM Transactions on Management Information Systems, 9*(1), 1–16. doi:10.1145/3183367

Menguc, B., & Auh, S. (2008). The asymmetric role of market orientation on the ambidexterity firm performance relationship for prospectors and defenders. *Industrial Marketing Management, 37*(4), 455–470. doi:10.1016/j.indmarman.2007.05.002

Meško, M., Suklan, J., & Roblek, V. (2017). *The Impact of the Internet of Things to Value Added in Knowledge-Intensive Organizations. In Knowledge Management Strategies and Applications.* IntechOpen. doi:10.5772/63142

Meyer, B. (2014). *Agile!: The good, the hype and the ugly.* Springer International Publishing. doi:10.1007/978-3-319-05155-0

Mikalef, P., & Krogstie, J. (2020). Examining the interplay between big data analytics and contextual factors in driving process innovation capabilities. *European Journal of Information Systems, 29*(3), 260–287. doi:10.1080/0960085X.2020.1740618

Miles, M., Huberman, M., & Saldana, J. (2014). *Qualitative Data Analysis: A Methods Sourcebook* (3rd ed.). Sage Publications Ltd.

Mioara, M. S. (2012). The impact of technological and communication innovation in the knowledge-based society. *Procedia: Social and Behavioral Sciences, 51,* 263–267. doi:10.1016/j.sbspro.2012.08.156

Mithas, S., Krishnan, M. S., & Fornell, C. (2016). Research note—Information technology, customer satisfaction, and profit: Theory and evidence. *Information Systems Research, 27*(1), 166–181. doi:10.1287/isre.2015.0609

Moisiadis, F. (2002). The fundamentals of prioritising requirements. *Systems Engineering, Test & Evaluation Conference,* 1-12. https://pdfs.semanticscholar.org/7395/4e283497f15c6b0d7d2ef615afbd1587450c.pdf

Monteiro-Guerra, F., Rivera-Romero, O., Mylonopoulou, V., Signorelli, G. R., Zambrana, F., & Fernandez-Luque, L. (2017). The design of a mobile app for promotion of physical activity and self-management in prostate cancer survivors: Personas, feature ideation and low-fidelity prototyping. *2017 IEEE 30th International Symposium on Computer-Based Medical Systems (CBMS)*, 761–766.

Morris, M., Schindehutte, M., & Allen, J. (2005). The entrepreneur's business model: Toward a unified perspective. *Journal of Business Research*, *58*(6), 726–735. doi:10.1016/j.jbusres.2003.11.001

Müller, R. M., & Thoring, K. (2012). Design thinking vs. Lean startup: A comparison of two user-driven innovation strategies. *Leading through Design*, *151*, 91–106.

Munch, J. (2011). Risk Management in Global Software Development Projects: Challenges, Solutions, and Experience. *2011 IEEE Sixth International Conference on Global Software Engineering Workshop*, 35–35. doi:10.1109/ICGSE-W.2011.35

Mura, M., Micheli, P. G., & Longo, M. (2020). Effects of performance measurement system uses on organisational ambidexterity and firm performance. *Academy of Management Proceedings*, *1*(1), 1–40. doi:10.5465/AMBPP.2020.13898abstract

Myers, M. D. (2019). *Qualitative research in business and management*. Sage Publications Limited.

Nambisan, S. (2013). Information technology and product/service innovation: A brief assessment and some suggestions for future research. *Journal of the Association for Information Systems*, *14*(4), 1. doi:10.17705/1jais.00327

Nambisan, S. (2017). Digital entrepreneurship: Toward a digital technology perspective of entrepreneurship. *Entrepreneurship Theory and Practice*, *41*(6), 1029–1055. doi:10.1111/etap.12254

Nambisan, S., & Baron, R. A. (2010). Different roles, different strokes: Organizing virtual customer environments to promote two types of customer contributions. *Organization Science*, *21*(2), 554–572. doi:10.1287/orsc.1090.0460

Nambisan, S., Lyytinen, K., Majchrzak, A., & Song, M. (2017). Digital Innovation Management: Reinventing innovation management research in a digital world. *Management Information Systems Quarterly*, *41*(1), 223–238. doi:10.25300/MISQ/2017/41:1.03

Nambisan, S., Lyytinen, K., & Yoo, Y. (2020). Digital innovation: towards a transdisciplinary perspective. In *Handbook of Digital Innovation*. Edward Elgar Publishing. doi:10.4337/9781788119986.00008

Nambisan, S., Wright, M., & Feldman, M. (2019). The digital transformation of innovation and entrepreneurship: Progress, challenges and key themes. *Research Policy*, *48*(8), 103773. doi:10.1016/j.respol.2019.03.018

Nathaniel, A. K. (2012). An Integrated Philosophical Framework that fits Grounded Theory. In V. Martin & A. Gynnild (Eds.), *Grounded Theory: The Philosophy, Method, and work of Barney Glaser* (p. 193). Brown Walker Press.

Nelson, S. D., Del Fiol, G., Hanseler, H., Crouch, B. I., & Cummins, M. R. (2016). Software prototyping. *Applied Clinical Informatics*, *7*(01), 22–32. doi:10.4338/ACI-2015-07-CR-0091 PMID:27081404

Ngugi, J. K., & Goosen, L. (2021). Innovation, Entrepreneurship, and Sustainability for ICT Students Towards the Post-COVID-19 Era. In L. C. Carvalho, L. Reis, & C. Silveira (Eds.), *Handbook of Research on Entrepreneurship, Innovation, Sustainability, and ICTs in the Post-COVID-19 Era* (pp. 110–131). IGI Global. doi:10.4018/978-1-7998-6776-0.ch006

Nguyen-Duc, A., Dahle, Y., Steinert, M., & Abrahamsson, P. (2017). Towards understanding startup product development as effectual entrepreneurial behaviors. *International Conference on Product-Focused Software Process Improvement*, 265–279. 10.1007/978-3-319-69926-4_19

Nguyen-Duc, A., Kemell, K.-K., & Abrahamsson, P. (2021). The entrepreneurial logic of startup software development: A study of 40 software startups. *Empirical Software Engineering*, *26*(5), 1–55. doi:10.100710664-021-09987-z

Nguyen-Duc, A., Seppänen, P., & Abrahamsson, P. (2015). Hunter-gatherer Cycle: A Conceptual Model of the Evolution of Software Startups. *Proceedings of the 2015 International Conference on Software and System Process*, 199–203. 10.1145/2785592.2795368

Niu, H.-J., & Chang, C.-J. (2018). A Novel Method Guiding IC Manufacturing R&D Direction: Perspective From Knowledge Integration Innovation. *International Journal of Innovative Computing, Information, & Control*, *14*(4), 1371–1388.

Nixon, J. D., Dey, P. K., & Davies, P. A. (2013). Design of a novel solar thermal collector using a multi-criteria decision-making methodology. *Journal of Cleaner Production*, *59*, 150–159. doi:10.1016/j.jclepro.2013.06.027

Njima, M., & Demeyer, S. (2017). Evolution of software product development in startup companies. *CEUR Workshop Proceedings*.

Nobel, C. (2011). Teaching a 'Lean Startup' Strategy. *HBS Working Knowledge*, 1–2.

Nonaka, I. (1994). A dynamic theory of organizational knowledge creation. *Organization Science*, *5*(1), 14–37. doi:10.1287/orsc.5.1.14

Nonaka, I., Toyama, R., & Konno, N. (2000). SECI, Ba and leadership: A unified model of dynamic knowledge creation. *Long Range Planning*, *33*(1), 5–34. doi:10.1016/S0024-6301(99)00115-6

Nonaka, I., Umemoto, K., & Senoo, D. (1996). From Information Processing to Knowledge Creation: A Paradigm Shift in Business Management. *Technology in Society*, *18*(2), 203–218. doi:10.1016/0160-791X(96)00001-2

Nowak, M. J., & Grantham, C. E. (2000). The virtual incubator: Managing human capital in the software industry. *Research Policy*, *29*(2), 125–134. doi:10.1016/S0048-7333(99)00054-2

Nunnally, J. C. (1978). *Psychometric theory* (2nd ed.). McGraw-Hill.

Nurdiani, I., Börstler, J., & Fricker, S. A. (2016). The impacts of agile and lean practices on project constraints: A tertiary study. *Journal of Systems and Software*, *119*, 162–183. http://ddo.org/10.1016/j.jss.2016.06.043. doi:10.1016/j.jss.2016.06.043

Nurdiani, I., Jabangwe, R., & Petersen, K. (2016). Practices and challenges of managing requirements interdependencies in agile software development: a survey. *2016 International Conference on Engineering, Technology and Innovation/IEEE International Technology Management Conference*, 1-8. 10.1109/ICE/ITMC39735.2016.9025919

Nyfjord, J., & Kajko-Mattsson, M. (2008). Outlining a Model Integrating Risk Management and Agile Software Development. *2008 34th Euromicro Conference Software Engineering and Advanced Applications*, 476–483. 10.1109/SEAA.2008.77

O'Reilly, C. A. III, & Tushman, M. L. (2013). Organizational ambidexterity: Past, present, and future. *The Academy of Management Perspectives*, *27*(4), 324–338. doi:10.5465/amp.2013.0025

Ode, E., & Ayavoo, R. (2020). The mediating role of knowledge application in the relationship between knowl-edge management practices and firm innovation. *Journal of Innovation and Knowledge*, *5*(3), 1–9. doi:10.1016/j.jik.2019.08.002

Oehmichen, J., Heyden, M. L. M., Georgakakis, D., & Volberda, H. W. (2016). Boards of directors and organizational ambidexterity in knowledge-intensive firms. *International Journal of Human Resource Management*, *28*(2), 283–306. doi:10.1080/09585192.2016.1244904

Oinas-Kukkonen, H., Hohtari, S., & Paekkoa, S. (2012). Organizing End-User Training: A Case Study of an E-Bank. In A. Dwivedi & S. Clarke (Eds.), *End-User Computing, Development, and Software Engineering: New Challenges* (pp. 335–354). IGI Global. doi:10.4018/978-1-4666-0140-6.ch016

Ojasalo, J., & Ojasalo, K. (2015). Using service logic business model canvas in lean service development. *Proceedings of the 2015 Naples Forum on Service*, 9–12.

Okatan, K., & Alankuş, O. B. (2017). Effect of Organizational Culture on Internal Innovation Capacity. *Journal of Organisational Studies and Innovation*, *4*(3), 18–50.

Olsson, H. H., & Bosch, J. (2015). Towards continuous customer validation: A conceptual model for combining qualitative customer feedback with quantitative customer observation. *International Conference of Software Business*, 154–166. 10.1007/978-3-319-19593-3_13

Ordanini, A., & Rubera, G. (2010). How does the application of an IT service innovation affect firm performance? A theoretical framework and empirical analysis on e-commerce. *Information & Management*, *47*(1), 60–67. doi:10.1016/j.im.2009.10.003

Osterwalder, A. (2004). *The business model ontology: A proposition in a design science approach*. Academic Press.

Osterwalder, A., & Pigneur, Y. (2010). *Business model generation: A handbook for visionaries, game changers, and challengers*. John Wiley & Sons.

Paetsch, F., Eberlein, A., & Maurer, F. (2003). Requirements engineering and agile software development. *Enabling Technologies: Infrastructure for Collaborative Enterprises, 2003. WET ICE 2003. Proceedings. Twelfth IEEE International Workshops On*, 308–313.

Palinkas, L. A., Horwitz, S. M., Green, C. A., Wisdom, J. P., Duan, N., & Hoagwood, K. (2015). Purposeful Sampling for Qualitative Data Collection and Analysis in Mixed Method Implementation Research. *Administration and Policy in Mental Health*, *42*(5), 533–544. doi:10.100710488-013-0528-y PMID:24193818

Parke, C. (2013). *Essential First Steps to Data Analysis: Scenario based examples using SPSS*. Sage Publications Ltd. doi:10.4135/9781506335148

Paternoster, N., Giardino, C., Unterkalmsteiner, M., & Gorschek, T. (2014). Software development in startup companies: A systematic mapping study. In Information and Software Technology (Vol. 56). Academic Press.

Paternoster, N., Giardino, C., Unterkalmsteiner, M., Gorschek, T., & Abrahamsson, P. (2014). Software development in startup companies: A systematic mapping study. *Information and Software Technology*, *56*(10), 1200–1218. doi:10.1016/j.infsof.2014.04.014

Patton, J. (2014). *User story mapping: Discover the whole story, build the right product*. O'Reilly.

Pearce, J. A. II, & David, F. (1987). Corporate mission statements: The bottom line. *The Academy of Management Perspectives*, *1*(2), 109–115. doi:10.5465/ame.1987.4275821

Peng, M. Y. P., Lin, K. H., Peng, D. L., & Chen, P. (2019). Linking organizational ambidexterity and performance: The drivers of sustainability in high-tech firms. *Sustainability*, *11*(14), 1–17. doi:10.3390u11143931

Pentland, B. T., Recker, J., Wolf, J. R., & Wyner, G. (2020). Bringing context inside process research with digital trace data. *Journal of the Association for Information Systems*, *21*(5), 5. doi:10.17705/1jais.00635

Perdana, R. A., Suzianti, A., & Ardi, R. (2017). Crowdfunding website design with lean product process framework. *Proceedings of the 3rd International Conference on Communication and Information Processing*, 369–374. 10.1145/3162957.3162994

Pergher, M., & Rossi, B. (2013). Requirements prioritization in software engineering: A systematic mapping study. *2013 IEEE Third international workshop on Empirical Requirements Engineering*, 40-44. 10.1109/EmpiRE.2013.6615215

Petersen, P., & Gencel, C. (2013). Worldviews, research methods, and their relationship to validity in empirical software engineering research. In *2013 Joint Conference of the 23rd International Workshop on Software Measurement and the 8th International Conference on Software Process and Product Measurement* (pp. 81–89). IEEE 10.1109/IWSM-Mensura.2013.22

Popli, R., Chauhan, N., & Sharma, H. (2014). Prioritising user stories in agile environment. *2014 International Conference on Issues and Challenges in Intelligent Computing Techniques (ICICT)*, 515–519.

Prencipe, A., Davies, A., & Hobday, M. (2003). *The Business of Systems Integration*. Oxford University Press. doi:10.1093/0199263221.001.0001

Quinn, J. B., Doorley, T. L., & Paquette, P. C. (1990). Beyond products: Services-based strategy. *Harvard Business Review*, *68*(2), 58–60, 64–66, 68. PMID:10106517

Racheva, Z., Daneva, M., Sikkel, K., Wieringa, R., & Herrmann, A. (2010b). Do we know enough about requirements prioritization in agile projects: insights from a case study. *2010 18th IEEE International Requirements Engineering Conference*, 147-156. 10.1109/RE.2010.27

Racheva, Z., Daneva, M., & Buglione, L. (2008). Supporting the dynamic reprioritization of requirements in agile development of software products. *2008 Second International Workshop on Software Product Management*, 49–58. 10.1109/IWSPM.2008.7

Racheva, Z., Daneva, M., Herrmann, A., & Wieringa, R. (2010a). A conceptual model and process for client-driven agile requirements prioritization. *4th International Conference on Research Challenges in Information Science*, 287-298. 10.1109/RCIS.2010.5507388

Rafiq, U., Bajwa, S. S., Wang, X., & Lunesu, I. (2017). Requirements elicitation techniques applied in software startups. *2017 43rd Euromicro Conference on Software Engineering and Advanced Applications (SEAA)*, 141–144.

Raine, L., & Wellman, B. (2012). *Networked: The new social operating system*. MIT Press. doi:10.7551/mitpress/8358.001.0001

Raisch, S., Birkinshaw, J., Probst, G., & Tushman, M. L. (2009). Organizational ambidexterity: Balancing exploitation and exploration for sustained performance. *Organization Science*, *20*(4), 685–695. doi:10.1287/orsc.1090.0428

Rajala, R., Rossi, M., & Tuunainen, V. K. (2003). A framework for analyzing software business models. *ECIS*, 1614–1627.

Ramesh, B., Cao, L., & Baskerville, R. (2010). Agile requirements engineering practices and challenges: An empirical study. *Information Systems Journal*, *20*(5), 449–480. doi:10.1111/j.1365-2575.2007.00259.x

Rasmussen, E. S., & Tanev, S. (2016). Lean start-up: Making the start-up more successful. In *Start-up creation* (pp. 39–56). Elsevier. doi:10.1016/B978-0-08-100546-0.00003-0

Ravichandran, T., Han, S., & Mithas, S. (2017). Mitigating diminishing returns to R&D: The role of information technology in innovation. *Information Systems Research*, *28*(4), 812–827. doi:10.1287/isre.2017.0717

Razdan, R., & Kambalimath, S. (2019). Super Lean Software Startup Engineering Management. *2019 IEEE Technology & Engineering Management Conference (TEMSCON)*, 1–6.

Reifer, D. J. (2002). How good are agile methods? *IEEE Software*, *19*(4), 16–18. doi:10.1109/MS.2002.1020280

Reis, D. A., Fleury, A. L., & de Carvalho, M. M. (2019). Toward a Recursive Stage-Based Framework for Supporting Startup Business Initiation: An Exploratory Study With Entrepreneurs. *IEEE Transactions on Engineering Management*.

Reisinger, Y., & Turner, L. (2009). Structural equation modeling with LISREL: Application in tourism. *Tourism Management, 20*(1), 71–88. doi:10.1016/S0261-5177(98)00104-6

ReVelle, J. B. (2004). *What is Quality Function Deployment (QFD)?* http://asq.org/learn-about-quality/qfd-quality-function-deployment/overview/overview.html

Richter, N., Schildhauer, T., & Jackson, P. (2018). Meeting the innovation challenge: Agile processes for established organisations. In *Entrepreneurial Innovation and Leadership* (pp. 109–121). Springer. doi:10.1007/978-3-319-71737-1_10

Rico, D. F., Sayani, H. H., & Field, R. F. (2008). History of Computers, Electronic Commerce and Agile Methods. In M. V. Zelkowitz (Ed.), *Advances in Computers* (Vol. 73, pp. 1–55). Elsevier. doi:10.1016/S0065-2458(08)00401-4

Ridder, H.-G. (2016). *Case Study Research: Approaches, Methods, Contribution to Theory.* Rainer Hampp Verlag.

Ries, E. (2011). *The Lean Startup: How Today's Entrepreneurs Use Continuous Innovation to Create Radically Successful Businesses.* Crown Publishing Group. https://books.google.com.au/books?id=tvfyz-4JILwC

Riņķevičs, K., & Torkar, R. (2013). Equality in cumulative voting: A systematic review with an improvement proposal. *Information and Software Technology, 55*(2), 267–287. doi:10.1016/j.infsof.2012.08.004

Ripsas, S., Schaper, B., & Tröger, S. (2018). A startup cockpit for the proof-of-concept. In *Handbuch entrepreneurship* (pp. 263–279). Springer. doi:10.1007/978-3-658-04994-2_21

Rissanen, O., & Münch, J. (2015). Continuous experimentation in the B2B domain: A case study. *2015 IEEE/ACM 2nd International Workshop on Rapid Continuous Software Engineering*, 12–18.

Ritter, T., & Lettl, C. (2018). The wider implications of business-model research. *Long Range Planning, 51*(1), 1–8. doi:10.1016/j.lrp.2017.07.005

Robert, L., & Dennis, A. (2005). Paradox of Richness: A Cognitive Model of Media Choice. *IEEE Transactions on Professional Communication, 48*(1), 10–21. doi:10.1109/TPC.2004.843292

Robinson, F. (2001). *A proven methodology to maximize return on risk.* Academic Press.

Rodden, K., Hutchinson, H., & Fu, X. (2010). Measuring the User Experience on a Large Scale: User-centered Metrics for Web Applications. *Proceedings of the SIGCHI Conference on Human Factors in Computing Systems*, 2395–2398. 10.1145/1753326.1753687

Roja, A., & Năstase, M. (2014, November 6–7). *Technology entrepreneurship and entrepreneurial strategies* [Conference session]. 8th International Management Conference Management Challenges for Sustainable Development, Bucharest, Romania.

Rosenberger, P., & Tick, H. J. (2021). Agile enhancement of critical PMBOK V6 processes. *Journal of Modern Project Management, 9*(1), 190–203. doi:10.19255/JMPM02613

Rot, A., & Sobinska, M. (2018). The Potential of the Internet of Things in Knowledge Management System. In *Position Papers of the 2018 Federated Conference on Computer Science and Information Systems* (pp. 63-68). Poznań: Polskie Towarzystwo Informatyczne.

Rubin, A., & Babbie, E. (2009). *Research Methods for Social Work.* Cengage. doi:10.1093/obo/9780195389678-0008

Runeson, P., Høst, M., Ohlsson, M. C., Regnell, B., Wohlin, C., & Wesslen, A. (2012). *Experimentation in Software Engineering.* Springer Science & Business Media.

Runeson, P., Host, M., Rainer, A., & Regnell, B. (2012). *Case Study Research in Software Engineering: Guidelines and Examples* (1st ed.). Wiley Publishing. doi:10.1002/9781118181034

Saaty, T. L. (1977). A scaling method for priorities in hierarchical structures. *Journal of Mathematical Psychology, 15*(3), 234–281. doi:10.1016/0022-2496(77)90033-5

Saaty, T. L. (2003). Decision making with the AHP: Why is the principal eigenvector necessary. *European Journal of Operational Research, 145*(1), 85–91. doi:10.1016/S0377-2217(02)00227-8

Saaty, T. L. (2008). Decision making with the analytic hierarchy process. *International Journal of Services Sciences, 1*(1), 83–98. doi:10.1504/IJSSCI.2008.017590

Sabatier, V., Mangematin, V., & Rousselle, T. (2010). From recipe to dinner: Business model portfolios in the European biopharmaceutical industry. *Long Range Planning, 43*(2-3), 431–447. doi:10.1016/j.lrp.2010.02.001

Sadi, M. H., & Yu, E. (2015). Designing software ecosystems: How can modeling techniques help? In Enterprise, Business-Process and Information Systems Modeling (pp. 360–375). Springer.

Saghir, S., & Mustafa, T. (2016). Requirements Prioritization Techniques for Global Software Engineering. *Pakistan Journal of Engineering, Technology & Science, 6*(1), 42-63. http://journals.iobmresearch.com/index.php/PJETS/article/view/1143

Salim, J., Takeuchi, H., Nonaka, I., Toyama, R., & Othman, M. S. (2006). Integrating Japanese Knowledge Creation Theory Into Knowledge Management Initiatives. *Knowledge Management International Conference & Exhibition (KMICE)*, 241-247.

Santos, J., Spector, B., & Van den Heyden, L. (2015). Towards a theory of business model innovation within incumbent firms. In N. Foss & T. Saebi (Eds.), *Business model innovation: The organizational dimension* (pp. 43–63). Oxford University Press. doi:10.1093/acprof:oso/9780198701873.003.0003

Santos, R., Albuquerque, A., & Pinheiro, P. R. (2016). Towards the applied hybrid model in requirements prioritization. *Procedia Computer Science, 91*, 909–918. doi:10.1016/j.procs.2016.07.109

Sapsford, R. (2007). *Survey Research* (2nd ed.). Sage Publications. doi:10.4135/9780857024664

Satyal, S., Weber, I., Paik, H.-y., Di Ciccio, C., & Mendling, J. (2019). Business process improvement with the AB-BPM methodology. *Information Systems, 84*, 283–298. doi:10.1016/j.is.2018.06.007

Saunders, M., Lewis, P., & Thornhill, A. (2016). *Research Methods for Business Students* (7th ed.). http://lib.myilibrary.com/Open.aspx?id=819487

Sauvola, T., Rontti, S., Laivamaa, L., Oivo, M., & Kuvaja, P. (2016). Integrating Service Design Prototyping into Software Development. *ICSEA, 2016*, 338.

Schmiedel, T., & vom Brocke, J. (2015). Business process management: Potentials and challenges of driving innovation. In *Bpm-driving innovation in a digital world* (pp. 3–15). Springer. doi:10.1007/978-3-319-14430-6_1

Schneider, T. W. (1998). Building a business plan. *Journal of Property Management, 63*(6).

Schnieder, M. (2006). *Theory Primer: A Sociological Guide*. Rowman & Littlefield Publishers Inc.

Schön, E.-M., Thomaschewski, J., & Escalona, M. J. (2017). Agile Requirements Engineering: A systematic literature review. *Computer Standards & Interfaces, 49*, 79–91. doi:10.1016/j.csi.2016.08.011

Seetaram, N., & Petit, S. (2012). Panel Data Analysis. In L. Dwyer, A. Gill, & N. Seetraram (Eds.), *Handbook of Research Methods in Tourism: Quantitative and Qualitative approaches* (pp. 127–144). Edward Elgar. doi:10.4337/9781781001295.00013

Seidman, I. (2013). *Interviewing as Qualitative Research: A guide for researchers in education & the social sciences* (4th ed.). Teachers College Press.

Sener, Z., & Karsak, E. E. (2012). A decision model for setting target levels in software quality function deployment to respond to rapidly changing customer needs. *Concurrent Engineering*, *20*(1), 19–29. doi:10.1177/1063293X11435344

Seppänen, P., Liukkunen, K., & Oivo, M. (2015). On the feasibility of startup models as a framework for research on competence needs in software startups. *International Conference on Product-Focused Software Process Improvement*, 569–576. 10.1007/978-3-319-26844-6_42

Serrano, N., Gallardo, G., & Hernantes, J. (2015). Infrastructure as a service and cloud technologies. *IEEE Software*, *32*(2), 30–36. doi:10.1109/MS.2015.43

Sestino, A., Prete, M. I., Piper, L., & Guido, G. (2020). Internet of Things and Big Data as enablers for business digitalization strategies. *Technovation*, *98*(102173), 1–9. doi:10.1016/j.technovation.2020.102173

Severgnini, E., Galdamez, E. V. C., & Vieira, V. A. (2019). The effects of exploration, exploitation, and ambidexterity on software firm performance. *Revista de Administração Contemporânea*, *23*(1), 111–134. doi:10.1590/1982-7849rac2019170330

Shaari, H., & Ahmad, I. S. (2016). Brand evangelism among online brand community members. *International Review of Management and Business Research*, *5*(1), 80.

Shahzad, K., Bajwa, S. U., Siddiqi, A. F. I., Ahmid, F., & Raza Sultani, A. (2016). Integrating knowledge management (KM) strategies and processes to enhance organizational creativity and performance: An empirical investigation. *Journal of Modelling in Management*, *11*(1), 154–179. doi:10.1108/JM2-07-2014-0061

Shanbhag, N., & Pardede, E. (2021). A Triple Cornerstone Framework for Software Startups: A Systems Thinking-Based Analysis. In Handbook of Research on Modeling, Analysis, and Control of Complex Systems (pp. 60–90). IGI Global. doi:10.4018/978-1-7998-5788-4.ch003

Shane, S., & Venkataraman, S. (2000). The Promise of Entrepreneurship as a Field of Research. *Academy of Management Review*, *25*(1), 217–226. doi:10.5465/amr.2000.2791611

Shao, A. T. (2002). *Marketing research: an aid to decision making.* South-Western/Thomson Learning.

Shaw, R. L., Holland, C., Pattison, H. M., & Cooke, R. (2016). Patients' perceptions and experiences of cardiovascular disease and diabetes prevention programmes: A systematic review and framework synthesis using the Theoretical Domains Framework. *Social Science & Medicine*, *156*, 192–203. doi:10.1016/j.socscimed.2016.03.015 PMID:27043372

Sher, F., Jawawi, D. N. A., Mohamad, R., & Barbar, M. I. (2014). Requirements prioritization techniques and different aspects for prioritization: A systematic literature review protocol. *2014 8th Malaysian Software Engineering Conference*, 31-36. https://ieeexplore.ieee.org/stamp/stamp.jsp?tp=&arnumber=6985985

Short, J., Williams, E., & Christie, B. (1976). *The Social Psychology of Telecommunications.* Wiley.

Siggelkow, N., & Levinthal, D. A. (2003). Temporarily divide to conquer: Centralized, decentralized, and reintegrated organizational approaches to exploration and adaptation. *Organization Science*, *14*(6), 650–669. doi:10.1287/orsc.14.6.650.24840

Silva, T. R., Hak, J.-L., & Winckler, M. (2016). Testing prototypes and final user interfaces through an ontological perspective for behavior-driven development. In *Human-Centered and Error-Resilient Systems Development* (pp. 86–107). Springer. doi:10.1007/978-3-319-44902-9_7

Simpeh, K. N. (2011). *Entrepreneurship theories and Empirical research: A Summary Review of the Literature.* Undefined.

Şimşek, Z., Veiga, J. F., Lubatkin, M., & Dino, R. N. (2005). Modeling the multilevel determinants of top management team behavioral integration. *Academy of Management Journal, 48*(1), 69–84. doi:10.5465/amj.2005.15993139

Skowron, M., Rank, S., Garcia, D., & Holyst, J. (2017). Zooming in: Studying Collective Emotions. In J. Holyst (Ed.), *Cyberemotions: Collective Emotions in Cyberspace* (pp. 279–304). Springer. doi:10.1007/978-3-319-43639-5_14

Smoczyńska, A., Pawlak, M., & Poniszewska-Marańda, A. (2018). Hybrid agile method for management of software creation. *KKIO Software Engineering Conference*, 101–115.

Snihur, Y., & Tarzijan, J. (2018). Managing complexity in a multi-business-model organization. *Long Range Planning, 51*(1), 50–63. doi:10.1016/j.lrp.2017.06.010

Solinski, A., & Peterson, K. (2014). Prioritizing agile benefits and limitations in relation to practice usage. *Software Quality Journal, 24*, 447-482. doi:10.1007/s11219-014-9253-3

Somaya, D., & Graham, S. J. (2006). *Vermeers and Rembrandts in the same attic: Complementarity between copyright and trademark leveraging strategies in software.* Georgia Institute of Technology TIGER Working Paper.

Soni, A. (2014). An evaluation of requirements prioritisation methods. *International Journal of Innovative Research in Advances Engineering, 1*(10), 2349-2163. https://www.academia.edu/11130987/IJIRAE_An_Evaluation_of_Requirements_Prioritisation_Methods

Soto-Acosta, P., Popa, S., & Martinez-Conesa, I. (2018). Information technology, knowledge management and environmental dynamism as drivers of innovation ambidexterity: A study in SMEs. *Journal of Knowledge Management, 22*(4), 1–19. doi:10.1108/JKM-10-2017-0448

Souza, R., Malta, K., & Almeida, E. (2017). Software Engineering in Startups: A Single Embedded Case Study. *2017 IEEE/ACM 1st International Workshop on Software Engineering for Startups (SoftStart)*. 10.1109/SoftStart.2017.2

Spanz, G. (2012). *Startup best practice: Business Model Canvas.* Academic Press.

Stettner, U., & Lavie, D. (2013). Ambidexterity under scrutiny: Exploration and exploitation via internal organization, alliances, and acquisitions. *Strategic Management Journal, 35*(13), 1903–1929. doi:10.1002mj.2195

Stevens, J. (2009). *Applied Multivariate Statistics For The Social Sciences* (5th ed.). Routledge.

Stewart, C. M. (1992). Innovation is in the Mind of the User: A Case Study of Voice Mail. In U. E. Gattiker & R. S. Stollemmaier (Eds.), *Technology Mediated Communication* (Vol. 3, pp. 151–186). Walter de Gruyter. doi:10.1515/9783110860542.151

Still, K., Seppänen, M., Valkokari, K., Suominen, A., & Kumpulainen, M. (2018). Platform Competences of Digi-driven Startups. *ISPIM Conference Proceedings*, 1–10.

Subramaniam, M., & Youndt, M. A. (2005). The influence of intellectual capital on the types of innovative capabilities. *Academy of Management Journal, 48*(3), 450–463. doi:10.5465/amj.2005.17407911

Sutherland, J. S. K., & Schwaber, K. (2012). *The Crisis in Software: The Wrong Process Produces the Wrong Results.* J. Wiley & Sons.

Sutton, S. M. (2000). The role of process in software start-up. *IEEE Software, 17*(4), 33–39. doi:10.1109/52.854066

Svensson, R. B., Gorschek, T., Regnell, B., Torkar, R., Shahrokni, A., Feldt, R., & Aurum, A. (2011) Prioritization of quality requirements: State of practice in eleven companies. *2011 IEEE 19th International Requirements Engineering Conference*, 69-78. https://ieeexplore.ieee.org/stamp/stamp.jsp?arnumber=6051652

Sverrisdottir, H. S., Ingason, H. T., & Jonasson, H. I. (2014). The role of the product owner in scrum – comparison between theory and practices. *Procedia: Social and Behavioral Sciences, 119*, 257–267. doi:10.1016/j.sbspro.2014.03.030

Taylor, A., & Greve, H. R. (2006). Superman or the fantastic four? Knowledge combination and experience in innovative teams. *Academy of Management Journal, 49*(4), 723–740. doi:10.5465/amj.2006.22083029

Taylor, S., Bodgan, R., & DeVault, M. (2016). *Introduction to Qualitative Research Methods: A Guidebook and Resource* (4th ed.). John Wiley & Sons Inc.

Teece, D. J. (2010). Business models, business strategy and innovation. *Long Range Planning, 43*(2–3), 172–194. doi:10.1016/j.lrp.2009.07.003

Teece, D. J., & Linden, G. (2017). Business models, value capture, and the digital enterprise. *Journal of Organization Design, 6*(1), 1–14. doi:10.118641469-017-0018-x

Teece, D., & Leih, S. (2016). Dynamic capabilities and organizational agility: Risk, uncertainty, and strategy in the innovation economy. *California Management Review, 58*(4), 13–35. doi:10.1525/cmr.2016.58.4.13

Teng, D., & Lu, P. (2016). Value proposition discovery in big data enabled business model innovation. *2016 International Conference on Management Science and Engineering (ICMSE)*, 1754–1759. 10.1109/ICMSE.2016.8365646

The Standish Group. (2014). *The Standish Group report chaos— Project smart*. https://www.projectsmart.co.uk/white-papers/chaosreport.pdf

Tiwana, A., Konsynski, B., & Bush, A. A. (2010). Platform evolution: Coevolution of platform architecture, governance, and environmental dynamics (research commentary). *Information Systems Research, 21*(4), 675–687. doi:10.1287/isre.1100.0323

Todeschini, B. V., Boelter, A. S., de Souza, J. S., & Cortimiglia, M. N. (2017). Risk Management from the Perspective of Startups. *European Journal of Applied Business and Management, 3*(3), 3. https://nidisag.isag.pt/index.php/IJAM/article/view/263

Tonella, P., Susi, A., & Palma, F. (2013). Interactive requirements prioritization using a genetic algorithm. *Information and Software Technology, 55*(1), 173–187. doi:10.1016/j.infsof.2012.07.003

Toro-Jarrín, M. A., Ponce-Jaramillo, I. E., & Güemes-Castorena, D. (2016). Methodology for the of building process integration of Business Model Canvas and Technological Roadmap. *Technological Forecasting and Social Change, 110*, 213–225. doi:10.1016/j.techfore.2016.01.009

Torrecilla-Salinas, C. J., Sedeño, J., Escalona, M. J., & Mejías, M. (2015, May). Estimating, planning and managing agile web development projects under a value-based perspective. *Information and Software Technology, 61*, 124–144. doi:10.1016/j.infsof.2015.01.006

Trimi, S., & Berbegal-Mirabent, J. (2012). Business model innovation in entrepreneurship. *The International Entrepreneurship and Management Journal, 8*(4), 449–465. doi:10.100711365-012-0234-3

Tripathi, N., Seppänen, P., Oivo, M., Similä, J., & Liukkunen, K. (2017). The effect of competitor interaction on startup's product development. *2017 43rd Euromicro Conference on Software Engineering and Advanced Applications (SEAA)*, 125–132.

Tripathi, N., Oivo, M., Liukkunen, K., & Markkula, J. (2019). Startup ecosystem effect on minimum viable product development in software startups. *Information and Software Technology, 114*, 77–91. doi:10.1016/j.infsof.2019.06.008

Turk, M. (2015). Vertical integration. *Computing in Science & Engineering, 17*(1), 64–66. doi:10.1109/MCSE.2015.27

Tushman, M. L., & O'Reilly, C. A. III. (1996). Ambidextrous organizations: Managing evolutionary and revolutionary change. *California Management Review, 38*(4), 8–30. doi:10.2307/41165852

Umemoto, K. (2002). Managing Existing Knowledge is Not Enough: Knowledge Management Theory and Practice in Japan. *Strategic Management of Intellectual Capital & Organizational Knowledge*, 463-476.

Unterkalmsteiner, M., Abrahamsson, P., Wang, X., Nguyen-Duc, A., Shah, S., Bajwa, S. S., Baltes, G. H., Conboy, K., Cullina, E., & Dennehy, D. (2016). Software startups–a research agenda. *E-Informatica Software Engineering Journal, 10*(1).

Unterkalmsteiner, M., Abrahamsson, P., Wang, X., Nguyen-Duc, A., Shah, S., Bajwa, S. S., Baltes, G. H., Conboy, K., Cullina, E., Dennehy, D., Edison, H., Fernandez-Sanchez, C., Garbajosa, J., Gorschek, T., Klotins, E., Hokkanen, L., Kon, F., Lunesu, I., Marchesi, M., … Yagüe, A. (2016). Software Startups – A Research Agenda. *E-Informatica Software Engineering Journal, 10*.

Urban, M., Klemm, M., Ploetner, K. O., & Hornung, M. (2018). Airline categorisation by applying the business model canvas and clustering algorithms. *Journal of Air Transport Management, 71*, 175–192. doi:10.1016/j.jairtraman.2018.04.005

Urbinati, A., Bogers, M., Chiesa, V., & Frattini, F. (2019). Creating and capturing value from Big Data: A multiple-case study analysis of provider companies. *Technovation, 84*, 21–36. doi:10.1016/j.technovation.2018.07.004

Urquhart, C. (2013). *Grounded Theory for Qualitative Research: A Practical Guide*. Sage Publications Ltd. doi:10.4135/9781526402196

Vähäniitty, J., Lassenius, C., & Rautiainen, K. (2002). An approach to product roadmapping in small software product businesses. *ECSQ2002, Conference Notes*, 12–13.

Van den Bergh, J., Thijs, S., & Viaene, S. (2014). *Transforming Through Processes: Leading Voices on BPM, People and Technology*. Springer. doi:10.1007/978-3-319-03937-4

Van Den Berk, I., Jansen, S., & Luinenburg, L. (2010). Software ecosystems: A software ecosystem strategy assessment model. *Proceedings of the Fourth European Conference on Software Architecture: Companion*, 127–134. 10.1145/1842752.1842781

Van Der Aalst, W. (2012). Process mining: Overview and opportunities. *ACM Transactions on Management Information Systems, 3*(2), 1–17. doi:10.1145/2229156.2229157

Van der Aalst, W. M., Weske, M., & Grünbauer, D. (2005). Case handling: A new paradigm for business process support. *Data & Knowledge Engineering, 53*(2), 129–162. doi:10.1016/j.datak.2004.07.003

van Gelderen, M., Thurik, R., & Bosma, N. (2005). Success and Risk Factors in the Pre-Startup Phase. *Small Business Economics, 24*(4), 365–380. doi:10.100711187-004-6994-6

Van Heerden, D., & Goosen, L. (2021). Students' Perceptions of e-Assessment in the Context of Covid-19: The Case of UNISA. In M. Qhobela, M. M. Ntsohi, & L. G. Mohafa (Ed.), *Proceedings of the 29th Conference of the Southern African Association for Research in Mathematics, Science and Technology Education (SAARMSTE)* (pp. 291-305). SAARMSTE.

Van Looy, A. (2021). A quantitative and qualitative study of the link between business process management and digital innovation. *Information & Management, 58*(2), 103413. doi:10.1016/j.im.2020.103413

Van Looy, B., Martens, T., & Debackere, K. (2005). Organizing for continuous innovation: On the sustainability of ambidextrous organizations. *Creativity and Innovation Management, 14*(3), 208–221. doi:10.1111/j.1467-8691.2005.00341.x

van Waardenburg, G., & van Vliet, H. (2013). When Agile meets the enterprise. *Information and Software Technology, 55*(12), 2154–2171. doi:10.1016/j.infsof.2013.07.012

Vanhala, E., & Saarikallio, M. (2015). Business model elements in different types of organization in software business. *International Journal of Computer Information Systems and Industrial Management Applications, 7*, 139–150.

Verona, G., & Ravasi, D. (2003). Unbundling dynamic capabilities: An exploratory study of continuous product innovation. *Industrial and Corporate Change, 12*(3), 577–606. doi:10.1093/icc/12.3.577

Voigt, K.-I., Buliga, O., & Michl, K. (2017). Entertainment on Demand: The Case of Netflix. In K.-I. Voigt, O. Buliga, & K. Michl (Eds.), *Business Model Pioneers: How Innovators Successfully Implement New Business Models* (pp. 127–141). Springer International Publishing. doi:10.1007/978-3-319-38845-8_11

von Briel, F., Davidsson, P., & Recker, J. (2018). Digital technologies as external enablers of new venture creation in the IT hardware sector. *Entrepreneurship Theory and Practice, 42*(1), 47–69. doi:10.1177/1042258717732779

Von Hippel, E. (1988). *The Sources of Innovation.* Oxford University Press.

Von Hippel, E., & Von Krogh, G. (2016). Crossroads—Identifying viable "need–solution pairs": Problem solving without problem formulation. *Organization Science, 27*(1), 207–221.

Wagner, L. (2001). Extreme requirements engineering. *Cutter IT Journal, 14*(12), 34–38.

Waldenström, S. (2018). *Lean Startup Approach to Develop Ideas for Internal Systems and Processes: Creating Guidelines for Working with Ideas within Software and Service Companies.* Academic Press.

Walther, S., Plank, A., Eymann, T., Singh, N., & Phadke, G. (2012). *Success factors and value propositions of software as a service providers–a literature review and classification.* Academic Press.

Wang, R., & Chebo, A. K. (2021). The Dynamics of Business Model Innovation for Technology Entrepreneurship: A Systematic Review and Future Avenue. *Sage Journals, 11*(3).

Wang, C. L., & Rafiq, M. (2014). Ambidextrous organizational culture, contextual ambidexterity and new product innovation: A comparative study of UK and Chinese high-tech firms. *British Journal of Management, 25*(1), 58–76. doi:10.1111/j.1467-8551.2012.00832.x

Wang, X., Zhao, L., Wang, Y., & Sun, J. (2014). The role of requirements engineering practices in agile development: An empirical study. In *Requirements Engineering* (pp. 195–209). Springer. doi:10.1007/978-3-662-43610-3_15

Wang, Y.-M. (2012). Assessing the relative importance weights of customer requirements using multiple preference formats and nonlinear programming. *International Journal of Production Research, 50*(16), 4414–4425. doi:10.1080/00207543.2011.596848

Wang, Z., & Wang, N. (2012). Knowledge sharing, innovation and firm performance. *Expert Systems with Applications, 39*(10), 8899–8908. doi:10.1016/j.eswa.2012.02.017

Waters, K. (2009). Prioritization using moscow. *Agile Planning, 12*, 31.

Weiblen, T., Giessmann, A., Bonakdar, A., & Eisert, U. (2012). *Leveraging the software ecosystem: Towards a business model framework for marketplaces.* Academic Press.

Wernerfelt, B. (1984). A resource-based view of the firm. *Strategic Management Journal*, *5*(2), 171–180. doi:10.1002mj.4250050207

White, M. A., & Bruton, G. D. (2011). *The Management of Technology and Innovation: A Strategic Approach*. Thomson-Southwestern.

Wiegers, K. (1999). First things first: Prioritizing requirements. *Software Development*, *7*(9), 48–53.

Williams, A. (2020). The Dawn of a New Era in Entertainment History. *Global Tides*, *14*(1), 7.

Winter, S., Berente, N., Howison, J., & Butler, B. (2014). Beyond the organizational 'container': Conceptualizing 21st century sociotechnical work. *Information and Organization*, *24*(4), 250–269. doi:10.1016/j.infoandorg.2014.10.003

Wölbling, A., Krämer, K., Buss, C. N., Dribbisch, K., LoBue, P., & Taherivand, A. (2012). Design thinking: An innovative concept for developing user-centered software. In *Software for people* (pp. 121–136). Springer. doi:10.1007/978-3-642-31371-4_7

Woodard, C. J., Ramasubbu, N., Tschang, F. T., & Sambamurthy, V. (2013). Design capital and design moves: The logic of digital business strategy. *Management Information Systems Quarterly*, *37*(2), 537–564. doi:10.25300/MISQ/2013/37.2.10

Wood, S., Michaelides, G., & Thomson, C. (2013). Successful extreme programming: Fidelity to the methodology or good teamworking? *Information and Software Technology*, *55*(4), 660–672. doi:10.1016/j.infsof.2012.10.002

Wu, J., & Ang, S. H. (2020). Network complementaries in the international expansion of emerging market firm. *Journal of World Business*, *55*(2), 1–10. doi:10.1016/j.jwb.2019.101045

Wu, J., Ma, Z., Liu, Z., & Lei, C. K. (2019). A contingent view of institutional environment, firm capability, and innovation performance of emerging multinational enterprises. *Industrial Marketing Management*, *82*, 148–157. doi:10.1016/j.indmarman.2019.01.018

Wu, J., Wood, G., Chen, X., Meyer, M., & Liu, Z. (2020). Strategic ambidexterity and innovation in Chinese multinational vs. indigenous firms: The role of managerial capability. *International Business Review*, *29*(6), 1–8. doi:10.1016/j.ibusrev.2019.101652

Xu, L., & Brinkkemper, S. (2005). Concepts of product software: Paving the road for urgently needed research. *The First International Workshop on Philosophical Foundations of Information Systems Engineering (PHISE'05)*, 523–528.

Yadav, M. S., & Pavlou, P. A. (2014). Marketing in computer-mediated environments: Research synthesis and new directions. *Journal of Marketing*, *78*(1), 20–40. doi:10.1509/jm.12.0020

Yang, S.-B., & Choi, S. O. (2009). Employee empowerment and team performance. *Team Performance Management*, *15*(5/6), 289–301. doi:10.1108/13527590910983549

Yau, A., & Murphy, C. (2013). *Is a Rigorous Agile Methodology the Best Development Strategy for Small Scale Tech Startups?* Technical Reports (CIS). https://repository.upenn.edu/cis_reports/980

Yeşil, S., Koska, A., & Büyükmeşe, T. (2013). Knowledge sharing process, innovation capability and innovation performance: An empirical study. *Procedia: Social and Behavioral Sciences*, *75*, 217–225. doi:10.1016/j.sbspro.2013.04.025

Yin, R. K. (2009). *Case study research: Design and methods*. Sage Publications Ltd.

Yin, R. K. (2011). *Qualitative Research from Start to Finish*. The Guilford Press.

Yoffie, D. B., & Cusumano, M. A. (1999). Building a company on Internet time: Lessons from netscape. *California Management Review*, *41*(3), 8–28. doi:10.2307/41165995

YooO. S.HuangT.ArifogluK. (2017). A theoretical analysis of the lean startup's product development process. doi:10.2139/ssrn.3070613

Yoo, Y., Henfridsson, O., & Lyytinen, K. (2010). Research commentary—the new organizing logic of digital innovation: An agenda for information systems research. *Information Systems Research, 21*(4), 724–735. doi:10.1287/isre.1100.0322

Yousuf, M., Bokhari, M. U., & Zeyauddin, M. (2016). An analysis of software requirements prioritization techniques: A detailed survey. *2016 3rd International Computing for Sustainable Global Development*, 3966-3970. https://ieeexplore.ieee.org/abstract/document/7725002

Yu, C. (2004). *Structural Equation Model*. https://www.creative-wisdom.com/teaching/WBI/SEM.shtml

Yu, X., & Petter, S. (2014). Understanding agile software development practices using shared mental models theory. *Information and Software Technology, 56*(8), 911–921. doi:10.1016/j.infsof.2014.02.010

Zagajsek, B., Separovic, K., & Car, Z. (2007). Requirements management process model for software development based on legacy system functionalities. *Telecommunications, 2007. ConTel 2007. 9th International Conference On*, 115–122.

Zaidan, A. A., Zaidan, B. B., Hussain, M., Haiqi, A., Kiah, M. L. M., & Abdulnabi, M. (2015). Multi-criteria analysis for OS-EMR software selection problem: A comparative study. *Decision Support Systems, 78*, 15–27. doi:10.1016/j.dss.2015.07.002

Zolnowski, A., Weiß, C., & Böhmann, T. (2014). Representing Service Business Models with the Service Business Model Canvas—The Case of a Mobile Payment Service in the Retail Industry. *2014 47th Hawaii International Conference on System Sciences*, 718–727.

Zott, C., & Amit, R. (2007). Business model design and the performance of entrepreneurial firms. *Organization Science, 18*(2), 181–199. doi:10.1287/orsc.1060.0232

About the Contributors

Varun Gupta is working as a Postdoctoral Researcher with Universidad de Alcalá (UAH), Alcalá de Henares (Madrid), Spain. He is also the co-Director of master's degree in Innovation Economics, Management and Technology (Online & Presential), Universidad de Alcalá (UAH). He was a visiting postdoctoral researcher with Software Engineering Research Group (SERG), Department of Computer Science, Lund University, Sweden. He is an Associate Editor of IEEE Access (published by IEEE, and SCIE indexed with a 3.367 impact factor), PeerJ Computer Science (published by PeerJ, SCIE indexed with a 1.39 impact factor), International Journal of Computer Aided Engineering & Technology (published by Inderscience Publishers, Scopus indexed), IEEE Software blog, and Journal of Cases on Information Technology (JCIT), and is a former editorial team member of the British Journal of Educational Technology (BJET)(published by Wiley, SCIE indexed). He earned the Bachelor of Technology (Hons.), Master of Technology (by research), and Ph.D. degrees in computer science and engineering. He holds an M.B.A. (general) and a Máster en Dirección Internacional de Empresas as well. He is serving as a Reviewer of IEEE Transactions on Emerging Topics in Computational Intelligence. He was awarded with the "Best Editor Award" by Inderscience Publishers for his contributions to the International Journal of Computer Aided Engineering & Technology (Scopus Indexed) as Associate Editor. His area of interest is evidence based software engineering and innovation management.

Chetna Gupta is a Professor in Department of Computer Science & Engineering and Information Technology at Jaypee Institute of Information Technology, Noida, India. She has more 17 years of experience in research and teaching at university level. She is currently serving as Associate Editor, in International Journal of Computer Aided Engineering and Technology (Inderscience) and Associate Editor, in Journal of Cases on Information Technology (IGI Global-USA). Her area of interest includes Software Engineering, Search-Based Software Engineering, Distributed Software Engineering, Risk Management, Automated Software Engineering, Cloud Computing, Blockchain Technology and Applications of Machine Learning.

* * *

Haneen Allataifeh is a Ph.D. student at the Faculty of Business & Accountancy at the University of Malaya. Her interest focuses on innovation management and the digitalization impact on innovation practices.

Özlem Atay is a professor of Management at the Faculty of Political Sciences, Ankara University in Ankara, Turkey since 1996. She is the Head of Management and Organization Chair in the Department of Management. She was Vice Head of Management Department between 1999 and 2002. She teaches Management and Organization, Human Resources Management, Enterprise Policy and Strategic Management, Modern Organization Theory, Organizational Behavior, Management of Multinational Enterprises, Introduction to Management, Management and Organizational Behavior, Principles of Management, Management, Management Practices in Turkish Enterprises, Successful Case Study Method in Turkish Enterprises, Human Resources Management Practices, Strategic Human Resources Management, Contemporary Management Practices in Turkish Enterprises and Women in Management. She worked at Turkish National Productivity Center as a specialist between 1988 and 1996. She has led a number of training/consulting/research missions in public and private sector enterprises. She specializes in management, organizational behavior, productivity improvement techniques, human resources management, strategic management, energy, quality management, gender and women studies. She is the author of five books, chapters in seven books published by international publication companies and many academic articles in English and Turkish. She has received research scholarships from the World Bank, the Turkish Academy of Sciences, Ankara University, Curtin University, Turkish Scientific and Technical Research Institute, Turkish Higher Education Institution, etc. She was a visiting professor at Curtin University Graduate School of Business, Perth, Australia, in 2006; at Aalborg University College of Business, Aalborg, Denmark, in 2008, at Valparaiso University College of Business Administration, Valparaiso, USA in 2011, at Northern Illinois University College of Business, Management Department, DeKalb, USA in the 2012-2013 academic years. She won two "Best Paper Award", "Success Award" and "Award of Excellence" with four papers presented at four different international conferences. She represents Turkey at the international gender research consortium, the Women in Higher Education Management (WHEM) Network. The WHEM Network brings together internationally-recognized gender in HE researchers in 14 countries–– Australia, Austria, Ireland, New Zealand, Portugal, Sweden, South Africa, Turkey, India, Czech Republic, the United Arab Emirates, Germany, USA and the UK. WHEM Network, published its first book with Palgrave - Gender, Power and Management - in April 2011. The Network's second book with Palgrave, Generation and Gender in Academia, is published in June 2013. The third multi-country research book with Palgrave- Gendered Success in Higher Education: Global Perspectives- is published in February, 2017 (https://wil.insightsme.net/whem/) She published four books titled "Electricity Service Privatization in Turkey(April 2016)", "Innovation Systems (November 2017) ", "Academic Women(2000)", "Work Study Practices in Turkish Enterprise(1996) with coauthors. She is the sole author of the book titled "Collaboration and Management (1999)". She can speak fluent English, good German. Turkish is her mother tongue. She has many international and national journal peer-review and "Editorial Board" membership responsibilities.

Anthony Bolton is the CTO and CIO of Global Telecommunications and Infrastructure in General Motors and holds a PhD (University of South Africa) in Information Systems focusing on the impact of Unified Communications technology on enterprise productivity and design. Anthony previously held Executive IT positions in Fortune 50 companies such as Dell Computers, Hewlett Packard and Price Waterhouse. Anthony's focus in academic research centres on Unified Communication and Collaboration technology, Zero Trust security design and Software Defined Networking.

Leila Goosen is a full professor in the Department of Science and Technology Education of the University of South Africa. Prof. Goosen was an Associate Professor in the School of Computing, and the module leader and head designer of the fully online signature module for the College for Science, Engineering and Technology, rolled out to over 92,000 registered students since the first semester of 2013. She also supervises ten Masters and Doctoral students, and has successfully completed supervision of 43 students at postgraduate level. Previously, she was a Deputy Director at the South African national Department of Education. In this capacity, she was required to develop ICT strategies for implementation. She also promoted, coordinated, managed, monitored and evaluated ICT policies and strategies, and drove the research agenda in this area. Before that, she had been a lecturer of Information Technology (IT) in the Department for Science, Mathematics and Technology Education in the Faculty of Education of the University of Pretoria. Her research interests have included cooperative work in IT, effective teaching and learning of programming and teacher professional development.

Zoe Hoy is a senior lecturer of strategic quality management at the University of Portsmouth. She earned an HND in computer science, an MSc in strategic quality management and is a certified scrum product owner. Prior to academia, she worked for sixteen years in software engineering and quality roles. As a part time doctoral student, the focus of her thesis is requirements engineering in agile software development.

Elmarie Kritzinger joined the University of South Africa's College of Science, Engineering and Technology (CSET) in 2000 and currently holds the position of Professor in the School of Computing. Prof Kritzinger completed her PhD in 2006 and Post Graduate Certificate in Education in 2012. She is currently enrolled for her Master's in Education (Online Technology). Her research primarily focuses on Cyber Safety awareness, training and education for school learners, teachers and schools. The main aim is to establish and promote social responsibilities within communities to establish and grow a cyber-safety culture within South Africa. Prof Kritzinger has established herself as a mature researcher and has published in accredited national and international journals, contributed to a chapter in a book and presented at peer-reviewed conferences across the globe. Prof Kritzinger currently hold a NRF C3 rating within her research field.

Sowmya M. received BE degree in Computer Science and Engineering from Visvesvaraya Technological University, Belagavi India in June 2010. She acquired Master's degree in Software Engineering from Visvesvaraya Technological University, Belagavi, India in Jan 2016. She is pursuing Ph D in Computer Science and Engineering from Visvesvaraya Technological University, Belagavi, India since 2020. At present she is working as Assistant Professor at GSSS Institute of Technology for women, Mysuru. Her research interest includes Internet of Things. Computer Networks and wireless Communication.

Subramaniam Meenakshi Sundaram is currently working as Professor and Head in the Department of Computer Science and Engineering at GSSS Institute of Engineering and Technology for Women, Mysuru, Karnataka State, India. He obtained his Bachelor Degree in Computer Science & Engineering from Bharathidasan University, Tiruchirappalli, Tamil Nadu State, India in 1989, M.Tech from National Institute of Technology, Tiruchirappalli, Tamil Nadu State, India in 2006 and Ph.D. in Science & Engineering from Anna University Chennai, Tamil Nadu State, India in 2014.He has published 53 papers in refereed International Journals, presented 3 papers in International Conferences and has delivered more than 40 seminars. He is a reviewer of Springer – Soft Computing Journal, International Journal of Ah Hoc Network Systems, Journal of Engineering Science and Technology, Taylor's University, Malaysia and International Journal of Computational Science & Engineering, Inderscience Publishers, UK. He has organized more than 40 seminars / Workshops / FDPs.He has attended more than 45 Workshops / Seminars. His area of interest includes Computer Networks, Wireless Communication, Software Engineering, Optical Networks and Data Mining. He is a Life Member of Indian Society for Technical Education (ISTE) and a member of Computer Society of India (CSI). He has 30 Years of teaching experience and 10 years of research experience. Currently 7 research scholars are pursuing Ph.D. in VTU Belagavi, India under his guidance.

Sedigheh Moghavvemi is Associate Professor of Technology Management and Entrepreneurship at the Faculty of Business & Accountancy at the University of Malaya. Her research experience includes business and management, technology adoption, innovation management, smart tourism, and social media. She has worked on different research and consultancy projects pertaining to entrepreneurship, marketing, tourism, human resource, the results of which have been published in peer-reviewed journals.

Tejaswini Murgod is presently working as Assistant Professor in the department of CSE at GSSS Institute of Technology for Women, Mysuru, Karnataka State, India. She received B.E. Degree in Computer Science and Engineering from Visvesvaraya Technological University, Belagavi, India in June 2008. She acquired her Master's Degree in Software Engineering from Visvesvaraya Technological University, Belagavi, India in Jan 2015. Mysuru. She has completed Ph. D in Computer Science and Engineering in the area of underwater wireless sensor networks from Visvesvaraya Technological University, Belagavi, India. Her research areas includes Underwater Communication, Optical Networks and Wireless Communication Networks. She has also published Book Chapters with leading publishers.

Anh Nguyen-Duc is an Associate Professor at the Department of Business and IT, College University of Southeast Norway. His research interests include Empirical Software Engineering, Data Mining, Software Startups Research and Cybersecurity. He has authored/co-authored more than 100 publications in peer-reviewed journals, conferences, and workshops on Software Engineering. Prior to joining research and development field, he worked as a software engineer and an IT consultant for several years in Vietnam.

Kağan Okatan worked as a manager in the field of Information Technologies for many years. He led large-scale digital transformation projects. He holds a doctorate in business administration and a master's degree in information technology. He is a university lecturer and research and development projects consultant. He has focused mainly on management information systems in the fields of knowledge-based management and innovation management of organizations.

Bobrova Olegovna is a 1st year student of magistracy in Computer Law and Information Security Jurisprudence of the Higher School of State Audit of the Moscow State University. M.V. Lomonosov.

Eric Pardede received a master's degree in information technology and a Ph.D. degree in computer science from La Trobe University, Melbourne, Australia, where he is currently an Associate Professor.

His research work has been published in more than 100 publications in international journals and conference proceedings. His research interests include data analytics, IT education, and entrepreneurship.

Konyukhova Galina Pavlovna is a Candidate of Pedagogical Sciences, Associate Professor of the Department of Management and Informatics in Technical Systems, Moscow State Technological University "STANKIN".

Leandro Ferreira Pereira is CEO and founder of WINNING Scientific Management. He has more than 18 years of experience in senior management positions in management consulting companies and university academic activity. With a degree in Management Informatics from the University of Minho and a PhD in Project Management from the Pontifical University of Salamanca, Leandro Pereira has in his curriculum several of professional and academic distinctions, among which, the best national manager award (from Best Team Leaders), the University Senate Award for having been the best student of the University and the National Prize "Youth and National Defense awarded by the Ministry of Defense". Currently, he divides his professional activity between management consulting, the academy, and advisory various entities, in particular, the Court of Auditors, and has supervisor of dozens of doctoral and master students.

Anastasia Samoylova is a 5th year student of the Faculty of Mechanical Engineering, Department of Technologies and Equipment of Mechanical Engineering, direction 15.05.01 Design of technological machines and complexes. Federal State Autonomous Educational Institution of Higher Education Moscow Polytechnic University.

Narendranath Shanbhag received his Master's degree in Information Systems Management from La Trobe University, Melbourne, Australia in 2013. He is currently pursuing a Ph.D. degree in Computer Science at La Trobe University, Melbourne, Australia. His research is in the area of entrepreneurship with a focus on software startups.

Sukran Sirkintioglu Yildirim is an assistant professor of Banking and Finance at Kastamonu University. She graduated a PhD from Ankara University in department of Business Administration. Her main research interests are strategic management, innovation, and structural equation modelling.

Nguyen Trung is a PhD candidate at ThuongMai University. His research interest is project management and software startups.

Britvina Valentina Valentinovna is a Candidate of Pedagogical Sciences, Associate Professor of the Department of Information Cognitive Technologies of the Moscow Polytechnic University, Associate Professor of the Department of Management and Informatics in Technical Systems of the Moscow State Technological University STANKIN.

Index

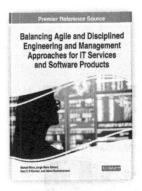

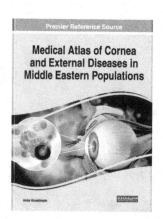
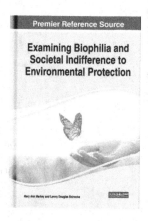
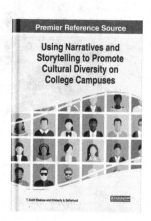

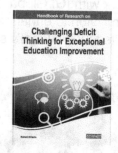

Printed in the United States
by Baker & Taylor Publisher Services